DIMENSIONS OF DRESS AND ADORNMENT: A BOOK OF READINGS

DIMENSIONS OF DRESS AND ADORNMENT:

A Book of Readings

Third Edition

Lois M. Gurel
Marianne S. Beeson

Illustrations by Clayton E. Peterson

KENDALL/HUNT PUBLISHING COMPANY
Dubuque, Iowa, USA   •   Toronto, Ontario, Canada

Cover design by Marianne S. Beeson

Copyright © 1975, 1977 by Lois M. Gurel and Marianne S. Beeson
Copyright © 1979 by Kendall/Hunt Publishing Company

Library of Congress Catalog Card Number: 74-20103

ISBN 0–8403–2038–8

Printed in the United States of America

B   402038   01

CONTENTS

Chapter 4
Clothing Behavior: Social and
Psychological Viewpoints

Chapter 5
Apparel as an Economic Good

PREFACE TO SECOND EDITION

The focus of this collection of readings is the diversity of meanings, symbolism, and significance which people attach to clothing and adornment—people of the past, people of today, people in various cultural and subcultural groups, people acting as consumers of clothing, people as producers of clothing, and people "using" clothing, consciously or unconsciously, in their daily lives.

We believe that understanding of a group or an individual, including the self, is enhanced by understanding his clothing. In our present world, with distances drastically reduced by satellite communication and jet travel, we are experiencing more and more contact with cultures different from our own. Mobility and urbanization affect interpersonal relationships within our culture, as we deal with strangers, to whom we are also strangers. An understanding of different customs and values regarding dress may help us to appreciate people and to be effective in people relationships. Knowledge about the universal influences which have brought about man's clothing and insight into forces affecting the individual's clothing behavior are means of understanding the self and the self in relation to the world of man.

Because dress is so closely allied to culture, to the history of civilizations, to individual and group behavior, and to systems of government and economics, there are numerous views to be considered in order to answer fundamental questions about clothing. We have selected, therefore, a multidiscipline, social science approach to the study of clothing. Anthropology, history, social psychology, and economics each have a different perspective on the role of clothing in the lives of people.

Anthropology contributes the interpretation of culture as related to the clothing and adornment of prehistoric peoples, existing nonliterate and preindustrial tribes, racial, ethnic, and national groups in varying degrees of social absorption, and in general, contemporary cultures of the world at whatever stage of development. Field work among the world's few remaining primitive peoples is the forte of the cultural anthropologist. Because of the relative simplicity of their lives, such groups are more or less controlled laboratories for study of customs, including dress and adornment, social structure, language, religion, and the methods of obtaining or producing the necessities of life. From investigations of primitive groups which have been isolated from other cultures, anthropologists are sometimes able to speculate about the culture of prehistoric man and offer insight into man's cultural evolution.

History adds the dimension of past civilizations to the study of clothing. What has gone before is often a key to understanding the present—what is happening now. Analysis of the relationships of forms and styles of dress to the technology, art, science, political events, and social conditions of a particular civilization is facilitated by a study of history.

Psychologists study the behavior of young children to gain insights into natural human responses, the assumption being that cultural influences and social conditions have not yet appreciably modified behavior. Psychology explores the mind and conscious and unconscious determinants of behavior.

The behavior and organization of groups of people is the focus of sociology. The sociologist investigates the collective behavior, social interaction, and structure of various cultural and subcultural groups.

Behavior of a group which is deviant from the mainstream of a society may be interpreted by the sociologist, while individual deviant behavior may be the concern of the psychologist. *Social psychology* is a broader field, combining the emphasis of psychology with that of sociology to analyze behavior. Social psychology helps to explain clothing behavior.

Economics is the study of the means man employs to satisfy his desires—the production, distribution, and consumption of goods and services. Economists investigate resource allocation; wealth and poverty; economic conditions, such as inflation and recession; the economic policies of government as they affect producers, consumers, and international trade; and the flow of goods, services, and income. All of these conditions influence consumers and producers in the markets for clothing goods and clothing related services, such as dry cleaning and laundering.

We propose that the social science aspects of clothing offer a broad foundation for further study, stimulating to the technical education of the textile scientist and the aesthetic experience of the textile or apparel designer, and enlightening to students in clothing and textiles fields leading to professions in advertising, promotion, sales, production, and consumer education. For students who do not anticipate additional formal education in clothing fields, we hope that the study of clothing is continued on an informal basis—people watching, traveling, when shopping for clothing, and even when dressing in the morning. Since everyone wears clothes almost all of the time, we feel that there is much to be gained through examination of such a uniquely human and integral facet of living.

It is fortunate that many social scientists and popular writers have considered clothing from the viewpoints of the various social sciences. We have grouped together those writings which seem to handle the topic within the broad perspectives of the particular discipline. We have left the challenging prospect of integration of these divergent theories and analyses to the students and teachers using this book. We expect that at least some of the readings will stimulate discussion and debate—even disagreement—along the way toward increasing knowledge and the understanding of dimensions of dress and adornment.

Lois M. Gurel
Marianne S. Beeson

PREFACE

Our first step in planning for the third edition of this book was to survey instructors who have adopted it in their own courses. We were gratified to receive a very high percentage of returns. Thank you to all who took time to describe how you use the book and to give us suggestions for the revised edition.

We learned how richly diversified are the courses which use this readings book as a text. The intriguing course titles alone were enough to conjure up a fantasy of a cross country course-auditing marathon! How much we could learn from a direct approach.

In the meantime we have tried to accommodate the needs of as many colleges and universities as possible. Realizing now that the book is being used at all class levels, including graduate, we have chosen readings for the third edition which should appeal to a wider audience. For those courses which use our book in addition to other texts and for those institutions which separate the social science aspects of clothing into two or more basic courses, we expect that the expanded third edition will be more than is needed. However, we know that as teachers you will be selective as always in the readings you assign. We are confident, too, that curiosity will lead you as students to read selections that are not assigned, on topics that are not part of the course. Therefore, these "unassigned" pages may actually contribute to general knowledge and background for future courses.

We have concluded from our survey that evaluating students' understanding of the concepts presented here, for the most part through testing, has been a problem for many instructors using this book as a text. The circumstances are understandable, since most of these readings are primarily essay in form, that is offering the personal view of the author. Often a particular view may be totally opposed by others who cite different evidence or make differing, but equally legitimate interpretations. We propose that this situation is in fact a positive one because it demands critical thinking. The instructor's position is crucial—helping students to analyze diverse essays in terms of reliability of supporting evidence and the logic of conclusions. We believe that central to a positive approach is encouragement to explore related topics and to search for additional examples and confirmation to sustain theories about dress and adornment. Specifically, we have found that student essays and reports, library assignments involving summarization of supplementary readings on note cards or through critiques, and "open book" tests, permitting the use of note cards as well as the text, are meaningful tools for evaluation.

Thus, with the aim of guiding students in assignments such as those mentioned above, we have added to the third edition lists of "Additional Readings" accompanying each chapter. Some entries contribute to a topic already covered in the chapter, and others are on subjects related to the social science discipline of the chapter but not represented in the readings. Another reason for developing these lists was to direct readers to important articles and books which we were unable to reprint due to limitations imposed by the budget for permission fees. Our objective to hold down the retail price of the book was often an overriding factor as we made selections from many interesting possibilities.

Of course, further sources can be located through the footnotes and reference lists connected with many of the reprinted articles. In cases where selections are excerpted from larger works, such as books, the entire reference may be worthwhile reading and also a good source of pictures. A visual presentation of the various clothing themes is essential we believe. We have indicated through annotations to "Additional Readings" which ones are particularly good sources of photographs or illustrations. By using an opaque projector, illustrations can be viewed by an entire class. Instructors assembling illustrations for class lectures and students preparing oral reports will usually find excellent illustrations by first examining the original books and periodicals which are quoted in this readings book, then through a check of references cited where possible, as well as by the use of the "Additional Readings."

It is satisfying and also humbling to know that our efforts in searching out the materials to produce this book of readings have been, for the most part, appreciated and that the book is considered useful to the education process. We continue to welcome comments and suggestions from the students and teachers using *Dimensions of Dress and Adornment*.

Lois M. Gurel
Marianne S. Beeson

CHAPTER 1

Clothing and Man

INTRODUCTION

Lois M. Gurel

One of the basic instincts of mankind is that of creativity. A universal expression of this instinct is the need for man to add beauty, as he sees it, to the immediate world in which he lives, his near environment. The most intimate part of this near environment is his own body, and the desire to add a decorative layer, a "second skin," to the basic form provided by nature is universal in mankind. Regardless of why, when, or where man first wore clothes, it is an established fact that once he began to do so he has never stopped. There are no peoples that have yet been discovered, past or present, that do not cover or decorate their bodies in some fashion.

Before we can describe and discuss the various ways in which man has tried to beautify the body provided him, certain terminology must be made clear, lest we get bogged down in semantics. Clothing or dress may refer to those items that are put on the body, that cover the body, and generally that have a functional utility. Adornment may refer only to those items or practices used for decoration with no utilitarian purpose. Often these terms are used interchangeably and we shall do so in this book. We will refer to clothing as dress *and* adornment.

It must, also, clearly be understood that the use of the word "man," both in the title of this chapter and in the articles that follow, has no sexual connotation. Other animals, in their adaptation to a variety of environmental conditions, have become differentiated into a wide variety of species. But all the races of mankind remain members of one specie, *Homo Sapiens*. It is to this concept that we direct the term "man" in these readings.

Thus by man we mean mankind **and** womankind, males **and** females, men **and** women. This idea by no means implies that there are not variations in physical characteristics among *Homo Sapiens* due to environment and heredity. But rather, the implication is that these variations are minor compared to the similarities that exist, and that man belongs to a single biological classification.

The first two articles in this chapter are presented by way of an introduction to the few known facts and the many conjectures about the beginnings and the purposes of clothing. So that you may begin to think of clothing in a broad sense, this background should provide a firmer base for future readings.

It is interesting to compare the points of view presented in these two selections with the third article. Coming from a discipline not usually associated with clothing, Desmond Morris is a well known zoologist who has expanded his interest in animal behavior to include human behavior. Among his several best selling books are *The Naked Ape, The Human Zoo* and the most recent, *Manwatching,* from which this article was taken.

However clothing may have "happened," or for whatever reason, its importance to the development of man is established. This importance of clothing was best expressed as follows:

> Of the biological inventions of the past, four were made before the dawn of history. I refer to the domestication of animals, the domestication of plants, the domestication of fungi for the production of alcohol, and a fourth inventon which I believe was of more ultimate and far-reaching importance than any of these, since it altered the path of sexual selection, focused the attention of man as lover upon woman's face and breasts, and changed our idea of beauty from the steatopygous Hottentot to the modern European, from the Venus of Brassemt to the Venus of Milo (J.B.S. Haldane in Daedalus).[1]

ADDITIONAL READINGS

On the universality of clothing and adornment:

Severin, Timothy. *The Horizon Book of Vanishing Primitive Man.* N.Y.: American Heritage Publishing Co., 1973.
  Excellent color photographs.

Wax, Murray. "Themes in Cosmetics and Grooming," *American* Journal of Sociology, May 1957, pp. 588–593.
  The universality of cosmetic and grooming practices in human societies.

On functions of dress:

Guthrie, R. Dale. *Body Hot Spots: the Anatomy of Human Social Organs and Behavior.* N.Y.: Van Nostrand Reinhold Co., 1976.
  Clothing, sunglasses, jewelry, and make-up are described as means of dramatizing or concealing body "hot spots."

1. Adams, J.D. *Naked We Came.* New York: Holt, Rinehart and Winston, 1967, p. 37.

Flugel, J.C. *The Psychology of Clothes.* New York: International Universities Press, Inc., 1971 (reprint of the 1930 edition).

Examples of body adornment:

Chagnon, Napoleon. "Yanomamo: the True People," *National Geographic,* Vol. 150, No. 2, August 1976, pp. 211–223.

Chagnon, Napoleon A. *Yanomamo: the Fierce People.* N.Y.: Holt, Rinehart and Winston, 1968.

MacLeish, Kenneth and Conger, Dean. "Help for Philippine Tribes in Trouble," *National Geographic,* Vol. 140, No. 2, August 1971, pp. 220–255.

Photographs of ear piercing among Ubo men and women.

Luz, Oskar and Horst. "Proud Primitives, the Nuba People," *National Geographic,* Vol. 130, No. 5, November 1966, pp. 673–699.

Scarification, patterned head shaving, lip plugs, and nose, lip and ear piercing are shown in photographs.

Mullar, Kal. "Taboos and Magic Rule Namba Lives," *National Geographic,* Vol. 141, No. 1, January 1972, pp. 57–82.

Process of knocking out a woman's front teeth is shown, symbol of her marital status.

Richie, Donald. "The Japanese Art of Tattooing,"*Natural History,* Vol. 82, No. 10, December 1973, pp. 50–59.

Schultz, Harald. "The Waura: Brazilian Indians of the Hidden Xingu," *National Geographic,* Vol. 129, No. 1, January 1966, pp. 130–152.

Body painting and hair dyeing are photographed.

Levy, Howard S. *Chinese Footbinding: The History of a Curious Erotic Custom.* N.Y.: Bell Publishing Co., 1967.

THE ORIGINS OF DRESS

Lois M. Gurel

Decoration of the human body has been universal among all of mankind for thousands of years, however, there is very little evidence to support a theory as to where or when adornment was first used or the form in which clothing first appeared. Archaeology has provided some evidence of dress and ornamentation from prehistoric times. However, the fibers, fabrics, and furs, materials used for clothing by early man, have rarely been preserved as have stone and ceramic tools and implements. Articles of adornment have been found in the forms of hard jewelry and body paint.

Ochre, a pigment used for body decoration, found at the Neanderthal burial sites of the early Paleolithic era of the Old Stone Age (about 50,000 years ago) provides the first direct evidence that man decorated his body. Also from this period, stone scrapers, similar to those used by some primitive tribes today to scrape fat and flesh from hides in preparing them for clothing, have been uncovered. The extreme cold of northern Russia has preserved a few skin and fur garments from the Old Stone Age, as well as beads of ivory and fox teeth (1, p. 4). Other evidence also indicates that man lived in Northern Europe during the Old Stone Age. In order to survive the glacial periods of this era he would have had to have some form of protection from the cold. Whole skins, furs, and eventually sheep fleece were wrapped around the body for warmth, and later in time, holes were punched in the skins with an awl like tool and the skins laced together. The Ice Age hunters of the New World lived about 20,000 years ago. They were not ape men, but made weapons, spoke a language, and wore furs for protection from the fierce cold of glacier gripped North America (2, p. 782).

Cave paintings, executed at a slightly later date, the late Paleolithic Era—25,000–40,000 years ago—depict forms that might be human decorated in ways that suggest bodily adornment, if not actual garments. As time passed cave paintings became more sophisticated and by 20,000 B.C. the figures were decidedly human and of both sexes—the women clad in feathered skirts, the men in ceremonial masks. Remarkable cave paintings made by ancient hunter-artists, found in Lascaux Cave, in southwestern France, were done about 15,500 years ago.

From this same period (25,000–40,000 years ago) archaeologists have found what may be considered reliable evidence that man knew how to sew—the first eyed bone needles, probably used to fashion simple skin and fur garments similar to those worn by the American Indians in the past and the Eskimos today. It is safe to guess that they painted these skin garments. Their use of color is seen in the cave paintings of this period and it is logical to assume that they extended this art to their clothing. They may even have printed off designs on their clothes using bone cylinders (3, p. 95).

Clovis-Folsom man (named from early discoveries in Folsom and Clovis, New Mexico) lived over 12,000–15,000 years ago. Discoveries of a crude paint pot from these excavations lend credence to the theory of an early use of paint for body adornment and clothing. Folsom man also wore ornaments. Beads and pendants made from lignite, bone, and red hematite have been uncovered from a camp site in Lindenneier Valley, Colorado (2, p. 797).

Although evidence is scanty, we can say with some degree of certainty that man did begin to wear clothes between 50,000 and 25,000 years ago and had reached a fairly sophisticated level of ornamentation by 15,000 B.C.

It is interesting to note how closely the dates provided by mythology parallel archaeological finds. According to Chinese legend, the first man and emperor was Pan Kon. He separated the heavens and earth 129,600 years ago. The period of the past, from then to the present day, was divided into twelve parts, called conjunctions, of 10,800 years each.

Sometime during the eighth conjunction "men covered themselves with vestments of leaves." However, the waters had not yet subsided and men were miserable. So, "they covered themselves with skins of beasts to preserve themselves from the colds and winds." If you figure these dates out mathematically you will find that according to ancient Chinese mythology man began to wear bodily coverings to protect himself from the cold sometime between 32,000 and 54,000 years ago (4, p. 2).

The oldest extant fragments of fabric were found in Switzerland in the year 1854. Following a severe drought, the water level of the lakes fell to such a low point that remains of an ancient Neolithic people were discovered. These people lived 10,000 years ago and had built their homes on wooden piles over the water's surface. These Swiss Lake Dwellers cultivated flax and wove linen fabrics with a high level of technical skill. No complete garments, or even very large pieces of fabric, were found. These Swiss Lake Dwellers probably did not cut, sew, and fashion their fabrics into tailored garments but simply draped them around the body in the manner of classical Greece and Rome. The oldest extant item of clothing found in North America is almost as old as those found in Switzerland. A pair of fiber sandals made from shredded sagebrush bark has been found at Fort Rock Cave, Oregon.

Dated by the carbon 14 method, these sandals are about 9,000 years old (2, p. 787).

> The atoms of carbon 14 are radioactive, like those of radium or uranium . . . this radioactive carbon is created high in the earth's atmosphere by powerful cosmic rays coming from outer space. The rays produce neutrons, which react with nitrogen in the air to create atoms of carbon 14, so named because each has a nucleus composed of 14 nucleons.
>
> Gradually the carbon 14 atoms descend to lower levels . . . and are absorbed by plants in their growing process. . . . Carbon 14 breaks down at a fixed rate. During life, the carbon 14 in humans, animals, and plants is constantly disintegrating and being replaced. After death the carbon 14 in the remains continues to disintegrate but is no longer renewed. Consequently, the time that has elapsed since death can be measured by determining how much carbon 14 is still present in proportion to the ordinary carbon which does not disintegrate (2, pp. 784, 787).

This completes the inventory of present evidence concerning the clothing of prehistoric times, the time prior to the beginnings of recorded history about 5,000 years ago—some ochre and other evidence of paint, a few cave paintings, and some scraps of linen cloth and sagebrush sandals.

REFERENCES CITED

1. Roach, M.E., and Eicher, J.B. *The Visible Self: Perspectives on Dress.* Englewood Cliffs, N.J.: Prentice-Hall, Inc., 1973.
2. Henry, T.R. "Ice Age Man, the First American." *National Geographic Magazine,* CVIII, No. 6, December, 1955.
3. Wells, H.G. *The Outline of History.* Garden City, N.Y.: Garden City Books, 1949.
4. Hiler, Hilaire. *From Nudity to Raiment.* New York: The Educational Press, 1930.

THE FUNCTION OF DRESS

Lois M. Gurel

Since the origin of clothing remains obscured in the past history of man, the next question that one may ask, then, if not "When?" or "What?" is "Why?" Why did man first begin to wear clothes? What made him give up the freedom he had enjoyed without them? Just as we cannot know for sure *when* man first began to wear clothing, so we only speculate on *why* he did. Although many theories have been suggested, four major ones emerge and have been agreed upon by most specialists in the clothing field: modesty, immodesty, protection, and decoration or adornment.

The Modesty Theory

The modesty theory is often called the Mosaic theory, or Biblical version for why man wears clothes. This theory implies that costume originated because of an innate sense of shame that led man to adopt a covering for his naked body. Foundation for this theory comes from the Old Testament, the Book of Genesis attributed to Moses (hence the term "Mosaic").

> Then the eyes of both were opened, and they knew that they were naked; and they sewed fig leaves together and made themselves aprons. . . . And the Lord God made for Adam and for his wife garments of skins, and clothed them (Genesis 3:7, 21).

This instinctual theory, while a popular one to this day, has been disputed by authorities for several reasons. It is true that most people in the world today use clothing to conceal parts of the body; it is also true that most people feel shame if these parts that are generally covered, are exposed. However, what is covered or left uncovered varies from group to group. The concept of modesty is not the same in all societies. As an example, in opposition to miniskirted America, Micronesian women wear waist to knee lava-lavas woven from hibiscus bark. ". . . a woman's thighs must be modestly covered, but her breasts may go bare (1, p. 708)." In most of the world, "Pornography matter of geography (2)."

Standards of modesty have also changed with time. There have been many periods in the history of Western civilization where the sight of an ankle was considered shameful and many where the "see-through" look was considered the utmost in fashion. During the mid-seventeenth century, the topless look was "in" at the court of Charles II of England, but by the early twentieth century something as radical as a V-neck dress was denounced from the pulpit as immoral and by physicians as likely to lead to pneumonia. One must remember that clothing itself is neither moral nor immoral. It is the breaking of traditions which makes it so.

The behavior of small children has also led to the unacceptance of the modesty theory by scholars in the study of clothing behavior. Small children do not have an innate sense of modesty. They are quite content to remove their clothing in public until the pressures of society and their parents dictate otherwise. And the concept of modesty changes with age, even within Western civilization. It is acceptable to undress a small child, to change a baby's diaper in public. Pictures of nude babies appear in magazines and newspapers, on television, and on walls and mantlepieces. At some age, some point in time, what is considered cute becomes indecent exposure, punishable by laws rigidly enforced in most Western countries. Modesty may be, indeed, a contributing reason for the use of clothing, both today and in the past, but it is unlikely that it was either the original or primary function of dress or body adornment.

The Immodesty Theory

A second and closely related theory to the modesty theory has been labeled the immodesty theory. Proponents of this theory believe that clothes were first used as a sexual lure, to call attention to parts of the body that were covered. Although we may point out articles of clothing, both modern and historical that seem to exist solely for sexual attraction, it is, nevertheless, difficult to conceive of primitive man, who had been naked, adopting clothes for this reason alone.

Vocal and persuasive proponents of the immodesty theory have been the late James Laver, who was costume historian and curator of the Victoria and Albert Museum in London, England, and Lawrence Langner, late director of the New York Theater Guild. Laver believed that the purpose of fashion and the objective of clothes was to draw attention to various erogenous bodily areas. The "theory of shifting erogenous zones" is based on the premise that the female body is so desirable and so alluring to men that they cannot see it all at once but must be compelled to pay attention to only one part at a time. Fashion plays the role of shifting this emphasis so that attention is not given to one part long enough to lose its power to excite men. Fashion may do this in many ways, by drawing clothes tightly around an area, exposing it, or exaggerating its size. We may use for examples the low neck, cinched waists, the bustle, and the miniskirt. In fact, the entire cycle of rising and falling skirt lengths can be used as an example of the shifting emphasis from and to legs.

Langner believed that the main purpose of clothing was to stimulate sexual interest, but by its use, not its absence. He believed that it is man's curiosity about what is under the clothing that keeps up interest in mating and so perpetuates the human race. If it were not for this curiosity, if everyone were naked, all interest in sex would be lost and the human race would die out (3, Chapter 3). Or, if all sex did not cease to be, then we would be reduced to a once a year spring mating season like most other mammals. Clothing, and the curiosity about what is under it, is really responsible for our year round sexual life.

> Man appears to be the only creature among the higher mammals of which the female, as well as the male, for better or for worse, maintains an interest in sexual activity, spring, summer, fall and winter, and morning, noon and night. . . . Among mammals, mating is usually a seasonal affair, related to the ovulation of the female. With most higher mammals this takes place in the spring and only during the limited period that fertile mating and therefore reproduction of the species is possible. Thus we find that the curiosity aroused by wearing clothes and the stimulus due to their removal is part and parcel of our all-the-year-round sexual life. This is merciful, for if we had a spring mating season like most other mammals, our babies would all be born around Christmas time, and we would never be able to find sufficient obstetricians, midwives, or hospital beds to bring them all into the world at once. Moreover, during the spring, mankind would have to cease most of its other activities, and concentrate on mating. We therefore should be grateful for the role played by clothing in helping to spread our sexual activities over all four seasons of the year (3, pp. 39–41).

Immodesty, as well as modesty, are culturally determined functions of clothing and not likely the original reasons that man covered his nakedness.

The Protection Theory

The use of clothing for protection from the weather came late in human development. Since man originated in tropical or subtropical lands, at the beginning of his life on earth he had little need for clothing to keep him warm. When he discovered the use of animal skins and furs, as well as shelter, to protect him from the cold, he was able to wander farther from his origins and extend his territories into more northerly climes. This cultural adaptivity made it possible for him to survive the approaching ice ages in the northern areas of the world. Without this ability, unique to man, he would likely still be confined to the tropical regions of the world.

Other physical hazards concerned prehistoric man; he needed protection from insects, thorns, and underbrush, particularly protection for the sexual organs. Langner believed that until man stood erect his posture served as protection, but when he no longer crouched or crawled his sexual organs were fully exposed, and so early clothing served to protect and not to hide these parts (3). Of course this theory does nothing to explain why women first began to wear aprons and eventually skirts. Mr. Langner does not address himself to the fact that women were no more exposed erect than they had been in a crouched position.

Psychological protection was also an early function of clothing, protection from the evil eye, from unseen spirits, and from gods. Particularly susceptible to evil spirits were the organs of fertility and reproduction, and many G-strings, sheaths, aprons, and supporters served to protect these parts from perils both physical and psychic.

It is important to observe that clothing, like other products of culture, is not to be explained in terms of biological needs alone. Clothing serves many functions other than the obvious one of protecting the wearer from weather, troublesome insects, and other environmental hazards. Some—perhaps most—of these functions are to satisfy culturally created needs, as is seen from the fact that their expression varies enormously from one society to the next. Even the biological function of clothing is strongly conditioned by the culture—sometimes . . . to the extent of rendering the clothing inadequate protection against the weather (4, p. 314).

The Adornment Theory

A fourth function of dress is that of decoration or adornment. This is probably the most important and the original function of clothing. Creativity is expressed in the urge to improve upon nature by decorating, altering, shaping, and covering the body. It is plausible to imagine that clothing began when some early ancestor of ours was attracted to a bright stone, or a pretty shell, or even a flower. He picked it up and carried it along with him. Then, needing his hands for whatever work he was doing, he tied the shell (or the flower, or the stone) to a piece of vine and hung it around his neck, or his waist—and so man began to wear clothes. This decorative instinct, this interest in something bright and shiny, can be observed among the primates—monkeys, apes, chimpanzees—both in captivity and in the wilds. Give them bright scraps of cloth, ribbons, straw flowers, fancy hats—they will often hang them about their bodies in some fashion.

Decoration of the body takes many forms, and in some societies there are variations totally divorced from and more important than clothing. Body painting, tattooing, scarification, and mutilation of parts of the body are some of the ways that people use to adorn themselves.

Body painting. Body paint may range from elaborate painted clothing found among many primitive South American Indian tribes to the cosmetics and fingernail polish used in more technologically advanced cultures. In the United States today we spend 4.2 billion dollars annually on body paint preparations, that is cosmetics (5). Painting is not permanent; it must be constantly renewed; even after many thousands of years of body painting the techniques have not appreciably changed. Paint comes off on clothing, upholstery, eating utensils, and occasionally our fellow men. Primitive man uses paint in a superior way. He simply paints on his clothing and uses his body as an artist uses his canvas. Modern man just patches up areas left uncovered by cloth or leather.

Hair coloring is also a form of body painting. Of the total amount spent on cosmetics today, 27% or over a billion dollars, is spent on hair preparation annually (5). Bleaching and dyeing of hair was known in antiquity, and blondes had more fun as long ago as the Renaissance. Artificial red heads lived and played in ancient Greece—shown by the statuary on the ruins of temples such as the Maidens of the Acropolis.

Tattooing. The problem with paint is that it does not last but must constantly be renewed. The solution to this problem—tattooing. The technique used is to puncture the skin with a needle carrying an indelible dye. It is a long, painful process, but very rewarding socially in some societies. Tattooing is found throughout the world, the two main centers of this art being Japan and Polynesia. There, the higher the status, the more tattooing. In parts of Polynesia, tattooing may extend over the face, torso, limbs, and in some overenthusiastic cases, the tongue. Tattooing is also used as a means of tribal identification and a part of initiation ceremonies or rites of passage.

Unusual tattoos are those of the Ainu, aboriginal inhabitants of Japan's Hokkaido island. Lip tattoos, now an obsolete custom and prohibited by Japanese law, can still be seen on older generation women. The tattoos are made with the soot from the bottom of cooking pots giving them their characteristic blue color. Coming from the sacred fire, the tattoos helped the women obtain good husbands and protected them from evil, particularly evil that might enter by way of nose or mouth (6).

The Japanese thought our tattooing a cruel practice, and so they forbade it. . . . Maybe it was, but tattooed lips meant we were marriageable. I was tattooed against my will at 17, but now I'm glad it was done. I found a husband right away (6, 278).

As modern society attempts to enforce their values on the remaining Stone Age civilizations, ancient tribal customs change. But in Polynesia tattooing remains a highly developed art rich in custom and tradition. However, many teenagers on the Island of Yap in Micronesia, now make their ritualistic tattoo marks with felt-tipped pens imported from the United States (1, p. 716).

Scarification. For dark skinned peoples, tattooing is not a practical decorative device since no white dyes have been discovered for this purpose. African and Australian tribes have resorted to scarification or cicatrization for body decorations. Scarification involves cutting the skin and rubbing irritants into the wounds to cause scar tissue in the form of raised lumps or welts. Generally a part of some rites of passage, the resulting scars are often produced in elaborate geometric designs and are highly symbolic.

Among the Bushmen in the Kalahari Desert in southern Africa, a boy cannot marry until he has made his first kill of a large game animal. The dead animal is used in the following initiation rites, an elaborate scarification ritual. Foam from the boiling meat is made into a paste which is rubbed into the cuts made in the body: between the eyes to give him good vision, on legs and arms for strength and good aim, and on the breast to ensure good lungs (7, p. 880).

Deformation. Of all the animals, only man has the urge to alter his body through deformation, mutilation, removal, or disfigurement of body parts. Among the many ways he has devised to do this, some actually inhibit the healthy functioning of the human body.

Least harmful, perhaps, is the practice of piercing the nasal septum, the lips, or the ears so a wide variety of objects may be inserted into the holes. Some tribes extend the ear lobes so that disks six to eight inches long may be inserted into the created openings. Even among "so called" civilized peoples ear piercing is a common practice. The invention of the screw back and clip earrings did not abolish this practice. In fact it has become increasingly popular in recent years, particularly among the younger generation. Noseplugs that block all entry of air and lip-plugs that reduce the diet of a people to soup and mush are found in many places.

Both head and foot binding have been practiced in many times and locales. Adherents of head binding lived in Ancient Egypt, among the American Indians, and with the provincial French as well as among some primitive tribes today. Styles ranged from cones, wedges, and cylinders to flat-tops with various devices and contraptions used to achieve the right degree of shaping. In many tribes mothers bind their infants' heads in bark cloth, rewrapping and tightening the binding daily for many months.

The most notorious deliberate use of foot multilations have been practiced by the Chinese. For 800 years they crippled their women by making the deformed Lily foot the ideal of female beauty. "The shape of the Lily foot is man-made; it is foreign to human anatomy." It is an artificial look that illustrates ". . . that man derives an infinitely stronger satisfaction from his art work . . . than from the products of Nature (8, p. 76)." But modern civilization also deforms the foot, perhaps unintentionally. The effects of years of squeezing feet into shoes designed by manufacturers for the ideal foot can be seen by looking at the bare feet of a middle aged person, particularly a woman.

"Human feet are defective. Their most obvious fault is their not being identical . . . after millions of years of human evolution, there still remains a right and a left foot (8, p. 75)." Shoemakers have been trying for just about the same length of time to overcome this difference by making shoes look as identical as possible. "The ultimate triumph of contemporary clothing is the symmetrical shoe, our deepest regret is our inability to develop a symmetrical foot (8, p. 74)."

Filing teeth or knocking them out is still another form of mutilation that occurs in scattered places in the South Pacific. Although one must be cautious about applying personal value judgments to the ways in which others beautify their bodies, this decorative practice imposed by man upon his body is perhaps the most foolish. Scarification and tattooing, while painful and perhaps repulsive to us, seldom cause death or illness (unless the wound becomes infected). They do not inhibit natural bodily processes. The deliberate destruction of the teeth does, however, since it interferes with normal digestion and often results in malnutrition and death.

Why do people wear clothes? Why did man first begin to wear clothes? A number of possible answers to these questions have been offered in the form of four theories commonly accepted by authorities in the clothing field. Pros and cons for accepting or rejecting them have been presented. It may be that more than one of these theories was the reason why clothing was first used. Or that one theory was operating in one culture while another theory was the primary reason in a different place. Or that none of these reasons was the original motive for wearing clothes. No one knows for sure. After careful study educated guesses may be made. Personal opinions are permissible about why man first wore clothes, but these opinions must be based on a careful evaluation of existing evidence.

REFERENCES CITED

1. Boyer, D.S. "Micronesia: The Americanization of Eden." *National Geographic Magazine.* 131, No. 5, May, 1967, pp. 702–744.
2. *Teahouse of the August Moon.* Play by John Patrick Goggan. Novel by Vern J. Sneider.
3. Langner, L. *The Importance of Wearing Clothes.* New York: Hastings House, 1959.
4. Beals, R., and Hoijer, H. *An Introduction to Anthropology.* New York: Macmillan Co., 1959.

5. *Standard and Poor's Industry Surveys.* July 19, 1973.
6. Hilger, Sister M.I. "Japan's 'Sky People,' The Vanishing Ainu." *National Geographic Magazine.* 131, No. 2, February 1967, pp. 268–288.
7. Thomas, E.M. "Bushmen of the Kalahari." *National Geographic Magazine,* 123, No. 6, June 1963, pp. 867–888.
8. Rudofsky, B. *Are Clothes Modern?* Chicago: Paul Theobald, 1947.

CLOTHING SIGNALS: CLOTHING AS DISPLAY, COMFORT AND MODESTY

Desmond Morris

It is impossible to wear clothes without transmitting social signals. Every costume tells a story, often a very subtle one, about its wearer. Even those people who insist that they despise attention to clothing, and dress as casually as possible, are making quite specific comments on their social roles and their attitudes towards the culture in which they live.

For the majority of people, Clothing Signals are the result of a single daily event—the act of dressing, performed each morning. At the top and bottom of the social scale this activity may lose its once-a-day frequency, with rich socialities changing several times daily as a matter of course, and poor vagrants sleeping rough in the same clothes they wear by day. Between these two extremes, the once-a-day routine is usually only broken for the donning of specialized clothing. The man who gets dirty wears working clothes, the sportsman wears high-activity clothes. People attending special ceremonies—weddings, funerals, garden parties, dances, festivals, club meetings, formal dinners—change into the appropriate costumes. But although these pursuits mean the doubling of the once-a-day act of dressing, the change is nearly always from 'everyday' clothes into 'special' clothing. The old pattern, in which social rules demanded the changing from 'morning dress' to 'afternoon dress' to 'evening dress,' as a matter of regular routine, has now virtually vanished.

The modern trend in dressing behaviour is usually referred to as one of increased informality, but this is misleading. In reality, there is no loss of formality, merely the exchange of old formalities for new. The wearing of a pair of jeans by a young male today is as much of a formality as was the wearing of a top hat by his equivalent in a previous epoch. He may feel that he is free to wear anything he pleases, and is rid at last of the suffocating rules of costume etiquette that once dominated social life, but what he is pleased to wear is as much a uniform today as the costumes of his predecessors were in earlier times.

The written rules of yesterday may have been scrapped, but they have rapidly been replaced by the unwritten rules of today.

To understand these rules we have to look back at the origins of clothing as a pattern of human behaviour. Basically, clothes have three functions: comfort, modesty and display. Comfort is, of course, the utilitarian function of garments, non-social and personal. Early man evolved in a warm climate, where his temperature control system operated efficiently. His constant internal body temperature of 37°C, combined with his naked skin surface, worked well enough without artificial aids. He was helped by several important physiological mechanisms that had the same effect as taking off or putting on a layer of clothing. He could, for example, change the flow of blood at the body surface by dilating or constricting the blood vessels in the skin, the maximum blood-flow through the skin being twenty times the minimum level. It has been calculated that pushing the hot blood to the surface in this way is roughly equivalent to the shedding of a woollen garment such as a pullover. Heat loss from the hot skin is further improved by the human ability to sweat copiously from almost the whole body surface. Early human hunters, engaged in violent physical activity, must have experienced a dramatic increase in the amount of heat produced by the internal metabolic processes of the body—something like five times the resting level—and their naked skin surface must have been a valuable aid to temperature control under these conditions, providing a large area for sweat loss and therefore for heat loss by evaporation. The human body is capable of a continuous output over an hour of up to one litre of sweat, increasing to as much as four times this rate for short periods.

Excerpted from "*Manwatching: A Field Guide to Human Behavior*" by Desmond Morris. N.Y.: Harry N. Abrams, Inc., 1977, pp. 213–220. Reprinted by permission of the publisher.

With its variable heat production and its variable heat loss, the unclothed human body was—and is—capable of maintaining the constant body-temperature so vital for our species, despite variations in physical activity and despite minor fluctuations in climate. But when man started to explore and strike out across the globe, to the burning hot deserts and the icy polar regions, the natural body-system could not cope with the demands put upon it. Protective clothing became essential, either to reduce heat loss from the skin surface or to shield the skin from the direct blast of the sun's rays. With the passage of time, as human activities became more and more complex, additional forms of protection were required—against sharp surfaces that could damage the skin, against intense light, against attack from sharp weapons, against loss of oxygen, and against excessive radiation. Each new demand gave rise to new forms of protective clothing, from thick shoes and heavy gloves to helmets and suits of armour, from deep-sea diving suits to space suits, from goggles and sun-glasses to snorkels and welding-masks, from overalls to bullet-proof vests.

From the very beginning, protective clothing of these different kinds created problems. Not only did they decrease the efficiency of the muscular actions of the body, but they also introduced special health hazards. They reduced skin ventilation and they interfered with the removal of sweat from the skin surface. Also they provided a haven of rest and a hiding place for a wide variety of tiny parasites. When naked, in primeval times, the human skin suffered none of these problems. The millions of microbes living on it were kept in a state of equilibrium. But unventilated, clogged with decaying sweat and besieged by parasites, the body surface quickly fell prey to all kinds of diseases. At best, there was unpleasant 'body odour'; at worst, epidemics. Unable to abandon his protective clothing, man was forced to develop the counter-balancing devices of perfumery and hygiene. Scents were widely used to mask smells, and washing, of both bodies and clothes, was used to remove them. Today, at last, with medical hygiene adding its weight to normal ablutions, modern man has managed to return to a comparatively healthy skin condition, similar to that of his primeval ancestors, without resorting to the naked state.

If clothing were simply a matter of comfort and protection, then there are many occasions when we could all abandon our costumes, thanks to modern technology. We have air-conditioning, central heating and soft furnishings in our homes and could easily wine, dine, entertain and relax in the nude without any protective problems arising. The fact that we do not do so leads on to the second basic function of clothing, that of modesty. In this role, clothing acts as a concealment device. Garments are worn to switch off certain body signals. Ever since early man went upright and walked on his hind legs he has been unable to approach another member of his species without giving a sexual display. For other primates this problem does not arise. They approach on all fours and are forced to adopt a special 'presentation' posture if they wish to display their genitals. The 'full frontal' human body can only reduce the sexuality of its approach by hiding the sexual regions in some way. It is not surprising, therefore, to find that the loin-cloth is culturally the most widespread of all garments. In any social situation demanding costume-shedding, it is the last clothing barrier to fall.

An additional factor supporting modesty in dress has been the dramatic increase in population size. After millions of years living in small tribal units, mankind now moves about in huge urban crowds, surrounded by comparative or total strangers. Under these conditions direct sexual displays have to be damped down. Body signals have to be switched off. Even in hot climates this means body coverage that extends well beyond the genital region, and the reason is not hard to find. The human body is a mass of gender signals, and every curve of flesh, each bulge and contour, transmits its basic signals to the eyes of interested onlookers. The female breasts, the buttocks, the hips, the thighs, the waist, the slender neck, the rounded limbs, and the male chest, the body hair, the broad shoulders, the muscles of the arms and legs, all these visual elements are potentially arousing to the opposite sex. If their messages are to be reduced, then they too must be hidden by enveloping garments.

At different times and in different epochs the social rules of modesty have varied, but the basic principle has remained the same. The more anti-sexual the demands of society, the more all-covering has been the clothing. Extreme examples were the heavily veiled females of certain Arab countries, where not only was the entire body covered with clothing, including the whole of the head and face, but its shape was also concealed by the voluminous nature of the garments. Peering through the tiny slit in her heavy veil, such a female could be either a raging beauty or a hideous hag, and only her husband knew the truth for she would never appear in public, at any time in her life, in a more revealing costume.

Today it is hard to credit some of the lengths to which civilized cultures went, only a century ago, in their quest for modesty in dress. At one point, even to speak the word 'leg' in English was considered an obscenity, and the legs of grand pianos had to be clothed for public recitals. Bathing machines, in which early bathers changed into their bulky swimming costumes, were required to have curtained steps, so that their occupants could descend into the water before becoming visible to others on the beach.

Descending from these extremes of modesty it is possible to locate a whole range of degrees of exposure, with certain parts of the body gradually dropping out of the 'concealment category.' In the world of entertainment as late as the 1930s it was necessary to conceal naked navels in Hollywood movies, and naked female nipples did not appear in newspapers until the 1960s. Since then, pubic hair has sprouted on the silver screen, but if it does so in a public place its owner is still liable to prosecution. The mono-bikini swimsuit, after initial skirmishes with the police in the south of France, has now started to appear with some regularity, however, and we are back once again to the fig-leaf or loin-cloth stage in at least some of our public social contexts. In other situations the rules are still almost Victorian in their rigidity, and even the rich and powerful may find themselves expelled from certain top restaurants for exposing their naked necks, tieless, to the gaze of the other diners.

With this neck-tie rule, we move on to the third basic function of clothing, namely display. For the expulsion of tieless diners from restaurants has more to do with their refusal to wear a social label than their attempt to expose their Adam's apples. The tie, like so many other details of costume, is unimportant either as a comfort device or a modesty covering. Instead it operates as a cultural badge, slotting the wearer neatly into a particular social category. This is the most ancient use of clothing, preceding even its protective and modesty roles, and it remains today of supreme importance. The bleak ,functional tunics of spacemen from the future, beloved of writers of second-rate Science Fiction, are about as unlikely as the return of total nudity. As fast as one set of decorative accessories is stripped away, it is replaced by another, and this state of affairs is likely to continue for as long as man remains a social being. Clothing is simply too good a vehicle for visual displays for it ever to become merely a bleak, protective covering.

In the past the display function of clothing has often operated with extreme ruthlessness. In 14th-century England, for example, it was not a matter of style or taste but of law, with the parliament of the day spending much of its time laying down firm rules concerning the fashions of dress permissible for each social class. If someone of a lower social station wore clothing permitted only for higher ranks, he or she might be fined or have the offending garments confiscated. The application of the laws seems to have met with some difficulty, however, such was the desire of people to display high status via their costumes, and monarch after monarch was driven to introduce more and more restrictions and heavier fines. The details are hard to believe when viewed from the present century. These extracts from a clothing-reform act in the reign of Edward IV are typical: 'No knight under the rank of a lord . . . shall wear any gown, jacket, or cloak, that is not long enough, when he stands upright, to cover his privities and his buttocks, under the penalty of twenty shillings. . . . No knight under the rank of a lord . . . shall wear any shoes or boots having pikes or points exceeding the length of two inches, under the forfeiture of forty pence. . . .' England was not alone in these restrictions. In Renaissance Germany a woman who dressed above her station was liable to have a heavy wooden collar locked around her neck as punishment; and in America, in early New England, a woman was forbidden to wear a silk scarf unless her husband was worth a thousand dollars.

These are isolated examples chosen from thousands of such regulations which together made up a vast network of limitations imposed on costume displays in earlier periods of history. They reveal not only the fact that clothing and social status were intimately linked, but also that many people were trying to improve their status by the wearing of costumes typical of their superiors and had to be penalized for transmitting Clothing Signals that were 'beyond their station.' Today there are no such laws for everyday clothes, the only surviving regulation being the prohibition of 'indecent exposure' in public places. It is still an offence, however, for a major in any army to wear the uniform of a colonel, and specialized 'costumes of office' remain as rigidly controlled as ever.

For those without official posts it might seem that the decay of the clothing laws would lead to decorative chaos, but nothing could be further from the truth. Instead of experiencing a costume free-for-all, society applied its own restrictions. At first the legal rules were replaced by rules of etiquette, carefully written down as before but now demanding obedience to good taste rather than to the laws of the land. Then, as etiquette books faded into history with the breakdown of rigid class structures, the rules went underground. They survived but they became unwritten, almost unspoken. Today, with social 'class' amost a dirty word, these rules are subtle and complex, and are often complete inversions of the earlier systems. A British earl, for instance, when asked recently if there were any benefits in holding his social rank today, replied: 'Only one—that I do not have to dress so damned smartly as my manservant.' This comment, which would have seemed sheer lunacy to his medieval ancestors, sums up in a single sentence the major trend that has overtaken male Clothing Signals in recent generations. It is a trend that has swept the world and now applies as much to Japanese bankers and Russian politicians as it does to Norwegian architects or Portuguese school-teachers.

The explanation of the new male trend is to be found in the need for a new source of high-status clothing. If any man can buy gaudy silks and satins and adorn himself like a displaying peacock, then clearly such excesses will soon become meaningless and even vulgar, and high-status seekers must turn elsewhere for their inspiration. Where they did in fact turn, back in the eighteenth century, was the sports field. High-status males were indulging in high-status sports. English country gentlemen were taking to the hunting field and adopting a sensible mode of dress for the occasion. For ease of riding, they wore a coat that was cut away in the front, giving it the appearance of having tails at the back. Big, floppy hats were replaced by stiff top-hats, like prototype crash helmets. Once this hunting outift became established as the high-status sports-costume of the day, it became synonymous with leisure and the lack of need to work. This made it appealing as a daring form of everyday wear for the 'young bloods' of the day, and it spread from the hunting field into general social use. Gradually it became accepted, lost its daring flavour, and by the middle of the nineteenth century the slightly modified costume of 'top hat and tails' was normal, everyday wear.

As soon as this costume was commonplace it lost its high-status quality and a new sporting area had to be plundered for further 'avant-garde' costumes. This time it was the turn of shooting, fishing and golf, all costly, leisured pursuits of the well-to-do and therefore excellent sources for new costume ideas. The tough shooting-tweeds became check lounge-suits, with only minor modifications, and Billycock hats became bowlers. The softer sporting hats became trilby hats. At first the lounge-suit was still considered daring and extremely informal. Only the tailcoat was permissible for formal occasions, even though it was clearly beginning to lose ground. In no time at all the lounge-suit, by abandoning its loud checks and becoming more sombre in colour and pattern, was pushing the tailcoat out of all daytime social events until, as 'morning dress,' it retreated into the formalized contexts of weddings and other such ceremonial events, and as 'evening dress,' it retreated into a fossilized black-and-white condition for special nights on the town. Relentlessly the lounge-suit pursued it, driving it even from these strongholds, until it sank to its present relic condition as the costume of head-waiters in expensive restaurants. In its place came the ubiquitous dinner-jacket, the newly fossilized black-and-white version of the lounge suit.

No sooner had the lounge-suit reached this hallowed status than it became necessary to replace it with some new and more daring sports wear. The answer was the hacking-jacket, worn by high-status horse-riders on cross-country canters. It quickly became the everyday casual wear known as the 'sports jacket,' and soon climbed the long social path to the boardroom and the executive suite. Today it is still locked in battle with the entrenched lounge-suit, but whichever choice they make, modern businessmen are, without exception, all wearing what can accurately be described as ex-sports clothing.

In recent years a new trend has appeared. With a growing distaste, in an increasingly egalitarian society, for 'privileged' individuals, it became necessary for high-status males to perform their clothing displays in an even more subtle fashion. The man who wore a smart yachting blazer with shiny brass buttons when going out for a drink at his local bar, in imitation of a rich sporting yachtsman, was now in serious trouble. Raiding high-status sports was no longer possible. Instead it became necessary to borrow costumes from distinctly low-status occupations, in order to demonstrate that, even though you were rich and famous, you were nevertheless one of the 'poor boys' at heart. The earliest symptom of the 'poor boy' syndrome sprang from the fashion for taking Mediterranean holidays, where the rough shirts and sweaters of the local fishermen quickly became absorbed into the everyday wear of wealthy young males, and have since spread to almost all countries as casual clothing—hence the tieless disputes at many a restaurant door. Even more important was the adoption of the denim jackets and jeans of poor cowhands in the American West, a trend that is still spreading today in a hundred subtly varying forms.

There is, of course, a catch in this latest trend, for the costumes of these new, high-status males must somehow be distinguishable from the real working clothes of the low-status males who still wear them in their original contexts. The clothing signals must transmit the perverse message that: 'I approve of "poor boys," but I am not one myself.' This is done in several ways. The first is to wear the sweaters or denims in just those social situations where the true 'poor boy' would be climbing into his 'best clothes.' The second is to have the 'poor' clothes beautifully tailored and elaborately styled, without robbing them of their superficial 'poorness.' The third device is one that belongs exclusively to the modern world of mass media, and could not have existed before it. This is the famous-face contrast. Anyone who is rich and well-known, and whose face appears regularly in newspapers and magazines and on TV and cinema screens, can afford to wear the scruffiest of 'poor boy' clothes to even the most glittering occasions. He is then, by the contrast between his famous face and his faded denims, making a violent silent attack on his affluence-oriented culture. If he is carefully photographed alighting from his gleaming Rolls-Royce, while wearing his crumpled, 'poor boy' clothes, he must be forgiven for the inconsistency.

This is only one of the many interwoven trends that can be observed in the complex world of Clothing Signals. Some are long-term, lasting for whole decades, while others are short-term, surviving only for a season or two. Not all are easy to explain. . . .

CHAPTER 2

Anthropological Perspectives on Dress and Adornment

INTRODUCTION

Lois M. Gurel

By understanding the past we can cope with the present and plan for the future. When we learn about our origins we begin to appreciate the variety of ways in which we have developed. Anthropology, a comparative study of mankind, attempts to discover and compare the universalities and differences among the peoples of the world, past, and present. It has been called a bridge between the natural and the physical sciences, between behavior and biology.[1]

Traditionally, anthropology may be divided into four categories: cultural or social anthropology, archaeology, linguistics, and physical anthropology. While the articles in the preceding section review factual evidence and theories which may be considered within the fields of physical anthropology and archaeology, the articles in this chapter are primarily within the scope of cultural anthropology.

One of the tools used by anthropologists is clothing. This is a useful tool with which to study man for several reasons: (1) it is obvious (2) all peoples use some form of dress, and (3) it is found in the tombs and temples of many ancient peoples, if not extant garments, then in the form of wall and cave paintings, pottery decorations, and statuary.

Clothing practices vary because they are influenced by the physical environment and the biopsychological makeup of man. Through an anthropological approach to the study of clothing, however, we are fascinated, not only by the diversity of clothing around the world, but we are equally impressed with the amazing cultural similarities shared by all men in their quest for the necessities of life—food, shelter, clothing and a meaningful existence.

We are living in a world where physical barriers between peoples are breaking down faster than cultural ones. We are forced into contact with peoples for whom we have not even begun to reach an understanding. Large numbers of people are ethnocentric in their views. Ethnocentrism projects one's own culture's meanings onto patterns of behavior occurring in completely different cultural contexts.

1. Fox, Robin. *Encounter with Anthropology.* New York: Harcourt, Brace Jovanovich, Inc., 1973.

Man is one entity with common cultural as well as biological characteristics; at the same time man possesses a diversity of unique cultures. It becomes necessary to understand these cultures, both on their own terms and in relation to a common humanity. A greater understanding is necessary because the most diverse types of behavior can stem from universal needs and qualities, and seemingly very similar types of behavior can be caused by very real differences. This type of understanding between peoples will not come easily without some background as to how and why cultures differ and some objective facts about man and culture that make up the body of anthropological knowledge.

The value of this type of study has been questioned with a "so what" attitude. It is argued that no amount of study is going to make us accept some customs and habits. Human sacrifice, cannibalism, and slavery, as well as scarification and mutilation may be momentarily interesting, but in the long run, irrelevant, because nothing will make us like these practices. Not only do we abhor certain customs, but whole peoples may arouse our intense dislike.

Understanding, however, means knowing the reason for, and does not mean liking or even accepting. This kind of understanding does not in itself solve any problems, does not tell us how to act in the face of cultural practices that we find distressing, but, our problem if neither how to like each other or how to be all alike, but how to live together. Such understanding does, in fact, provide an essential foundation for deciding how to live together with regard for other's individual and societal differences.

Cross cultural differences that are studied within a broad framework need, also, to be studied within our own culture. In the United States there are cultural differences between north and south, east and west, urban and rural, black and white, rich and poor, and young and old. In understanding other cultures we try to look beyond customs that to us are strange, even shocking, and see recognizable people in real situations doing real things. The next step, then is to apply these same principles to a better understanding of ourselves, to look at our own cultural patterns as objectively as possible.

Alerted to the order and variation in human behavior by the study of other cultures, we can see our behavior as it is affected by our own customs and culture.

The opening articles in Chapter 2 continue with the ideas presented previously, that man, alone among animals, has an insatiable need to decorate and adorn his body even to the point of painful mutilation. Rudofsky and Morris discuss their views on overall body adornment with emphasis on the antecedents of many present day practices. Harris, on the other hand, traces the historical path of just one—the ritual of sun tanning.

Since many of the things that man does to his body are symbolic and ceremonial, Beeson's introduction to the various regalia used in the rituals associated with rites of passage allows the reader to integrate the practices of folk societies with those that occur in our own culture for similar, even if more obscure, reasons.

The remaining articles in Chapter 2 discuss the ritualistic clothing of individual countries, tribes, social, or religious groups. These are several among many more, selected by no particular criteria other than to give the reader a broad view of anthropological evidence of the diversity in the use of dress by the people of the world. Some of the articles are about practices unique to a particular country—the Kimono of Japan and the costumes of Mexico; others apply to specific parts of the world—the Eskimos and Eastern costumes; and several concern subcultural groups within a larger society.

One need not go beyond the borders of the United States to find those whose clothing differs from that of mainstream American societal norms. That they display this difference in the way they dress is especially meaningful to us in pursuing the "why's" of clothing. The dimensions of dress and adornment serve the purpose of group identification both among themselves and to those outside the fold. The last three articles are about people who cling to their old order ways of dress so as to deliberately set themselves apart from the main culture. All serve to illustrate again the universalities and diversities in dress among the cultures of the world.

ADDITIONAL READING

On rites of passage:

Kirk, Malcolm S. "Change Ripples New Guinea's Sepik River,"*National Geographic,* Vol. 144, No. 3, September 1973, pp. 354–381.

> Photographs show scarification as a rite of passage for adolescent boys. Body painting and masks for other rituals are shown.

Turnbull, Colin M. *Man in Africa.* Garden City, N.Y.: Anchor Press/Doubleday, 1976.

> Clothing, including masks and headdresses, and initiation rituals are discussed.

Lamp, Frederick, "Frogs into Princes: The Temne Rabai Initiation," *African Arts,* January 1978, pp. 38–49.

On national costume:

"Beauty of Kimono," *Japan Illustrated* Vol. 9, No. 2, 1971, pp. 28–55.

Urabe, Makoto. "Internationalized Japanese Fashion," *Japan Illustrated.* Vol. 10, Autumn, 1972, pp. 6–15.

On the dress of specific subcultures:

Firm, Jo Ann. "Parkas," *Alaska* magazine, November 1972, pp. 42–50.

> Many photographs are featured, some showing the decorative detail of parkas.

Garland, Phyl. "Is the Afro on Its Way Out?"*Ebony,* 28, February 1973, pp. 128–136.

Vine, Deloria Jr. "Largest Collection of Indian Items is Put on Display,"*Smithsonian,* Vol. 9, No. 5, August 1978, pp. 58–65.

> Masks, a wedding costume, and a patchwork counselor's coat are shown in color.

Koch, Ronald P. *Dress Clothing of the Plains Indians.* Norman: Univ. of Oklahoma Press, 1977.

Cordry, Donald and Dorothy. *Mexican Indian Costumes.* Austin: Univ. of Texas Press, 1968.

> Many color photographs of garments such as the huipil and quechquemitl. Spinning and weaving are also shown.

Neal, Avon. "It's a Big Deal Posing for Camera in Guatemala,"*Smithsonian,* Vol. 5, No. 12, March 1975, pp. 66–71.

> Color photographs of Guatemala Indians in regional costumes posing in front of non-traditional painted backgrounds.

Neal, Avon. "Molas: Jungle View of 'Civilization,' "*Smithsonian,* Vol. 6, No. 8, November 1975, pp. 124–126.

> Color photographs show the reverse applique pieces—molas—of the Cuna Indians (living on the San Blas Islands off Panama). Molas form the front and back panels of the women's traditional blouses.

Priebatsch, Suzanne and Knight, Natalie. "Traditional Ndebele Beadwork," *African Arts,* January 1978, pp. 24–27.

Joseph, Marietta B. "West African Indigo Cloth," *African Arts,* January 1978, pp. 34–37.

African Arts. April 1978, pp. 18–47.

> Several articles in this issue describe various costumes used by Yoruba peoples in different parts of Nigeria for celebration of Egungun masquerades, rituals honoring ancestors and also serving as status symbols for the living.

Fischer, Eberhard. "Dan Forest Spirits: Masks in Dan Villages," *African Arts,* January 1978, pp. 16–23.

Borgatti, Jean M. "Okpella Masking Traditions," *African Arts,* July 1976, pp. 24–33.

On religious subcultures:

Gehman, Richard. "Plainest of Pennsylvania's Plain People: Amish Folk," *National Geographic,* Vol. 136, August 1965, pp. 228–253.

Willians, Richard L. "The Shakers, Now Only 12, Observe Their 200th Year," *Smithsonian,* Vol. 5, No. 6, September 1974, pp. 40–49.

> Black and white photographs and text descriptions of traditional Shaker costume.

Miller, Sister Mary C. and Roach, Mary Ellen. "Religious Garb: Significant or Sentimental," *Journal of Home Economics,* Vol. 58, November 1966, pp. 731–734.

Mintz, Jerome R. "Brooklyn's Hasidim," *Natural History,* January 1977, pp. 45–59.

Singer, Isaac Bashevis. "The Extreme Jews," *Harper's,* Vol. 234, No. 1403, April 1967, pp. 55–62.

Rubens, Alfred. *A History of Jewish Costume.* N.Y.: Funk & Wagnalls, 1967.

Frazer, John E. "India's Energetic Sikhs," *National Geographic,* Vol. 142, No. 4, October 1972, pp. 528–541.

BODY ADORNMENT:
SOCIAL MUTILATIONS AND COSMETIC DECORATIONS

Desmond Morris

The wearing of clothing is only one of many ways in which the human animal decorates itself. In addition, skin may be scarred, flesh pierced, hair lopped, necks scented, nails painted, faces powdered and teeth filed. Some of these Body Adornments persist for a lifetime while others last for only a few hours; but they all act as important human displays, indicating the social status, the sexual condition, the aggressiveness, the group allegiance, the playfulness, or some other quality of the decorated body.

The many temporary adornments, such as make-up, jewellery, nail-varnish, wigs and hairstyles, and perfume, are little more than extensions of clothing. Like garments, they can be put on and taken off at will, and do not commit the wearer to any lasting social bond. They can be used again and again, but can be varied for special moods and contexts. Or they can be discarded as fashions change.

The permanent adornments—those involving some form of body mutilation—are more typical of rigid societies, where allegiance to the group is of massive importance. These are badges that can never be taken off, and that set their owners apart from all other groups until the day they die. Frequently the application of the decoration is performed at a special ceremony, a tribal initiation, with the initiate suffering great pain in the process. This pain is an important part of the bonding—a physical horror that binds him even tighter to those who share it with him. Acquiring the status of belonging to the group is made such an ordeal, so difficult to endure, that forever afterwards it will be felt as something vitally important in his life. The very intensity of the experience helps to widen the gulf between him and those who have not shared it.

Frequently the mutilations are genital and applied at the age of puberty. For the first time the child cannot turn to its parents for protection from pain and, in this way, is turned away from them and towards the social group of the tribal 'club'.

Other mutilations are performed by parents themselves on their infants, long before the children know what is happening to them. In these cases the child, as it grows, accepts its special body qualities almost as if they are biological features making him into a different species from the members of other tribes who lack them.

The best way to study these adornments, both temporary and permanent, is to look at each part of the body in turn, and see what kind of attention it receives. Starting with the hair, there are obviously enormous possibilities for decorative modification, but always of a temporary kind, since whatever is done is soon undone by the death of old hairs and the growth of new ones.

The curious thing about human head-hair is that it is so long. If left to itself it would grow to great and cumbersome lengths in both males and females, and it seems likely that some sort of attention must have been paid to it even by our earliest ancestors. The male beard also attains great length if uncut, and there is a case on record of a man whose beard was longer than himself—so long, in fact, that one day he tripped over it and fell to his death. What prehistoric hunters were doing with hirsute appendages of these dimensions remains a mystery, unless they were useful specifically as an encouragement to increase social grooming. Monkeys and apes spend a great deal of time grooming one another's fur, and this action helps to cement friendly relations between them. If early man was in constant need of barbering, this could conceivably have increased his friendly grooming ritual and helped him improve his social relationships.

Whatever its original value, the head-hair of mankind has for centuries been a vital decorative organ, often being employed as an additional gender signal by dressing it differently on males and females. It has also been worn

From "*Manwatching: A Field Guide to Human Behavior*" by Desmond Morris. N.Y.: Harry N. Abrams, Inc., 1977, pp. 222– 229. Reprinted by permission of the publisher.

in a hundred different styles as a badge of age or status, and elaborated by the employment of waxes, ointments and wigs. The use of artificial hair is at least 5,000 years old. Ancient Egyptians commonly shaved their head and then donned special wigs for ceremonial occasions. They used either human hair or vegetable fibre, holding it in place with beeswax. Wigs were also popular with Roman women, who had them made from the hair of conquered peoples. Roman prostitutes could be identified by the colour of their wigs, which were dyed yellow. Roman men, like those of modern times, wore wigs only to hide hair defects and tried to keep the matter secret.

The early Christian church hated the artificiality and vanity of wigs, and bishops refused to give a blessing by the laying on of hands if it meant touching a hairpiece that might have come from a pagan head. Even the natural flowing locks of female Christians became looked upon as tempting and devilish and in medieval times women were urged to hide their hair under tight hoods. Not until the Elizabethan age did wigs and elaborate hairstyles make a full comeback. When the great queen decided to cover her own poor hair with a full wig, she was quickly copied by other women anxious to emulate her, and the wig again became a high-status display. At the same time, in France, Henry III lost his hair as a result of dyeing it with dangerous chemicals and was forced to wear a velvet cap with tufts of hair stitched inside it. Again the courtiers followed suit and by the seventeenth century large, decorative wigs were seen everywhere in Europe. Louis XIV, becoming bald at the age of 32, kept the tradition alive with a magnificent black wig that was handed to him each morning through closed bed-curtains and was then handed out again in the same way at night, so that no one ever caught a glimpse of his royal bald pate. The Christian church was now deeply divided on the subject of these decorative aids to personal appearance, and ugly scenes occurred in vestries as wigless priests tried to knock off the wigs of their more stylish colleagues.

During the eighteenth century European wigs became more and more elaborate and over 110 different wig-styles for men are recorded from this period, the tallest being the extraordinary Macaroni wig, which was stuffed with horsehair and reached a height of 18 inches. Wigs were expensive and only a rich man could afford the really large ones, which required several real heads of hair to make them up, hence the words 'bigwig' for an important person.

Eighteenth-century wigs were so obviously false that they were frequently removed in public, to scratch the head, to wash it, or simply for comfort when relaxing amoung friends. As in ancient Egypt, the male head was shaved or cropped beneath the wig.

There were several advantages in wearing wigs at that date. Hygiene was poor and the removal of the wig for washing was an aid to cleanliness. Also, wigs could be changed to suit the mood or the occasion and could be sent to the hairdressers without the owner leaving his home. The wig-wearer could also go out incognito, so vast was his head-covering. But above all the wig was a display of fashion and of social status.

In the later part of the century female wigs outdid those of the males in sheer extravagance, reaching heights of 30 inches in extreme cases and requiring the lowering of carriage seats and the raising of doorways. France was the centre of inspiration, where a fashionable woman would spend half a day erecting her wig and then sleep in it for as long as a week, propping it up on special bed supports. The real hair was swept up into these creations, causing severe problems with hair-parasites and much pin-scratching of heads.

When the guillotine fell at the end of the French Revolution, the fashion for wigs fell with it and was never to be seen again in such extreme forms. At the same time in North America, where, despite the ragings of puritan ministers and the introduction of wig-taxes, wigs had flourished for many years, the newly won independence of the United States led to similar changes. The elaborate, old hair-styles of Europe were fading fast everywhere and a new simplicity was on the horizon. Throughout Victorian times the wig was reduced to a secretive role, employed only to remedy defects and referred to discreetly as 'an imperceptible hair-covering'. Hairstyles remained restrained in both sexes, and apart for the usual minor shifts of fashion, there was little extreme activity until recent years.

In the 1950s, synthetic hair was invented in the United States and cheap, dramatic wigs became possible. By the 1960s there was a new boom, with an estimated one-third of all fashion-conscious females in Europe and the United States owning a 'wig of convenience'. The fun-wigs of the affluent, buoyant 60s came in all sizes, shapes and colours, and were once again being worn openly as wigs, rather than secretly as pseudo-hair. Modern males have not, as yet, returned to this condition. Instead they have gone further and further towards creating a naturalistic hairpiece. The culmination of the trend has been the invention of hair transplant techniques, in which hair and skin is cut from one part of the head and sunk into the bald patch on the top of the skull. In 1970 an American entertainer was reputed to have paid 12,000 dollars for a hair-by-hair treatment of this type, undoubtedly the most expensive piece of Body Adornment since the construction of Marie Antoinette's finest three-foot-high court wig.

As the 1960s faded, obvious wigs once again lost favour, and women returned to a more naturalistic approach to hairstyling. But it is doubtful if we have seen the last of blatant, decorative hairpieces. As an extension of the natural hair-signals they will undoubtedly reappear before very long. They have one great advantage over many other types of Body Adornment—their conspicuousness. Today, with most of the body draped in clothing, the key sites for adornment devices are the head and hands, and artificial hair can easily take the lion's share of available space.

The next region to consider is the face. Like the hair, this has been subjected to endless forms and styles of adornment over the centuries. Ancient cosmetic boxes reveal the minute attention that was paid by early Egyptians to their facial make-up, and ancient wall-paintings show us with remarkable clarity some of the results of their labours.

Make-up does several things to the human face. It may disguise it, or protect it from the sun; it may make it look younger and healthier, or it may label it as belonging to a particular social category; it may signal aggressiveness or sexuality. As with hair adornments, there have been periods when any form of make-up has been spurned as 'unnatural', and others when to be without it would be tantamount to indecent exposure.

In tribal societies make-up plays an important role in establishing the status of the individual within the community, and gives him a cultural 'badge'. It may also be thought of as protective, defending the wearer against imagined evils, but in reality this amounts to the same thing, since the true protection it affords is that of group membership.

In ancient societies an underlying motive in using make-up was protection, not against evil but against the sun. Like modern sunbathers with their sun-lotions, the early Egyptians protected their faces against the damaging glare of the sun's rays. One of the ingredients of their famous eye make-up was hydrosilicate of copper, which acted as an immediate remedy for suppuration caused by the intense glare. But their interest in cosmetics grew beyond the purely protective and became highly decorative in its detailed application. Cleopatra, for instance, used black galena on her eyebrows and painted her upper eyelids deep blue and her lower eyelids bright green. An upper-class Egyptian lady would spend much time at her toilet, employing special elbow cushions to steady her pivoting arm as she applied the delicate eye-lines. Her toilet box included a tube of eye-pencils, a container of shadow-powder, bottles of coloured ointments, cosmetic pots and a bronze mixing dish. Some of her make-up was antiseptic as well as decorative and some was heavily scented. Some, such as face masks of egg white, were used to conceal wrinkles. A reddish ochre was used to add a healthy colour to the cheeks and carmine was added to the lips. Lipstick, often thought of as a modern invention, is in reality 5,000 years old at the very least.

There is therefore little that is new in the world of facial adornment. All that has happened over the centuries is that different cultures have approved or disapproved— exaggerated or restricted—to varying degrees, the cosmetic activities of ancient and tribal peoples. Sometimes,

as in ancient Greece, the more elaborate application of cosmetics was confined to one particular class—the courtesans (both male and female)—while at others it spread from royalty downwards. Tragically, in later centuries, the chemistry of make-up became increasingly dangerous and frequently damaged the faces it was meant to improve. This led in turn to even more frantic attempts to cover up the ravaged surfaces. Disease was also playing havoc with smooth skins and marks and blemishes were repeatedly smothered in layers of powder and paint. In the seventeenth century a craze developed for 'beauty spots', small patches that were used to cover small scars and spots. Before long these had developed their own language and became specific facial signals. In London they were even used as political devices, the right-wing Whigs wearing them on the right cheek, and the (then) left-wing Tories wearing them on the left. The simple black spots soon grew into fancy shapes, such as cresents and stars, and at the court of Louis XV the precise position of these facial adornments became loaded with meaning: the corner of the eye indicated passion, the centre of the cheek gaiety, the nose sauciness, the forehead majesty, and so on, around the face.

In modern times there have been two great changes. In the first place, advanced medical care reduced the damaged done to skin by disease, and in the second place advanced chemistry made modern cosmetics safe and even beneficial. The result was that the make-up of the twentieth century could, at the same time, become less of a mask and less of a danger. Caked faces became shaded faces, and skin-painting became skin-care. As before, the features, such as the eyebrows, eyes and lips, were specially modified or exaggerated, but there was now a completely different approach to the general surface of the smooth skin. Previously this had nearly always been powdered or painted white, with or without the addition of rouge. This was a high-status signal based on the fact that only low-status females would have to work out-of-doors and ruin their cheeks with a horrible tan. Since high-status females were protected from the sun, a super-white face heightened this status value. The rouge, when added, was to indicate good health. For the modern female, the situation has become completely reversed. Now, in a predominantly industrial world, it has become important to demonstrate that long holidays in the sun can be taken. The longer the sunning, the higher the status, so suntan, real or *artificial,* has become the new facial badge to wear, and cosmetics have changed from white to brown.

Another facial device belonging to recent years is the more drastic phenomenon of cosmetic surgery, involving the cutting away of sections of skin and then stretching what is left to pull out the wrinkles of old age. Face-lifts and nose-bobs are still viewed as extreme measures by most people today, but cosmetic dentistry, another modern development, is now widely accepted, as is the use of contact lenses for the eyes. The 'Bionic Man' may be an escapist fantasy, but the bionic face is almost with us already.

Apart from making modern faces look younger and healthier, and therefore more appealing, the application of careful make-up means three things: time, materials and services. Time means money, and materials mean money, and where specialized services are needed the cost is even higher; so, on these three counts: make-up = affluence = status. On this basis make-up has always been, and always will be, a facial signal saying 'I have money to burn'. Also on this basis, the more elaborate the make-up, the better. In other words, if a woman presents an elaborately made-up face of unashamed artificiality, she is performing a threat display. In the boisterous 1960s, this led to wild facial adornments in Western countries, rivalling those of tribal warriors; but in the more restrained and increasingly egalitarian social climate of the 1970s, these overt displays have receded. In their place is something much more subtle. Make-up has not vanished, it has instead become devious, reflecting a more devious attitude to affluence itself. Affluence and high status are still sought after, but they must not be *seen* to be sought after. It is an age of pseudo-puritanism, and the effect this has on facial displays is precisely what we might expect from looking back at history. It was the purity of the Ancient Greeks, the puritanism of the Christian Church, and the prudery of the Victorians that led, in the past, to the suppression of flashier styles of make-up. Only courtesans, whores and tarts were painted ladies in those periods. We are returning to those conditions now and, once again, the female face must appear fresh and innocent. The difference is that now she has a whole range of advanced cosmetics to help her look even fresher than fresh, and even more natural than nature herself can manage. To the experienced eye the adornment signals are still there, but they are no longer blatant. Like the expensively tailored, faded denims, the face cleverly contradicts itself and transmits two messages at once: 'I take care to look careless'.

Descending from the face and looking at the body skin in general, there is an obvious draw-back in fully clothed cultures, where the skin is only exposed on special occasions. In semi-naked tribal societies body painting and tattooing were widespread and, in many cases, a work of art—perhaps the *original* form of art for our species. A third form of skin ornamentation was the more drastic process of cicatrization, in which patterns of raised scars were made by rubbing charcoal and other materials into freshly cut slits on the body-surface. The bas-relief effect, like the coloured patterns of the tattooist, provided a lasting 'badge' of adornment.

Despite modern clothing, all three of these devices have continued to survive in some form. Body painting made a brief comeback in the 1960s. Tattooing has never completely vanished, but has merely withdrawn to the vicinity of naval dockyards and other sailors' haunts. Cicatrization has been less successful and its last appearance was in Germany, where it took the form of deliberately inflicted duelling-scars.

Tattooing and scarring, being more or less permanent mutilations of the skin, are essentially badges of allegiance, and it is significant that many of the designs favoured by sailors are symbols of pair-bonds (hearts and arrows) or culture-bonds (patriotic flags and national emblems). From time to time it has been suggested that tattooing should be employed on a widespread basis, specifically for its permanence; and there was a serious proposal in the last century that the tattooing of a coloured ring on the wedding finger should be made a compulsory part of the marriage service. This was to defeat unscrupulous bigamists and other males who removed their wedding rings to prey on unsuspecting women. If widowed, a tattooed star was to be added; if divorced, a bar; and if re-married, a second ring. In this way no one could escape having their marital status identified. In the early part of the present century, American husbands were similarly urged to follow the custom of New Zealand natives and tattoo their wives to reveal to other men that they were married and were not to be molested.

Despite these attempts, the only widespread forms of permanent body mutilation that still survive, apart from sailors' tattoos, are the piercing of ears for earrings and the cutting-off of the foreskin in the ritual of circumcision. Tribal mutilations, such as lip-plugging, tooth-filing, ear-stretching, and the removal of parts of the female genitals, have failed to find favour in the modern world. Circumcision is, in fact, the only really severe form of primitive mutilation to have resisted the modern trend toward abhorrence of body-violation. If, as used to be the case, it was performed at puberty instead of at infancy, that too would no doubt have vanished long ago, swept away by the outrage of the initiates. But the protests of babies are more easily ignored, and with the false accolade of medical hygiene to help it on its way, the genital deforming of young males continues unabated.

One early form of infant violation that has failed to survive is the curious and previously widespread activity of head squashing. At birth the human skull is soft and easily moulded. Various cultures, in Africa, North and South America, and Europe, indulged in skull-moulding, employing a variety of tight bindings of squeezing-boards to achieve the desired shape. The most popular head-style was one with a flattened forehead, producing a tapering, pointed crown. The preference for this shape is linked to high status, like so many body adornments. The reason for the linkage in this case is that individuals with pointed heads cannot carry burdens on their heads, and display throughout their lives their inability to perform menial tasks.

European head-squashers seem to have had different motives. Like some of the Ancient Egyptians, they preferred elongated heads that ballooned out at the back of the skull, an effect easily produced by mothers binding their babies' heads tightly soon after birth. This practice was still active in certain provincial regions of France up until the last century, kept alive by the teaching of phrenologists that head shape could influence intelligence.

In modern times heads have been left unsquashed, and this particular form of body deformation has been relegated to the feet, twentieth-century shoemakers having taken over the role of human bone-crushers. This is more true of female shoes than male; but fortunately for modern women, the extremes of foot-squeezing seen in Old China are no longer perpetrated. There, the crushed feet of high-status females made walking difficult and working impossible—again a deformation to display the owner's inability to perform menial tasks. The 'elegant' pointed shoe of modern Western women is also less than perfect for hard physical work, but the foot deformities it causes are less devastating.

There are, of course, a thousand other ways in which the human animal seeks to adorn its body and enhance its display qualities. Some are exotic rarities, such as nipple-rouge and nipple-rings, male chest-wigs, and female pubic tufts trimmed to heart-shapes; others are commonplace and widespread, such as necklaces, bracelets, finger-rings and nail-varnish. Taken together they amount to a set of wide-ranging 'frozen' gestures, items of display that are long-lasting and highly efficient in relation to the actions that produce them. The visual impact of a shaken fist lasts only as long as the arm is moving, but the visual impact of the act of putting on any form of Body Adornment lasts long afterwards. It is this efficiency of the ratio of action-effort to display-impact that ensures that Body Adornments will be with us for as long as our species walks the planet.

THE FASHIONABLE BODY

Bernard Rudofsky

The urge to alter his body is felt by man only; animals, enjoying the advantage of healthier instincts, do not share it. Although the human shape was designed by the greatest of artists, His taste does not necessarily coincide with ours; at no time did man accept the image in which he was created as final, and he early decided that there was room for improvement. Neither prehistoric cave dweller nor late industrial urban man considered the human body aesthetically satisfactory, the Aurignacians and Magdalenians practiced mutilation of the hands with the same confidence that modern man brings to crippling his feet. Uneducated and oversophisticated alike seem to act on an uncontrollable impulse to rearrange their anatomy; no part of the body is spared some more or less violent interefence. With all the points of similarity, however, there is one significant difference: Primitive man sets up an unvarying body ideal and sticks to it. Industrial man, on the other hand, has no clear idea of what he wants; his aims are erratic, his tastes ephemeral. Whatever the reasons for wanting to change his physique, whatever the relevance of his narcissistic or autoerotic inclinations, the factor that goes farthest to account for this unholy obsession is his boredom. Bored with the natural shape of his body, he delights in getting away from himself, and to judge from past and present performances, the resources at hand for making his escape are inexhaustible. Not that there is much method in his endeavors; instead of striving for perfection he is consumed by a passion for unceasing experimentation. Only rarely does he exercise self-restraint. To the ancient Greeks, for instance, the human body was inviolate, or almost: they plucked their pubic hair. As a rule, however, man sees in his body little more than the raw material for his creations. The fact that his exertions can be traced back to prehistoric times does not sanction the results but endows them with a certain respectability.

In the beginning, man himself was clay and canvas. Body painting and body sculpture were fused into a single production and thus accounted for a harmonious work of art. Indeed, we should not hesitate to regard them as the oldest art. At any rate, the use of the body as the artist's medium rather than his inspiration antedates the more conventional categories of plastic art.[1]

Works of art often exist only in the minds of those who create them, and the so-called improvements perpetrated on our anatomy are no exception. "It is certainly not true," observed Charles Darwin, "that there is in the mind of man any universal standard of beauty with respect to the human body. It is, however, possible that certain tastes may in course of time become inherited." Without going into the deeper motives of why certain human forms give us pleasure and others do not, Darwin scoffed at Western man's conceits. "If all our women," he argued, "were to become as beautiful as the Venus de' Medici, we should for a time be charmed; but we should soon wish for variety; and as soon as we had obtained variety, we should wish to see certain characteristics a little exaggerated beyond the then existing standards."[2] As we shall see, a little exaggeration goes a long way.

It is of course doubtful that a modern woman blessed with the proportions of a Greek statue would be happy. Broad hips have not been fashionable for a long time, and what modern shoe could accommodate a classical foot? But then, even in Darwin's time, the shape of the Medicean Venus (a mere copy of a Greek sculpture) was thought to be on the dowdy side. Far more desirable than everlasting perfection were, and still are, changeable beauty ideals, and with good reason:

Our laws permit a man to have as many wives as he pleases, provided he marries them successively. Since, however, this staggered sort of polygamy is often beyond a man's means, the way to make the monotony of marital life tolerable is to split a wife's personality. To appease her husband's promiscuous appetites, a good wife will impersonate as many divers types as her talents permit. Masquerading alone won't do the trick. A new dress or a sun tan do not turn her into a new woman; the change has to be more than skin-deep. In the following pages we shall examine, if ever so rapidly, some of the alterations that she—or he—were able to accomplish in their pursuit of physical variety. Let us begin at the top.

One of the boldest ways to interfere with human anatomy is the molding of the skull. Among tribes who practice this art, it is part and parcel of a child's upbringing. It calls for special skills and has traditionally been a mother's duty and, we may presume, pleasure. The first provocation to a mother's pinching and kneading her baby's skull was perhaps its yielding softness. Playful handling developed into more conscious efforts at deformation, to which racial and aesthetic concepts were added later. Thus, broad heads were broadened, flat noses flattened closer to the face, a tapering occiput sharpened to a point—a shape mostly associated today with humanoids from outer space. These spectacular forms were achieved with the aid of contraptions no more ingenious than a common mousetrap.

Admiration for elongated heads was widespread among such dissimilar peoples as the ancient Egyptians, American Indians, and provincial French. In some parts of France the custom of binding children's heads was still observed as late as the past century. Contrary to what one would expect from a nation known for setting ideals of elegance for the better part of the world, the motives for this kind of head deformation were eugenic rather than aesthetic. Educational systems being what they are, people believed that a child's vocation could be guided, literally, by shaping his brain. One Jesuit, Father Josset, for instance, advised mothers to work on their new-born children's heads so that they might become great orators.

It was a time when phrenology was the last word in head control. Purportedly a science, it dealt with the conformation of the skull. The shape of a person's head was supposed to determine his aptitudes and moral character. Indeed, it was thought that a direct relationship existed between the faculties of the mind and the separate portions of the brain, each portion representing a distinct mental or moral disposition. Their number varied from twenty-seven to thirty-six, depending on the phrenologist's persuasion. They were classified in what strike us today as rather whimsical categories: Religion; Wit; Ideality; Cunning; Marvellousness; Mimicry; Murder; Wonder; and so forth. Persons who had their heads examined late in life often realized with dismay that they had missed a chance of being massaged into a genius. Eventually, the "art of reading bumps," as it was called in the United States, was so successful that an American university established a professorship of phrenology.[3] Observed the Encyclopaedia Americana: "The most necessary thing for a professor of phrenology was a happy faculty for flattering everybody."[4] Alas, not only art but also science is subject to the fashions of the day. Thus, phrenology has given way to aptitude tests, while squeezing heads has been abandoned in favor of squeezing toes.

Another, far more enduring, not to say endearing, sort of body deformation is obesity. Admired in many parts of the world, obesity rates—as far as women are concerned—as a secondary sexual characteristic. To judge from prehistoric art, fat women either predominated or were chosen by artists for their models, and in the course of time the well-upholstered woman was favored over the scrawny one. A similar taste can frequently be found in modern art; the artist who does not limit his sympathies to the fashionably disembodied female, sides with the primitive, and celebrates massive womanhood. Moreover, a fat body is often thought of as a strong body, and since only women of leisure can afford the luxury of being immobilized, the overfed woman came to represent the well-to-do and beautiful; obesity was promoted to a mark of quality. Hence among those primitives who gauge female beauty by sheer bulk, brides-to-be go through preparations of excessive fattening.[5] Upon reaching puberty, a girl is placed in a special fattening-house. The time of seclusion varies from several weeks to two years depending on the wealth of her parents.

Some tribes discriminate in their admiration for obesity between over-all bulk and specific, strategically placed cushions of fat. The most celebrated among salient features is steatopygia, the overdevelopment of the subcutaneous fat that covers a woman's hind parts and upper thighs. Unlike the judges of our beauty contests who have their eyes on a prominently cantilevered bosom, buttock lovers make their selection by "ranging their women in a line, and by picking *her* out who projects farthest *a tergo.*"[6] Western woman, whom nature forgot to endow with a magnificent rear end, had at times to rely on make-believe to render herself desirable; witness the bustle of the eighteen-seventies, a gross illusion of steatopygia. Subsequently, man's admiration shifted to the stout woman with a tiny waist, a combination that does not occur in nature. It cannot be produced by crossbreeding or special exercise; it exists only as a sartorial illusion, achieved by applying a vise known as corset.

In approaching this subject we have to keep in mind that the woman who lived at the turn of the century barely resembled today's woman. She had missed an important phase in the evolution of mankind for she could not stand straight unaided. To insure her upright position she needed support, and it was the corset that saved her from having to walk on all fours.

Precautions against her breakdown had to be taken early in life. The little girl was securely encased in a junior corset that promised Perfect Health, and visibly improved the contours of her shrimplike body. (To be sure, the use of a child's corset was not limited to occidental countries. Circassian girls—to give but one foreign example—wore from the tenth year on a broad girdle of untanned leather. The wealthy locked it with silver hooks whereas common people sewed it tightly around the waist. One writer, familiar with Circassian lore, tells us that mothers fastened their daughters "into saffian leather garments for seven years to give their figures symmetry."[7] This cuirass was worn until the wedding night "when the bridegroom with a sharp-cutting dagger unties the Gordian knot, which ceremony is frequently attended with danger."[8]

The corset of our grandmothers was a masterpiece of functional design. It operated on three levels—mechanical, aesthetic, and moral. "The corset," wrote Thorstein Veblen, the foremost portraitist of the leisure class, "is in economic theory substantially [an instrument of] mutilation for the purpose of lowering the subject's vitality and rendering her personally and obviously unfit for work. It is true, the corest impairs the personal attractiveness of the wearer [Veblen refers of course to the naked woman], but the loss suffered on that score is offset by the gain in reputability which comes of her visibly increased expensiveness and infirmity."[9] The natural outline of the female waist, unredeemed by art, was not savory enough for man. It was the corsetière's business to attack the aesthetic problem at its roots by bending women's bones into an alluring shape.

The whalebone corset marked an advanced technique of disfigurement. Athough the mechanism with its stays and ribbons was a comedown from the all-metal corset, the results were complex enough. Not only did the corset claw into the flesh, it played havoc with the inner organs by displacing them, eventually leading to a number of ailments. Occasionally, it caused miscarriages. On the credit side was the heightened seductiveness of the wearer, her embraceability, so to speak: the pressure applied to the waist produced the desired simultaneous inflation of the chest and buttocks, the latter still further accentuated by the bustle.

The corset's crippling effects on the female body were persistently ignored, much as today we ignore the consequences of wearing deforming shoes. The would be guardian of our health, the physician, whose business it is to keep us in good working order, was then as reluctant to interfere with fashion's dictum as he is today. His warnings were sounded timidly, or at any rate ineffectively. He plied his trade oblivious of, or in tacit agreement with, the abuses of the day. As a man he was not immune to the corset's fascination; as a doctor he hesitated to condemn the corset for fear of being considered immoral. Respectful of manufacturers and their products, he did not permit himself much criticism. Occasionally, he was even known to pimp for them or, better, turn predatory and go into business himself.

To give an example—in the eighteen-eighties, a Dr. Scott put on the market an unbreakable electric corset, guaranteed quickly to cure paralysis, rheumatism, spinal complaints, dyspepsia, constipation, impaired circulation, liver and kidney troubles, nervous debility, numbness, and so forth. "Constructed on scientific principles," the advertisement assured the gullible woman, "the therapeutic value is unquestioned." When constantly worn, "nightly, if desired," the corset also imparted to one's system "the required amount of *odic force* which Nature's law demands."

Odic force, a now forgotten nineteenth-century discovery, was then much on people's minds, thanks to the persuasive power of advertising. *Od* was a gift of nature, like perfect pitch. Those who had it were endowed with excruciating sensibility. They could divine a vein of ore in a mountain or, more spectacularly, start a pendulum swinging without touching it. Those whom nature had neglected could, if they wished, have recourse to odic contraptions such as Dr. Scott's corset whose miraculous powers were attested to, believe it or not, by the late surgeon general of the United States. Eventually, the scientific theory collapsed and *od* became odious.

Everything considered, doctors' knowledge of the female anatomy was less than perfect mainly because they based their observations on the deformed body. They were misinformed about such an elementary performance as breathing; not only woman's skeleton but also her breathing apparatus was thought to function differently from man's. "Until recent years," wrote Havelock Ellis in 1910, "it was commonly supposed that there is a real and fundamental difference in breathing between men and women, that women's breathing is thoracic and men's abdominal. It is now known that under natural and healthy conditions there is no difference, but men and women breathe in a precisely identical manner."[10] If doctors had wanted to they could easily have found "natural and healthy conditions" among non-corset-wearing women the world over.

Withal, corset manufacturers did not overlook the male body as potential modeling clay in their hands. Although the wearing of a corset was mainly a woman's prerogative (and duty), the fops and drones among men were not long in adopting it. "The corset mania," we read in the *Springfield Republican* of 1903, "began with the military men—they compare notes on corsets in some of the army clubs as gravely as they discuss the education bill at the National Library Club."[11] In all fairness, however, we must grant them in retrospect their inalienable right to body deformation. They were not the first to squeeze their waists; wasp waists were common as far back as archaic Greece. The last holdout for male waist constriction is Papua, provided the old customs are still honored.

At a distance of more than three generations, our great-grandmothers' fanatical loyalty to the wasp-waist ideal would seem absurd were it not that we now understand its deeper significance much better. Far more than a crutch, the corset was the hallmark of virtue. The belief that clothes are designed in good measure to punish the flesh never really lost its hold on us; in a way we are still doing penance for Adam's sin. Though clothes may not always be the best protection against nature's rigors, they often represent instruments of moral philosophy. The attraction of the agreeably punitive hairshirt has not worn off; metamorphosed variously into garter, girdle, waistband, and brassière, it plays on some of the focal points of the body, leaving an imprint. The bruises are accepted as the inevitable consequences of wearing clothes. Perhaps there lingers in women's mind the consoling thought that *their* mothers endured far greater inconvenience.

When the harm that resulted from wearing a corset had been belatedly recognized—and cavalierly dismissed—the fashion that lent an edge to men's inexhaustible appetite for swooning females was vindicated on moral grounds. People who lived in what was, from the point of view of costume history, a crustaceous age, thought of the whalebone corset as a kind of Jeanne d'Arc armor. Uncorseted women reeked of license; an unlaced waist was regarded as a vessel of sin. A heretic like Isadora Duncan, heralded by Rodin and other connoisseurs of the human physique as the embodiment of Greece, helped only to strengthen further the popular belief that the lack of a corset (and shoes) was the visible sign of depravity.

Every generation has its own demented ideas on supporting some part of the human anatomy. Older people still remember a time when everybody went through life ankle-supported. Young and old wore laced boots. A shoe that did not reach well above the ankle was considered disastrous to health. What, one asks, has become of ankle

support, once so warmly recommended by doctors and shoe salesmen? What keeps our ankle from breaking down these days of low-cut shoes?

Ankle support has given way to arch support; millions of shoe-buying people are determined to "preserve their metatarsal arch" without as much as suspecting that it does not exist. Nevertheless, the fiction of the arch is being perpetuated to help sell "supports" and "preservers" on an impressive scale.

The dread of falling arches is, however, a picayune affair compared to that other calamity, the feet's asymmetry. I am not talking about the difference within a single pair of feet, that is, the difference between the right and left foot of a person; I mean the asymmetry of the foot itself.

Few of us are truly aware that an undeformed foot's outline is *not* symmetrical. It is distinctly lopsided. Let us have a close look at it: The big toe extends from one to two inches beyond the fifth toe. More importantly, the five toes spread out fanlike. They do not converge to a point in front as one would expect from the shape of the shoe. Quite the contrary, they converge to a point in back of the heel. It should be obvious, even to the least observant person, that to conform to the outline of a shoe, the big toe ought to be in the place of the third one, i.e., in the center.

Shoe manufacturers have shown admirable patience with nature. Despite or because of the absence of feet that live up to their commercial ideals of anatomy, they doggedly go on producing symmetrical shoes. And although their customers' feet have not changed in the course of time, they spare no effort and expense to come up every season with a new (symmetrical) shoe for the same old foot. (The pathological hate of the natural form of the foot is nowhere more forcibly expressed than in the commandments of the Shakers which say that "it is contrary to order to have right and left shoes.")

By some atavistic quirk of nature, every normal baby is born with undeformed feet. The forepart of the foot—measured across the toes—is about twice as wide as the heel. The toes barely touch each other and are as nimble as fingers. Were the child able to keep up his toe-twiddling, he might easily retain as much control over his feet as over his hands. Not that we see anything admirable in nimble toes; they strike us as freakish perhaps because we associate prehensile feet with primitive civilizations. To our twisted mind, the foot in its undamaged state is anachronistic, if not altogether barbaric. Ever since the shoe became the badge of admission to Western civilization—in rural countries such as Portugal and Brazil the government exhorts peasants to wear shoes in the name of progress—we look down on barefooted or sandaled nations.

Since wearing shoes is synonymous with wearing *bad* shoes, the modern shoe inevitably becomes an instrument of deformation. The very concept of the modern shoe does not admit of an intelligent solution; it is not made to fit a human foot but to fit a wooden last whose shape is determined by the whims of the "designer." Whereas a tailor allows for a customer's unequal shoulders and arms; an optometrist prescribes different lenses for the right and left eye, we buy shoes of identical size and dimensions for our right and left foot, conveniently forgetting—or ignoring—that, as a rule, they are not of the same width and length. Even in countries where it is still possible to find an artisan willing to make a pair of shoes to order, chances are that he works on mass-produced lasts and comes up with a product that, shapewise, is not much different from the industrial one.

In both the manufacturer's and the customer's opinion the shoe comes before the foot. It is less intended to protect the foot from cold and dirt than to mold it into a fashionable shape. Infants' very first shoes are liable to dislocate the bones, and bend the foot into the shoe shape. The child does not mind the interference; "never expect the child to complain that the shoe is hurting him," says podiatrist Dr. Simon Wikler, "for the crippling process is painless." According to a ten-year study of the Podiatry Society of the State of New York, 99 percent of all feet are pefect at birth, 8 percent have developed troubles at one year, 41 percent at the age of five, and 80 percent at twenty; "we limp into adulthood," the report concludes. "Medical schools," says Dr. DePalma, "fail almost complctcly in giving thc studcnt a sound grounding and a sanc therapeutic concept of foot conditions." And in *Military Medicine* one reads that "there has been no objective test that could be readily incorporated in physical examinations, or taught to medical students, pediatricians, or physicians in military and industrial medicine, that would enable them to recognize deformities of the foot. . . ."[12] In sum, physicians leave it to the shoe designer to decide the fate of our feet.

To top it all, modern man, perhaps unknown to himself, is afflicted with a diffuse shoe-fetishism. Inherited prejudices derived from the Cinderella complex; practices whose origins and reasons escape him, and traditional obtuseness combine to make him tolerate the deformities inflicted by his shoes. In this respect his callousness matches that of the Chinese of old. In fact, if he ever felt a need to justify the shoes' encroachments on his anatomy, he could cite Lily feet (provided he had ever heard of them), the Chinese variety of the "correctly shaped" foot.

This exotic custom which lasted nearly one thousand years did not extend over the whole country; the Manchu, including the imperial family, never practiced foot-binding. Small feet are a racial characteristic of Chinese women, and the desire to still further reduce their size in the name of beauty and for reasons indicated earlier, seems to have been strong enough to make women tolerate irrevocable mutilation. As so often happens, people derive infinitely greater satisfaction from an artifact, however

crude, than from nature's product. Besides, not only were a woman's stunted feet highly charged with erotic symbolsim, they made her eligible for marriage. Without them she was reduced to spinsterhood.[13] Her desirability as a love object was in direct proportion to her inability to walk. It ought to be easy for our women to understand the Chinese men's mentality; "every woman knows that to wear 'walking shoes'—as derogatory a term as 'sensible shoes'—puts a damper on a man's ardor. The effect of absurdly impractical shoes, on the other hand, is as intoxicating as a love potion. The girl child who puts on a pair of high-heeled shoes is magically propelled into womanhood."[14]

Modern woman is not averse to maltreating her feet for reasons similar to those of her Chinese sisters, and therefore makes allowance for bunions, calluses, corns, ingrown toenails and hammer toes. But she draws the line at a major interference with her foot skeleton. Unwilling to bother with growing her own, organic high heels, she has to get along with artificial ones.

As costume props go, the high heel's history is relatively short. In the middle of the seventeenth century this new device for corrupting the human walk was added to the footwear of the elegant, putting them, as it were, on tiptoe. The ground, indoors and outdoors, came to a tilt, so to speak, and, for fashion's sake, people began to walk on a portable incline. As the ordinary folk continued to wear flat-bottomed shoes, heeled footwear, combined with a strutting walk, became a mark of distinction. Withal, the times were anything but favorable to the new invention. On the street the well-heeled had to avail themselves of a sedan chair to avoid the cobblestones underfoot, while indoors they found it difficult to negotiate the polished parquets and marble floors that were the pride of the epoch. And yet, men took to high heels as enthusiastically as women did. To judge from paintings of the time, fashionable men could not have cared less for "walking shoes."

Did men's high-heeled shoes and fine stockings turn a woman's head? Were women smitten with the sight of a man's well-turned ankle and slender leg? For whereas their own legs remained hidden by crinolines, men proudly displayed their calves and gave as much attention to them as to their wigs. Silicon injections still being centuries away, a skinny fellow made up by padding for any natural deficiency. Eventually, the French Revolution brought men and women down to earth. Dandies and *élégantes* wore paper-thin flat soles without, it seems, depriving themselves of their mutual attraction. Years later, when high heels reappeared on the fashionable scene, they were relegated to woman's domain; men never left the ground again.

In lucid moments we look with amazement at the fraud we perpetrate on ourselves—the bruises, mutilations, and dislocated bones—but if we feel at all uncomfortable, it is not for long. An automatic self-defense mechanism blurs our judgment, and makes right and wrong exchange places. Moreover, some violations of the body are sanctioned by religion, while others are simply the price of a man's admittance to his tribe, regardless of whether he lives in the bush or in a modern metropolis. The sense of superiority he derives from, say, circumcision is no less real than that of the owner of a pair of Lily feet. Physicians have always been of two mind about it; "to cut off the top of the uppermost skin of the secret parts," maintained the intrepid Dr. Bulwer, "is directly against the honesty of nature, and an injurious unsufferable trick put upon her."[15] And a contemporary pediatrician, E. Noel Preston, writing in the *Journal of the American Medical Association,* considers circumcision "little better than mutilation." The very real dangers of the operation such as infection and hemorrhage outweigh the fancied advantages of cancer prevention. "If a child can be taught to tie his shoes or brush his teeth or wash behind the ears," said Dr. Preston, "he can also be taught to wash beneath his foreskin."

A change of allegiance may lead to double mutilation, as in the paradoxical phenomenon of uncircumcision: After the subjugation of Palestine by Alexander the Great, those Jews who found it desirable to turn into Gentiles, underwent a painful operation that restored to them the missing prepuce. (1 Cor. 7:18 ff; I Macc. 1:15)

Sometimes such mutilation reaches a high degree of ferocity. Among some Arabian tribes circumcision is performed as an endurance test for youths who have come of age; "it consists," writes the Hebrew scholar Raphael Patai, "in cutting off the skin across the stomach below the navel and thence down the thighs, after which it is peeled off, leaving the stomach, the pelvis, the scrotum, and the inner legs uncovered and flayed. Many young men are said to have succumbed to the ordeal which in recent times has been prohibited by the Saudi Arabian government."[16] However, the custom has not disappeared, doubtless as a result of its sex appeal. The ceremony takes place in female company, that is, in the presence of the young men's brides-to-be, who may refuse to marry their intended if they betray their agony by as much as an air of discomfort.

Man's obsession with violating his body is not just of anthropological interest, it helps us to understand the irrationality of dress. The devices for interfering with human anatomy are paralleled by a host of contraptions that simulate deformation or are simply meant to cheat the eye: bustles, pads, heels, wedges, braguettes, brassières, and so forth. Once, thirty years marked the end of a woman's desirability. In time, this age limit was gradually extended and pushed to a point where it got lost altogether. In order not only to look eternally young but also fashionable, woman had to obey everchanging body ideals. Thus a woman born at the turn of the century was a buxom maiden in accordance with the dictates of the day. Photographs testify to the generosity of her charms although her tender age ought to raise doubts about their authenticity. In the nineteen-twenties, when maturity and motherhood had come to her, pictures record an angular, lean, flat-chested creature. Since she did not want to renounce her attractiveness, she had to submit to an extremely unfeminine beauty ideal. Twenty years later, she was rotund again and commanded the undiminished attention of the other sex. Today, she is still in the running, ever ready to overhaul her body to prolong her youth beyond biological limits. She has inflamed three generations of men each loyal to a different image of perfection.

Alas, an aged body, however arresting and deceptive be the results of its updating and remodeling, imparts to its owner only a limited sense of youth. It serves mainly as a stylish peg for clothes. In other words, it is the clothed body that triumphs, not the naked one. As Herbert Spencer said: "The consciousness of being perfectly dressed may bestow a peace such as religion cannot give."

REFERENCES

1. Eckart von Sydow, "Primitive Kunst und Psychoanalyse" (*Imago-Bucher,* Leipzig, 1927, Band 10, p. 153).
2. Charles Darwin, *The Descent of Man.* New York, n.d., p. 890.
3. James Hastings, *Encyclopaedia of Religion and Ethic.* New York, 1951, p. 898.
4. *Encyclopedia Americana.* New York, 1957, vol. 22, p. 22.
5. L.W.G. Malcolm, "Note on the Seclusion of Girls among the Efik at Old Calabar" (*Man,* London, 1925, p. 113).
6. Darwin, op. cit., p. 886.
7. Hermann Heinrich Ploss, *Woman, an historical, gynaecological and anthropological compendium.* London, 1935, vol. I, p. 447.
8. Peter Simon Pallas, *Travels through the Southern Provinces of the Russian Empire in the Years 1793–94.* London, 1812, p. 398.
9. Thorstein Veblen, *The Theory of the Leisure Class.* New York, 1911, p. 172.
10. Havelock Ellis, *Studies in the Psychology of Sex.* New York, 1942, vol. II, part 1, p. 172.
11. "Modern English Dandy" (*Current Literature,* New York, 1903, vol. 34, p. 228).
12. Simon J. Wikler and Thomas Hale, "Gross Non-painful Foot Defects" (*Military Medicine,* October 1965, vol. 130, no. 10).
13. Adolfo Dembo and J. Imbelloni, "Deformaciones" (*Humanior,* Buenos Aires, 1938, section A, tome 3, p. 3).
14. Bernard Rudofsky, *The Kimono Mind.* New York, 1964, p. 50.
15. John Bulwer, *Anthropometamorphosis,* London, 1653, p. 379.
16. Raphael Patai, *Sex and Family in the Bible and the Middle East.* New York, 1959, p. 201.

THE RITES OF SUMMER

Marvin Harris

Circumambulate the city on a sunny afternoon and what do you see? In Herman Melville's day it was "thousands and thousands of mortal men fixed in ocean reveries." Far more abundant in our own times are the souls fixed in solar reveries—seminude men and women who crowd rooftops, parks, and beaches hopeful of a suntan.

As the history of the parasol indicates, civilized peoples have always considered it a privilege to be able to avoid the heat and glare of the sun's direct rays. Parasols were adopted with as much enthusiasm by the kings of West Africa as by the Chinese emperors and the popes of Rome. The kings of Siam even insisted on taking their multitiered parasols with them as they rode into battle on the backs of elephants. Everywhere ordinary mortals were forbidden to protect themselves with such devices, just as they were forbidden to wear silk clothing or carry swords.

The umbrella, incidentally, has always been the parasol's poor relation. To keep from getting wet, royalty mainly stayed indoors or inside enclosed vehicles. England's upper crust accepted the parasol long before they accepted the umbrella. They did not want to give the impression of not being able to afford a proper carriage.

By staying out of the sun, royalty—from Japan to Spain—kept itself several shades lighter than the peasants who worked in the fields. Where people's skin could be appreciably darkened by exposure to solar radiation—and this includes almost everyone of Asian and European descent—pallid skin became a mark of upper-class status. To be untanned was to be noble; to be noble was to be untanned. Also, since noble skin was pallid, the veins were more visible than in ordinary mortals; they looked bluer than the veins in the temples and wrists of peasants. And so there arose in Europe the notion of "blue blood."

The doctrine "white is beautiful" became an esthetic canon among the upper classes. Beautiful women were described by European court poets as having necks as "white as alabaster" or breasts "as white as snow." Members of the so-called yellow and brown races used the same metaphors of whiteness to characterize their own leisure class women.

In China, as far back the Early Han period, 202 B.C. to A.D. 25, the nobility of both sexes used face powders, made out of lead or glutinous rice and millet to enhance the impression of pallor. Suntanned European explorers arriving by sea in the eighteenth century were greeted, appropriately enough, as "red-faced barbarians" or "redskins."

In Japan, according to anthropologist Hiroshi Wagatsuma, the skin of the court ladies was described by the word *shiroi*, which is also the word used to denote the whiteness of snow or of paper. From A.D. 710 onward, white powder was applied to the face, cheeks were rouged, and teeth were blackened, creating an effect of stark pallor. During the Tokugawa period (1603–1867), women steamed their skin and then polished it with a cloth bag containing rice bran.

For many years after their initial contact with European explorers, Japanese artists painted Europeans with brown, gray, or pinkish faces. Japanese women appearing in the company of Europeans were always depicted in whiter shades than Caucasians.

Eventually, "whiteness" was internalized by the Eurasian lower classes and became their own ultimate psychological standard of beauty and excellence. This conformed to the normal process of diffusion of esthetic criteria downward from the upper classes. For, to paraphrase Thorstein Veblen,* the tastes of the highest social or pecuniary strata usually determine what a community accepts as decent or honorific. It was in this way that the pink, brown, yellow, and red peoples of Europe and Asia acquired a prejudice against skins darker than their own.

In Europe, during the course of the nineteenth century, leisure class evaluations of suntans underwent a reversal. The change was closely correlated with the advance of industry and the decrease of agriculture. As the factory system spread, the upper classes developed an intense interest in the outdoor life; they began to cultivate vigorous, open-air sports such as tennis, polo, and mountain climbing. "Back to nature" became a favorite theme in literature and the arts. The man of action, bronzed by a tour of duty in India or Malaya, became the new paragon of leisure class male pulchritude, and the lithe, suntanned, tennis-playing, outdoor woman became a respectable alternative to the cloistered, snow-and-alabaster ideal of the old regimes.

Why did the suntan suddenly find favor? I think the underlying cause was in the reversal of the prevalence of sun and shade with respect to social class. With the spread of the factory system, the main locus of menial labor was moved indoors. A pallid complexion ceased to be the prerogative of the parasol-wielding blue bloods; it became instead the indelible mark of the men, women, and children whom Karl Marx described as capitalism's "wage slaves."

Industrialization made shade cheap and sunlight expensive. High-density urban settlements proliferated upward along narrow alleys, preventing sunlight from pen-

---

*See "Dress as an Expression of the Pecuniary Culture," pp.154–159.

etrating to ground level. Also, the industrial slums were characterized by high crime rates that made open-air diversions dangerous for working-class families. And most important perhaps, the high-density consumption of coal cast a permanent pall over working-class districts.

William F. Loomis of Brandeis University has shown that the permanent shadow produced by coal smog during th nineteenth century was the main reason for the epidemic of the crippling disease known as rickets. Without exposure to ultraviolet radiation from the sun, the human body is incapable of synthesizing the hormone calciferol, which is released into the bloodstream by the skin and is essential for hardening calcium in growing bone.

The relative lack of the skin pigment melanin in European populations represents an evolutionary adaptation to the need for maximum exposure to weak and intermittent sunshine during the long northern winters. Tanning, on the other hand, is thought to be a protective device that mobilizes available melanin to screen out the more intense and potentially lethal radiation of the summer months. Incidentally, the blackest African skins are produced by precisely the same pigment, melanin, occurring in greater abundance in the epidermal layers, probably as an adaptation against overdoses of solar radiation in tropical latitudes. With industrial smog blotting out the sun, therefore, the European working class fell victim to rickets, especially during the winter.

Indoor confinement under crowded conditions was also associated with a higher incidence of tuberculosis among urban factory workers and their families. At the start of the twentieth century doctors began to prescribe "heliotherapy"—sunbathing—as a specific cure for this disease. So there was a definite health advantage to be gained by wealthy Europeans and Americans who embraced the outdoor life and elevated the esthetic value of suntan over that of pallor.

Nonetheless, a suntan as the new badge of leisure class identity should not be overlooked. Sunshine per se had nothing to do with curing tuberculosis and only a few minutes a day of ultraviolet radiation on translucent pink cheeks will keep the average pale-faced infant well supplied with calciferol, even during the winter months.

The intense mass irradiation that now goes on under the summer sun, however, is a definite menace to public health. In the words of Harold F. Blum of the National Cancer Institute, "an impressive amount of evidence converges to indicate sunlight as a cause of human skin cancer." This risk is greatest precisely among people of European descent whose skin contains the least amount of melanin. Contrary to popular expectations, the more one indulges in sunbathing, the greater the risk of developing skin cancer. A deep tan is the sign of a deeply injured skin.

At the moment, I see little prospect for moderating the cosmetic value attributed to the well-tanned face and body. The consumption of sunlight has grown into one of the major focuses of our economy. Under the influence of the tourist and real estate industries it has been democratized and no longer draws its main strength from the popular desire to emulate the superrich, who, I suspect, have once again begun to seek shade. In the arena of middle-class consumerism, keeping a year-round total body tan has replaced the Cadillac as a status symbol. For the average, pale-faced, installment plan vacationer, one conspicuous tan is worth a thousand picture postcards.

And what about all those sundrenched condominiums whose investment value will plummet if people get around to thinking of them as cancer traps?

I do see one ray of hope in all of this—more people may eventually be forced to concede that color prejudice is for the birds.

THE REGALIA OF RITUAL: RITES OF PASSAGE

Marianne S. Beeson

Anthropologists have studied rituals and ceremonies around the world. Rites of passage are the rituals which celebrate or mark the passage of an individual from one position or state into another life stage. Birth, puberty, marriage, and death are accompanied by traditional ceremonies in almost all cultures.

While the form of ritual varies of course, it is significant that special, symbolic clothing is usually part of rites of passage. Festive foods and beverages, including alcoholic drinks, music, dance, and presentation of gifts may be integral to rites of passage in cultures ranging from non-

literate African tribes to the upper social class levels of the American culture.

The French anthropologist Arnold van Gennep delineated three stages in rites of passage—separation, transition, and incorporation (5, p. 14). Marriage includes separation from one family and incorporation into another. In Western cultures it is the bride who is separated from her parents and siblings (Her father "gives her away."); the transition is the honeymoon, and incorporation is into the family of the groom. In some matrilineal societies, the groom is separated from his family, and he lives with or is incorporated into his wife's family.

The elaborate customs of dress for the marriage rite are as traditional and ritualistic as the throwing of rice—a symbol of fertility. White in the United States is the traditional color for wedding gowns, a symbol of festive joy originally, but since the Victorian era respresentative of chastity and purity. As is the case with most symbols, misrepresentation does not preclude continuance of the tradition. In China brides wear red, and, in fact, during the American Revolution red was popular for patriot brides as a symbol of rebellion (4, p. 126). In other cultures brides wear black, or green, or no particular color, but a special costume.

In spite of a degree of youth rejection of certain longstanding values and attitudes in the United States, brides tend to be ultra-traditional in the selection of wedding dresses.

> . . . tales of paper wedding dresses and plastic dresses and gaucho pants and hot pants and scuba-diving suits make for lively reading in *Life* magazine but have nothing to do with what's really happening in our country. When a lass dreams about the magic moment, she is not visualizing herself in seethrough-micro-mini with vinyl boots. She is the fairy princess, period (4, p. 127).

The anti-establishment, iconoclastic mood is not often expressed in wedding garb.

> Regardless of their lifestyle at the moment, when it's time to get married they harden back to some ancient tribal voice. Store after store reports the same behavior: lass enters as a tie-dyed hippie, leaves as a vanilla ice cream cone (4, p. 128).

The current Women's Movement has led to a few changes in some of the legal and financial arrangements of marriage; for example, there is a modest trend toward the retention of the bride's family name after marriage or the joint adoption of a hyphenated combination of bride's and groom's surnames. However, when it comes to the presentation of self for the wedding ceremony, even feminists find pleasure in selecting the most traditional—and sexist—of wedding gowns. Anna Quindlen, a reporter for the New York *Times*, recounts her childhood desire for a Madame Alexander bride doll and how her dreams were fulfilled in her own wedding.

> What I wanted was to be the feminist I'd always been, the journalist I'd managed to become, and the—let's face it—vision of loveliness I'd always hoped for one shot at being. . . . I did not want to wear a sensible suit, a chaste column of crepe, or a Mexican dress for my wedding. I wanted to *be* a Madame Alexander doll (2, p. 73).

For the members of the wedding party, ritual clothing involves a bit of play-acting, too. At a splashy wedding of New York City blacks, the rental bill for the men's tuxedos was $70 each. The best man's attitude is revealing.

> "It's just a big dress-up, that's what it's all about. . . . How often you get decked out like this and have a blast? The main draw is the reception and then the parties afterward, goin' all night. You're in the groove anyway, so it's a ball! (4, p. 67)"

Rites of passage are often performed within the context of religious practices. The Jewish Bar Mitzvah, when the thirteen year old boy passes into manhood, the Catholic's confirmation, baptisms and christenings are religious rites of passage requiring special clothing for the ritual subject. Marriages and funerals are also usually religious ceremonies.

Death as a rite of passage calls for nonordinary clothing and adornment. In America the elaborate preparation of the body includes hair styling and cosmetics. The success of such preparation seems to be measured by the approving comments of friends and relatives, "He (she) looks so natural!"

In Jessica Mitford's exposé of the funeral trade, *The American Way of Death,* portions of promotional material describing attire for the deceased are quoted.

> "The No. 280 reflects character and station in life. It is superb in styling and provides a formal reflection of successful living." . . . refers to the Fit-A-Fut Oxford, which comes in patent calf, tan, or oxblood. . . . The same firm carries the Ko-Zee, with its "soft, cushioned soles and warm, luxurious slipper comfort, but true shoe smartness." Just what practical use is made of this footwear is spelled out. Burial footwear demonstrates "consideration and thoughtfulness for the departed." . . . for the ladies is the "new Bra-form, Post Mortem Form Restoration," offered . . . at the demonstrably low price of $11 for a package of 50—they "accomplish so much for so little (1, p. 56)."

At a convention of funeral directors, a line of gowns for the departed was displayed; there were street-wear type dresses, negligees, hostess gowns, and brunch coats (1, pp. 56–57). The day of the burial shroud has passed. Americans expect their dead to look lifelike for this rite of passage.

Puberty rites in primitive cultures are often involved and lengthy rituals dealing with taboos associated with menstruation; sometimes circumcision is performed during puberty rites. Stoicism during periods of isolation, evidence of bravery, and endurance of pain, such as in scarification, mutilation, or during circumcision may be expected of the adolescent. In preindustrial cultures puberty means leaving childhood and emerging as an adult of marriageable age. The addition of a symbolic article of clothing, a change of hairstyle, or adult cosmetics are cultural means of conveying availability to the opposite sex.

In the industrialized nations, puberty is regarded primarily as a physiological change, accompanied by very few changes in status or rank. Adolescents who are physically adults do not often assume adult roles. Western cultures extend into several years the period in which the young adult remains dependent upon his parents for financial and emotional support. Professions and jobs require such extensive education and training that adult responsibilities must be delayed. Thus, puberty alone does not mean transition from childhood to adulthood in such societies; rites of passage at puberty would be insignificant by definition.

However, other ritualized ceremonies may accompany changes in position, even though they are not associated with the life crises of birth, puberty, marriage, and death. Graduation or commencement entails prescribed clothing, the customary congratulatory handshake, and at the proper moment, transfer of the tassel from the right to the left side of the mortarboard—all symbolic of completion of one stage in life and a beginning or *commencement* of another.

*   *   *

A personal experience of this writer may serve to illustrate how tenaciously a society clings to symbols of ritual. In 1972 I had the privilege of serving on a student-faculty committee charged with the responsibility of planning a commencement ceremony for the College of Home Economics, one of seven colleges at Virginia Polytechnic Institute and State University. Due to pressures from students and others in favor of a more personalized ceremony and because of the impracticality of individually handing "sheepskins" to 2,650 graduates, it was decided to confer degrees *en masse* at a University commencement in the stadium and then to have additional commencement programs following in each College. The numbers of graduates and guests were thus reduced to manageable proportions, and each College was given complete freedom to plan the proceedings. In our College committee, the faculty assumed advisory roles and let the students make their own decisions.

I *anticipated* the unconventional, something "way out" and original: guitar music, barefoot parades through the trees, casual dress, guests seated on the grass. I envisioned a light but meaningful program which would be the antithesis of the many pompous, boring, and sunny-hot commencements I had endured for several years. I should have been more culturally attuned, because I was actually *surprised* at the outcome of the planning sessions. Tradition was observed to the last detail: caps and gowns, faculty in full academic regalia, organ processional, an inspirational speech, and the walk across the stage of an auditorium to shake hands and receive the certificate bearing further proof of college graduation! Obviously this group

of graduates felt more secure and perhaps more definitely graduated amid the familiar rituals and symbols. Proud parents and relatives were pleased, and rightfully deserving of any rewards or satisfactions. Perhaps it was an expression of gratitude to parents for the "gift" of a college education which was the underlying motivation for the conservative commencement. At any rate, given the same freedom to plan commencement, each succeeding graduating class has planned and carried out almost identical traditional ceremonies.

*   *   *

At least one writer has classified the following experience as a popular rite of passage.

> David, a youth in his middle teens, was led away from his parents by one of the officials dressed in a dark uniform. He was taken to a room somewhere on the other side of the building. There he and several other young men began the examination. Seated in neat rows they underwent the examination under the stern eye of another official. Later they were required to manipulate a giant machine under the watchful eye of still another official. Finally, after waiting at home for a period of up to several weeks, they were welcomed into the community of their brothers (5, p. 13).

The account pertains to the procedure for obtaining a driver's license, a test for entry into the adult world of automobile drivers.

Other rites of passage are those of initiation into societies, clubs, or cults. Schwartz and Merten recount one phase of initiation into high school sororities.

> Early Saturday morning all pledges arrive at the park in bizarre and exotic dress. Though it is difficult to capture the impression they make assembled at this park, perhaps a "typical" example might convey the visual impact of this gathering. A girl wears a bathing suit over men's pajamas and has a woman's stocking on one leg with a high-heeled shoe and a sock on the other foot with a flat-heeled shoe. Her hair is separated into many braids to which ballons are attached, and she wears a necklace composed of onions and sardines. She has a rope belt from which tin cans are hanging. Her face is painted in unmistakably strange patterns, perhaps one side is red and the other is black. No one sees this as a costume in the usual sense of the word. While it is obviously absurd and obtrusive, it nevertheless exaggerates dress styles socies [socialities—the top level of the status system] see as common to other strata of the adolescent community. In addition to this garb, pledges are required to bring catsup, eggs, garlic salt, chocolate syrup, shaving cream, and the like with them to the park.
>
> When all the pledges from these three sororities are present, they begin a race for six blocks to another park where the final phase of mock begins. The members drive to the other park shouting encouragement to their pledges who run along one of the main streets of the community. The pledge who arrives at the park first "wins" for her sorority although there is no special recognition of this accomplishment. Each sorority takes its pledges to a separate section of the park and starts to cover them with an amazing assortment of difficult to re-

move substances. The aim of this activity is to smear the pledge so that she looks as messy as possible. Special attention is paid to their hair. The substances are handrubbed (by the pledges) into the hair, and those who have been through this ritual claim that it takes weeks to completely remove all the odor and traces of this treatment. The official rationale for this event is that it is fun. Though the members engage in considerable hilarity, they also do a thorough job and work in a rather systematic fashion on each pledge. While the treatment is going on, the pledges are made to play in the sand or on the slides. After thirty to forty minutes have elapsed, the pledges are driven home in the open trunks of cars and mock has ended.[1]

The events described above occurred near the end of a nine week period of pledging. A formal tea and then *Hell Night* preceded the episodes in the park. During *Hell Night* pledges were insulted, yelled at, and commanded to cry. "If she cannot (cry), members scream at her until she does (3, p. 1124))." The final stage was a formal rite of induction with an exchange of gifts between pledges and their "pledge mothers" (3, p. 1127).

The duration of pledging in this example, up until actual induction into the sorority, represents the isolation stage in rites of passage, a transition period in which the position of the ritual subject is ambiguous. He does not belong to, nor is identified with, either his former level or his impending state. Turner further characterizes the transition period.

> . . . neophytes in initiation or puberty rites, may be represented as possessing nothing. They may be disguised as monsters, wear only a strip of clothing, or even go naked, to demonstrate that as liminal beings they have no status, property, insignia, secular clothing indicating rank or role, position in a kinship system—in short, nothing that may distinguish them from their fellow neophytes or initiands. Their behavior is normally passive or humble; they must obey their instructors implicitly, and accept arbitrary punishment without complaint. It is as though they are being reduced or ground down to a uniform condition to be fashioned anew and endowed with additional powers to enable them to cope with their new station in life (6, p. 95).

1. Schwartz, Gary and Don Merten, "Social Identity and Expressive Symbols: The Meaning of an Initiation Ritual." Reproduced by permission of the American Anthropological Association, from the *American Anthropologist,* 70 (6), 1968.

Turner has implied that the lack of any national rites of passage in modern Western society has placed adolescents and young adults of the counter-culture in the isolation or transition stage of self-imposed rites of passage. His analysis of clothing and behavior draws a rough parallel to the nonstatus conditions of initiates during puberty rites in preindustrial societies.

> . . . members . . . "opt out" of the status-bound social order and acquire the stigmata of the lowly, dressing like "bums," itenerant in their habits, "folk" in their musical tastes, and menial in the casual employment they undertake (6, p. 112).

The fact that members of the counter-culture often do emerge from their radical experience to assume conventional societal roles seems to suggest that the "drop out" period may indeed be a transition—a kind of marathon puberty rite after which the subject is welcomed into adulthood.

In continuing to mark with ritual some of the significant transitions in various stages of life, diverse cultures share a common experience. Through preservation of the manner of dress and the other symbols of rites of passage, each culture expresses a tie to the past and with preceding generations. Styles of dress and clothing customs so firmly entrenched in cultural rituals are very slow to change.

REFERENCES CITED

1. Mitford, Jessica. *The American Way of Death*. New York: Simon and Schuster, 1963.
2. Quindlen, Anna. "Ms. Goes to a Wedding," *Ms.,* December, 1978, pp. 73–75.
3. Schwartz, Gary, and Don Merten. "Social Identity and Expressive Symbols: The Meaning of an Initiation Ritual." *American Anthropologist,* 70 (Dec., 1968), pp. 1117–1131.
4. Seligson, Marcie. *The Eternal Bliss Machine: America's Way of Wedding*. New York: William Morrow & Co., Inc., 1973.
5. "The Rites of Passage: Milestones on the Road of Life." *Senior Scholastic,* January 8, 1973, pp. 13–15.
6. Turner, Victor W. *The Ritual Process: Structure and Anti-Structure*. Chicago: Aldine Pub. Co., 1969.

KIMONO, FROM ITS 12th-CENTURY ORIGINS, IS RECOGNIZED AS A LASTING SARTORIAL TRIUMPH

S. Chang

Despite the inroads of the miniskirt, the Japanese still love their traditional dress and don it for special occassions.

In Japan for the umpteenth time, Eliot Elisofon earlier this year had a new litany. "Kimono," he gushed, "is visually the most glorious of things invented by Man." A renowned photographer and documentary film-maker, Elisofon never changed. Whatever his current enthusiasm, he gave himself up to it completely. Typically, he chanted his new litany with such gusto that his Japanese friends could only smile. "Here goes Eliot-*san* again," said one of them. "Don't ever take him to a Japanese restaurant, or he will kill you with his kimonology." Alas, the assignment on kimono from this magazine was to be his last. Only a week or so after he left Japan, he died unexpectedly in New York.

To most Japanese, of course, his last enthusiasm is perfectly understandable; kimono is nothing less than the apex of their sartorial arts. But, unlike Elisofon, the Japanese take it for granted. They use understatement in praising it. Indeed, some of them have been even critical of it, and these critics have included women. Take, for instance, a 19th-century empress of Japan. Her Imperial Majesty said kimono was "unnatural to human body." But this should by no means be mistaken for an imperial attempt at downgrading it. The truth of the matter is quite the opposite. In the time-honored Japanese esthetics, nothing, you see, is perfect without at least one flaw. These critics of kimono were striving to find a flaw in it, but only in order to make it perfect in their eyes. Such is the way in Japan. Elisofon knew this, but he seems to have found it hard to accept.

Kimono, like most other components of Japanese culture, must be traced to China for its origins. But it was never a direct import on yesteryear's slow boats across the Yellow Sea; it can only be described as the result of processes for which the Japanese have long been noted: adaptation and refinement. The first written record of Japanese garb seems to underline the point. There is an eyewitness account in the chronicle of a Chinese traveler who showed up in Japan toward the middle of third century A.D. "They [the Japanese] wear simple clothes that take the form of a square fabric with a hole in the center," he wrote. "They wear it by penetrating the hole with their head." He was describing the garment worn by women of the lower classes, which must have looked like a poncho. Men of these classes simply draped a straight piece of cloth over their shoulders.

With the introduction of Buddhism sometime after A.D. 500, the Japanese court began to copy Chinese costume, and at a tempo reminiscent of the pace with which Japan centuries later adopted the miniskirt. In 682 a code was drawn up for the imperial household which prescribed, among other things, the mode of dress for each level of the hierarchy. Specified were all things Chinese, including a lacquered headdress running up to a point and a flowing robe with pleats and broad sleeves that almost touched the ground. It was an unabashed transplant from the Chinese court. But the Japanese, here again, were already improvising. For example, with colors: Each rank at the Japanese emperor's court was distinguished by the color of the dress uniform. At the bottom of the color scheme was black, for the lowliest attendants, and at the very top, *oni* (a reddish yellow) for the monarch. Wearing a color assigned to a higher rank was cause for arrest.

The chromatic sense was particularly sharp among ladies of the ancient Japanese court. This is amply demonstrated in *The Tale of Genji,* written around the year 1000 by the talented Lady Murasaki. This famous novel, the first in the annals of Japanese letters, is actually about the loves and life of a prince charming in Kyoto—Hikaru Genji. But the author crammed her novel with chatty commentaries on which character wore what. And her discussions of color are, to most male Japanese readers today, painfully long. In the novel a lady appears for dinner in a dress "too pale in color," which is but another excuse for a lengthy dissertation on the psychology of colors and the wearer's presumed state of mind for the evening. And small wonder. There was little else to talk about as far as dress was concerned. In that period a court lady's costume was, in effect, a uniform; they all wore the *juni-hitoe*—literally, "12 layers."

The penchant was for downright overdressing. Sometimes the 12 layers multiplied into 20 for a really sumptuous cascade. To top it all off, they often wore one or more pairs of *hakama* (divided overskirts) and a sweeping *mo* (train), over which trailed a cataract of glistening black hair. A modified version of *juni-hitoe* is still in existence, but it is donned only by female members of Japan's imperial family on state occasions such as royal weddings and coronations. So rigidly uniform was the styling of it that ladies of the court in the days of Lady Murasaki could try for individuality only in their color combinations. A sensible trend soon emerged. With their changing color schemes, these ladies began to reflect or anticipate the seasons. For spring, the combinations of colors often reflected the blossoms of the plum and cherry; for summer, the colors of azaleas; for the fall, blazing foliage colors were fashionable; and in winter the thing to do was to dramatize the contrast between the green of pine trees and the purity of snow. All this they managed to do by mixing the colors of the various layers of the *juni-hitoe.* Even today, the color scheme is an over-riding factor in Kimono, and the reason is the same as it was almost a thousand years ago: Since the style has not changed at all, color is the only way of expressing one's own taste.

Kimono in more or less its present form surfaced in the 12th century. Then it was called *kosode,* which means "small sleeve." Originally it was an undergarment worn by Japanese court ladies beneath the broad-sleeved *juni-hitoe* and by samurai warriors under their armor. Then the samurai wives adopted it for everyday outer wear, tying it at the waist with a narrow *obi* (sash).

To begin with, Chinese silk was the regulation material for *kosode.* Then, at the end of the 16th century, Hideyoshi Toyotomi—the greatest hero in Japanese history —gave the local silk industry a remarkable boost. This samurai general of humble peasant origin, whom Westerners call the "Napoleon of Japan,"was a great patron of the arts. Hideyoshi invited Chinese weavers, fugitives from the faltering Ming Dynasty, to come to Kyoto and set aside a special quarter of the city for them. The descendants of their Japanese colleagues, the Nishijin weavers, are today among the most versatile of kimono craftsmen in the country. At the same time, a flood of foreign techniques and materials began to pour into Japan, such as the magnificent Indian silks and the Gobelin tapestries brought in by the Dutch. A blending of all these techniques resulted in a great period for kimono. The Nishijin weavers' contribution is particularly noteworthy. They outstripped their emigré Chinese confreres and came up with a technical break-through that enabled them to imitate embroidery by means of weaving. This was the invention of the celebrated weaver Tawaraya, who achieved the effect by "floating" patches of colored threads on the surface of the fabric.

The Yuzen dyers a century later—circa 1700—developed a technique for painting designs on kimono with colorfast dyes. Their method was somewhat akin to that of Indonesian batik, in which the pattern is drawn in dye-resistant hot wax that is later removed. The Yuzen dyers' innovation was to use, instead of wax, a thin paste of glutinous rice flour and egg white which enabled them to draw incredibly fine lines.

Refinements followed. The rich merchant class, for once turning into arbiters of taste, demanded sophistication. Then the Japanese theater, the pantomimic noh and kabuki plays, respectively inspired angularity of form and a flood of exploding colors for the decoration of kimono. Courtesans of the Edo period (1615–1867) also made a contribution in the astonishing development of the *obi.* Once a narrow sash used by samurai women, it became a gaudy ornament almost as important as kimono itself. Kimono today is a summation of all these diverse elements in tradition. The peak of elegance was reached about 200 years ago. Since then kimono has undergone no notable changes.

For all its subtle refinements, kimono has seldon ceased to be baffling to Westerners. Among the first Americans to see it was Commodore Matthew Perry 120 years ago. He promptly disapproved. In the record of his memorable mission to Japan, the Yankee seadog calls it, of all things, "an ungraceful drapery—with much of the undress look of dressing gowns." The chronicle doesn't make it clear just where Perry studied kimono. Some Japanese today pointedly recall the presence of bordellos not far from where his "black ships"dropped anchor after their transpacific crossing. Was it perhaps in one of them, they wonder, that he made his studies of kimono? Even though history provides no answer, the fact of the matter is plain: Under no normal circumstances would kimono achieve an "undress look,"even though in American dictionaries the word has a secondary meaning as "a loose dressing gown usually worn by women." But that is obviously a different garment.

No Damper on Eroticism

Baffling to the Japanese is the fact that *keto* (literally, hairy ones, but derogatorily, foreigners) misunderstanding could take the opposite direction, too. Typical of this phenomenon is the way a British film producer reacted to kimono last spring. After a stroll through the Ginza on a national holiday, he discussed the many kimonoed girls he had seen. Then he allowed himself to be blunt. "What's so good about kimono?" he demanded. "It covers your women's anatomy so completely." After a pause he asked again, this time sotto voce: "You cover them up so that we foreigners won't become excited over them—right?"

Not right. Kimono could and does excite eroticism among Japanese males, but they look for it where foreigners are not accustomed to—in the nape of a woman's dainty neck. That's why the neckband of kimono, or its position over the nape, is a telling guide to a woman's attitude toward life and sex. For the information of the uninitiated, the geisha throws it back to expose as much of her nape as is technically possible.

In its long history, kimono has gone through only one critical period. That was during and immediately after

World War II, when a singular brand of patriotism on the part of a Japanese housewives' association almost completely drove kimono off the streets. To flaunt the luxuries of kimono, officials of the association decided, was against the interests of the Japanese empire. "Think of our soldiers battling far away from home." they argued. "We Japanese women back home must at least look patriotic, too."

Quickly, the meddlesome ladies went to work. Wearing aprons over their own purposely drab kimono, they would accost the more colorfully attired members of their sex and thrust at them a handbill from the association. "Cut off your kimono sleeves," the message sternly said. "And work for the empire." Frightened, the women thus warned hastened to lock up their Sunday best in their chest of drawers. For a dully patriotic substitute, they began wearing what was perhaps the ugliest costume in the whole history of kimono. This consisted of a course cotton kimono of indigo color and *mompe*, baggy pants akin in style to those donned by the masses in China during the Great Proletarian Cultural Revolution. Soon that combination became a woman's uniform of sorts for a Japan at war.

Kimono's future looked grayer still at the war's end. With the institutions of emperor worship and empire building collapsing, the Japanese desperately needed a new national cult. And they found one in what GIs on occupation duty in Japan had brought along with chewing gum—the American concept of efficiency. Professor Takashi Motoi of Kyoto City University, a foremost authority on kimono, recalls: "The more we brainwashed ourselves on this new concept, the more did kimono look obsolete." True; down the ages kimono has stood for anything but efficiency. "In no time,"says Professor Motoi, "we all were convinced that in the new society that was about to develop in Japan after the war, there would be no place left at all for kimono."

Motoi, and his fellow prophets of doom for kimono, couldn't have been more wrong. It is true that far more Japanese girls than ever before now adopted Western clothes for everyday wear. Kimono as working garb disappeared almost completely. But it didn't die with the Japanese empire. On the contrary, the more Japan recovered in economy, the more did kimono regain its traditional importance. Today, as wear for ceremonies and parties, it is having what could only be called a renaissance. The proof of this is only too visible in the streets of Japan on festival days. The streets then will be practically awash with the radiance of kimono worn by lovely parades of Japanese women. In this fast-changing land, kimono in fact is one of the few visible links between today and yesterday.

But kimono, to say the least, is costly. There was a time when American tourists in Japan would pop into department stores for a "$10 set" to take home as a souvenir. Few Americans do so now. For an antique set of silk kimono and matching *obi,* the price can go as high as $10,000. One Tokyo business tycoon, in fact, is known to have paid as much as $20,000 for his daughter's bridal costume. These incredibly high prices have led to the birth of a new business in Japan—the kimono rental. Commercial wedding halls in Japan invariably have a rental section to fill the needs of many brides-to-be. This is one difference between the old days and now. Once upon a time, a silk wedding costume was like a household fixture: It was handed down from generation to generation for use by all of the family brides.

Another difference concerns the art of wearing it. Professionals like geisha never get dressed for work without assistance from those experts called *hakoya.* For ordinary Japanese women, it was a different story altogether. Until the close of the war, most women were able to put it on alone and tie those heavy *obi* with no assistance from others. No more. Now few girls seem to be able to do it without help from their mothers or sisters. The fact is that there are more than a hundred classes in Tokyo to teach them how to do it.

A Test of Patience

Nevertheless, the art is declining, for it is complex and demanding. First off, you wear *koshimaki* (scarlet waist wraparound). Then come, in turn, *hada-juban* (soft undervest), *naga-juban* (long undergarment)and finally kimono. To place them all in proper position and keep them there, you need at least half a dozen cloth belts tied as tightly as possible around the waist. For the *obi* itself there have to be *datemaki* (undersash) and padding to give it proper fullness. And then, at last snow-white *tabi* (socks) for the feet. To wear kimono, in short, is tantamount to a test of patience. But it is often too much for many Japanese girls, to the annoyance of kimono connoisseurs. Another source of annoyance to these connoisseurs concerns panties that young Japanese girls now wear under kimono. Flimsy as the Western piece of garb is, they insist, somewhat improbably, that it breaks the "purity of line." In the past no one wore panties under kimono, but now only geisha seem to abide by the old rule.

All the same kimono perseveres. And that magic still seems to happen when Japanese women climb out of their minis, midis or Pierre Cardins and into kimono. In the process, they always seem to undergo a transformation. Once kimonoed, they appear to assume what can only be called the kimono mind. And that is supposedly everything that once made Japanese women infinitely desirable—obedient, witty and lovely. There is no denying that they look their best in kimono. And some Japanese males with a dreamy turn of mind wish their favorite *keto* women were dressed in it, too. At an old Buddhist temple in Tokyo this past summer, a Japan Marilyn Monroe

Admiration Society sponsored a memorial rite to mark the anniversary of the passing of the star. Then a shaven-pated monk at the temple wistfully observed: "Monroe-*san* was one of those foreign girls who would have looked just right in kimono—that's why we loved her so much."

MEXICO'S MANY COSTUMES

Elizabeth Snoddy Cuéllar

"Do you wear shoes, *huaraches,* or go barefoot?" If you live in Mexico this is one of the questions the census taker asks you, and how you answer is a factor in deciding into which of the socioeconomic levels you fit. Although in most modern societies clothing has become standardized, today's Mexican, like his ancestors, accentuates the social differences by his dress.

In his book *Viva Mexico,* published in 1908, Charles Flandrau discusses the habit, which one still acquires in Mexico, of watching the world go by from a bench in a plaza or a chair on a hotel balcony. He tells of seeing in the space of a few minutes big-hatted carriers waiting in the street for a job, burros carrying cobblestones, an endless stream of biblical-looking girls bearing huge water jars to and from a circular fountain, ice cream vendors crying their wares, old women with handfuls of lottery tickets, basket sellers and flower sellers, houseboys dawdling along on errands, and ladies draped in black lace on their way to church. One of the reasons for the picturesqueness of the scene is the variety in the costume of its actors.

The Mexicans who wear shoes usually belong to the upper class groups who, if judged by their dress, could be from any place in the western world. The wearers of *huaraches,* the typical Mexican sandal hand made of strips of leather and soles cut from discarded rubber tires, include the villagers and many of the people of the rural areas. They are the ones who show the greatest mixture of Spanish and Indian in their dress and in their customs.

The third group, those who go barefoot, are the Indians. Perhaps their ancestry is no more pure Indian than that of the average Mexican *mestizo,* a blend of the great Middle American Indian races and the conquering Spaniards, but because of their clothing, their tradition-bound way of life, and often their language, they are classified as *indios.*

The Indians had been weaving beautiful fabrics for several thousand years before the arrival of the Spaniards in 1519. The long history of weaving has had a profound effect on all types of art and decoration in the Americas. Here, perhaps more than elsewhere in the world, the geometric patterns to which the weaver is largely restricted

by the warp and weft are repeated in the decoration of pottery, in stone carving, and in painting.

Cloth in early Mexico was woven of fibers of wild cotton, cactus, and the maguey or century plant. Cotton was the most important of these because of its affinity for dyes and thus its great ornamental value, and great fields of it were cultivated by the Indians.

The art of weaving was highly valued by the Indians. Men do a large part of the weaving in present-day Mexico, but in ancient times it was woman's work. Fray Bernardino de Sahagún, a priest with a great interest in the ancient customs, wrote in the 1560s: "If the newly born was a girl, when they baptized her they put into the glazed tub all the implements of woman, with which they spin and weave, because the life of a woman is to be reared in the home and live and remain in it." He also wrote that the Indians considered a lack of weaving ability as among the worst possible faults of a woman. "A woman born under this sign (Cecalli) was likewise unfortunate; she was good for nothing; she could not spin or weave; she was stupid, a smiling rustic, overbearing, vociferous and (they say) always eating Tzictli (called chicle today . . . and even to this day chewed and cracked between the teeth by lewd women)."

The Indians placed great value on woven goods. Aztec households were largely self-sufficient; most utensils and clothing were made in the home. But, according to the *Codex Mendoza* and the Tribute Roll of Moctezuma, in addition to this home-produced cloth the Aztecs demanded over a million lengths from their subjugated tribes as part of their annual tribute.

Woven goods were considered appropriate gifts on important occasions. Sahagún tells of newly elected chieftains offering great festivities to the other chiefs of a district: "Whenever the newly elected chieftain prepared such a festival he gave a great number of blankets and richly ornamented belts to the chiefs who gathered around him, so much so that the latter left more loaded with what they received on such occasions than they had been upon

Reprinted from *Américas,* monthly magazine published by the General Secretariat of the Organization of American States in English, Spanish, and Portuguese. Vol. 28, No. 5, pp. 5–13.

arrival with their own gifts to the chieftain. The blankets presented to the latter were all made in his house, very beautifully woven or embroidered in many patterns, according to the status of the person to whom they were to be given." Offerings were also made by the Aztecs at the temples of each of the *calpulli,* or clans, and included woven blankets as well as fowl, corn, beans, and flowers.

Bernal Díaz del Castillo, the soldier-chronicler of Cortez' conquest of Mexico, relates that the first gifts sent to Cortez by Moctezuma included much gold and that "over thirty loads of beautiful cotton cloths were brought worked with many patterns and decorated with many colored feathers." He also wrote of the fabrics and clothing that were sold in the great Tlaltelolco market (in present-day Mexico City): "feathers, mantles, and embroidered goods. . . . Next there were other traders who sold great pieces of cloth and cotton and articles of twisted thread. . . . There were those who sold cloths of henequen and ropes and the sandals with which they are shod, which are made from the same plant. . . . In another part there were skins of tigers and lions, of otters and jackals, deer and other animals and badgers and mountain cats, some tanned and others untanned."

The range of colors used by the Indians gave a richness to their fabrics. They had learned to make dye from many of the things around them, among them scarlet from the cochineal, the tiny insect that lives on the nopal cactus, blue from the indigo plant, and purple from a little shellfish found along the Pacific coast. The Indian women were also expert with their needles of bone and copper, and their embroidery added to the beauty of their costumes.

The richest garments of the time were adorned with featherwork, possibly one of the most beautiful arts of all time as the colors of feathers have a richness that no man-made paints or dyes can match. The Indians used the tiny, fine feathers from small birds in their work; their favorite was the hummingbird because of its irridescent sheen, and the feathers from thousands of these little birds were used in the making of a single cloak for a rich noble. Feathers were demanded as tribute from conquered tribes, especially those from the tropical jungles.

Featherworkers needed great skill and patience. The feathers were separated according to color and stripped so that only the delicate tip was left on the barb. Copper tweezers were used to pick up each little feather and lay it on the cloth being woven, the stem being woven into the cloth and the colored tip fixed in place with a drop of gum. The feathers were laid on in overlapping rows and formed beautiful patterns and rainbow effects of color. This made the cloaks as fine and warm as fur and they were greatly prized, for there was no wool in Mesoamerica before the arrival of the Spaniards.

Great changes took place in weaving in Mexico with the arrival of the Spaniards. Wool-bearing animals were introduced, as well as the upright loom and the spinning wheel. The Indians had spun on a wooden hand spindle weighted with an often beautifully decorated clay whorl called a *malacate.*

Horizontal or backstrap looms had been used earlier for weaving, as they still are in many parts of Mexico. The backstrap loom is a simple one made of two bars of wood with the warp, or lengthwise thread, stretched between them. One end is fastened to a tree or house post and the other to a belt of leather or woven palm around the weaver's waist. The weaver stands or sits on a stool or a reed mat and leans back to hold the warp taut for weaving. These looms work well for making belts and bags or fabric strips that aren't too wide for the weaver to pass the shuttle through the warp with ease; thirty inches is about the greatest width that can be reached. The European upright loom, in which the warp is fastened in a frame, makes possible the weaving of fabrics of almost any width, as the weaver can move back and forth beside the loom.

Wool was the greatest contribution the Spaniards made to Mexican weaving. They brought with them many domesticated animals—horses, burros, cattle, pigs, goats, and sheep. Sheep's wool was eagerly adopted by the Indian weavers as it was warmer and more durable than cotton, and it almost immediately became a part of the costume of many groups.

Silkworms were also introduced and mulberry trees planted shortly after the Conquest. Silk was produced until the end of the sixteenth century, when a flourishing trade with China brought in the finer silks. With the new fabric available and with Spain's restrictive production and export laws for the Colony, the raising of silk was reduced to small home industries in a few isolated communities.

Soon after the Conquest the Spaniards took advantage of the skilled Indian weavers and local sources of cotton and dyes to set up weaving work-shops. These were sufficient to fill the needs of the Spaniards but not those of the Indians; because the Indians continued to depend on their home out-put, traditional Indian techniques, equipment, dyes, and articles of clothing survived. Today there are still two distinct types of weaving in Mexico, the Indian and the Mexican, which is a mixture of Spanish and Indian. Indian weaving, using the backstrap loom and old techniques, is principally done by women, while men are almost always found at the upright loom.

The most important and the best-known article made in Mexico on the upright loom is the serape, the blanket and cloak of most of the *huarache*-clad men of rural and small-town Mexico. It is woven either in one piece or in two strips that are sewed together. The serape is probably a descendant of the *tilma,* the cloak of the Indians that was worn about the body and knotted over the right shoulder, and the Spanish-Arabian *manta,* or wool travel blanket. A most useful garment, it is a man's overcoat and his covering at night; he can spread his merchandise out on it in the market or stretch it over poles to make a shelter, and in the end his serape serves as his shroud.

To be carried, the serape is doubled lengthwise and the narrow folded cloth hung over one shoulder. When it is cold the man throws it around his body in such a way that his neck and ears are protected. Some serapes have slits in the center for the head, and hang like cloaks. Although it dates from after the Conquest, the serape was immediately accepted by almost all Indian groups and has become a traditional part of the Mexican scene. The design and color of serapes vary considerably from one area to another and one can often tell where a man is from by the serape he wears.

Many areas in Mexico are noted for their serape weaving. Well-made serapes can be found in the Toluca and Texcoco markets; heavy and tightly woven, they are often used for rugs. More loosely woven serapes that make soft, comfortable blankets are woven in Teotitlan del Valle in Oaxaca, and these are the ones constantly peddled in the Oaxaca city plaza.

Distinctive serapes are woven in Jocotepec, Jalisco; they are of dark brown or white decorated with stylized roses, wreaths, and sprigs of small flowers in pastel colors. Little-known but beautiful natural color wool serapes are made by the Mayo Indians and can be purchased in and around Navojoa, Sonora. The most primitive serape looms are used by the Tarahumara women in Chihuahua State, and their heavy vegetable-dyed serapes can often be found in small stores in Creel, southwest of the city of Chihuahua, where they are put on the scales and sold by the kilo. Handsome loopweave serapes woven of burro hair are made in Silao, Guanajuato, and can be bought there or in the market in the city of Guanajuato.

Santa Ana Chautempán in the State of Tlaxcala has long been noted for its serapes; the famous old Saltillo serapes were probably first woven by the colony of Tlaxcalans who were moved to Saltillo by the Spaniards in 1591 and who furnished the entire area with woven goods. The Saltillo serapes were very famous during the colonial period, and probably represent the finest tapestry weaving in all Latin America. Although they are called Saltillo serapes they were actually made in other areas as well, but were taken to the great Saltillo Fair to be sold.

In areas of heavy tourist demand some weavers have succumbed to turning out serapes in loud colors and wild designs of Aztec calendars and Indian gods. It is still possible, however, to find the simple, traditional designs in soft colors used by the villagers themselves. These are usually woven in the natural wool colors of off-white, gray, brown, and black, sometimes with accents of pleasingly dyed wools.

What the serape is to the Mexican man the *rebozo,* or shawl, is to the woman. The *rebozo* serves as her hat and coat, as the cradle for the baby on her back or hip, or the cover for the baby lying beside her; it is her market basket or the cover for a pot of *tamales* or other food she sells in the market. It can also be formed into a roll and placed on her head to help balance a jar or basket being carried.

The origins of the *rebozo* are obscure, but its use can be traced back to the end of the sixteenth century. In 1532 an edict was issued by the Royal *Audiencia* of New Spain which prohibited mestizo, mulatto, and Black women from using Indian apparel, and the *rebozo* may have been adopted at that time to give character to the dress of these groups as well as to provide a head covering for church.

Rebozos are often still woven on backstrap looms and on each end the fringe is knotted in lacy patterns. While there are many elegant *rebozos* of wool and silk, a poor woman wears a simple, dark-colored cotton one, often with a pinpoint allover design in white that is achieved through the ikat or warp tie-dye process. In ikat dyeing the skeins of thread that will form the warp are wrapped at certain places with fibers or cotton thread, and when dyed these areas remain white, forming the design.

The finest and most authentic *rebozos* are woven today in Santa María del Río in the State of San Luis Potosí and in Tenancingo, State of Mexico. The Tenancingo *rebozos* are usually cotton and those of Santa María silk. The test of the best *rebozos* in the colonial period was whether they could be drawn through a wedding ring, and those of Santa María were the ones that most often passed the test.

The U.S. anthropologist George Vaillant gives a good picture of how the Aztecs dressed. The common man "left his head uncovered, his hair long, and customarily wore a *maxtli,* or loin-cloth, a mantle knotted over one shoulder, and sandals of leather or woven maguey fibre in cold weather. Women wrapped about their loins a finely woven cloth, which they sustained with a narrow belt. A sleeveless slipover, or *huipil,* completed their costume. They plaited their hair into braids, sometimes interlacing them with ribbons, and these they wrapped around their heads."

The garments of the poor were made of maguey fiber or coarse cotton; the rich wore the same articles of clothing but made from finer fabrics and decorated with elaborate embroidery. The warriors wore rich mantles and ornate feather headdresses or costumes modeled after eagles or jaguars. On certain occasions priests dressed like gods and goddesses in sumptuous and ornate costumes. Elaborate jewelry of copper, gold, silver, shell, precious stones, and mosaics added to the brilliance of the scene.

The Spaniards almost immediately adopted one article of Indian clothing. The Aztecs had a body armor of quilted cotton that had been soaked in brine. It was such an effective protection against the clubs and missiles used by the Indians that the Spaniards gratefully put aside their cumbersome steel armor.

One of Bernal Díaz' first comments on the people of Mexico's east coast was a favorable one: "These Indians were clothed in cotton shirts made like jackets, and covered their persons with a narrow cloth, and they seem to us a people superior to the Cubans, for the Cuban Indians go about naked." The friars did, however, insist on putting pants on the Indian men and by 1601, it was already reported that the Indians of Yucatán were wearing shirts, wide breeches, hats, and cotton sandals. Those shirts and pants were of *manta,* a heavy, unbleached muslin, and still form the basic costume of many Indians and rural mestizos.

Differences, however, have developed over the years so that one can often tell where a man is from by whether his pants are long or short, or tied at the ankle or left loose, whether the shirt has a yoke, is gathered or pleated, is tucked in or left hanging out, and by the type of embroidery on the costume.

One of the most distinctive articles of the Mexican man's dress today is his hat, and most men would not consider venturing out without it. They are usually of straw but each area has its own style as to the width and curl of the brim, and the height and shape of the crown. Some of the Indian hats are decorated with ribbons, flowers, seed pods, and squirrel tails.

The *fajas* (belts) and *morrales* (bags) used by both men and women add greatly to the beauty of their costumes. The *fajas* are used by women to hold up their wrap-around skirts and by men for decorative or ceremonial purposes. They vary in length and width, some being as little as an inch wide and others as much as a foot. Some are of woven cotton, but the finest ones are usually of wool with woven designs. Embroidered and woven *morrales* are much used. Most of them have a strap or strings for wearing over the shoulder, and carry almost anything the Indian uses. Many of the bags are made of *ixtle* fiber from the maguey.

The dress of the Indian woman changed very little with the Conquest because the priests found her to be modest and well covered. Her basic garments are still a skirt and a *huipil,* the straight, sacklike blouse, or a *quechquemitl,* the small pointed shawl worn over the shoulders. Some groups also wear a headdress or head covering.

The traditional skirt is a long strip of handwoven wool or cotton, wrapped about the body length-wise in sarong fashion or with the fullness pleated out in front or in back. It is held in place by tucking in one corner or by wrapping the waist with one or more *fajas*. Most of the wool skirts are of natural brown or black, or are dyed dark blue, while many of the cotton ones are white. In pre-Conquest times most of the skirts had borders and fringes, but stripes and contrasting weaves furnish the only pattern found in most

of them today. In some areas skirts are now attached to a band so that the wearers are spared the task of arranging them each time they are put on.

The *huipil* is a simple garment made of two or three long strips of fabric sewed together length-wise. It is then folded over and the sides sewed together, leaving the seams open at the top for armholes, and a neck opening is cut. Like most truly Indian garments the *huipil* is not fitted, nor is the fabric shaped or cut except for the neck opening. Depending on the region it may be long or short, tight or loose, and of cotton or wool. In a few areas the sides of the *huipil* are sewed up only a few inches from the bottom, or are left completely open.

While the *huipil* is the almost universal garment in southern Mexico, the *quechquemitl* is found in the central and northern part of the country. It is formed of two woven rectangles joined to make a covering for the shoulders; sometimes the points are worn in the front and back and sometimes over the shoulders. In Nahuatl, the language of the Aztecs, *quechquemitl* means neck garment, and it was probably used in ancient times for ceremonial occasions. Like most Indian garments, it is versatile; in some places it is also used as a head covering, babies can be wrapped in it or put under it to be nursed, and small articles can be twisted into it to be carried.

Indian children usually dress like miniature versions of their parents, except for little boys in the hot country, who are seldom encumbered with pants. Little girls, on the other hand, are always modestly covered.

Indians wearing traditional costumes can be seen by the visitor to Mexico in a number of areas. One of the best places is at Oaxaca's Saturday market, for which members of many different groups make the long trek into the city. The State of Taxaca has more different costumes, and more non-Spanish-speaking Indians, than any other. A fine place, too, is San Cristóbal de las Casas, high in the mountains of Mexico's southernmost state, Chiapas. Here every day is market day and some of the country's most traditional and interestingly dressed Indians come to buy and sell. Numerous different regional costumes are worn by the Tarascans in the State of Michoacán; their clothing forms a mosaic of colors against the background of their high lakes and evergreen-forested countryside.

On Mondays hundreds of Otomí Indians can be seen along the old Pan American Highway on their way to and from the market at Ixmiquilpán, State of Hidalgo, and as both the men and women walk along they spin *ixtle* fiber into thread. Picturesquely dressed Indians from the mountains of the State of Puebla travel down to a number of markets, two of the most interesting being in Cuetzalán on Sunday and Huauchinango on Saturday. And at the Sunday market at Atlacomulco in the State of México the Mazahua women make a picture worth seeing as they come in to do their shopping dressed in their dark blue embroidered *quechquemitls*.

The Totonac Indians who live around Papantla, Veracruz, are a joy to behold dressed in immaculate white, the men with fresh flowers on their hats. The descendants of the Maya, too, in the State of Yucatán, make one wonder how their clothing can stay so white in that largely waterless country; it calls to mind that in ancient times a Maya husband could divorce a wife who didn't have his bath ready when he came in from the fields.

A few Huichol in their beautifully embroidered clothing may be seen by the lucky traveler in Tepic, Nayarit, or at the edge of Guadalajara at the Basilica of Zapopán,

the home of the Franciscans who work with them in their isolated mountains. And lucky, too is the traveler who happens to see a primitive Tarahumara in the city of Chihuahua, or a nomadic Seri in Bahía Kino, Sonora.

Most exciting of all, however, is to happen upon a group of Indians dressed in colorful traditional costumes in Mexico City to see the sights or to sell their handicrafts. They could have stepped out of the sixteenth century, and they form a striking contrast to the tall buildings and rushing traffic of one of the world's largest cities.

TRADITIONAL HAIRDRESSING IN NIGERIA

Titus A. Ogunwale

The Nigerian woman, like women everywhere, pays particular attention to natural adornment. Special hairdos not only enhance but also emphasize her femininity. So, for most Nigerian women, hairdressing is among the notable traditional occupations. Young girls learn the techniques from their mothers or from female friends of the same age group. Hairdressing is an elaborate and involved art which requires skill and keen imagination. While every Nigerian woman knows the rudiments of hairbraiding, some have become professional hairdressers who establish stalls or sheds in the market places of cities, towns or even villages. Her working tools are simple: combs (wooden or plastic), black thread, a mirror, a long needle *(ikoti)*, a blade, a locally made perfume *(adin)* and different kinds of pomade and vaseline. The wooden comb, the *ikoti* and the *adin* are traditional tools still widely used despite some innovation.

Nigerian women, particularly the Yoruba, have evolved an endless variety of hairstyles, each braided to symbolise an object, a particular event or occasion. The following are common: *suku* (basket), *orunkunaro* (the knee of a cripple), *kolese* (lines of hairdo but without "legs"), *panumo* (a name for a bus), *kohin-sorogun* (turn your back to the rival-wife), *Aja nloso* (a dog sits), *Ipako elede* (a pig's occiput); *Pakunpo* (knock-knee), *Koroba* (a bucket), *Aladade, Adile,* or*onile-gogoro* (a skyscraper), *Akete Kano* (a hat from Kano), *Arin-omo-ni-ng-o-sun* (I will sleep among the children), *Awoyoyo* (a troop of marching soldiers) and *Agogo*. Most of these hairstyles are traditional, and the translation of their names into present-day English is unfortunately difficult to do without making them appear somewhat absurd.

The *Koroba* (bucket) hairstyle is woven in six, eight, ten or more rows starting from the center of the head to the sides, giving the shape of a bucket. *Suku, Kolese,* and *Ipako elede* are worn by women in almost all the tribes in Yorubaland. They are about the simplest of the hair-

styles, and, except for careful braiding, do not involve elaborate design. *Kohin-sorogun* must have been the creation of jealous women. In those polygamous families where the man marries more than one wife, the wives often regard each other as rivals. Part of that rivalry is a jealousy of one another's hairstyles. The interpretation of *Kohin-sorogun* is "Turn your back to a jealous rival;" and as the *kohin-sorogun* hairstyle is best admired from behind, the wearer must turn her back for the jealous rival to see better. *Ipako elede* is shaped like the pig's occiput. The *arin-ono-ni-ng-o-sun* has a wide line formation supported by thinner ones, while the *Akete Kano* describes a kind of hat which is made in Kano. Generally, hairdos fall in rows like a land-plot of ridges and furrows. While most hairstyles have from 4 to 8 or 12 rows, in the *Awoyoyo* style, the rows can reach up to 30 or 60. This is painstaking to arrange and usually carries special charges.

The *Awoyoyo* and *Agogo* are generally worn by members of the royal family—wives of Yoruba obas, princesses and new brides. Devotees of some Yoruba gods (i.e. Sango, the Yoruba god of thunder), or goddesses (Oya and Oshun, both Yoruba deities and wives of Sango) have also traditionally worn *Awoyoyo* or *Agogo*. *Awoyoyo* and *Agogo* would therefore seem to be among the earliest forms of hairdo. This point is further illustrated by the *Agogo* hairdo on the Yoruba deity at Ile-Ife, Esu Ilare. From the look of this deity, *Agogo* represents the peak of feminine hair fashion. It is worn by both men and women during the traditional festivals like the Oshun festival at Oshogbo, the Igogo festival at Owo and the Oke 'Badan festival in Ibadan. During the *Edi* festival at Ile-Ife, girls between the ages of 7 and 11 have their heads decorated

From "Traditional Hairdressing in Nigeria." *African Arts,* No. 3. Spring 1972, pp. 44–45. Pictures are omitted. Reprinted by permission of the publisher.

with one-tenths of a penny, ha'pennies, and pennies, and afterwards parade about the town dancing and collecting gifts.

Regional differences in hairstyles are, at times, quite strong, sometimes permitting an observer to geographically identify a woman. For example, in some sections of the Federation, particularly the Midwest and Eastern States, plaiting the hair with black thread is preferred over other forms of hair-dressing. In the Northern area, the Hausa and Fulani women have a hairstyle and elaborate head ornament which are peculiar to themselves.

Some comparatively recent hairstyles reflect a particular trend in fashion or mark an event. Examples include: Gowon, named after Nigeria's Head of State, Major-General Yakubu Gowon who is known as the "Soldier of peace"; *ogun pari* (end of the civil war); Eko bridge (the new Lagos bridge); and *Bebedi* (beads worn around the waist of a woman). These hairstyles are common in the cities—Lagos, Ibadan, Benin and Ilorin.

Hairdressing is carried out with a definite procedure. A woman ready for braiding first of all disentangles the previously plaited hair and combs it out thoroughly. After the combing, she dictates the style she wants to the hairdresser, and settles down with her head facing either down or up, between the thighs of the hairdresser. The latter applies her comb (*oya* or *iyarun*) and the long needle

(*ikoti*) to draw contours on the head of her customer. The design must be near-perfect. At infrequent intervals, the woman looks into the mirror to see that the coiffeur keeps to the particular hairstyle desired, and if necessary, orders a correction or an amendment. Morgan's pomade, liquid paraffin, or Vaseline hair cream is then applied as may be desired by the customer. When black thread is used to plait the hair, a blade is employed to tidy up any loose ends. The hairdresser's salon is usually full to capacity on Saturdays, as the women prepare for their "Sunday best." And it is not unusual to find a number of suitors around, ready for courtship.

In the past, hairdressing was virtually free, a good turn exchanged among friends. But nowadays, hairdressers charge from 1/- to £1.1/- for different hairstyles. Despite the influx of imported wigs, traditional hairdos are still commonly worn by Nigerian women. Some foreigners, especially those from other parts of Africa, America and the West Indies have begun to copy the Nigerian hairstyles. A number of Nigerians who train abroad in hairdressing return home to create new forms, patterned after traditional styles. Although the traditional patterns are being modified to suit modern trends in fashion, there is no immediate fear that traditional hairdressing may fade out.

ESKIMOS: CLOTHING AND CULTURE

Lois M. Gurel

One cannot read about the Eskimos' struggle for survival against the brutal elements of nature without being impressed with their ingenuity in using scant supplies and their undaunting courage against seemingly impossible conditions. Perhaps no place in the world have a people made better use of natural resources. By a unique process of adaptation, they have won a victory by bending to nature at the same time that they make the best of all that she provides. The study of Eskimo clothing reveals but one aspect of a constant dual role that nature plays with these people, that of provider and antagonist.

Across the arctic reaches of the Western Hemisphere, from the Bering Sea to the shores of Labrador and Greenland is a vast expanse of 3,400 miles. It is here that the Eskimo people live and wage their battle with nature for survival. The most widely distributed of primitive people, the Eskimos have a unique cultural sameness which is at the same time distinct from every other culture in the world (1, p. 1). This similarity in culture is due to the similarity of materials with which they cope with life in their hostile environment. Fur clothing is tailored in the same style, they travel by dog sled and kayak, they heat

and cook with shallow open lamps of stone or pottery, and they burn animal fat in these vessels. The harpoon is the universal weapon. Religious practices are similar, and when rites vary they do so only in detail. The myths and legends told in a snow hut of the central Eskimos will be repeated in all its detail by the Eskimos of both the Pacific and Atlantic coasts.

Climate is the most often misconstrued fact about the region inhabited by the Eskimos. It is neither as cold in winter nor as warm in summer as many writers have stated. However, it is certainly an arctic climate in all but a few sections of the Eskimo lands. Although a long hard winter is an outstanding feature, no area of Eskimo occupancy is snow-covered perennially. On the other hand, too much has been written about the shorter, warmer summer which is shorter and less warm than popular fancy has it. Although the dominant season is winter, it is not the cold of the arctic winter that is important, but its length coupled with the feeble summer heat. Dominating all Eskimo life is the process of getting through the arctic winter.

Eskimo religion is predominantly made up of a number of taboos, mainly concerning the food and clothing supply. In order to have the raw materials necessary for survival, the unseen spirits of the invisible world must be properly appeased. Practically all material needs are supplied by hunting; most of the Eskimos' taboos are directed toward the spirits of the game animals upon which they depend. The list of taboos that pertain to the sewing of caribou skins, the most important source of clothing, are numerous. Since it is essential to keep the products of the sea and the land separate, there is an elaborate system of when and under what conditions an Eskimo woman may sew on caribou clothing. The restrictions are lifted for necessary mending, but otherwise she must not work on caribou hides: if she has touched a seal that day; when her people are living on the sea; at the fishing creeks when the salmon are running; when the walrus is being hunted while the ice is still firm; for three nights after the killing of a whale (1, p. 363). Since they are also prohibited from sewing on deer skins during the summer caribou hunts, "The result is that there is often difficulty in getting the new clothing finished in time for the winter" (2, p. 169).

An elaborate system of ritual has grown out of these taboos. Dress for these rites comes in two forms—no clothing and more clothing. Nudity is the ceremonial dress for many Eskimo men and boys. Women may be topless but are always covered below the waist. Among the more well-to-do, very elaborate ceremonial robes are made and saved, however, in most places new clothes are also symbolic and thought to please the spirits (3, p. 95).

Ceremonial garments are generally the same as everyday clothes in cut and form; they would be cleaner and more elaborately decorated. The exact significance of many robes is difficult to determine since the people themselves do not often understand the basic concept of clothing symbolism. It is believed that the gut parka worn by a boy for his first catch was worn to ward off evil. The garment, called a *kamleika,* covers the body completely and is drawn tight with a string through the middle. It is completely waterproof and so should also keep out the evil spirits. Mittens are used during ceremonies to protect against contact with evil. Ermine is used in Alaska because this fur is supposed to give the wearer a great deal of power. This primitive belief may be linked to ermine as a modern day symbol of royalty. Ceremonial masks are prevalent; worn mainly by the Shamen, or medicine man, the people believe that the man who uses a mask actually becomes the spirit that the mask represents. Made in pale colors with grotesque features, these masks are oversized and too heavy to be worn. They are hung from the hut or tent and moved by a man behind them. Finger masks are used by the women; they stand still and move their arms so that the little masks seem to dance.

The spirits they fear most are those of dead relatives and friends, so mourning procedures are very rigorously enforced among all the Eskimo tribes. In order to protect the rest of the family from the possible return of the ghost, there is a taboo against uncovering the head for a period of time. Parkas are turned inside out and often mittens are worn continuously (1, p. 270). Among the Polar Eskimos, the practice is to throw away all the clothing they had been wearing at the time of the death. There are several reports of a ceremony of honor for the dead where one person is chosen to sit naked for three days without food or water to show special reverence for the departed relative.

Modesty is a very unimportant motivation for wearing clothes. The Eskimos go almost completely naked in the interior of their hot winter homes. Sexual pleasure is never concealed, and the simple triangular apron, similar to a masonic apron, is worn over the sex organs to protect them from magical influence.

It is here, in ritual and ceremonial dress, that the differences among the tribes are the greatest, even though the variations are of kind rather than essence. The belief in spirits, the lack of a strong concept of a divine judgement, and the many taboos are all part of a single cultural entity. Clothing plays a large part in these ceremonies. In a land of scarce but varied resources, one group may use a fox tail while another may trim their robes with wolverine claws. To the Central Eskimo the spirits of the land animals are most important, while along the coast The Great Festival of the Whale is primary. The end results are very much the same.

The Eskimos are very warm and supportive of their closest relatives. A successful hunter must supply, not only his nuclear family, but also members of his patriclan who are in need, one of the reasons why Eskimo families have few extra possessions. In a land where bare existence is difficult, no one is allowed to be cold or hungry. Those who have share with those who have not, without being asked and without any specific promise of return, just a knowledge that if they are ever in a similar situation, some one of their relatives will be there to help them out. This practice has great implications for clothing acquisitions. Skins and furs are hard to come by; a great deal of time is spent in hunting; sources are not always predictable. The construction of skin and fur garments is an arduous and time consuming job. By the time the men in the family have provided enough raw materials and the women have done the sewing to clothe not only their immediate family, but their needy relatives, there is generally no surplus.

The role of men and women in the culture, though sharply defined, is not as stringent as one would expect in a primitive society. The men are the hunters; they provide the sustenance—food, fuel, and furs. All of the housework is done by the women, preparations and cooking of food, care of the house and its furnishings, repairs to the tent and the winter house. After the raw materials necessary for the winter garments are provided by the men, their job is over. The care and making of the clothing supply is the sole responsibility of the women. In fact, lack of skill in this important task is considered grounds for divorce in many Eskimo communities (4, p. 34). "A man is the hunter his wife makes him," say the Polar Eskimos, for they know that a well-made dress will make a hunter independent of the weather and so more certain of his prey (2, p. 112).

The Eskimos have never learned to spin or weave. Since 1964, the University of Alaska has been experimenting with the domestication of the musk ox. Their thick under wool, called qiviut, is exceedingly warm and light weight. Textile specialists are attempting to teach the Eskimos how to knit this rare yarn in hopes of establishing a profitable Arctic economy based on the wool of these animals. Qiviut fibers are very expensive; most of the finished garments are sold and few are used locally (5). With the possible exception of a few items made from qiviut, therefore, most Eskimo textiles are made entirely from the skins of animals. In recent years they have traded their skins for woolens and cottons for summer use because these fabrics are cooler than hides. They are the only North American natives to make full-tailored clothing. The women are excellent seamstresses, their windproof and waterproof garments the results of years and generations of experience.

> Their waterproof seams are probably the only really waterproof sewing in the world . . . if an Eskimo seamstress sees you oiling boots that she had made, she is likely to become angry. She consider it an insult to be suspected of stitching so poor that it needs to be greased before it will keep out moisture (6, pp. 72–73).

All waterproof sewing on boots is done with three-ply sinew thread on overlapping seams.

Eskimo clothing is the most suitable apparel ever developed for cold climates. "The male dress of the Central Eskimos is without doubt the warmest and most practical arctic clothing in existence (4, p. 199)." It is made on the double window principle. An isolated layer of air is kept between the inner (*artigis*) and the outer (*kulitak*) garments. In warm weather, only the inner layer is worn. The many skins of arctic animals give the people a wide choice and years of experience have shown them which skins are best for different uses.

> Seal skin is strong and to a certain degree waterproof; but in very cold weather it is not warm enough. Bear skin is exceedingly warm, and one can fall into the water wearing a pair of bear-skin trousers without getting wet; but they are tremendously heavy. Musk Ox skin has the same disadvantage and it is also almost impossible to keep the shaggy fur clean of blood and dirt. Hare, eider—duck, and fox skins combine great warmth with extreme lightness; but they are too delicate for general use (2, p. 111).

Rainproof bags and coats are made from fish skins; bird skins make bags and hand-wipers. The white whale is much prized for boot soles and boat covers. Fox skins may be used for outer clothing, but only if nothing better is available.

Of all the animals available to these northern people, the caribou is the absolutely essential and the only one necessary to keep the Eskimos alive and warm during the long arctic winter. Their skins are strong, but also light and warm. The air cavities in the hairs serve as an insulator and keep the warm air in while at the same time it keeps the cold air out. The only problem with caribou skins is that the hairs break off easily and,

> . . . in a snow-house inhabited by a family of deerskin-clad Eskimos there is a constant rain of hair which sticks to the greasy implements and floats in the soup pot and the water pail. But when faced with the alternative of being either cold or finding a few hairs in one's food, the choice is not difficult (2, p. 111).

The whole foundation of the following years' economy is laid by the important autumn caribou hunts. Later the hides are too tough to handle, in winter the hair is loose, and in summer they are apt to be full of holes and bare spots. This seasonal nature of the caribou results in the only style cycle of the Eskimos. It is fashionable to wear old clothes all summer and appear in the new outfits at the start of the winter season (6, p. 62). Although a successful hunter may have several outfits for himself and his family, it is the usual practice to have only these two sets of clothing—last year's for every day, and this year's for special occasions.

Dryness is of the greatest importance in the arctic. Skin clothing, because it is not porous, becomes damp through perspiration. If perspiration freezes on the body it can be fatal. The loose fitting styles of the clothing allow a layer of warm air to lay close to the body, but at the same time permit the evaporation of any wetness that develops. Skin dress must, however, be completely dried after each wearing and the Eskimos are very careful to brush off all snow and ice before bringing their garments into the house. A special tool, called a snow-beater, is used for this purpose. It is much harder to keep footwear dry, and so all Eskimos carry several pairs of skin stockings and other footwear, changing these items often. The same is true for mittens. In summer, drying is no problem; wet clothes are strung on lines outdoors to dry. Those Eskimos that use blubber lamps in winter have devised a special drying rack that is hung or propped over the lamp and here footwear and mittens dry overnight. Among the central tribes where blubber is not used, drying becomes a serious problem. "For a time one may manage by putting stockings and mittens under the sleeping blanket or in dry snow, but when this no longer helps, there is nothing else to do than to lay the wet articles aside and use new ones (7, p. 199)." When the wet skin clothing finally dries it is stiff and cold.

The women, then, have to make these garments pliable by either rubbing them with their hands or in some cases chewing them soft again. Although cleanliness of clothing, like cleanliness of person, is very unimportant, great care is taken of the clothing. It is protected from tears and wear, mended promptly, dried carefully, and extra items stored in skin bags.

Temperature changes create great clothing problems for the Eskimos. In winter the thermometer ranges between −10 degrees and −30 degrees; when properly clothed this is considered very pleasant. It is only when the temperature drops to −40 degrees and below that it is considered cold. "In the middle of winter, the sun never rises above the horizon, and the temperature remains fairly constant throughout the day, making selection of clothing easier than in times of seasonal change (8, p. 236)." The problems arise when the days are warmer. At zero degrees, caribou skin clothing is too warm, and boots get wet walking through the relatively warm snow.

The main garment of the Eskimos, the parka, can be traced to similar garments worn by primitives throughout history. Basically, the poncho of South American origin, it is merely two skins sewn together at shoulders, hanging loosely, with an opening for the head. "If this two-skin poncho is also sewn up the sides and fitted with sleeves, we have a skin shirt similar to that worn by many Indians, and if, finally, it is fitted with a hood, the fundamental cut of the Eskimo frock is complete (2, p. 113)."

This basic Eskimo garment is a simple style, made up of two skins, one front and one back, with a third skin for the sleeves. Fur is turned out for the *kulitaks* or winter garments except for the mitten palms and shoe soles. Variations are many but minor, mostly that of length, fullness, or trim, not a change in basic form. The Hudson Bay Eskimos wear their frocks to the knees and slit at the hem at both sides into two side flaps, one back and one front. These may be of equal or of unequal length. On the Northwest Passage the Eskimos wear a parka that looks much like a modern tailcoat. In Greenland, Eskimos like their parkas short and very tight fitting, while those in central areas fringe the bottom of this basic dress and wear them full to allow for air circulation. Keeping them very long prevents the cold air from becoming a problem. Among the Copper Eskimos the cut is quite short at both waists and wrists. In Northern Alaska the parka has a fur border on the bottom, at the wrists, and around the edge of the hood which varies from round to pointed (2, p. 114).

Generally, Eskimo parkas are worn loosely, without a belt, but in severe cold or driving wind they are belted tightly to keep the warm air in and the cold wind out. These belts may be made from leather thongs, antlers, skins, wolverine claws, or porcupine quills.

The main difference between the basic garments of men and women is that the women's parkas are longer gen-

erally almost ankle length, and they have an enormous hood with a sack in back in which Eskimo children spend the first year of their lives.

> There they sit, warm and comfortable against their mother's naked back, at first wearing only a little cap, later a vest of velvety fawn skin. When hunger begins to call, there is plenty of room under the wide frock for them to be taken round to the breast without having to be brought to the outside (2, p. 114).

There are no sex restrictions on the use of materials. Both sexes wear garments of the same skins, although the warmer and stronger ones are saved for the hunters. If there is a shortage of deerskin the women may make their clothes of less durable foxskins.

The *artiggis,* or underfrock, worn by both sexes, also has a hood. It is made from some short haired skin and worn with the hair next to the body. In warm weather this garment becomes an outer garment and so these inner clothes are often lavishly decorated with bead embroidery, fringe, fur trimming, and in later years, printed cotton. Many of the designs on these beautiful summer costumes come from the Indians in the area.

Under the *artiggis* they wear birdskin shirts with the feathers inside. These are the only tight fitting garments. Otherwise the skin clothes are loose and do not overlap too much, so as to allow for ventilation (9, pp. 49–50).

The women decorate their garments more than they do those for the male members of the family. In some areas certain colors are reserved for a particular sex but this is not the general practice. However, colored skins are more likely to be seen on women's boots than on men's. Fringe and beading, along with jewelry such as necklaces, bracelets, rings, and ear ornaments are used by both sexes.

There is some variation in the ornamentation used among the different tribes. However, the aim of embroidery is not social superiority for the wearer (1, p. 193). Some of the ornamentation has a religious connotation, such as the amulets sewn across the shoulders, however, most of the decoration is merely local fashion. In some areas skins are not only carefully matched, but contrasting colors are inserted. A very popular decorative effect, particularly among the Greenland Eskimos, is skin mosaics. Small strips and squares of skin are dyed different colors and painstakingly sewn together by the women into many intricate shapes and patterns. Amulets of fox-tails and caribou teeth are sewn across the back at shoulder height. Some tribes have replaced these amulets with symbolic bead ornamentation. In Alaska, wolf or wolverine fur is used for trimming, while in Victoria Island strips of leather ribbon are dyed with red ochre and used for trimming. Bone buttons and weasel tails are used for decoration or carried as charms. Decoration of Eskimo garments almost exclusively follows natural seam lines or trims openings and edges. The simulated amulets across the shoulder, mentioned above, are just about the only type of decoration used in the middle of a garment.

These amulets, real and simulated, are worn by both sexes to ward off evil spirits. An individual may own several of these charms all serving different purposes. They represent a mystical alliance between the wearer and the power they symbolize. If given to someone else the power is lost whereas a charm, such as a lucky coin, keeps its effect regardless of who has it.

Although sometimes obscure, generally the symbolism behind the amulets is clear. Owl claws are worn so that the wearer will have strong fists; caribou ears make the wearer quick of hearing on the hunt; the skin of a loon in the kayak gives speed; the side line on a salmon, which resembles a seam will make a girl a good seamstress. Among the Nelsilk Eskimos, girls wear belts of amulets much like a charm bracelet. The following is a description of one such belt worn by a girl in order to give certain qualities to her future child.

> Swan's beak (it will be a boy); bear teeth (he will be fat); owl feet (powerful fists); ptarmigan feet (good runner); gull head and trout decory (lucky fisher); brow band containing a bee (a strong head); ermine skin (strength and dexterity); caribou front teeth (luck when hunting caribou); head of a great northern diver (manly qualities); piece of ice scoop of a dead hunter (luck in sealing); tarsal bone of a wolf (fast runner) (2, p. 161).

Trousers, also, are similar, with the variations slight among the tribes. They almost invariably wear inner and outer trousers made exactly alike. The inner pair is worn hair inward, and the outer pair is worn with the hair side out. The length and width may vary from tribe to tribe and is related to the length of the parka. In many places the bottom of the pants and the top of the boot do not meet. Only in the most extreme weather is this section of leg covered with a piece of animal skin.

Footwear is the most important item in an Eskimo's wardrobe. The feet must be kept warm and dry, and since evaporation is not possible here, this presents a problem. The basic items include stockings, short socks, boots, and outer shoes with double soles—all made of hairy deerskin. The stockings are made of thin-haired deerskin worn hair inward; the height of the stockings depends upon the length of the trousers. They always fit up above the trouser openings.

Eskimos possess many different kinds of boots. The very long-legged ones used in spring when the snow is deep and wet, are made of seal skin and are called *kamiks*. The winter boots are shorter and made of deerskin and vary from the sleek and narrow boot of Greenland to the enormous, oversized, baggy boot found west of Hudson Bay. Deerskin shoes, worn hair inward are used over the boots to protect them. On a long journey with much walking, a sandal is sometimes tied under the sole. For further protection of the feet, always the most exposed part of the body, they put a layer of dried grass in between the two pairs of soles and this is changed every day.

Except for their unusual parkas, the rest of the women's outfit is very similar to that of the men. Although in warm weather many Eskimo women may be found now in calico dresses and woolen shawls bought from the traders. This is particularly true among the Alaskan Eskimos where acculturation has been the greatest (10, p. 130). In winter all the women wear the traditional clothing because it is warmer. Their *kamiks* may be much longer than the men's boots are, sometimes reaching all the way to the crotch. Then instead of trousers they wear short panties made of foxskins. There is also a unique garment, worn only by the women when traveling during the winter. It is a legging-like arrangment that is combination of boot, stocking, and pants that ties around the waist.

The Eskimo adults are of medium stature (5′4″ to 5′5″ for men) with broad shoulders and narrow hips. They are a hardy race of uncommon strength and endurance. Pure bred Eskimos have a light brownish-yellow complexion, round broad faces with large features, oblique or Mongoloid eyes and flat noses. Their hands and feet are small; their hair, which is coarse and black, is usually straight, somewhat greasy and unkempt. Boys and men wear their hair combed down in front and cut off square across the forehead, long in back and on the sides. Hair is the pride and joy of Eskimo women. They wear it in a tuft on top of the head as stiff and straight as possible. In order to get it stiff and at the same time get the glistening appearance that is prized as beauty, they steep it in urine, making it moist and easier to tighten (9, pp. 28–29).

There is little distinguishable difference in dress between the children of different sexes. Infants are dressed in soft jackets and caps made of fawn skin. Their legs are kept bare since they are carried inside their mother's hood. At about two years of age they are put into a trouser, boot, parka arrangement, similar for boys and girls. Boys of eight are dressed like men, but girls do not wear the typical women's dress until ten or twelve years of age (11, p. 149).

* * * * *

The Eskimos are a serious and sober race, not surprising in a region where all human effort must be concentrated on the most elementary requirements for survival. An essential feature of Eskimo life is that of uncertainty. Dependent as he is upon the weather, the seasons, and the hunt, it is no wonder that he lives for today and is not overly concerned about the future. All an Eskimo can do is to prepare for his hunting expedition with good tools and warm clothing and hope.

> Strip him of his clothing, deprive him of his tools and implements, his dwellings, and his ability to create these things

essential to life, and he would be scarcely more fit to survive in his northern environment than a savage from the tropical jungle. Clearly, with no more than his natural physical attributes he would soon perish. He has neither the protective fur of the caribou, the polar bear, and the musk ox, nor the warmth-conserving fat of the seal, the walrus, and the whale. He cannot live on the scanty vegetation of the tundra as can the caribou, nor has he the migratory range of these browsers. He lacks the physical aids to hunting and fighting of the bear and the wolf.

The Eskimo cannot compete with the animals as an animal. He is not compelled to. What he lacks as a physical organism he acquires through ingenuity and invention. He survives, not chiefly through physical strength and endurance, as the animals do, but through mental capability. An ingenious hunting device can take the place of fleetness of foot or sharpness of tooth or talon; the use of fire and clothing can compensate for weak resistance against cold (1, p. 65).

An so, like many primitive peoples, the Eskimo adapts himself to his environment; the mores, cultural pattern, traditions, and skills that he has developed make him a cultural success. "He survives farther north than any other people on earth, in exceedingly wretched and difficult conditions—an exemplification of man's cultural adaptability to nature in the raw (1, p. 66)."

In looking for the "whys" of Eskimo clothing practices, much can be said about the availability of raw materials, the Eskimos' need for decoration in clothing because of his drab surroundings, religious implications, whether or not he is modest or immodest, the effect of kinship groups,

and numerous other factors. However, one must always come back to the severity of the northern winter with its long and sunless days, and the too short and not warm enough arctic summer. It is here that the answer to Eskimos' clothing behavior can be found. It seems only too obvious that protection from the elements is the outstanding motivation behind traditional Eskimo dress.

BIBLIOGRAPHY

1. Weyer, E.M. *The Eskimos*. New Haven: Yale University Press, 1932.
2. Birket-Smith, K. *The Eskimos*. London: Methuen and Co., Ltd., 1959.
3. Lantis, M. *Alaskan Eskimo Ceremonialism*. New York: J.J. Augustin Publisher, 1947.
4. Giffin, N.M. *The Roles of Men and Women in Eskimo Culture*. Chicago: The University of Chicago Press, 1930.
5. Griffiths, H.M. "Arctic Handknitting." *Handweaver and Craftsman*, 22, No. 2, Spring, 1971, pp. 6–9.
6. Stefansson, V., and Schwartz, J.A. *Northward Ho!* New York: The Book League of America, 1929.
7. Birket-Smith, K. *The Caribou Eskimos*. Copenhagen: Gyldeddalske Boghaddel, 1929.
8. Gubser, N.J. *The Naunamiut Eskimos, Hunters of Caribou*. New Haven: Yale University Press, 1960.
9. Nansen, F. *Eskimo Life*. London: Longman's Green, and Co., 1893.
10. VanStone, J.W. *Eskimos of the Nushagak River*. Seattle: University of Washington Press, 1967.
11. Boas, F. *The Central Eskimo*. Lincoln: University of Nebraska Press, 1964.

COSTUMES OF THE EAST

Walter A. Fairservis, Jr.

Some years ago a special exhibition on the arts of ancient Peru was held at The American Museum of Natural History. The lovely, masterful, and infinitely colorful metal, pottery, stone, and fabric objects on display represented the cultures of civilized and aboriginal Peru before the white man. The opening of this splendid exhibition was attended not only by representatives of the Museum, the press, and the city, but also by members of New York's social and business elite. The men wore business suits, all cut approximately the same way and made grave by the shades of gray, black, and brown conventional to the modern American male. The ladies, conscious of current fashion, wore dresses that differed slightly from one another in cut, but almost all shared one color—black. Most of these dresses, regardless of design, were adorned by strings of pearls.

The appearance of modern man as represented by this sample was funereal and conformist. When one considers how many individuals in this group commanded wealth

and power suitable to the ambitions of past monarchs, the factors that created this costuming must have been stringent indeed. These people, as well as most urbanized citizens of the West, are heirs to the whole colorful tradition of costume that runs from ancient western Asia, through *Godey's Lady's Book,* to the current French fashion mart. There was, and is, no reason why this incredible resource in history could not be drawn on to produce variety in the costumes of modern man—except for limitations imposed by cultural conventions.

Costume is basic to man's culture and is as much a part of his natural history as the courtship dance is to the ruffed grouse or social behavior is to the African lion. With its vast variety of form and ornament, costume provides the anthropologist with a graphic choice for sorting out the ethnic, occupational, and social categories to which individuals of the species *Homo sapiens* belong.

Conventions of dress have always been rooted in the value system, the technology and economics, and the communicative aspects of one's culture. Until recently, whether you worked on Madison Avenue or on New Bond Street, wearing a pair of bright red socks or an emerald green tie to the office might have provoked a barrage of joking remarks. Costume deviations have, in the past, even led to circumstances in which an individual lost his job. While attitudes today are somewhat more relaxed, conformity is still the general rule.

One manifestation of today's youth revolt is costume. Barefooted, long-haired young men will wear T-shirts and dungarees, African shirts, or Asian costume jewelry so that they may be in direct contrast to the establishment exponents of Western cities and towns, with their shirts and ties, coats, pressed pants, and shoes. Their female counterparts present similar contrasts. Ironically, however, once the rebellious generation establishes its costume conventions, it adheres to them as rigidly as does the "other" generation. Costume on either side of the generation gap is now so conventional that little of the unexpected is found. Indeed, Western man appears to have decisively limited his costume repertory to what is conformist, generally drab, and efficient. In part this is the result of the mass production of inexpensive clothing, but more important, Western man candidly admits he likes his clothing that way.

One may ask why this is so, for if the present costumes of Western man are the end result of the cultural evolution that created Western civilization (and we have no reason to think that the development of costume is divorced from that evolution), then conformity in modern costume is perhaps symptomatic of conformity on a deeper and more meaningful level. From Moscow to San Francisco most men and women wear the same kind of clothes, varying only slightly from the norm according to occupation or wealth. The Japanese, Chinese, and urbanized inhabitants of Southeast Asia, India, western Asia, and Africa have also adopted this type of clothing, as have Australians and most Latin Americans. All who are involved with modern industrialization and its expression in the production and control of goods and services, whatever their nation, wear the same basic costume.

Costume is unique to man. But why does he wear clothes at all? Over-all dress may have evolved as *Homo sapiens* lost his presumed hirsuteness toward the end of the Pleistocene, or as his peregrinations brought him from warmer climes to more arctic ones. But man is wonderfully adaptive biologically, and there is no reason to believe that he could not have retained relative or even absolute nudity through natural selection under different climatic conditions.

It is possible that the first clothing was worn simply to cover the vulnerable genitalia and other specific areas of the body. The genitalia of both sexes, as well as the female breasts, are highly sensitive; thus, it would seem sensible for man to provide artificial protection for these parts of the body. Furthermore, even among surviving aboriginal peoples, both the excretory and menstrual functions are regarded as antisocial. Concealment of the organs of such functions appears to be the result of this attitude.

Critical to our understanding of the character and role of costume is, of course, man's attitude toward sex. It has been said that costume should be regarded, not as the concealer of one's sexual character, but rather as its revealer. Too many in the West regard the genitalia rather than the men or women who possess them, as the symbols of sex. Oddly, as students of erotica well know, the simple exposure of genitalia is not as erotic as the partly clothed body. The difference between the sexes is not simply a matter of plumbing, but in its ideal sense, a matter of the whole person who possesses a form of body and a state of mind that complement or supplement the opposite sex. It is a mutuality that transcends biological identity, and yet in its fullest expression emphatically identifies the individual as a woman or man. One's culture determines what is masculine and feminine by a whole pattern of attitudes and behavioral emphases that have to be understood within each cultural setting, for they are by no means identical from culture to culture.

All this suggests that the development and enhancement of those traits that graphically distinguish maleness and femaleness have been critical to *Homo sapiens*. In this, certainly, ideals of beauty have an important role. Body painting, tattooing, sweet scents, athletic or dance exhibitions, vocal expression, and the wearing of flowers or certain animal pelts have been among the graphic enhancers of one's sexual identity. Costume was and is a firm supporter of this identity. The recent vogue among Western women for men's clothing may be part of their drive for parity with men.

Whatever the early social forms of man, whether band or tribe, the identification of one's group through graphic representation is so commonplace among all peoples, past and present, that we can assume it was a part of prehistoric life. Here, costume, whether in terms of horned headdresses, painted skin robes, or adorned fur pieces, certainly had its place.

The Eurasian and North African region saw the beginnings of civilization in the latter part of the fourth millennium B.C. These early civilizations of western Asia and Egypt were heirs to rich weaving traditions that were already at least five thousand years old. Animal hair and a variety of plant fibers, including flax, were spun and woven, and dyeing seems to have been on the scene as early as 6000 B.C. The woven cloth was basically used as a wraparound or drape. This elementary, yet practical form has characterized the garments of the Mediterranean, North African, and western and southern Asian regions until comparatively recent times. Early and elaborated expression of it can be seen in the arts of ancient Egypt and western Asia.

Tailored clothing appears in the historical record from about 2000 B.C., but it probably emerged earlier than that, as the sewed skin robes of the late Stone Age in Europe suggest. However, to both central Asian pastoralists and arctic hunters, pants and sleeved shirts had obvious advantages over the draped garments of the more southerly peoples. Pants allow for free movement of the legs, while insulating the flesh from weather and wear.

Thus we find that by the time of Christ, the peoples of the Mediterranean world, the Near East, India, and China wore varieties of draped clothing' skirts, pullovers, and wraparounds, while the peoples of central Asia and Europe beyond the Mediterranean realms wore varieties of pants and skirts. The latter group made their clothing largely from wool and animal hair: the former used cotton, linen and silk. Not that these softer materials were unappreciated by the people of Europe and central Asia: rather, they were difficult to obtain since they had to be imported. But there was another, perhaps equally basic reason.

Both the ancient Egyptians and the Chinese had strong feelings about wool. Those who wore the rough material were regarded as "barbarians" outside the pale of civilization. In turn, there are records of Europeans and central Asians contemptuously remarking on the effeminate silken clothing of "civilization." To have a beard and to wear wool was to be a barbarian or a bandit in the eyes of the Chinese. To wear silk and be clean-shaven was to be weak and unmasculine in the opinion of the Turk. In such ways clothing marked the cultural affinity of people in ancient times. The idea that draped clothing is effeminate and tailored clothing masculine is still found in such remarks as the one supposedly typical of a family dispute: "Who wears the pants in this family, you or I?"

The history of Western costume is comparatively well known and can be found in many fine books. What is apparent in these histories is the rapid change in the costume of the European elite almost century by century. The costume of the peasantry, which formed the largest portion of the population, changed slowly—until the nineteenth century. Anthropologists recognize two complementary traditions in civilization: a "great tradition" carried by the overriding national, usually urban institutions such as government, church, the military, and business: and a "little tradition" expressed through local traditions and beliefs and often referred to as the folk order. Folk orders tend to be conservative, preserving elements of cultural styles for an astoundingly long time.

While the everyday costumes of the peasantry were generally designed for the ease of movement required by farming, and were correspondingly simple and utilitarian, the clothing worn for church, for festivals, or for weddings, styled by centuries of tradition was colorful and locally distinctive. Such costumes can be seen in the folk museums of Europe and, rarely on festival occasions in a few "unspoiled" sections of that continent. However, this does not mean that the local tradition of costume is nearly dead, for among the many ethnic groups of Europe that claim a degree of autonomy, costume still has nationalist meaning.

The finest folk costumes were made at home or by the best seamstresses in the village or district. They were prized possessions carefully stored, cleaned, and mended. Often the combination of intricate sewing, painstaking work, and pride in the result produced a work of art as precious or, indeed, more precious than the products of the weavers' guild in the courtly cities. Such costume treasures were characteristic of much of Europe's folk culture. Into the creation of these costumes were fed the traditional symbols, the colors, and the iconography that marked the folk belief and gave meaning to the end result. When a peasant girl appeared in her traditional costume, she emphasized her pride in tradition and her identity with it. What she wore, when she wore it, and what she did while wearing a given costume derived from centuries of tradition not in a stultifying sense (for the pragmatic peasantry rarely burdened itself for long with the stiff collars, high pantaloons, and agonizing corsets that the aristocracy forced itself to endure in history), but in a very personal and often mystical sense.

What one wore reflected the spirit of the past, the reality of the present, and the hope of the future—a future that would see one's children doing the same things as the parents. It is this personal, tradition-bound quality that marks folk culture generally and that has to be understood if one is to ascertain the true motivation for folk costume.

The personal and the traditional characteristics of the little tradition contrast markedly with the impersonal and style-conscious character of the great tradition. The bewildering changes in the history of Western costume reflect the political, social, and economic fortunes of the elite and their supporters. Class consciousness, individual accomplishment, patriotism, wealth, and occupation strongly influenced members of the institutions of the great tradition. One can detect the concern of the time in costume development, from the wealthy ostentation of the Renaissance courts, through the imperial classicism of the Napoleonic era, to the stamped-out conformity of the twentieth century. International contacts, political events, a theatrical personality, war, the state visit of a dignitary, the automobile, a new dance—all have contributed to changes of costume style. The plethora of Asian- or African-derived fashion elements, which the Westerner eagerly placed in his costume repertory and as eagerly discarded when it was "out of style," bewilders the mind: burnooses, turbans, kimonos, saris, Tartar hats, caps, pajamas, sandals. Napoleon revived the styles of ancient Rome—and some famous personages wore togas; while late in the nineteenth century Donizetti's opera *The Daughter of the Regiment* put fashionable women into fashionable uniforms. The discovery of Tutankhamen's tomb in 1922 had American women dressing like Nefertiti; when Walt Disney did "Davy Crockett," coonskin caps swept the nation. Beau Brummell, Greta Garbo, Tarzan, Grace Kelly, the Beatles, and many others have caused widespread costume change.

The great traditions of costume in Asia are not, of course, like those of the West. A tendency prevails in Asia to observe a tradition of costume rather than to change according to "style." Richness, history, and religion are major factors in Asian elite dress. The gold and silver saris of Benares, the Tartar-style cap said to have been worn by Genghis Khan, and the green turban of those who have made the pilgrimage to Mecca are examples. Asians have always put great stock in the symbols of faith, heritage, and princely wealth.

However, the folk order is yielding before the massive assault of modern industrialization and its spokesmen, the mass media. National states that link their future to standardization at every level, to the conditioning of their citizenry to one body of laws, to one political theme, to one educational philosophy, and to mass values regard the folk order as not only backward but inconceivable in an age when jets span the earth and man walks on the moon. So resentful of the folk order are national states that deliberate efforts are made to undermine its hold by sub-

verting its youth, "modernizing" its traditions, and deriding its faith. National states thus obtain their goals—one nation, one people, one government, one belief, and of course, one costume repertory. The exponents of change through time overwhelm the exponents of tradition. Western costume is covering the earth.

This conformity of appearance, with its roots in conformity of culture, confronts Asian people as they look to the West and accept Western ways. The almost infinite and kaleidoscopic variety of Asian cultures is already being extinguished by the massive onslaught of the West. China, for example, once one of the most varied and colorful of all Asian cultural forms, is now one of the most conformist and colorless of Asian cultures. And if the present governments of India and Iran have their say, cheap, machine-made cloth and national "cottage" industry styles will become the manifest destiny of every citizen, no matter what his belief, his cultural heritage, or his income. This in the very lands from which sprang the splendors of design and craftsmanship that have ennobled mankind since early civilizations arose there thousands of years before the first smokestack darkened the skies of the West.

The great hope of the earth is that the proponents of Western culture can be made to consider not only the vulnerability of the physical earth but also the mortality of man's cultures. The reality of this mortality is made graphic in man's costume.

FOUR HUNDRED YEARS OF CUSTOM AND TRADITION: THE DRESS OF THE GENTLE FOLK

Lois M. Gurel

In North America, most subcultural groups, bound together by ethnic and religious traditions and customs, have been absorbed into the American "melting pot." Few have managed to keep their identity, resisting the temptations of modern civilization, and still live within the larger American society. Three of the most successful groups that have met the challenge and surmounted obstacles, legal and social, have been the surviving Anabaptists that originated in Central Europe during the Protestant Reformation in the 16th century—the Mennonites, the Amish, and the Hutterites. As nonconformist groups they rejected many of the prevailing religious beliefs of that day, particularly forced membership in a state or universal church.

Because their views challenged the existing European social, political, and economic, as well as religious order, they were persecuted, martyred, and finally forced to leave their homelands, first to other sections of Europe and

finally to North America. Here in the New World they found religious and cultural freedom and retained their old world beliefs and life styles. One of the most noticeable manifestations of their beliefs and life styles that has set them apart from their neighbors, has been their clothing. Although the three groups differ in their religious convictions, in the authorization for their customs and dress, and in the strictness to which they adhere to overt examples of their beliefs, they are similar in many ways. There are very often misunderstood and mistaken for each other.

The Peculiar People

The largest group in numbers of members, and the most scattered geographically, are the Mennonites. They live in more than half of the United States and the provinces of Canada. They are also the most diversified in outward interpretations of their religious beliefs, particularly clothing. Some women wear no jewelry or makeup, others frequently patronize beauty parlors. There are several Mennonite groups in North America, the largest, the Old Mennonite Church, traces its origin to Switzerland. In the transfer from the Old World to the New, this group has taken a more moderate path in transforming dress, culture, and worship to prevailing American patterns.

Peculiar Things

The most "peculiar" thing about Mennonites are their beliefs. Their dress is not nearly so distinctive as that of the Amish. An Amishman can rarely be mistaken for anything but an Amishman, but recognizing a Mennonite on the spot is often impossible.

Women in the more traditional groups wear white caps or prayer veilings, a practice based on a passage from the Bible: "Any woman who prays or prophesies with her head unveiled dishonors her head" (1 Corinthian: 11:5). Head coverings symbolize for them the functional relationship of God's order in creation—God, Christ, man, woman. These "coverings," as they call them, are made of transparent net material. They are attractive when properly fitted and give dignity and meaning to the role of the Christian woman. They are worn for public worship and often in daily work. The most distinguishing feature of women is the general absence of makeup and jewelry.

Some of the more conservative Mennonite women wear the "cape dress." This is a modern version of the old Halsduch (neckpiece). It consists of an extra piece of cloth over the shoulders, fastened at the waistline and at the shoulders, but not at the sides. It has helped to keep out low-necked, sleeveless, too-short dresses, and has tended to discourage showy styles.

Mennonite men generally follow conventional hair-styles and wear readymade clothes. Some ministers wear the "plain coat," which buttons straight to the top and has no lay-down collar.

In some conservative congregations the men wear ordinary business suits with no necktie. Conscience tells them the tie is worldly. With this dress one could mistake them for members of Pentecostal or similar sects. Most Mennonite men, and many Mennonite women, dress no differently from other people.

The use of the "Pennsylvania Dutch" dialect among Mennonites has been disappearing with the passing of parents and grandparents of the present generation. Except for the persons of Amish upbringing who join the Mennonites and some individuals in eastern Pennsylvania, very few can speak the dialect.

Dancing, gambling, card playing, smoking, and drinking are taboo. Fellowship and recreation are obtained by socials, intragroup sports, home crafts, social services such as singing in hospitals, and benevolent work projects. Disasters by fire, tornado, death, heavy financial loss, and other emergencies are alleviated by a system of mutual aid, and by generous labor and gifts-in-kind. [1]

A mixture of custom, tradition, and kinship binds the Mennonites together. Their distinctive dress has been one of the outward signs of a strong positive membership reference group. There is evidence today that the "peculiar"

1. Reprinted by permission from *Mennonite Life,* copyright 1954, 1959, and 1974 by Herald Press, Scottdale, Pennsylvania, 15683.

garb is changing—modified and modernized. In most places the men now dress like those around them. And although the women still place modesty first in their choice of clothing, they, too, are gradually adopting a contemporary clothing style. They are certainly the least conservative and most worldly of the three groups.

The Plain People

The Amish separated from the Mennonites in the late 17th century and took their name from Jacob Amman of Switzerland. Today's Amish, because of their deep respect and admiration for their ancestors, have clung tenaciously to the style of dress and traditions of centuries ago. How their forefathers managed 400 years ago satisfies their needs and desires today. The Amish have managed to resist modern civilization and 20th century technology by adhering strictly to their old country religious doctrines while settling within the modern culture. The three Amish groups are the House Amish, the most liberal of the three, the Church Amish, and the Old Order Amish, the most conservative. Amish country is located around Lancaster, Pennsylvania, although other groups reside in Wisconsin, Illinois, Ohio, and other sections of the United States.

Nicknamed the "Plain People" because they generally dress in colorless and undecorated clothes, they are a very gentle people who resist outside forces such as reporters, tourists, and photographers. They also have very few social contacts with outsiders, the "gay people," because they don't want to be influenced by the unbelievers. The Old Order Amish forbid the use of electricity, powered farm equipment, telephones, and automobiles. The covered, horse-drawn carriage is used by families and members of the same sex, while the uncovered carriage is used by courting couples. Some of these practices are slowly changing. The same automobiles that were considered sacrilegious a few years ago (and still are by some of the elders) are rapidly becoming the style for the younger generation. The cars are not taken home at night, however, but left behind stores in town to be used primarily on weekends. Only the familiar buggies travel the road to the house.

The basic belief of the Amish is that nothing is approved merely because it is the custom. All behavior must be based on the Bible. Clothing is strictly governed. The styles have not changed since the 17th century and all dress is regulated by Biblical interpretations. Apparel must be substantial (Genesis 3:7, 21) and modest. "Also that women should adorn themselves modestly and sensibly in seemly apparel, not with braided hair or gold or pearls or costly attire. . . . (I Timothy 2:9)." Clothing of the opposite sex must not be worn. "A woman shall not wear anything that pertains to a man nor shall a man put on a woman's garment. . . . (Deuteronomy 22:5)." The wearing of jewelry is prohibited.

In that day the Lord will take away the finery of the anklets, the headbands, and the crescents; the pendants, the bracelets, and the scarfs; the headdresses, the armlets, the sashes, the perfume boxes, and the amulets; the signet rings and nose rings; the festal robes, the mantles, the cloaks, and the handbags; the garments of gauze, the linen garments, the turbans, and the veils.

Instead of perfume there will be rottenness; and instead of a girdle, a rope; and instead of well-set hair, baldness; and instead of a rich robe, a girding of sack-cloth; instead of beauty, shame. (Isiah 3:18–24).

Some of their clothing is regulated by the local bishops in the districts where they live. Some is also regulated by the manufacturers on which they depend for the clothing they cannot produce at home. Their practical, rugged ways of living also influence their styles. Delicate fabrics and bright and fragile colors, would be impractical for their simple farm life.

Bonnets and Broad Brims

The Amish have retained dress styles which were common in their part of Europe during the seventeenth and eighteenth centuries. There has been gradual change among them, so that dress varies in regions, but they have not adopted the styles and fashions of the American society.

The beard is required of all adult male members of the church, and it must begin to appear at the time of baptism or marriage, depending on the local practice. Mustaches are taboo. Buttons are used on men's shirts, trousers, and underwear, and on children's dresses, but hooks and eyes are required on men's coats and vests, especially on Sunday clothing. Men's trousers are the old broad-fall type, also called "barn-door britches" (like sailor pants), and they are homemade, as are most Amish garments.

Peculiar to men's dress (for adult members of the church) is the *Mutze,* a special kind of coat with a split tail which must always be worn for church. This was the name for the ordinary coat worn by all men in the Palatinate region where the Amish lived. It was originally made of undyed flax, therefore light in color rather than dark as now.

Women wear a head covering, tied at the neck, which they call a *Kapp* (cap). All women, even very little girls, wear a white cap—except that teen-age girls until marriage wear a black cap with a white organdy apron for full Sunday dress. Baby boys wear dresses and little bonnets but no *Kapp.*

Mennonites and some of the more progressive Amish groups justify the wearing of the white cap with a passage from the Bible, but with the Old Order Amish it is simply a part of the daily dress and custom. The Amish *Kapp* is an exact replica of the headpiece worn generally by Palatine women long ago.

Another part of woman's dress, originally functional but now ornamental, is the *Lepple* (bustle), a rounded piece of cloth attached at the waist on the back of the dress. It is found in eastern United States and among the "Swiss" Amish in Indiana. Its origin is also European. To many of the Amish women today it is a symbol of humility.

Women wear black bonnets over their *Kapp* as extra protection in winter. Bonnets were earlier worn by the fashionable people of France and England. The Quakers adopted them later. With a small group of extremely conservative Pennsylvania Amish the bonnet is still taboo. They wear a kerchief and a flat hat which was probably the practice of all colonial Amish women settlers in this country.

Amish hats for men are made of imported Australian rabbit fur and are manufactured by special firms. One firm makes twenty-eight different sizes and nearly as many styles. The brims and crowns range in size and shape to fit a two-year-old boy or his grandfather and all ages in between. The bishop sometimes wears a special hat with a rounded crown and different curl of the brim. Adult young men may have a "telescopic" hat.[2]

The purpose of the women's headgear and dress is for protection and warmth. According to Amish law nothing should accentuate, enhance, or adorn the female figure. So the Amish women neither bob, curl, nor braid their hair. The young girls do braid their hair but do not allow it to hang from their heads. Women wear no jewelry, wedding rings, or cosmetics. The dresses of the women always have a high neckline and are always of a solid color, usually purple, royal blue, or red. They have little to say about their choice of dress other than color; the style, cut, length, and number of pleats are all decreed by the district bishop. Prints, flowered materials, stripes, plaids, and mixed colors are not worn. Undergarments may be white, but only the dead are dressed in white for outerwear. Unmarried girls wear white aprons while married women wear aprons to match their dresses.

Buttons are considered a sign of the military. The Amish, being a peace loving people, refuse to use them on their outer wear or their Sunday best clothing. Therefore, Amish women buy hooks and eyes by the gross as well as cotton cloth such as muslin, net, denim, and corduroy by the bolt.

Women wear their hair parted in the middle, combed smoothly back and rolled under a fine net prayer cap. They never appear without this *Kapp*. The woman is in subjection and subordination to her husband and the head covering is symbolic of this relationship. In some districts, a change from this custom would mean immediate expulsion from the group.

The men appear without hats only inside the house, school or at Sunday meeting. The hat symbolizes his role within the social structure. When the two year old boy begins wearing long pants, he receives a stiff black hat with a three inch brim. The bridegroom wears a telescopic hat during the early years of marriage. This hat must have a permanent crease around the top of the crown. The grandfather's hat has a four inch crown and a four inch brim. The bishop's hat has a four and one half inch crown and a wide seam around the crown. A hat with a flatter crown is worn by Amish fathers. The flat crowned, wide brimmed straw hat which was preferred for summer is no longer being made by the manufacturers (1, p. 135). The outsider may never notice these differences, or if he does he may regard them as accidental. But to the Amish these symbols indicate whether people are fulfilling the expec-

2. Reprinted by permission from *Amish Life,* copyright 1959 by Herald Press, Scottdale, Pennsylvania, 15683.

tations of the group. A young man who wears a brim that is too narrow is liable for sanction (1, p. 135).

The Amish men wear blue, black, or gray work clothes but their Sunday suits are always blue-black. Lapelless coats, standing collars, and hooks and eyes distinguish the men's clothing from modern styles. Undergarments and trousers have button closings and the barndoor flap instead of zippered or vertical varieties. Leather belts are forbidden so cloth suspenders are used—their width determined by the bishop. The Amish use rubber only in overshoes or galoshes.

Store-bought shirts are worn by some but they must be white or blue, or sports shirts in modest colors. Homemade shirts are recognized by their lack of collars, longer length, and sewed-up front. Neckties are forbidden. The men are allowed to wear a silver or nickel pocket watch on a cloth or leather band. A sleeveless black vest is often a part of the Amish men's attire.

When a man comes of marriageable age and has joined the church, he wears a beard. He also shaves his upper and lower lips to avoid being offensive to the congregation. This was especially noticeable when the communion cup was passed and drops were left on the hair. Depending on the rule of the congregation, he may shave his cheeks.

The bishop of the district prescribes the length of the men's hair. It may be ordered as short as the upper tip of the ear or as long as the finger's width below the lobe of the ear. No current hair style may be worn, and combing, parting, and dressing up are all forbidden—patting of the hair with the hand will bring it into order.

The Amish clothing contributes to group identity and signifies their values and beliefs. To the Amish themselves their clothing communicates their beliefs to one another. Their dress forms a boundary maintenance which permits their culture to be unaltered by that of outsiders.

A Colony of Heaven

The Hutterites, the third Anabaptist group to come to North America in the 16th century, have successfully perpetuated a vastly different life style than either the Amish or the Mennonites, or their American and Canadian neighbors. The Hutterites live in Montana, South Dakota, and the three western provinces of Canada and are the oldest continual communal group in the Western Hemisphere. About 150 colonies, known as Bruderhofe are scattered through this area, averaging about 100 persons in each.

The Hutterites are attempting to establish a colony of heaven here on earth and although they have many utopian ideas they have no illusions concerning their present imperfections. They believe in common property ownership and like the Amish have kept the dress and customs of their early ancestors. Their German Tirolean dialect, distinctive clothes, and geographic isolation have separated them from the surrounding society. They have had

unusual success in transmitting their distinctive heritage to every new generation. Their colonies are small but they have one of the highest birth rates in the world. They have been more successful in resisting assimilation into the dominant culture than any other ethnic or religious group.

> Thus, whether regarded as a fragment of the Protestant Reformation that has survived unchanged in the modern world, as a *Germeinschafts* group that has proved uniquely resistant to the encroachments and segmental relationships of individualistic society, or because of their nonconformist response to many widely held beliefs, as a test case of cultural pluralism, the Hutterites deserve closer attention than they have generally received (2, pp. 4–5).

Definitions of need and equality vary from one Hutterite community to another, but they are among the most central concepts that govern daily life and the distribution of material goods. All members are not necessarily equal or have the same needs, but food and clothing are allotted according to a societal heirarchy with individual needs considered.

Among the regulations imposed upon the community members, they are admonished to spend little time, effort, or money on clothing or appearance. Therefore, clothing is distributed according to this concept of need. Since styles don't change, if a woman takes care of her clothes she can accumulate quite a substantial wardrobe for her family and for herself. The women often buy less durable fabrics just so they will wear out faster and so they can have new outfits more often.

Clothing or fabric is distributed by the head tailoress to individuals or family heads according to the number of members in the family and their ages. Careful records are kept of all clothing allowances. The fabric need not be used for its intended purpose or person and may be saved or traded within or outside the community.

> The rule book specifies to the inch how much yardage each person shall have on the basis of his age. Ten-year-old boys shall have material for a jacket annually at the rate of 3 yards and 6 inches. Eleven-year-old boys shall be allotted 3 yards and 12 inches, and men over fourteen shall receive 4 yards. When someone is overweight he shall have 9 additional inches. Clothing allotments change most dramatically when boys and girls become adults. . . . The rule book allows 9 yards of material for a modern dress. It takes only about 5 yards to make a modern dress, but the traditional allotment is still passed out (3, p. 51).
> Each woman sews for her family. All women's clothes and all underclothes are homemade, and so are most of the men's shirts. Men's suits too are made at home after a plain pattern. Buttons for shirts and blouses are bought, but dresses and men's suits are fastened with hooks and eyes made by the man. . . . (2, p. 114).

Clothing is a very important part of group identification and a recognized pattern in the lives of the Hutterites. Strong bonds of group identity result and enforce the positive effects of reference group membership.

Customs such as the beards worn by the men after they marry, or the garb, serve to set the members of the group apart. The Hutterian who leaves the colony on a business trip to the city or the nearest town does not feel uncomfortable or timid because he is different in his ways and appearance. Rather he feels like an ambassador of a nation who is fully aware he is away from home, but is more concerned with what people at home think of him than with what the people think whom he is dealing with at the moment.

Except in isolated instances, and then among the young, there is no objection among the Hutterians to the clothes they are required to wear (2, p. 188).

The Hutterites' failure to emerge from "self-imposed cultural and physical isolation" is looked at askance by the dominant cultural groups in the states and provinces where they live. In a society where homogeneity is the mode, any nonconformist group is a threat to the majority. Cultural assimilation and uniformity are required by the few for the emotional stability of the many. Recent years have shown gradual change in attitudes toward subcultural problems as more voices are raised in defense of those who choose to set themselves apart and resist cultural leveling.

Indeed, the Hutterian communities provide a natural setting for the study of human relationships and behavior that no artificial control group could offer. Meanwhile the Hutterians will carry on in their old ways. Whatever contribution they have to offer to society in the form of scientific knowledge will have to be pried from them. They themselves are satisfied to work, but not to work too hard; to extend their hospitality to friends and strangers, but never to press it on them; to be in this world, but not of this world (2, pp. 189–190).

REFERENCES CITED

1. Hostetler, J.A. *Amish Society*. Baltimore: Johns Hopkins Press, 1962.
2. Peters, V. *All Things Common*. Minneapolis: The University of Minnesota Press, 1965.
3. Hostetler, J.A., and Huntington, G.E. *The Hutterites in North America*. New York: Holt, Rinehart and Winston, 1967.

THE PIOUS ONES

Harvey Arden

Maybe we should have parachuted in. That would have seemed much more appropriate somehow for two travelers dropping out of one world into another. Instead, mundanely, photographer Nathan Benn and I took the subway, boarding on Manhattan's lower East Side and emerging ten minutes later. . .

"Welcome to Williamsburg in Brooklyn," Nathan said. "Or to Satmar in old Hungary. It depends on how you look at it."

Passing shopwindows hieroglyphed with square-block Hebrew letters, we entered the extraordinary world of Williamsburg's Hasidic Jews, or Hasidim—meaning "pious ones." Here, wedged amid Brooklyn's ethnic hodgepodge, sprawls a 40-block enclave of ultra-orthodox Judaism, where most of the men wear flowing beards and dangling earlocks in accordance with God's command in the Book of Leviticus 19:27: "Ye shall not round the corners of your heads, neither shalt thou mar the corners of thy beard."

Their clothing, derived from styles long worn by Jews in eastern Europe, is a striking study in monotone—black or dark-toned suit, wide-brimmed black hat, white shirt buttoned at the neck, no tie. "It may seem plain to you," one Hasid told me, "but to me it's beautiful!" On Sabbaths and holidays the married men don great sable-trimmed hats called *shtreimels,* giving them a noble, almost regal air as they stride along.

The women, not limited to their menfolk's color scheme, wear modish but distinctly modest garments as they push their baby carriages and strollers along Lee Avenue. Only after you've been told are you likely to notice that most of them are wearing wigs. Often styled in the latest coiffure, these are worn to conceal their real hair—which is cropped after their wedding and henceforth hidden from men's eyes as prescribed by a centuries-old tradition.

"A few minutes more on the subway and we'd already have broken the law." Nathan said. "The *Jewish* law, that is, against traveling or working on a Sabbath or religious holiday. For an Orthodox Jew to ride a subway or even to push the buttons on an elevator is forbidden. And put on your yarmulke, too." He referred to the skullcap traditionally worn by Jews. "The Hasidim wear them all the time—even when they're sleeping."

I later inquired of a Hasidic acquaintance why he wore his yarmulke even when he went to bed.

"Because a Jew covers his head as a sign of his respect for God," he answered. "And—tell me, please—am I not still a Jew when I'm sleeping?"

Excerpted from "The Pious Ones" by Harvey Arden in *National Geographic Magazine,* Vol. 148, No. 2, August, 1975, pp. 276–298. Reprinted by permission of *National Geographic Magazine.*

Note: Readers are urged to review the entire article, "The Pious Ones," particularly for the excellent photographs.

Though I had become bar mitzvah—a "son of the commandment" or a "man of duty"—at age 13, I had only occasionally attended a synagogue since then. Certainly, I had no sense of obligation to follow all of the multitude of mitzvahs, or commandments, that God had charged the Jews of Moses' time to obey in fulfillment of their covenant with Him. To the Hasidim, however, these mitzvahs are as important today as they were in ancient times.

No fewer than 613 such mitzvahs are enunciated in the five books of Moses comprising the Torah, or Pentateuch. They range from the Ten Commandments and such sub-lime moral precepts as "thou shalt love thy neighbour as thyself" to so technical a regulation as "neither shall a garment mingled of linen and woollen come upon thee."

These latter two mitzvahs, seemingly worlds apart in significance, appear in consecutive verses of the Book of Leviticus (19:18, 19). The Hasidim hew as strictly to the latter as to the former. To heed and safeguard the 613 mitzvahs, plus literally thousands of other laws and traditions that have evolved from them over the millenniums, becomes the very fulcrum of their daily existence.

ECCLESIASTICAL VESTMENTS IN THE MODERN CHURCH

Reverend Monsignor John T. Doherty

Ecclesiastical vestments in the past reflected the art and culture of the times and represented, to some degree, the Church's view of herself and her mission. Even the dominant theological themes of an age found expression in vestment decoration, just as they did on Dante's pages and in Michelangelo's frescoes. When the "kingly" model of the bishop's role prevailed and the "court" model of the liturgy strongly influenced the sacred ceremonies, vestments and insignia of office tended to be ornate, rather regal, and strongly concerned with visual impact and symbolism. When the "shepherd" model of the bishop and priest prevailed, vestiture tended to return to the more simple, austere, and functional. It is this latter mood that has emerged recently as the Church has undergone radical self-study and the ecclesiastical arts have caught the mood.

The Second Vatican Council, which ended in 1965, left a heritage of reform and renewal that will be felt for many years. It was the Council that brought together developing awarenesses of the Church's self-image as "the people of God," the "pilgrim people," characterized by simplicity in form and practice. These concepts left their mark almost everywhere in the Church, including the attitude toward official and liturgical vestiture.

The liturgical vestments of the bishop are a good point of departure for understanding the attitude of the Church in this field, because the bishop is seen as the chief celebrant of the Eucharist in his diocese. Every priest and every gathering of people for Eucharist within a diocese have a direct relationship to the bishop and his celebration of Mass. When he celebrates in the most solemn fashion, especially in his cathedral church, it is called a pontifical Mass and the full vestments of the Church are used. An example of a theological implication can be seen in the long tradition of the bishop's wearing not only a chasuble that represents his priesthood, but also the vestments of

lesser orders as well, such as the deacon's dalmatic and the sub-deacon's tunic. In 1960, after many requests from the bishops of the world, the Sacred Congregation of Rites in Rome removed the obligation of wearing these extra vestments, leaving it optional to each bishop.

After the Council had greatly simplified all the sacred rites, bishops made urgent appeals that the *Ceremonial of Bishops* (the book governing their rites, insignia, and vestments for sacred use) be quickly revised in order to conform to the total liturgical renewal. Since this would necessarily take time, an interim document was issued in June 1968, which can be summed up by its own reference to "elements which are obsolete and out of harmony with our age." It asks for the preservation of "the venerable traditions of ancient liturgical services," especially in the bishop's liturgy that is so central, but at the same time its overall tone is set by phrases such as "returning sacred rites to a noble simplicity and to an authenticity of sign." This is a long step from the twelfth-century concept of a bishop's wearing nine vestments in order to represent nine different aspects of his pastoral office! Some changes covered by this document are significant. The dominant note is simplicity. The traditional canopy over the bishop's chair (*"cathedra"*—hence the word "cathedral") was abolished, as were the kneeling cushion, thrones for other bishops present, and genuflection before the bishop.

Within nine months the Papal Secretariat of State issued another instruction, concerning the dress and insignia of cardinals. Pope Paul was quoted as wanting to bring the exterior forms of ecclesiastical life "into closer correspondence with the changing circumstances of the

From "Ecclesiastical Vestments in the Modern Church." *The Metropolitan Museum of Art Bulletin*, Vol. 29(n.s.) No. 7, March 1971, pp. 310–312. Pictures are omitted. Copyright © 1971 by the Metropolitan Museum of Art.

times, and of making them now accord better with the higher spiritual values which they should express and promote." The Secretariat noted that "the modern mentality is particularly sensitive [to this subject], one that demands the avoidance of possible extremes in one direction or the other, and an ability to bring correctness and decorum into harmony with simplicity, practicality, and the spirit of humility and poverty." As a result, the simple black cassock became the dress for optional use on ordinary occasions. The mantelletta (a sleeveless, knee-length vestment) was abolished, as well as the traditional sash with tassels and the "galero"or red cardinalatial hat. Some items of dress were left optional; still others were suppressed.

The liturgy of the Roman Rite was dramatically revised almost in its entirety and the revisions became effective in March 1970 in most parts of the world. Of interest to those viewing this exhibition of medieval ecclesiastical vestments are two principles laid down in this revision regarding vestments. The first principle is this: "the beauty of a vestment should derive from its material and form rather than from its ornamentation. Any ornamentation should include only symbols, images, or pictures suitable for liturgical use and anything unbecoming should be avoided." The second principle is that "in addition to traditional materials, vestments may be made from natural fabrics of the region or artificial fabrics in keeping with the dignity of the sacred action and the person wearing them." Judgments regarding the second principle are left to the body of bishops in each country or cultural region. In the United States, the National Conference of Bishops saw fit simply to repeat that principle and then to turn the judgment over to the local bishop in any cases of doubt about suitability. What is

significant is the opening up of liturgical vestiture to development in all parts of the world: vestments now can depart from the traditional materials, decorations, and form to meet the cultural needs, resources, and wishes of each locality. Synthetic and local natural materials will supplement the traditional silk and linen we are so accustomed to. It is of interest to view the medieval examples of vestments in the light of these developing principles.

One additional note should be made. The revised liturgy provides for the Mass being offered with the celebrant facing the people, instead of having his back to them. This is now common practice and will probably have considerable effect on the designing of vestments in the future. When the people were more in a "spectator" role than in a "participant" role, the back of the chasuble became the center of visual attention and was often decorated with a cross, a liturgical symbol, or even a picture of the Last Supper. It harmonized with the sanctuary and with the vestments of the assisting ministers . Now, with the priest facing the people, his face, hands, words become the center of attention and the vestment falls into a secondary visual role. Thus the first principle stated above comes into a context where the material and the form rather than decoration dominate the vestment.

In summary, the Church's attitude toward the use of vestments in our time grows out of her present view of her mission and image. While firmly committed to sacred vestments in the performance of the liturgy and to maintaining the basic tradition of the past, the Church will see adaptation and creativity grow and increase, based not on a Roman or a Catholic or a baroque model, but arising from varying cultures and local expression.

CHAPTER 3

Historical Influences on Costume

INTRODUCTION

Marianne S. Beeson

Renier has defined history as "the story of the experiences of men living in civilized societies."[1] There is no reference to time in his definition; Renier believes that contemporary history is not a contradiction in terms. The review of last season's fashions is a study of fashion history, and the records of what people are wearing today—newspaper accounts, photographs, fashion magazines, commentary, and garments now being collected for costume museums—will shortly become history. Clothing as one of man's experiences is one key to the story of civilizations.

The history of costume (the term costume used to mean clothing, adornment, and accessories, such as fans, muffs, and walking sticks) is derived from many sources: written, pictorial, and actual surviving articles. The earliest evidence regarding dress has been discussed in Chapter I. Archaeology is considered by some authorities to be a separate discipline and by others to be an auxiliary of history.[2] At any rate the physical evidence of ancient civilizations is uncovered through archaeological methods.

Art history is an important source of costume information, although not without its limitations. Portrait painting, for example, while wonderfully rich in detail of dress, provides a record of the clothing of only relatively wealthy people who could afford to engage an artist.

The lower socio-economic classes are rarely depicted in portraits. In addition, it is generally assumed that costume shown in portraits is not exemplary of "everyday" dress for the upper classes portrayed. The individual in history sitting for the portrait painter was most likely to don his or her most elegant, sumptuous, and fanciest "best" outfit, jewelry, and hairdo, for the same reasons people today get themselves and their children decked out in "Sunday best" for the 88-cent 8 × 10 portrait special down at the supermarket.

Because customs of dress and details of costume have an historical tradition, what people *have* worn continues to influence what people wear today. In fact, some styles

of Western dress and adornment, in and out of contemporary fashion, have been given names of the people and places associated with their historic origins: the Chesterfield coat, cardigan, raglan sleeves, sideburns, Wellington boot, Norfolk jacket, and Eaton jacket, to mention a few.

Textile and apparel designers find inspiration in history, and formal study of history of costume is part of the designer's education. Fashion repeats some of the style ideas of previous periods. Nostalgic interpretations of styles from the 1920s, 1930s, and even the 1950s have enjoyed recent vogue. Movies, such as *The Great Gatsby, The Sting,* and *Grease,* have played a part in popularizing these periods in fashion history.

Usually, styles have been repeated with enough differences in fit, fabric, and other subtle changes to prevent people from simply storing old clothes and waiting for them to come back in fashion. If it was retrieved from mothballs, the men's double-breasted suit of the 1940s did not look just right in the 1960s when double-breasted suits were back in style. Today, however, there seems to be considerable interest in authentic clothes of the past. Used clothing stores have been doing a brisk business with young customers for several years. Now, some stores, describing their merchandise as "antique clothes," are achieving success also. The owner[3] of an antique clothing store in Roanoke, Virginia, reports that her best sellers (in approximate order of popularity) are men's pleated trousers from the 40s, long white cotton and lace skirts and blouses from the turn of the century, and the "movie star" look of the forties—women's suits with padded shoulders and slim skirts, satin and sequined slinky evening gowns, high-heeled shoes with platforms and ankle straps, and rhinestone jewelry.

According to Laver's "Law of Fashion" regarding the bias people maintain on viewing dress of the past, fashions of as recent a period as thirty years ago would be considered "amusing." (See "Why You Wear What You Do," p. 144.) Is "amusing" the mood that purchasers of antique clothing seek to create through their attire? It remains to be seen whether this interest in clothes from the past is a fad or a trend. If it is a trend, it is bad news for apparel

1. Renier, G.J., *History: Its Purpose and Method.* London: George Allen & Unwin, Ltd., 1950, p. 38.
2. Charles-Picard, Gilbert, editor, *Larousse Encyclopedia of Archaeology.* New York: G.P. Putnam's Sons, 1972, p. 9.

3. Source: Interview with Julie Hunsaker of Jezebel's.

producers. People will not have to buy very many new clothes if they can depend upon what is stored in the attic!

There are a number of clothing anachronisms that are with us today because of historic tradition. In men's clothes:

1. The watch pocket in trousers—when most men no longer carry pocket watches.
2. The vest—originally protective underwear worn under armor, today not much more than a bib.
3. Lapels on suit jackets and sports coats, which no longer function since they cannot be turned up to close the neckline.
4. A buttonhole in the lapel with no function.
5. Shoulder pads, originally for protection in combat, today to create a broad shouldered ideal of manhood.
6. Buttons at the wrist of coat sleeves—without function.

Rudofsky enumerates several of what he calls "absurdities" in today's dress—antiques which have lost significance and function. He diagrams the location and number (totalling 70) of buttons on the various layers of clothing of a fully dressed man, and applies the same scheme to pockets—totalling 24.[4]

There are details in women's clothes which are also maintained in deference to tradition. In garment construction, for example, there are several conventional ways of handling construction processes for no other reason than because the eye is accustomed to seeing and expecting a certain effect. The triangular folds of fabric which form darts are always designed to be pressed toward the center front or center back of a garment. It makes no difference to the fitting function of darts, but the effect on the right side is different, and it is the "toward the center" rule which is observed, solely because of tradition.

Perhaps the most obvious carry over from the past has to do with direction of lapped closures in apparel: women's clothes lap right over left in a button closure; men's garments lap left over right. Several different explanations have been offered for this convention. Battista says that the initial purpose for the direction of men's closures was to involve the right hand as little as possible in buttoning and unbuttoning, leaving it free for fighting. He says that women's button fastenings require primarily the right hand, so that the left is free to hold a baby.[5]

There are more observations of contemporary clothing which could be made to show how closely styles are linked to the past. The thesis of Rudofsky's book, *Are Clothes Modern?*, is that clothes are indeed *not* modern, but entrenched in historical traditions. Thus, history helps to explain today's dress. Conversely, study of costume of a particular period and culture is necessary to the story of history.

The articles in this chapter deal with different aspects of the history of dress and adornment. The first outlines the long history of fabric production, spinning and weaving, from the ancient spindles of prehistory to the shuttleless looms of a modern textiles plant. From an anthropological viewpoint, highlights in the evolution of Western dress are outlined in Johnston's article, concluding with analysis of today's moods expressed in dress and predictions for the future. "Sumptuary Legislation in Four Centuries" discusses laws which have attempted to regulate expenditure for dress. "Our Ancestors as Fashion Plates" traces developments in styles of military uniforms and considers parallel changes in women's fashions.

The various efforts to promote dress reform in the nineteenth century are revealed in articles on Amelia Bloomer and Dr. Mary Walker. Historical perspectives on hair and teeth are provided by two articles on those subjects. The chapter concludes with "The Song of the Shirt," based on two historical themes—the history of apparel manufacture and the history of women's employment in apparel production, both seen from a women's rights point of view.

ADDITIONAL READINGS

On costume history:

Laver, James. *A Concise History of Costume and Fashion.* N.Y.: Harry N. Abrams, 1969.

Hollander, Anne. *Seeing through Clothes.* N.Y.: Viking Press, 1978.

> A "Newsweek" review calls this book a history of fashions in undress since about a third of the illustrations are nudes.

Batterberry, Michael and Ariane. *Mirror, Mirror: A Social History of Fashion.* N.Y.: Holt, Rinehart and Winston, 1977.

> Michael was trained as an art historian, Ariane as an archaeologist. Lavish illustrations, many in color, for this history of Western dress.

Stannard, Una. "Clothing and Sexuality," *Sexual Behavior,* Vol. 1, No. 2, May 1971, pp. 25–33 and 64.

> How the custom of women wearing skirts and men wearing trousers developed and some possible implications for the similarity in dress of men and women.

Woolson, Abba G., editor, *Dress Reform: A Series of Lectures Delivered in Boston Dress as It Affects the Health of Women.* Arno, 1974, reprint of 1874 edition.

Kunz, George Frederick. *Rings for the Finger.* N.Y.: Dover, 1973, republication of 1917 edition.

> History and symbolism of rings.

Kidwell, Claudia B. *Women's Bathing and Swimming Costume in the United States.* Washington, D.C.: Smithsonian Institution Press, 1968.

> Includes some photographs of actual bathing garments from the Smithsonian collection.

Heinrich, Peggy and Worssam, Ray J. "Bathing Machines Brought Elegance to Skinny Dipping," *Smithsonian,* July 1974, pp. 56–61.

> A history of bathing customs and costumes, especially as related to ideas about health and modesty.

4. Rudofsky, Bernard. *Are Clothes Modern?* Chicago: Paul Theobald, 1947, pp. 120–121.

5. Battista, O.A., "Why We Dress the Way We Do," *Science Digest,* 46 (Oct., 1958), p. 29.

Glynn, Prudence. *In Fashion: Dress in the Twentieth Century.* N.Y.: Oxford Univ. Press, 1978.

>   Black and white photographs. Part Two, "Special Clothes," includes royalty, menswear, sports, and children.

Carter, Ernestine. *The Changing World of Fashion: 1900 to the Present.* London: Weidenfeld and Nicolson, 1977.

>   Influence of dance, sports, wars, etc. Lavish photographs of fashions by designers in Paris, London, and America.

North, Rene. *Military Uniforms,* 1686–1918. N.Y.: Grosset & Dunlap, 1970.

>   Illustrated by drawings in color.

On the history of apparel manufacture:

Cooper, Grace Rogers. *The Invention of the Sewing Machine.* Washington, D.C.: The Smithsonian Institution Press, 1968.

>   A detailed study with numerous black and white photographs.

Stein, Leon. *The Triangle Fire.* Phil.: Lippincott, 1962.

Stein, Leon. *Out of the Sweatshop: The Struggle for Industrial Democracy.* N.Y.: Quadrangle/NY Times Book Co., 1977.

TEXTILES

In one of Grimm's fairy tales a dwarf named Rumpelstiltskin taught a miller's daughter how to spin straw into gold. Without the dwarf's help mankind has spun threads of many kinds into the equivalent of gold, creating comfort, luxury, beauty and great wealth in one of the world's oldest arts.

The making of cloth has spurred commerce, invention, an industrial age, a chemical age, most recently a space age by creating a portable environment within a suit of clothes. In its course textile technology has challenged physicians with a spectrum of new and baffling allergens.

Four Threads

Modern manmade fibers have diminished but not replaced the four historic threads from which the art of clothmaking flowered through the ages. Linen from Egypt, wool from Mesopotamia, silk from China, and cotton from India clothed the world until this century.

The concept of thread was born out of the need to clothe the relatively hairless body. European man's first thread was a strip of hide or a strand of animal sinew. When the ice receded and Europe became a vast forest, the lake and bog dwellers experimented with vegetable fibers to make traps, fishing nets, and carrying bags by knotting, netting and looping.

Men wove before they learned to spin: on the model of spider web and birds' nests they made mats, baskets, the walls of wattle and daub huts, and the first primitive textiles out of fibers as they were found in nature. The idea of twining fiber ends together to make a continuous weaving yarn developed independently in widely separated places. The long inner fibers of the flax stem became the choice thread of the Nile dwellers. Woven fabrics found in Egypt, dating from 5000 B.C., make linen the oldest textile known.

Wool came next: Eurasian peoples may have begun by spinning yarn out of clumps of animal hair caught on bushes. Woollen cloaks, caps and tunics have been found in early Bronze Age graves in Switzerland and Scandinavia. Woollens were the first and for many centuries the only fabrics worn in Europe and Asia, and the peoples of early Mesopotamia and the Mediterranean coast of Asia who domesticated sheep and goats were the first wool weavers.

Eventually the finest woollens came from goats, such as the Angora goat of Anatolia that yields angora and mohair yarns, and the Kashmiri goat whose soft silky undercoat is the source of cashmere. The Bactrian camel of Asia was also a source, shedding its fleece seasonally in clumps so that it did not need shearing.

In South America an early source of wool was the llama and its related species the alpaca, guanaco and vicuña. Cat and rabbit pelts, cow's hair produced in Siberia and horsehair in European Russia were among the other sources that today are used mainly as fillers in textile manufacture.

Silk originated so early in China that its discovery is legendary: one tale ascribes it to an observant princess of about 5000 B.C. who watched a caterpillar spinning its cocoon on a mulberry tree in the palace garden. Another credits Si Ling-chi, an empress of 2640 B.C., who encouraged the nurture of the silkworm and discovered how to unreel the cocoon. Immersed in a bowl of warm water, a cocoon can be unwound in a continuous filament from 300 to 1600 yards long; the greater the length, the finer the filament. Other species spin a silklike filament but the Chinese chose their indigenous mulberry moth, *Bombyx mori,* for sericulture so long ago that the moth itself is no longer found in the wild state. The Japanese have a larger silkworm, the *yamamai,* and both China and India derive wild or tussah silk (called *shantung* in China, *pongee* in India) from *Antheraea mylitta.* This silkworm is cultivated on groves of dwarf oak trees.

Cotton, called the crop that clothes the world, can be grown in tropical and subtropical climates. Paradoxically, it was the last of the great fibers to become worldwide.

From "MD" Medical Newsmagazine, Vol. 18, No. 4, April, 1974, pp. 99–110. Reprinted by permission of the publisher.

Joseph's coat of many colors and the handsome hangings with which Solomon adorned the first temple in Jerusalem are thought to have been the finely woven, brightly printed or painted cottons of India. Herodotus wrote of trees in India that produced fleeces as their fruit, and Florentine artists a millennium later were still picturing these "trees" with a sheep's head at the end of each branch.

Of the great fibers only linen is archeologically older than cotton: fabrics of twined cotton, an early weaving technique, have survived in the dry air of Peru from 2000 B.C. In the Old World its first users were the Indus valley people of 3000 to 1500 B.C. The invading Aryans who are thought to have destroyed the Indus city of Mohenjo-Daro took over the art and developed it to such expertness that their diaphanous fabrics were described by ancient travelers as "the woven wind of India." Dacca muslins, reputedly woven of continuous threads 200 miles long, were of such gossamer texture that when spread on the grass and wet with dew they were said to become invisible. The cobweb-thin yarns were spun on bamboo slivers the thickness of a needle, twirled inside a cocoanut shell.

The Art

Clothmaking advanced from primitive experiment to skilled art in the settled life of villages: spindle whorls and loom weights of stone and clay at neolithic sites indicate that the first farmers were spinning and weaving. Egypt's tombs preserved the continuous record from Menes to Tutankh-amen, a 2000 year span including practically every kind of weave known today. Other sites have also revealed the sophistication of the first clothmakers from astonishingly early cultural stages. From a Danish grave of about 1000 B.C. came a girl's jacket of a weave resembling homespun; the skirt with it was made of string, tied and knotted. A woman's long full skirt of a few centuries later is woven in a colorful plaid.

Often only a discarded rag remains of the early textile art, tossed on a rubbish heap with broken pottery as in the kitchen middens of the Swiss lake dwellers. At Mohenjo-Daro one fragment of fine cotton was found resting on a silver vase and another on a copper razor, the oxidation of the metals acting as a preservative. Excavations at Megiddo in Palestine, the Armageddon of the Bible, revealed primitive spindle whorls and loom weights from 3000 B.C.; later levels yielded bone spindles, clay loom weights with impressed seals, beautifully decorated whorls of bone and ivory. Minoan Crete left no actual textiles but the wall paintings of the palace at Knossos depict court ladies of high fashion in gowns with fitted bodices and crisp flounces that could only be made with fabrics fine enough for dressmaking.

The excavators of ancient Troy also found no shred of cloth, but 8000 clay spindle whorls testified to a Trojan textile industry. The second settlement, of about 2500 B.C.,

shows evidence of a 43 inch horizontal loom with one end fastened to the house wall and the other to two posts set in the floor. The clay warp weights lay in orderly rows as they fell when the roof collapsed, probably 1000 years before the fall of Homer's Ilium.

Homer sang of embroideries, laces and Sidonian dyes. An art that was already so ancient was inevitably woven into legends like that of the Lydian maiden Arachne who challenged Athene to a weaving contest and was turned into a spider for her presumption. Ariadne's thread guided Theseus out of the Labyrinth of Minos, and Penelope wove her father-in-law's shroud by day and unraveled it by night, holding the suitors at bay until Odysseus' return. The bridal gown presented to Jason's royal bride by the jealous Medea killed the princess on her wedding day.

Most awesome in Greek myth were the symbolic three fates: Clotho who spun the web of a man's life, Lachesis who measured its length and Atropos who cut it at the foreordained hour of his death. The clothmaking arts are ascribed to the teaching of a god or a legendary godlike ancestor in the mythology of many lands.

Tools and Techniques

All the yarns of antiquity from the coarsest to the finest were hand spun, rolled between the palms or against the cheek or thigh of the spinner, then twisted and wound on a whirling spindle. The spinning wheel of Europe, the first step in mechanization, was a late medieval invention; the familiar distaff was no more than a stick with a ball of carded fibers, called the tow, stuck on one end, the other end supported under the spinner's arm or belt.

A loom was any device to stretch the warp threads: they might be strung from the roof beam of a hut, a stake in the ground or between a convenient tree trunk and the weaver's waist. Later came top and bottom beams to form a frame, eventually a cloth beam to roll up the finished fabric and bobbins to supply continuous warp threads. The loom might be either horizontal or vertical. The weaver separated the warp threads by hand or with a rod, passed the weft through on a stick spool as the shuttle and pushed it into place against the preceding threads with another stick called a beater. Heddles and shed rods were added to separate the warp threads in various patterns for different weaves, treadles to operate the shedding devices by foot and leave the hands free for the shuttle.

The cloth as it came from the loom was still far from finished: woollens and linens had to be "fulled" by trampling and beating to thicken the fibers and make them adhere for an even texture. Fulling was done in a bath of some natural detergent, such as plant ashes, stale human urine or fuller's earth (a form of aluminum silicate occurring in certain soils) that absorbs fats. For centuries this was done by human feet stamping on the fabric in a trough; in the Middle Ages the first fulling mills built by the side of streams harnessed water power to beat the cloth with mallets. The handy supply of running water also served for the washing and scouring of the cloth.

For a soft finish, woollens were repeatedly brushed with a teazle, a rough brush made from thistles or hedgehog skins, and the raised nap of fiber ends was then sheared off. Pressing completed the finish: a wall painting in Pompeii shows a standing cloth press in a fuller's workshop, with twin plates pressed together from above by giant screws. Other methods were ironing with a heavy wooden block and rubbing the surface with rods, smooth stones or a heavy marble ball.

Each kind of cloth had its own bleaching process. Linens were boiled in lye and spread in the sun for as long as 16 weeks, depending on the thickness of the weave. Cottons were laid on grass wet with dew and similarly whitened by sunlight. Woollens were spread on a hemispheric cage over a pot of burning sulfur, and afterwards rubbed with fine fuller's earth for extra whiteness. The Dutch in the Middle Ages had a near monopoly of the bleaching process with a technique of alternately steeping the fabrics in an alkaline solution and washing the excess alkali out with sour milk. The Chinese, to avoid too rigorous bleaching of their delicate silks, whitened them in advance by feeding the silkworms on leaves of the white mulberry.

Next came dyeing either of the whole cloth or in designs, if these had not been woven in with yarns already dyed in the fiber or after spinning. Batik, tie-dyeing, silk-screen and block printing were all known in ancient India and China. So was embroidery, and the goldsmiths of ancient Ur were skilled in drawing gold thread for the weavers.

Cloth Trade

Among the first trade goods of value along the sea lanes and caravan routes were textiles and everything related to them. From the weavers' looms also came the sacks and bales in which goods were carried and the sails of cargo dhows and galleys. Phoenician merchants sold their rich crimson dyes from the *Murex* shellfish, called Tyrian purple, to Egyptian pharaohs. They carried woollen goods and raw wool as far west as Cadiz in 1000 B.C.

Nineveh and Babylon were textile centers for the ancient world, and their sumptuous fabrics were famous, threaded with gold and embroidered with scenes of war and hunting. Roman empire poets wrote of *Babylonica stromata,* the animal tapestries, and one Metellus Scipio reputedly paid 800,000 cisterces for a special cloth called *Trichinaria babylonica.*

Sericulture remained a closely guarded Chinese secret for some 3000 years while innumerable legends grew up of its being smuggled westward by monks and missionaries; in one romantic tale a Chinese princess brought the silkworm larva concealed in her headdress as a wedding gift to her Indian bridegroom.

The women of Cos, the island made famous by Hippocrates, produced the *Cos vestis,* the transparent silk shift that shocked Athenian matrons; their silk yarns may have come from Persia.

Silk began traveling westward before 100 B.C. by the Silk Road, which was opened by the Han emperor Wu-ti. India, Persia and the Middle East received silks and silk yarns by this route for 1000 years; Palmyra in Syria, one of the road's terminals, became enormously rich on the shimmering fabrics carried by trains of some 100 camels on a 6000-mile journey that took about eight months. Julius Caesar bedazzled his countrymen with the silk canopies he imported for his Roman triumph, giving Romans the insatiable appetite for silk. In return for its silk the road carried back to China Mesopotamian wool, Indian Buddhism, Christian missionaries, and eventually Marco Polo who returned with a length of Mongolian gold-striped silk that the Italian weavers were quick to copy.

The great trade item of medieval Europe was woollens, the indigenous textile. Spain, which bred merino sheep, and Britain were competitors in producing the raw staple and the Flemish weavers were the leading producers of the cloth. For centuries the wool trade, which began England's commercial history, consisted of selling English and Scottish wool in Antwerp and buying finished goods. Medieval merchants traveled throughout England, as on the continent, their bales of wool or woollen goods strapped to shaggy ponies, displaying their wares at the cloth fairs.

William the Conqueror brought skilled weavers from Flanders and several successive kings sought to develop a native weaving industry. Many of the textile workers' guilds date from medieval times. But only with the Tudors did England become a textile manufacturing country. Elizabeth I, pursuing a policy begun under Edward VI, took advantage of the religious persecution in France and offered sanctuary to Flemish Protestant and French Huguenot weavers. The Weavers' Guild became the most powerful in London, and a law of 1666 required that a dead person must be buried in a woollen garment.

Britain gave its own place names to famous woollens such as the soft hairy tweeds woven of thick loosely spun yarn and the sturdy worsteds of a tight twist that gave a long-wearing cloth. As a reminder of England's staple trade the Lord Chancellor has sat on a woolsack when presiding in the House of Lords since the fourteenth century reign of Edward III, although today the sack is only symbolic, taking the form of a properly upholstered divan.

Cotton also came to England in Elizabethan times. The art of making cotton cloth moved westward from India across northern Africa with the Arabs and in the ninth century the Moors brought it into Spain. But it was Sir Francis Drake's capture of a Portuguese merchantman in the India trade that first made Indian cottons fashionable in Europe and brought calico, gingham, chintz and fine muslins, all named for their eastern sources, into the western world's textile vocabulary. England went into cotton manufacture, as did France, adding French names for new cotton yarns and fabrics such as lisle (from Lisle, now spelled Lille), batiste (from Baptiste, its inventor), lawn (from Laon), chambray (from Cambrai) and corduroy (Corde du Roi).

Machines

Long before machines transformed the textile industry, the unmarried girls who were the "spinsters" of the family, and their fathers and brothers who did the weaving on the family loom, were unable to keep up with the demand. By the fourteenth century a primitive form of factory production by journeymen and apprentices in a master's shop was formed, with woollens woven on hand looms in Bristol and worsteds in Norwich. In 1663 some 40,000 women and children in and around London were "throwing" silk (twisting and doubling it to the needed thickness) for the weavers.

In 1685 the revocation of the Edict of Nantes deprived French Protestants of the freedom of religion and in the next 15 years some 750,000 emigrated to England, many of them skilled weavers and cloth workers. Thousands of French linen workers settled in Ireland where one of them, Louis Crommelin, an expert in linen production from the growing of flax to the finished cloth, established an Irish linen industry that still thrives today.

By the eighteenth century the surge in cloth production for export, combined with Britain's plentiful resources in iron for machinery and coal for power, made textiles part of the industrial revolution. Inventors appeared, sometimes in unlikely places: Dr. Edmund Cartwright, who invented the first power loom, was a country clergyman in Leicestershire who had never invented anything nor ever seen a weaver at work, but on a holiday he had heard some Manchester businessmen talk of the need to speed up weaving to keep up with the cotton yarn being produced by the new spinning machines.

An American counterpart was Eli Whitney, the Yale graduate who was tutoring a plantation owner's children when he invented his cotton gin, which mechanically separated the fibers from the seeds. Some inventors like Whitney made little or no money out of their inventions and some were persecuted as a threat to the textile workers' livelihood. John Kay, who invented the flying shuttle, was driven out of England to France to die in poverty.

Kay's shuttle flew back and forth at the pull of a cord, freeing one of the weaver's hands to push up the weft. This acceleration of weaving in 1733 was followed by Lewis Paul's carding machine in 1748 which increased the production of fibers ready for spinning. The spinners, working at wheels that had hardly changed since the fif-

teenth century, fell behind. Then within the decade 1765–75 came James Hargreaves' spinning jenny, Richard Arkwright's spinning frame, finally Samuel Crompton's mule spinner, which combined the best features of both in a machine that drew, twisted and wound the yarn in a single operation. All these devices were designed for cotton but were soon adapted to wool.

At the Paris Exposition of 1801 Joseph Marie Jacquard exhibited his great pattern weaving loom on which a complex design could be set at the start and the warp and weft threads automatically produced it. Himself a silk weaver, Jacquard designed his loom to speed the weaving of the French silk damasks. But his principle has been found adaptable to other textiles and problems of pattern weaving. English cotton and linen weavers changed to the new loom and the weavers of Paisley in Scotland made the weaving of patterned woollen shawls a new industry. More recently Jacquard's system of punched cards and needles to guide the interchange of colored threads has been converted to copper plates and electric current.

The new machines, expensive and power driven, spelled the end of the cottage industry and the handicraft way of life. The exploitation of women and children as cheap labor in the textile factories occupied reformers throughout the nineteenth century. The movement of populations to the factory towns created a new urban poor class which the textile industry clothed in cheap woollens made of reclaimed rag wool, called "shoddy."

American Textiles

New England followed a parallel industrial development from the cottage industry of colonial times to an explosive growth of factory towns humming with machines, turning southern cotton and western wool into northern finished goods. In the 1680s woollen mills were producing cloth in three Massachusetts towns and by 1750 the industry was seen as a threat to Britain. The British parliament's attempts to restrict competition aroused fierce resentment and textiles were more provocation than tea for the American Revolution.

In 1793 Samuel Slater, a recent immigrant from England, built Cartwright looms from memory and set up the Slater mill in Pawtucket, Rhode Island (today it is a museum and the looms still operate). Americans also contributed their own inventions: from 1823 the Lowell loom designed by Paul Moody, the first to use a belt instead of iron gears to transmit power, became the standard power loom of New England's cloth mills.

George Washington had admired the quality of broadcloth produced in a Hartford mill in 1780 and in the same decade the first cotton mill went into operation in Beverly, Massachusetts. There were 8,000 spindles turning in New England in 1807, 350,000 in 1820, and more than five million at the start of the Civil War.

Test Tube Threads

The next revolution was chemical: man by-passed nature to produce weaving yarns out of test tubes, as the English scientist Robert Hooke prophesied in 1664 in his classic work, *Micrographia*. Two centuries later, when Europe's silk manufacture was being wiped out by a silkworm disease, the young French scientist Hilaire de Chardonnet, working with Louis Pasteur on the disease, evolved a method of dissolving cellulose from wood pulp into a viscous fluid, expelling it through a jet and hardening the resulting filament by evaporation of the solvent. Manufacturing began in 1889.

Three other methods were developing at the same time, the Bemberg and viscose processes using wood pulp with different solvents and the third beginning with waste cotton fibers after ginning to make acetate. Rayon, as it was eventually named, became the first commercially successful synthetic fiber for textiles and ultimately numerous other uses, and the viscose method using alkali and carbon bisulfide became the leading process for inexpensive silk-like fabrics. Bemberg silk, produced with copper oxide and ammonium and stretched to considerable fineness, was found useful for hosiery and sheer fabrics. Acetate, which was resistant to stains and creasing and could be plasticized with heat for a moiré effect, continued in use for upholstery and drapery fabrics, dress fabrics such as faille, crepe and taffeta, textured knits and lingerie.

Rayon was not a created but a regenerated natural fiber: it began and ended with cellulose. Other efforts were made to create textile fibers with soybeans, corn, seaweed, even whale meat (by the Japanese). Casein from milk was actually made into fibers to supplement wool during World War II but unfortunately when wet it smelled like sour milk.

The authentic chemical revolution of man-made fibers began with nylon, a true creation from the molecular level. A decade of experiments produced nylon bristles in 1938 and nylon yarn for hosiery in 1940. The nylon family expanded into dozens of variations, mainly derived from coal tar or petroleum and built by complex processes into molecular structures unknown in nature.

The new fibers had the advantages of continuous supply and uniformity; they were invulnerable to natural enemies such as moths and mildew and their properties could be varied almost at will by changes in the molecular structure. But unlike cotton and wool which when wet hold about their own weight in water, nylon takes up only 25 percent water. This was quickly recognized as an advantage ("drip-dry") but gave difficulty to the dyers.

Elasticity was another problem. The four great natural fibers are built of long-chain polymers that stretch in only one direction and recover their original length when released, but the man-elaborated polymers when overstretched by wetting or heating might shrink in distorted ways or not at all. This was overcome by a heating process that hardened the yarn, limiting its elasticity but guaranteeing that it would return to its original shape; out of this grew the convenient "permanent press."

The warmth combined with lightness of silks and certain fine woollens was another challenge. The natural yarns owe their warmth to their porousness which traps air between the fibers to form a natural insulation. This problem was met by bulking, that is, by twisting and heating the yarn to form a hollow spiral capable of trapping air. The spiral was also elastic and lightweight, and a new class of synthetic fibers was born which closely matched the natural ones in their three most desirables properties of warmth, lightness, elasticity.

Spurred by the competition, the producers of natural yarns developed their own processes: woollens and other fabrics were rendered crease-resistant, shrink-controlled and water-repellent by chemical treatment, and woollen yarns were also rendered "bulky." In consequence textiles whether of natural or synthetic yarns or an inventive combination of both have taken on a chemical complexity unimaginable to the spinners and weavers of a century ago.

Textile Medicine

The chemistry of the textile world has brought new problems to the medical profession, mainly dermatologic. Although no statistics are available, according to the Allergy Foundation physicians are seeing an increasing number of cases of contact dermatitis, a large proportion of which seem to be associated with textiles, as often with natural as with synthetic fabrics. Dyes, the processes with which fabrics are finished and the soaps and detergents with which they are washed are now so many and various that they defy most efforts to isolate a particular allergen. One preventive measure recommended is to wash the garment thoroughly before wearing.

The flammability of some synthetics, a property especially of downy robes and nightwear, was dealt with by legislation. The industry has made progress with flame-retardant fibers to meet this hazard.

Occupational health hazards to workers in the early textile factories were difficult to separate from general poor health resulting from long hours, unhygienic working and living conditions and malnutrition, but high rates of respiratory diseases including tuberculosis were evident well into this century. Most of the incidental health problems of poverty and poor working conditions have since abated.

"Woolsorters' disease" was identified as anthrax, but "weaver's cough," long associated with cotton workers, remains an industry problem. It has been diagnosed as byssinosis, a form of pneumoconiosis ascribed to the inhalation of untreated cotton dust. Ventilation systems have not reduced the dust particles (7–5 μ diameter) to the required 1 mg./cc.

A $250,000 research project initiated in 1969 by the American Textile Manufacturers Institute and executed by the Industrial Health Foundation produced a work practices standard. The program involves identifying areas of the plants according to degree of risk, screening and periodic rechecking of workers for respiratory and pulmonary function, education to avoid unnecessary exposure and the use of respirators where high risk cannot be avoided.

Textiles Today

A quarter century of dramatic change has brought shuttleless looms, including a Japanese machine that weaves by jets of water, color matching of dyes by computer, machines that knit at dizzying speed without an operator, brightly lighted textile plants that spread over acres of ground in single story structures instead of the dark, prisonlike mills that still dominate many towns.

Clothing is still the largest textile user, with home furnishing second. The 1969 controversy over skirt length made women reluctant to buy new clothes and resulted in a disastrous year for the clothing industry; currently the "layered look" has kept looms humming. A fall in home building has repercussions in the textile mills. A few large manufacturers have expanded into making every kind of color coordinated fabric for the house, as well as for its inhabitants. Most American textiles are produced by small, often family concerns; of about 1,000 companies only five produce more than $400 million worth of fabrics a year.

Among their hundred of uses (from typewriter ribbons to book bindings, book covers, even some books, from umbrellas and window shades to tea bags and life preservers) the most challenging textiles to produce were those for the Apollo astronauts. Teflon coated yarn and Fiberglas fabric protect against high fire hazard in an oxygen atmosphere; aluminized and other fabrics give reflective insulation against extreme temperatures. Layers of various nylons, some neoprene coated, some elastic (spandex) provide specific protections both outside and within the space vehicle in garments that must be highly mobile and relatively lightweight while carrying a complete life support system. Yet the space age bows to an ancient natural fiber and its harmony with the human body: the one garment that goes under all this and against the skin, labeled the "constant wear garment" and the "comfort layer" is made of cotton.

Summing Up

By textile historian L. Lamprey: The cloth makers have not only been part of history, they have made history.

WHAT WILL HAPPEN TO THE GRAY FLANNEL SUIT?

Moira Johnston

Some years ago, a writer titled her book *Fashion Is Spinach*. Immediately the phrase caught on and became an easy way to label fashion as one of life's absurdities. But students of history discover that style trends emerge over and over in similar patterns. To the perceptive, fashion is not spinach but a sign of the times and often significant in its sociopsychological implications.

As the American frontier spread westward, settlers pulled a sameness of dress across the land as they moved from one cleared patch of ground to the next. On this continent there never have been the centuries of isolation needed to develop richly individual regional dress. Today, the drab clothes of the West are universal, dulling the brilliant saffrons, batiks, and indigo of other cultures.

At first, standardized Western dress—essentially the suit—spread around the world as a prime symbol of progress and industrialization. The 19th century British suit brought clothes to the greatest separation of the sexes ever—with men, upright phallic symbols and women, glorified tea cozies. Now the development of an international dress parallels the supranationalizing of the world politically and economically—the direction many futurists see as the only way to go. The world of the future will undoubtedly be influenced by Asian and African cultures that, in spite of the suit, still have some color and sensuality left to feed into the sartorial melting pot. But, essentially, nations will have to lose themselves in the larger idiom. International costume will probably express the new set of values now being altered to fit the postindustrial age. The traditional Western ethic, like its clothes, will probably be too old fashioned to work. The earth's ecological crisis is already forcing a compromise between the manipulated, architectural shapes of the West and the natural flow and fatalism of Eastern robes.

From "What Will Happen to the Gray Flannel Suit?" *Journal of Home Economics,* Vol. 64, No. 8, November 1972, pp. 5–12. Drawings are omitted. (Drawn from *Figleafing through History: The Dynamics of Dress,* Moira Johnston and Christie Harris, Atheneum, 1971.) Reprinted with permission of the publisher.

But will humans ever be willing—or able—to give up altogether the little differences, the nuances that continue to make every person, town, city, nation, and civilization visually distinctive? Will history, with its ego building tales of territorial victories and gorgeous ethnic costume be a threat to a globalizing world? I don't think so. For humans haven't changed much. At times of upheaval, people have always clutched traditional clothes like a security blanket, giving volatile emotions something familiar to focus on . . . to hold on to. People have always found the confidence to face the future in the clothes of the past. And though forms will change, universal principles of dress will continue.

Historic Identity

This persistence of historic identity in the face of change struck me last year in Europe. All the young people of both sexes in America, England, and France were wearing essentially the same costume—flared pants, long skinny knit sweaters or shirts, and wide leather belts. They had all responded to one of the most basic universals—the compulsion to identify with what seems admirable. It's the dynamic force that has spread the business suit around the world and puts small boys into cowboy hats. It's the force that ties the army, the school, the team, the office, the nation together visually. And it is the force that has made bell bottoms, belts, and knit tops—originally an American style—an international uniform of the young.

But in each country at the time of my visit something was spontaneously changing the effect. And that something was history. In the States, the outfit was raw, like the frontier. It was a direct and dishevelled challenge to the impeccable dress of the establishment. Minimal wardrobes of jeans and shirts, worn until they fell apart, were a sacrificial purge of parents' overstuffed closets. The young were wearing like a hair shirt the accumulated guilt of a rich society. They'd gone back to the honest clothes, the cooperative effort, the closeness to the earth of their own frontier, and with jeans, boots, and belts slung on like Western gunbelts, were throwing this earlier image of America back in the faces of parents who had apparently lost sight of the founding values. And girls with masculine hip-slung belts and no brassieres were belligerently deemphasizing the ancient fertile image of lavish breasts and hips and defined waists, groping for a redefinition of sex roles.

Last year, in France, I saw a different trend in dress. The sleekness of the cut and fit, the sophistication of the colors, and the elegance of the belt lifted the look beyond social comment and revolt to the French tradition of taste and fashion. The spirit of the 18th century salons was alive and well on the Boulevard St. Germaine. There was still more concern for refinement than for raw innovation. The tight top and pants that left no confusion about sex

and the polished buckle that weighted the belt down in front like a sassy fertility girdle showed that the French young were not involved in Women's Lib. They were still using clothes to play the old seductive roles and to advertise to the world that France still cares about keeping up appearances.

In England, the fluid shirts and pants of both sexes were just a base for the romantic flow of long hair, long capes, rich blue and maroon velvets that gave any group of young people queueing up for a rock concert the appearance of a medieval procession. The English young have been left hanging without the confident identity the empire gave their parents. In a search for alternatives, the English youth had dipped unconsciously into their own medieval past. Their low-slung belts were worn like sword belts.

In all three countries, clothes seemed a dynamic assertion of nationalism, of individuality, in the face of what seems an irresistible tide of global uniformity. I see this urge to resist a collective image even within San Francisco where little microcultures manifest themselves in the Ivy League suits of bankers; in the hand-decorated levis of a Berkeley student, in the white gloves and British tweed suits of the ladies; in the trousers of the black school boys whose mothers won't let them wear jeans because jeans "look poor"; in the lacquered beehive hairdos and toreador pants; and in the calico sacks of adolescent earth mothers. Beyond the uniform of slacks, knits, and belts is this seemingly chaotic range of styles. But this is just the kind of clue that indicates we are in the midst of a social revolution that is very big and very deep. What we're seeing on our streets, what San Francisco (which gave birth to the costumes of counterculture and student activists) is experiencing, is the chaotic period that some futurists consider inevitable as people respond to change at different speeds.

A Glance Backward

But the chaos falls into order if we look back into history, for history shows us patterns that seem to repeat themselves at times of transition. I have detected three forces that motivate people in their manner of dress. Some cling to tradition, hanging on the old ways of dressing. Others hunt desperately for alternatives to what seems a bankrupt present and uncertain future. These persons search through the past, grab at mystical cults, the dress of other cultures, and escape into fantasy. But a third force, the future, pushes through spontaneously. And most of us become schizophrenic trying to integrate in our style of dress all the conflicting forces of our society. We tend to end up with the kind of ambiguous statement Dinah Shore made on television last season in her long midi skirts, split up the front, revealing hot pants. It was an assertion of female dependency and seduction fighting it out with liberation before our eyes. This confusion of clinging, escape, and change always leads to extravagant and exciting periods of dress such as we have today.

One of the earliest, biggest changes in dress took place when men shifted from hunting to farming. Men had always hunted and had always worn furs and skins. At the time, farming didn't seem much of an improvement. Settled towns were vulnerable, and the whole way of life lacked the old excitement and stimulation of the hunt Men now had woven fabrics and rectangles of wool and linen. But they were reluctant to give up their skins. So they went to the enormous trouble of making a fake fleece that combined both. They took loosely woven cloth and pulled tufts of real sheep or goat wool through it in horizontal rows, creating a shaggy cloth called "kaunakes." It had the look, feel, smell, and bulk of the real thing but used the new technology of weaving, too. It helped them get through the neolithic transition.

Compare that with the popularity of fake furs today. The postwar prestige of mink stoles shows that fur has continued as a prime status symbol. And although the killing of animals to drape women in pelts is beginning to seem immoral, downright primitive, and a threat to the balance of nature,* the need for the status associations of fur is so strong that a technology that can produce a moonsuit bends its talents to duplicating leopard, lamb, and chinchilla in manmade fibers.** They are our kaunakes. In the same way, the new plastics are meant to be poured, molded, and bonded, but we are emotionally unready to leave weaving behind. So we go to the excruciating trouble of spinning polyester threads and weaving simulations of cotton, linen, and wool the neolithic farmwoman was weaving 10,000 years ago. It is still difficult for us to feel affection for a vinyl tunic. Thus we accept the new only in the guise of the old.

Rome and the Toga

Looking back through history, we see that another great and painful point of transition occurred with the decline of Rome. The end of Rome was the end of the classical world and the end of the domination of the earliest civilizations ringing the Mediterranean. The state religions and bureaucracy had become hollow and impersonal, and people searched desperately for a way out of the emptiness. They imported mystical religions from the East, dressing one cult in complete Persian regalia. The Christian sect hid in catacombs and took on the humble tunics of the servant class to look like "the servants of the Lord," and often replaced the toga with the rectangular pallium wrap that had become a symbol of asceticism. As they began to gain strength and courage, they wore their clothes as a form of defiance against decadent Romans who were finding their escapes in makeup and jewels,

*See "Spotted Cats in Trouble," pp. 198–199.
**See "It's Fun and Fashionable to be Fake," pp. 200–201.

blond wigs, lovers, silks, and astrology. Officials, feeling the threat, imposed the toga with renewed vigor. For centuries, the toga had been the visible symbol that had rallied Romans and motivated them to greatness. The establishment felt that to lose the toga—the pride of every citizen—was to lose the fiber of Rome. Augustus tried to force its wearing by law. Consuls and officials throughout the empire paraded the toga with increasing determination. And the toga grew bigger, more complicated, more visible impressive—like a monumental arch. But all that the insistence achieved was more alienation, for as the toga became more elaborate, working men could scarcely afford it, could not work in it, and, without servants, could not even put it on. They stored their togas away in chests, bringing them out only for ceremonial occasions, and by the 4th century A.D. stopped wearing the toga altogether. No longer a live garment, the toga had shrunk to little more than a jeweled ceremonial scarf.

While the toga was weakening, the clothes of the future were creeping in—the wool cloaks and bright plaids of the barbarians of the northern frontier. Roman women were importing blond German hair for their wigs. Soldiers were adopting the barbarian trouser. These trends, I think, are valid clues to the end of the Roman Empire. For the power to influence dress has always pulsed out from the centers of political, economic, and cultural power. And the appearance in Rome of barbarian dress meant that there had been a subtle shift of power from Rome to the North and to the struggling new religion. Christian robes and barbarian pants show that the impressive facade of Rome had begun to crack several centuries before historians admit to the fall of Rome. And reviewing it now, I get a strong sense of *déja`vu.*

Transition in the Middle Ages

In the 14th and 15th centuries, we come to another transition that might compare with our own. Call it Renaissance, Reformation, Age of Science and Reason, or what-have-you . . . it was a shift from the other worldly superstition of the medieval soul, from volatile emotions and fears held in check by costumed spectacle, and religion made real by church statues carved in the fashionable clothes of the day. The transition then was a shift to the outer-directed, rational humanism of the Industrial Age.

It grew out of the gloom of dark European forests and the specter of death. Towns were replacing castles, guns had made armor obsolete, trade was replacing war; and the Black Death had wiped out what little confidence remained after the disaster of the Crusades, which had undermined the strength of the Church. The old way was failing, and people tried to hold on to it a little longer.

The Church, one of the pillars of the Middle Ages, increased its production of ceremonial vestments, for threatened symbols tend spontaneously to reassert themselves before they give up. Capes and chasubles reached a peak of elaboration, as gold and silk embroideries turned them into works of art, countering the secular threat of the Renaissance.

The old gear of the knight was dragged out, exaggerated and distorted, and paraded up and down the land in public ceremonials that turned the waning Middle Ages into a poignant Mardi Gras. Never have so many fountains spewed so much wine nor have so many birds flown out of so many room-sized pies. The knight's old heraldic motifs, which had identified and rallied him in battle, were blown up like supergraphics and spilled over into everything—wives' dresses, servants' clothes, banners, pennons, canopies, stockings.

Parti-color, the old divisions of color in the coat-of-arms that identified the families that had married into the knight's family, now turned up in men's hose, with one leg green, the other red-and-yellow stripes. The skin-protecting underwear of the knight came out from under the armor as doublet and hose that now dressed shoemakers and merchants. And knights in great suits of plate armor, engraved and polished to a dazzle, were hoisted up on plumed and caparisoned horses at tournaments that turned war into flamboyant ritual. The new armor was more impressive than the old coats of mail, but it was no longer functional for war. It grew heavier and more awkward, and gradually clanked into retirement, much as the toga had faded into retirement. And as the business suit may do in the future. For when garments lose their vital function and become ceremonial, we're headed for a new way of dressing.

Despite all this glorification of knightly symbols, the Renaissance was pushing through. There was a new interest in man, new wealth, great social competition. And after centuries of medieval robes that enshrouded the figure, the desire to display man was becoming irresistible. Hose and doublet fitted like skin, and display became more and more extravagant as heraldry, fantasy, and Renaissance ego and wealth fused together. Loose medieval sleeves grew into huge trailing sleeves that swept back like butterfly wings. Poulaine shoes stretched out to ridiculous lengths, and modest veils stretched out on yard-high pointed hennins and flaunted from the tips like banners. There were tournaments, masked balls, ceremonial entries in which diplomats paraded into cities with huge retinues all dressed in cloth-of-gold.

But not all the lavish display could keep the Renaissance from emerging. In fact much of the ostentation *was* Renaissance. But the spectacle gave people something reassuring on which to focus wild emotions during the transition.

I do believe strongly in the social functions of clothes. They communicate, motivate, attract or separate, show discipline or rebellion. And though these fantastic clothes of the 14th and 15th centuries had moved from function, in the utilitarian sense, to a ritual role, they were still working hard to control the chaos that was always hovering.

The Influence Today

I think clothes are doing the same things today. I see the power to influence clothes pulsing out now from colleges, communes, and the street; from the working class; from Blacks; from England, California, Peking, shifting from the establishment here as Rome shifted from its bureaucrats. I see our traditional institutions—municipal governments and IBM—fighting like Augustus to hold the line on our toga—the business suit—with rules and regulations that restrict long hair and jeans at work. I see the President of the United States reverting to 19th century palace guard uniforms for the White House guard. I see the suit becoming a hollow shell as men lose faith in the complex ethic of work, technological progress, manipulation of nature, utilitarianism, and material success the suit has symbolized. They toss it aside as disaffected Romans did the toga and search for alternatives. Today we see strung-out hair, Indian headbands, donkey beads, amulets, embroidered vests, and knitted ponchos. Will any of them prove to be the barbaric plaids and Christian palliums of our future? The three forces—tradition, escape, and the future—are all here keeping each other in balance, helping us through to a new age.

Look back on the last 5 years: First, the young people of this continent joined in a massive migration from reality, with drugs, clothes, and music that broke all the rules their daddies played by. Young people involved their senses in color and texture, something Galileo warned us against over 300 years ago. They stripped the structure out of clothes—the unnatural silhouettes that were one of the best ways the West had of showing how well it could twist nature to new forms. Rather than working life away, the young celebrated it in outrageous costumes. They aimed in every way at what has now been called the "new naturalism," and expressed it all with clothes—their desire to get back to the land and nature; to take the artificiality out of relations between the sexes; to return to tribal community; to let themselves be moved by feeling rather than reason; to find more pleasure in display of found objects such as feathers and shells than in possessions such as stocks and country clubs.

At first youth looked absurd, because our eyes simply could not accept a way of dressing that was not scrubbed, neat, plain, and practical. But gradually their way began to take on a coherence and pattern of its own.

Then, some women over 25 began tentatively to try out the new styles, occasionally wearing pantsuits to cocktail parties and accepting the soft bras that turned breasts from architectural monuments back into mammary glands. Men toyed with color and pattern in ties and shirts. On this continent people began to understand that the suit was not essential to social and business functioning; that drab colors and hampering skirts were not instinctive; that men had been *men* in past cultures in plumes, wigs, and blazing jewels. A new idea was groping for expression in clothes.

The threat was real, and the establishment had to respond, as it always does. The reaction set in several seasons ago. Fashion proclaimed a return to the conservative suit and to the madras and seersucker sports coat of the fifties. In women's clothes, the garments that could be considered American classics—blazers, pleated skirts, shirtwaist dresses, plaid coats—were revived. The thirties and forties were shaken out and paraded again.

As in the 15th century, the symbols of the old order were exaggerated: wide-lapeled, pinch-waisted suits became parodies. President Nixon and his aids—on their visit to China—sold the American way with an impenetrable wall of dark worsted. The draggy skirts, come-hither red lips, and frizzed hair of pre-Women's-Lib days were being flounced around.

"The party's over," and "sanity returns," the reports said. And *Women's Wear Daily* recorded the colors of the cashmere sweater sets Jackie Onassis had bought.

A Look Ahead

But if I have a premise about clothes, it's that they are the outward expression of the inner condition. If this is so, then the party is not over. For though the conservative reaction dominates fashion right now, even its intensity proves the threat is still there. Clothes are still saying "loud and clear" that the dress of the Western world has been profoundly changed, as survival forces us to soften our commitment to progress at any cost. Jeans, symbol

of alienation from the business suit, are now the most coveted garment in the world. Levis sell for $90 on the Russian black market. Organic forms wake a slumbering need for contact with nature's rich vocabulary of pattern and sense pleasure. Ancient status symbols—rare furs, jewels, and gold—are under attack as a squandering of the earth's resources. And now that pants, bodyshirts, and miniskirts have given women the freedom and pride of body that Christian morality denied them; will they go back willingly to constriction and limitations?

It may be, as some students of counterculture claim, that by avoiding the business suit and its obligations, youth avoids the rites of passage into manhood and clings to adolescence.* But unless the adult world begins to look more appealing, will the young give up the jeans and shirts they were raised in?

Hippie dress or Levi's, though, have not taken over the world, but they are the cutting edge of revolution, going to excess as revolutionary dress always does to make its point. The extremes may already be past, and even the passion for jeans could subside.

But the shabby trousers that rallied the "sans-culottes" of the French Revolution were cleaned up after the revolution and have been with us ever since. Homespun Christian robes have had more power in the long run than the toga. Obviously we cannot say for certain what's ahead. All we do know is that in our time the young caught the vibrations of a new idea first and expressed it in their own way. And I, for one, think the idea is here to stay. I believe that despite closetsful of somber suits all across the land today, by the end of this decade, the business suit will be something we will look back on with nostalgia and amusement.

*See p. 29 in "The Regalia of Ritual: Rites of Passage."

SUMPTUARY LEGISLATION IN FOUR CENTURIES

Joana W. Phillips and Helen K. Staley

In the four centuries from 1300 to 1700, "sumptuary regulation" in European countries and the American colonies underwent a period of growth, change, and decline. This discussion is based on a study of the sumptuary legislation and other regulations pertaining to personal appearance in the English Colonies in North America and in Western Europe to include Italy, German, Switzerland, France, and England. Research for the study was undertaken in the Library of Congress in Washington, D.C., in the archives of the Virginia and North Carolina legislatures, in the libraries of the University of North Carolina

in Chapel Hill, the Woman's College in Greensboro, Duke University in Durham, and in the libraries in the cities of Raleigh and Greensboro.

Definitions

Regulations which attempt to control the personal and individual expenditure of funds are sumptuary in char-

From "Sumptuary Legislation in Four Centuries." *Journal of Home Economics,* Vol. 53, No. 8, October 1961, pp. 673–677. Reprinted by permission of the publisher.

acter and have been termed *sumptuary laws*. Webster defines the term *sumptuary* as, "relating to or regulating expenditure," and the term *sumptuary law* as:

> . . . a law to prevent extravagance in private life by limiting the expenditure for clothing, food, furniture, etc., a law designed to regulate habits primarily on moral or religious grounds, but regarded as justified under the police powers of the state.[1]

Sumptuary law and *sumptuary legislation*—any regulation concerning personal appearance which carried a penalty to be enforced by state or church bodies.

Clothing—all forms of bodily ornamentation and portable articles which are worn or carried by a person, also decorations such as body painting or mutilations, ornaments, and garments.

Growth—the frequency of occurrence and the northwestward spread of sumptuary laws through Europe to America.

Change—in character as well as from simple to complex.

Decline—related to the strictness of enforcement and the frequency of occurrence of sumptuary regulations.

Historical Background

Historians have evidenced interest in this aspect of life in the Middle Ages and Renaissance period, primarily for its incidental sidelights on manners. A study of sumptuary laws of any age, however, offers insights into the economic, social, and spiritual concepts of a government, as well as the customs, dress, and furnishings of its people.[2]

Sumptuary laws originally encompassed the entire scheme of living and were enacted in an attempt to regulate excesses and extravagances of personal life in general.[3] There is evidence that such laws were used in ancient Greece.[4,5]

The first sumptuary law in regard to dress in Rome was passed in 215 B.C. and was directed against the extravagances of dress and jewelry.[6] The repeal of this law in 20 years typifies the fate of many of the personal regulations which followed through the centuries and which attempted to control, direct, or dictate the kind of garments and decorations which the populace could wear. Throughout history such laws were generally ignored, flagrantly opposed, only slightly enforced, and gradually became obsolete.[7]

There are few evidences available of sumptuary laws or diatribes against extravagances of dress during the Dark Ages. Laver says this is due, in all probability, to the fact that clothing was somewhat ragged and uncouth during that period.[8] It was Charlemagne who revived the use of sumptuary laws with decrees against dress and furniture during his reign.[9]

Moralists of the early Middle Ages took up the crusade once again against elegance and fashion. As civilization developed with the Renaissance movement, Italy appeared to become the first European country to make frequent use of sumptuary laws in an effort to control excessive display and extravagance. Soon, all of Europe was caught in the Renaissance movement and made use of this method of controlling expenditure.

The great mass of sumptuary laws in Europe occurred between 1300 and 1700—the period covered by this study.* During the early part of these four centuries, the simplicity of the Medieval governmental structure favored sumptuary legislation. Government was a paternalistic ruling body that sought to regulate the lives of its subjects not only legally and politically but morally and spirtually as well.[10] Sumptuary legislation was a pronounced expression of this concept of government.

The church, too, exhibited powerful control in the matter of extravagance.[11] In part because the church was intricately bound up in the affairs of the state as well as in the daily lives of the people.[12] The church was, however, very sumptuous and extravagant itself.

The Reformation brought a change in this ecclesiastical sumptuosity, as well as contributed to a sharpening of conscience among the people, but it was not a strong force in originating sumptuary laws.[13] Long before the influences of Protestantism were felt, sumptuary laws had existed as a normal part of the legislation.[14] The sumptuary laws were not products of the Protestant Reformation, nor were they directly church originated. Devised by secular ruling bodies, they were secular in origin.

Sumptuary laws were seldom as effective as the governing bodies might have desired.[15] Whatever the motives behind them, they were largely ignored by the people and often by the lawmakers themselves. As this approach to the limitation of extravagance spread with the westward flow of civilization, sumptuary laws appeared in Italy,

1. *Webster's New International Dictionary,* 2d edition. Springfield, Mass.: G. & C. Merriam Co., 1959.
2. Kent Roberts Greenfield, *Sumptuary Law in Nurnberg.* Baltimore: The Johns Hopkins Press, 1918, p. 8.
3. Sumptuary Laws, *Encyclopedia Americana,* 1955 edition, Vol. XXVI, p. 18.
4. Sumptuary Laws, *Everyman's Encyclopedia,* 3d edition, Vol. XII, p. 112.
5. Sumptuary Laws, *The New International Encyclopedia,* 2d edition, Vol. XXI, p. 666.
6. *Encyclopedia Americana,* op. cit., p. 18.
7. Ibid.

8. James Laver, *Clothes.* New York: Horizon Press, 1953, p. 30.
9. *Encyclopedia Americana,* loc. cit.
10. John Martin Vincent, *Costume and Conduct in the Laws of Basel, Bern, and Zurich,* 1370–1800. Baltimore: The Johns Hopkins Press, 1935, p. 1.
11. Greenfield, op. cit., p. 11.
12. Vincent, op. cit., p. 2.
13. Greenfield, op. cit., p. 25.
14. *Ibid.,* p. 12.
15. Greenfield, *op. cit.,* p. 134; Vincent, *op. cit.,* p. 4; *Encyclopedia Americana,* loc. cit.; Quentin Bell, *On Human Finery,* New York: A.A. Wynn, Inc., 1949, p. 19.
*See "Clothing Signals" by Desmond Morris, p. 9.

Switzerland, Germany, France, the British Isles, and the English Colonies in North America.

Review of Literature

References to legislation of a sumptuary nature are widespread throughout history texts and books of costume. There are, nevertheless, very few books that deal with the subject at any length. A serious search in the literature available for this study revealed that little specific information existed locally for the student of sumptuary regulations.

The subject of sumptuary legislation is intricately connected with the subject of clothing. In an effort to portray the various facets of clothing, authors in the fields of economics, philosophy, sociology, and psychology have developed and discussed theories of dress, and have included the subject of sumptuary legislation in their studies. Their views, as well as those of historians, have offered insight in the use and purposes of sumptuary laws.

Three authors—Greenfield, Vincent, and Baldwin—provided the primary sources of reference for this study. Their works were restricted to translation of the recorded laws from the original language into English and the interpretation of such regulations in light of their special interests. These books dealt with sumptuary legislation in particular and are valued by students of clothing for their detailed descriptions of costume.

Baldwin[16] presented a complete review of the sumptuary laws of England from the time of Edward III to James I. Her study made possible a more complete compilation of the laws of England than of any other country considered in this study and provided the background for consideration of the changing character of sumptuary laws. Also, Baldwin's monograph provided the background for understanding the sumptuary laws of the English Colonies in North America.

Greenfield's interest was directed toward an understanding of medieval governmental structure. His study of paternal government extended from the inception of Nurnberg in the eleventh century through the seventeenth century. The motives of the early laws were interpreted as the protection of morals, and those of later laws as that of maintaining class distinctions. He cited examples of legislation which demonstrated the strength of these motives. It was difficult, however, to relate the laws to their place in history or to each other, since no complete collection of laws appeared in his study.

Vincent's small volume is a condensation of materials found in the printed laws of Switzerland and the manuscript deposits in the archives of Basel, Bern, and Zurich. This, too, is a study in paternal government and is rich

in detailed information regarding the costumes of the times.

Historians of Colonial life in the seventeenth century supplied information which aided in the interpretation of laws recorded in the four English colonies considered in this study. These authors were in agreement that class distinctions existed in seventeeth century America, although they made no direct statements regarding sumptuary laws.

The collection of literature on the Blue Laws of Colonial America proved to be the most valuable source of information concerning the laws of a sumptuary nature which existed in the English Colonies in North America. Two Blue Laws, dated 1634 and 1676, respectively, were selected as representative of the type of controls which were attempted in the Colony of Connecticut and which were common to other New England settlements.

Plan of Procedure

Digests of 472 sumptuary laws and other regulations found in the literature were arranged by countries and in chronological sequence. Tables 1 and 2 are taken from this classification chart. The chart shows the span of sumptuary laws for the various countries, and table 3, the frequency of occurrence.

A study of the chart revealed eight classifications of stated or implied purposes for sumptuary regulations as they were used within each country:

1. *Maintenance of Class Distinctions*

Sumptuary laws enforced class distinctions by attempting to classify society through the medium of clothing. This classed social structure was considered natural and was accepted by society until the time of the French Revolution.

2. *Preservation of Morals*

Sumptuary laws supported moral motives by curbing luxuries when they were considered an evil. The government took for granted the right to check extravagances, since the desire for luxuries promoted immorality and crime in individuals. This presumably led to corruption of the state, thereby endangering its national existence.

3. *Protection of Home Industries*

Sumptuary laws often favored certain political and commercial interests. The wealth of a country hinged on keeping money within the country; therefore, foreign styles and foreign-made clothing were prohibited.

4. *Retaining Revenue for the State*

Sumptuary laws increased the amount of possible income to the state by restricting individual expenditure.

5. *Reduction of Government Expenses*

Sumptuary laws, by limiting extravagances, helped pre-

16. Frances E. Baldwin, *Sumptuary Legislation and Personal Regulation in England.* Baltimore: The Johns Hopkins Press, 1926.

vent poverty and thereby reduced the cost of the state of supporting the poor.

6. *Emergency Measures or War Acts*

Sumptuary laws sometimes appeared in times of emergencies as remedial measures against shortages or for individual protection.

7. *Consumer Protection*

Sumptuary laws were sometimes directed toward manufacturers or retailers of goods to meet certain standards or retain certain prices.

8. *Protection of Health*

Sumptuary laws curbed the use of commodities that were considered dangerous to health or morals. From ancient to modern times governments have felt a moral responsibility to control products which are considered dangerous to man.

The above purposes which occurred most frequently were:

1. Maintenance of class distinctions, which appeared as the most frequently used purpose in the total number of laws.

2. Protection of morals, which appeared as the most frequent concern in Italy, Germany, Switzerland, and the Colonies but of little concern in France and England.

3. Retaining revenue for the state and the reduction of government expenses, which appeared as the second most frequently used purpose in each country.

Summary of the Findings

From an analysis of the data, the following conclusions were drawn:

As fashion changes increased in frequency, there was an increase in the number of sumptuary laws, but the phenomenon of fashion had no direct influence on the purposes, spread, and decline of sumptuary laws.

The sumptuary laws spread westward as they developed in use and frequency in Europe.

The existence of other laws that have not been translated, or that have been lost, introduces possibilities of alterations in the patterns of development and spread of sumptuary laws.

Sumptuary laws increased in frequency as a financially strong middle class grew out of the development of commerce in Continental Europe and England.

The maintenance of class distinctions appeared as a purpose in the fourteenth century laws of Italy, when wealth began to increase, and appeared during the fifteenth century in Middle Europe.

The economic motive gained strength in sumptuary laws about 1500 when governments sought additional protection for home industries.

It was noted that the use of sumptuary laws began to decline in frequency of occurrence just as the economic motive appeared to be developing a marked degree of strength.

TABLE I

Sumptuary Laws of England

DATE	TO WHOM DIRECTED	RESTRICTIONS	PERMISSIONS — EXCEPTIONS DIRECTIONS FOR WEARING	PENALTIES
1406	All	Trimmings cut into the shapes of trefoils, roses, or similar devices Silver spurs		Same as 1402 law with this addition: All offenders in these matters were to be excommunicated from the Church
	Tailors	Forbidden to make the outlawed trimming shapes		Subject to punishment at the King's will
1420	All	Shall not gild on sheaths or metal	Except: On apparel of Barons, spurs of knights, ornaments of the Holy Church	Fine of ten times the value of the article Imprisonment for one year
1430	Common strumpets		To wear: Striped hoods	
1463	All	Jackets too short Shoes split at sides Shoes with peaks before and behind Cloth of gold Cloth with gold threads Any sable fur	Except: Lords and above	
		Figured velvet, silk, or satin Ermine Damask Satin	Except: Lords and their families Servants of the King's household	Fine of ten marks
		Cloth of velvet upon velvet	Except: Knights of the Garter	Fine of twenty marks
		Purple silk	Except: Knights of the Garter	Fine of ten pounds

TABLE 2
Sumptuary Laws of English Colonies in America

DATE	TO WHOM DIRECTED	RESTRICTIONS	PERMISSIONS — EXCEPTIONS DIRECTIONS FOR WEARING	PENALTIES
16??	Tanners in Connecticut Massachusetts		To put seals only in leather which has been properly tanned	
1634	All in Massachusetts Connecticut	Garments with lace trim Garments with silver, gold, or silk thread as trim Slashed garments Any cutwork, embroidery or needlework caps, bands, or rayles	Other than one slash per sleeve and one in back	Forfeiture
1636	All in Massachusetts		No one to make or sell any bone lace, or other lace to be worn on any garment or linen	Five shillings per yard
	Tailors in Massachusetts All in Massachusetts		No tailor shall set on any lace Small bindings of lace may be used on garments	Ten shillings for each offense
1634	All in Massachusetts Connecticut	No garments with immoderate great sleeves Slashes Immoderate great rayles Longewings	Those who have garments with lace on them may wear them except for those prohibited	
1639	All in Massachusetts Connecticut	Clothes ornamented with lace	No one to make, buy, or sell any manner of lace	

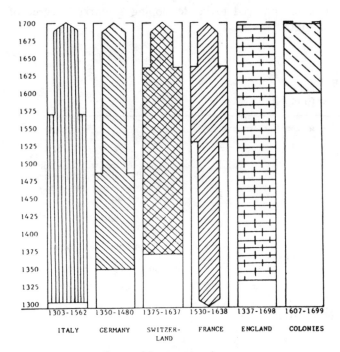

Span of Sumptuary Laws

TABLE 3
Frequency of Occurrence of Sumptuary Laws by 25-Year Spans

YEAR	ITALY	GERMANY	SWITZERLAND	FRANCE	ENGLAND	COLONIES	ALL COUNTRIES
1675–1700					2	2	4
1650–1674					3	19	22
1625–1649			37	10	4	23	74
1600–1624			4		7	6	17
1575–1599					38		38
1550–1574	4		4	19	10		37
1525–1549	3		3	20	34		60
1500–1524	4				37		41
1475–1499		13	5		16		34
1450–1474	3		7		28		38
1425–1449					1		1
1400–1424	1				23		24
1375–1399	3		14		1		18
1350–1374	1	21			27		49
1325–1349	7				2		9
1300–1324	6						6
Totals.....	32	34	74	49	233	50	472

The sumptuary laws of England were different in development from those of Continental Europe because of certain political, social and economic differences in history.

Although the sumptuary laws of England began at approximately the same date as those of Italy, the conclusion that the laws spread in a westward direction is maintained because the use of sumptuary laws as a type of governmental control increased as European civilization spread westward.

Impending or existing states of war affected sumptuary laws indirectly but caused no significant changes in their growth, spread, and decline.

Sumptuary regulations were short-lived in the English Colonies in North America because a decline had begun in Continental Europe and England about 1600 and resulted in a change in character and a virtual disappearance of such laws by 1700.

The economic trends of the seventeenth century were so well established and had gained such momentum that no effort could save the use of sumptuary laws from declining before the forces of free trade, democratic rule, and individual self-assertion.

The concentration of sumptuary laws in the Colonies of Massachusetts and Connecticut indicated that the Puritan movement had a measure of influence in their use.

Sumptuary laws were legislative acts designed to control personal expenditure and habits, but they reflected social and economic forces and changes that characterize the four centuries of this study.

After 1700, sumptuary laws changed in character from a concept of personal regulation by legislative groups to one of protection of public welfare.

OUR ANCESTORS AS FASHION PLATES

Peter F. Copeland

From early colonial times, military uniforms of our fore-fathers developed side by side with the high fashions of our distant matriarchs.

It is reported that Maurice de Saxe, Louis XV's German marshal of France, remarked as he lay upon his deathbed, "Life Doctor, is but a dream, and I've had a fine one!" A good portion of the dream of this military genius—aside from the wine and women with which he indulged himself in prodigious quantities—was involved in the design of military uniforms. In his remarkable little book, *Reveries on the Art of War* (1757), Saxe railed against the ridiculous military fashions of his period, and spent a good deal of time designing an infantry uniform surprisingly like the type adopted by the armies of Europe some 150 years later.

His labors, of course, were in vain. Aside from his own household regiment, which he maintained under strict discipline on his private estate, the retired marshal of all the armies of France was unable to effect a change in the military dress of his time.

The frivolities and vanities of feminine costume in the 18th and early 19th centuries are well known. Hogarth, Gillray, Rowlandson and many others made much of them in lampoons and caricatures, but American ladies dutifully copied their sisters abroad. Equally absurd were the affectations of military dress. Today soldiers go about their work in combat dress resembling the garments of garbage men. How quaint, then, is the foppery affected by regiments in bygone days.

Early military uniforms imitated the fashions of the aristocracy—an important factor in the success of 18th-century recruiting parties. A fancy cocked hat with button loop and cockade, a fine regimental coat with lapels and buttonholes often bound in ornately designed gold or silver lace, tight knee breeches, stockings and buckled shoes, brass-hilted sword—all these were items that the average peasant lad could never hope to afford. They were a long way from his own mean garments. To such a boy, a soldier's life must have seemed a fine one indeed.

Regular regimental uniforms began to make their appearance in Europe in the late 17th century, but officers often refused to wear them. They considered it demeaning for a gentleman to wear any man's livery, even the king's. Naval uniforms, for officers at least, did not appear until sometime later, and then were patterned on the dress of army officers. Naval enlisted men had no uniforms until well into the 19th century.

There was some connection between the affectations of female dress and the design of military uniforms. The first uniform for officers of Britain's navy was decided upon by King George II in 1748. According to one tale, his Majesty had selected a blue uniform faced with white for naval officers after having seen the Duchess of Bedford riding in Hyde Park wearing a handsome habit done up in those colors. This decision may, of course, have been prompted less by the habit that the duchess wore than by the way she wore it. And this might lead one into an intriguing conjecture concerning the relationship between duchess and king which would not be germane.

Before the advent of an officially prescribed dress, it seems that many officers of the British fleet wore fanciful uniforms of their own devising. A story is told about Captain William Burnaby, an accomplished fop, who joined

Admiral Edward Vernon in the West Indies in 1741. Upon announcing himself to the crusty (and somewhat slovenly) old admiral as commander of a bomb vessel just arrived from England, Vernon observed, eyeing him up and down, "Gad, sir, I really took you for a dancing master!"

The frivolity of military dress is well illustrated in the problems of the gentlemen of horse regiments in the closing years of the 17th century. Cavalrymen of those days wore huge periwigs, ornately curled, reaching to their shoulders, upon which was fixed (by means of a hatpin) a large hat with feathers, sometimes cocked up on three sides, sometimes only on one. After a thundering cavalry charge, the battlefield would be littered with flowing wigs with feathered hats fastened to them. Presumably, shaven-headed gentlemen of horse would spend the evening (if they had won) searching the smoldering turf for their headpieces.

Soldier dress tended to be somewhat international, for the armies of Europe often aped one another. They would adopt peculiarities of dress especially devised for some specific purpose, as in the case of the grenadier cap. Originally designed for a picked body of men whose duty it was to hurl grenades, the tall, brimless grenadier cap allowed a man to sling his musket and throw his bomb without knocking it off. As with many such utilitarian ideas, however, the cap soon became more and more exaggerated in size and less and less functional. It finally evolved as the absurd and towering bearskin cap of the 19th century.

Another example of this tendency to transform a practical military item into a travesty of uselessness is the hussar uniform. Hussars were originally companies of Hungarian irregular light horse. They caught the imagination of all of Europe, and by the late 18th century many nations had raised regiments dressed in the colorful Hungarian outfit. And gradually the elements of this uniform became so stylized as to be useless, indeed an impediment, in combat.

The small, fur-trimmed horseman's cap became an unwieldy high-crowned fur busby. The crown of the cap grew into a ridiculously long, tasseled appendage which flapped about the wearer's waist. The short fur-trimmed jacket turned into the pelisse, a garment so made that it was impossible to wear. It could only be slung over the shoulder by a cord—pretty perhaps, but also foolish and cumbersome. The sabretache, originally a dispatch case hung from a belt, became a purposeless encumbrance that dangled about a hussar's ankles when he dismounted. His breeches became so tight that he could not mount his horse without aid.

Although in many ways colonial Americans differed from Europeans, in the field of fashionable dress they slavishly copied their cousins across the sea. Countrymen and pioneers wore Indian moccasins and buckskin breeches, but ladies and gentlemen from Boston to Sa-

vannah ordered well-cut garments from London tailors whenever they were able.

In their military dress, too, Americans generally imitated European uniforms. Officers strove for the sort of smartness that they so admired in the soldiers of the king, but in colonial days and in the American Revolution the common soldier often got no uniform at all—only a musket and cartridge box and, if he were lucky, a blanket.

"Rheumatics" from Wet Pipe Clay

When in the early 1770s, white smallclothes (vest and breeches) became part of the soldiers' dress, great labors were undertaken to whiten garments that had become dirty and stained. Aching joints were a common complaint as a result of troops having to spend the greater part of each day in wet clothing in the name of military smartness. Smallclothes were bleached with pipe clay and water; leather crossbelts were vigorously whitened with pipe clay; the soldier's hair was combed with lard or tallow, whitened with a dusting of rancid flour, curled at the side and tied behind.

During the Revolution, despite shortages of every kind, the habit continued. A contemporary description of a Continental Army regiment noted men clad for the most part in rags, many without shoes, but all with hair meticulously curled, tied and whitened with flour.

In Continental regiments the "hunting shirt," or rifle shirt, often became the coat of the soldier. This was the common garment of the farmer, laborer and wagoner: a long, full shirt of coarse canvas linen, usually pulled over the head and reaching to the knee. These plebian garments were given a military connotation by dyeing them, with cuffs and collars a different color from the shirts.

The American officer, whenever he was able, got himself up to emulate European smartness, sporting plumes, epaulets, sashes, lace and gorgets. Affectations of foppery were practiced so widely that George Rogers Clark reportedly once ordered a sedan chair so that he might be sedately borne in the manner of a gentleman through the forests and swamps of Illinois and Ohio.

The most distinctive costume features of a lady of fashion at this time were her headdress and skirt. By 1770 headdresses had assumed truly alarming proportions. Supported by crinkled crinoline, false hair and wire frames and fantastically decorated, they had achieved such lofty heights that a hairdresser would be forced to ascend a ladder to finish off a coiffure. Plastered with pomade and flour paste, these towering creations were often topped with such figures as a ship under full sail, or the Battle of Bunker Hill, and they became such a nest of parasites that ladies used slim jeweled rods to scratch themselves without disarranging their headpieces.

Fifty years before the Revolution the hoopskirt returned. Hoops, made usually of cane or whale-bone, swelled skirts from waist to ankle to such a degree that it became difficult for a lady to navigate through a doorway. Then came elliptical hoops, which further increased the width of the skirt to the point where one could not proceed through a room without considerable disarrangemen of furniture. A lady had to be a very marvel of intrepidity; her lofty coiffure swayed perilously close to the candles of the chandelier, while her enormous skirts set end tables and chiffoniers atottering. Presumably the train of her dress collected the wreckage.

Imagine her upon the arm of a gallant officer whose bespangled regimental coat, worn fashionably open, is cut to flare generously outward at the hips. His large cocked hat nods with plumes, his hands are almost concealed beneath cascades of ruffled linen. His dainty small sword dangles about his thigh, and his absurdly trailing coat cuffs constantly threaten the tea cups—and the composure of his hostess.

By 1812 enormously high collars had come into military fashion, together with the preposterous *chapeau bras,* the fore-and-aft cocked hat favored by Napoleon and thereafter much exaggerated in size and festooned with plumes. This was adopted by naval as well as army officers. Picture an admiral navigating himself out of a bobbing whaleboat, up a Jacob's ladder and over the bulwarks of a man-o'-war while wearing this overpowering headpiece. Soldiers at this time wore a bell-crowned leather shako with a worsted pompom at the front.

Feminine dress, meanwhile, affected dramatic changes. Hoopskirts and headpieces gave way to the classic simplicity of ancient Greece. The dress became a straight sheath with low, square neckline and short sleeves. It was belted or gathered just under the breasts in a simple but elegant fashion—if the lady had the figure for it. In the 1820s there was a fashionable enthusiasm for military details. Froggings and epaulets began to appear in ladies' wardrobes, along with Wellington hoods and mantles.

Next, dresses began to spread again from hips to ankles as hoopskirt fashion returned. By the 1850s, skirts had resumed their enormous breadth, but the modesty and sobriety of the Victorian era rendered the styles far more somber and dismally chaste than in the 18th century. As this unfortunate fashion progressed, ladies were so bundled in padded petticoats, heavy skirts and bustles that the charms of the most shapely were entirely submerged. This, Victorians felt, was as it should be.

By mid-19th century, too, the gaudy plumes and ornate laced coats of 18th-century soldiery had disappeared, except for a reminder in the elegant and aristocratic "silk-stocking" companies of some large Eastern cities. Trousers had emerged triumphant in civilian male fashion, and soldiers were appearing in "pantaloons," though some officers clung to knee breeches until well into the 19th century.

Wars have always had a practical effect upon uniforms, making them less ornate, looser in fit, more comfortable. "Mad Anthony" Wayne, known for his neatness among Revolutionary War officers, wore a rusty red coat when he commanded at Fort Ticonderoga in 1777. Zachary Taylor led his men into the Mexican War in the 1840s dressed in a hickory shirt, a plain sackcloth coat and a straw hat. Ulysses S. Grant favored private's dress, devoid of braid and tinsel, and an old slouch hat.

Also, amusingly, nations tend to copy the uniforms of other countries that have been recent victors in whatever conflicts have been raging. Both Union and Confederate troops went into the Civil War in uniforms copied from the French, for during the Second Empire of Napoleon III France was considered Europe's most powerful nation. But when Napoleon III was defeated by the Prussians in 1870–71, Americans dutifully adopted Prussian-style uniforms, even to the spiked helmets. Similarly, at the end of World War II, many Western nations picked up Britain's battle dress or America's Eisenhower jacket, while Communist countries all wore a variation of the Soviet uniform.

AMELIA BLOOMER'S CURIOUS COSTUME

Mary Curtis

The 1850's debate started as a joke: Replace impractical hoop skirts with Turkish trousers. But, with her suggestion, Bloomer managed to alter fashion and feminist history.

Some claimed Amelia Bloomer cut off her long skirts and donned pantaloons because she knew how to cultivate a good publicity campaign. Amelia herself said that she did it for the cause of women's rights, that she never dreamed it would bring her name a dubious kind of immortality.

Whatever the reason, in the winter of 1850, young Mrs. Bloomer took to wearing knee-length skirts and pantaloons. And, within less than a year, the English-speaking world was calling it the Bloomer costume.

Reprinted with permission from The National Historical Society, publishers of *American History Illustrated,* June 1978, "Amelia Bloomer's Curious Costume" by Mary Curtis.

Amelia Jenks entered life as the unassuming daughter of an upstate New York shopkeeper. A month before her 22nd birthday, she became the equally unassuming Mrs. Dexter Bloomer, wife of a small-town newspaper editor.

When Elizabeth Cady Stanton and friends began to put her home town of Seneca Falls on the map as a feminist stronghold, Amelia was an interested observer. In 1848, when the Women's Rights Convention met at the local Wesleyan Chapel, Amelia and Dexter sat in one of the pews, but neither signed the famous Declaration of Sentiments.

However, Amelia had entered the fray as a temperance reformer. When women came under fire for their public activity in that movement, the newly formed Seneca Falls Ladies' Temperance Society founded a newspaper, with Amelia as editor.

Although others chose the name and supported the idea, *The Lily* was essentially the voice of Amelia Bloomer. She later claimed that it was the first paper owned, published, and edited by a woman, devoted strictly to the interests of women.

When Mrs. Stanton walked into the post office where the Bloomers were working and offered her services as a columnist for *The Lily,* the editor and the paper moved irrevocably into the feminist camp. In retrospect, Amelia insisted that she had been a feminist from the age of 15, when she was told about an elderly widow evicted from her home because of sexually discriminatory inheritance laws. Others, less charitably, accused her of calculated mimicry. Whatever the reason, she was now truly committed to the cause of women's rights.

Writing under the pseudonyms "Sunflower" and "Gloriana," Amelia and Elizabeth defended temperance, called for prohibition, exposed discrimination against women, advocated changes in the property laws, promoted liberalized divorce laws, disputed chauvinistic interpretations of the *Bible,* and moved toward support of women's suffrage. In the process, Amelia found herself in the midst of a heated debate on dress reform.

Although the debate began as something of a joke, the problem was a real one. Women's clothing of the 1850's could scarcely have been termed practical. Heavily corsetted waists and bodices pinched the form unmercifully, and the "Great Pyramid" style of long skirt was so wide at the bottom that a dress required eighteen to twenty yards of material. A woman within warming distance of the fireplace was in danger of having her hem catch fire. And some doorways were so narrow as to cause her to be left frustrated in the hallway.

With tongue firmly in cheek, the conservative editor of *The Courier* suggested that women exchange their long dresses for Turkish pantaloons. Amelia, half playfully, congratulated her perennial critic for his far-sighted idea. At that time Amelia was quite willing to support dress reform in a semi-serious newspaper debate. But she was not yet prepared to cut off her own long skirts. It took Elizabeth Stanton's cousin Libby to bring that about.

Elizabeth Smith Miller was the daughter of Gerrit Smith, a liberal-minded lawyer who encouraged his little girl to play the tomboy and wear whatever clothes she found comfortable. Her role as a conscious feminist is uncertain: Some historians portray her as a pious, otherworldly soul, a less ardent feminist than her father; others see her as a committed nonconformist. But it was certainly Libby, and not her father, who created and wore the outfit that came to be called the Bloomer costume.

On their honeymoon in Europe, Libby and her husband, Charles, visited Swiss sanitariums where women were recuperating from the ill effects of fashionably tight corset lacing. For comfort and freedom of exercise, the patients wore full Turkish trousers made from black broadcloth, partially covered by a skirt reaching just below the knee. The costume was not totally innovative. Less than half a century earlier, Parisian and English fashion plates had featured full ball dresses with pantalets.

The earlier fashion was marked by such low cut, scanty gowns that they were dangerous to the health in cold weather. An anonymous wag commented in verse.

> Plump and rosy was my face
> And graceful was my form
> Till fashion deemed it in disgrace
> To keep my body warm.

Libby and her imitators, more concerned about warmth and modesty than fashionable form, favored neck to toe covering.

The pantaloon style caught on quickly. Libby had been visiting the Stantons for only a few days when Elizabeth saw its practicality, and took up the fashion. Amelia, feeling that she had an obligation to practice what she preached, soon followed suit, *The Lily* broadcasting her attitude and actions.

To her avowed amazement, the New York *Tribune* and other papers across the country picked up the story. Some condemning, others praising, they carried headlines introducing the new terms, "Bloomerism," "Bloomerites," and "Bloomers." Amelia repeatedly attributed the costume to Libby Miller, but the name stuck.

Letters streamed into *The Lily,* adding hundreds of names to the mailing list and bringing in requests for patterns and illustrations. Caught up in her own advocacy role, Amelia wore the pantaloons for all occasions.

Cartoons in England's satirical *Punch* ranged from showing a Bloomerite on bended knee proposing to her chosen man (his response: "You must really ask Mamma"), to a lady in Bloomer costume shopping for a high silk hat.

Bloomer farces appeared on the stage, on both sides of the Atlantic. In the fall of 1851, Punch's Playhouse and Strand Theatre in London produced "A Figure of Fun, or the Bloomer Costume," with its rival Adelphi Theatre showing "Bloomerism, or the Follies of the Day."

Amid the uproar, adoption of the bloomer fashion seemed a stroke of genius for feminists. It fitted their message of liberation, and drew much desired publicity to the movement. Many other leading feminists—Theodosia Gilbert, Susan B. Anthony, Sarah and Angelina Grimke, Lucretia Mott, Paulina Wright Davis—adopted the short skirt and pantaloons, though not with uniformly happy results.

Amelia herself looked remarkably good in the costume. Dexter wrote of her "exceedingly pleasant and winning smile," but few others thought of her as beautiful. However, her small figure—5 feet 4 inches, about 100 pounds—was well suited to the outfit she wore.

Elizabeth Stanton's experience with the Bloomer costume was, perhaps, more typical, but less satisfactory. Her husband Henry approved of the outfit, but commented: "The worst about it would be, I should think, sitting down. Then ladies will expose their legs somewhat about the knee to the delight of those gentlemen who are anxious to know whether their lady friends have round and plump legs, or lean and scrawny ones."

The unkindest cut of all came from her young son, away at boarding school. Parents' visiting days were coming up, and the boy wrote to his mother begging that she appear in conventional long skirts. Elizabeth wrote back, explaining that she no longer owned any long skirts, that she considered them both restricting and dangerous. Showing that she understood his feelings, she added, "You want me to be like other people. You do not like to have me laughed at. You must learn not to care for what foolish people say."

Even for Elizabeth herself, that was easier said than done. With the baggy trousers and short skirts doing little to flatter her generous figure, Elizabeth was jeered. Initially committed to the pantaloons, she soon gave them up and lengthened her skirts.

Susan B. Anthony suffered, too. Her tall, awkward figure was as badly suited to the costume as Elizabeth's dowdy one. At best, she felt conspicuous. Reduced to tears by ugly comments, she took her friends' advice and went back to long skirts.

In time, the Bloomer costume became more of a burden than an asset for virtually all feminists. Even Amelia and the beautiful Lucy Stone, who were petite enough to wear the costume well, soon realized that more attention was being focused on their curious clothing than on their serious message.

In later years Amelia wrote to a friend and talked about other, practical reasons for giving up the costume:

> After retiring from public life and coming to this land of strangers [Iowa] where I was to commence life anew and make new friends, I felt at times like donning long skirts and did so. I found the high winds which prevail here much of the time played sad work with short skirts, when I went out, and I was greatly annoyed and mortified by having my skirts turned over my head and shoulders on the streets.

At first she tried modifying the Bloomer by weighting the hem with shot. But the winds still held the upper hand, lashing the weighted skirts against her, bruising her legs. Even her devoted Dexter admitted Amelia "was deficient in the quality of humor and took life too seriously." Without a sense of humor, bruised legs on top of embarrassment over skirts flying above the head literally added injury to insult.

When the lightweight "bird cage" style of wire hoops replaced the heavy layers of petticoats, Amelia found excuse enough to go back to long skirts.

By 1860 the Bloomer costume had faded into obscurity. But twenty years later Florence Wallace Harberton, wife of England's Viscount Harberton, revived it as a fashion approved by her National Dress Society (later, the Rational Dress Society). A highlight of the society's first meeting at Westminster Town Hall was what amounted to a fashion show featuring the Bloomer.

A year after that first meeting, the society began publishing its own quarterly, *Gazette,* advocating a costume they called the "Divided Skirt." Essentially, it was a Bloomer without benefit of overskirt.

Rational Dress and the Divided Skirt became increasingly popular in the nineties, when the safety bicycle (with pneumatic tires) was introduced. Physical exercise, including walking, dancing, playing tennis, and cycling, was now considered both healthy and respectable for young girls, although some of the old school still worried about, "how dreadful it would be if, by some accident, she were to fall off into the arms of a strange man!"

But the fully liberated young woman of the '90's was likely to breeze along country lanes in the recommended cycling costume of the day: a thick woolen vest, a pair of tweed knickerbockers, a close-fitting, water-proofed skirt "rather long in front so as not to display too liberal allowance of ankle," Norfolk jacket, and a small felt hat.

Amelia Bloomer, by then an elderly lady living quietly in Council Bluffs, Iowa, heard that cyclists had dubbed their comfortable modern outfit, Bloomers. She approved.

PANTSUITED PIONEER OF WOMEN'S LIB, DR. MARY WALKER

Allison Lockwood

*Civil War medic, often arrested for not dressing "like a woman,"
but was only female to win Medal of Honor*

"Why don't you wear proper clothing? That toggery is neither one thing nor the other!" So General William Tecumseh Sherman greeted Dr. Mary Walker in the jaunty pantsuit she wore as a surgeon during the Civil War, the only woman ever to win the Medal of Honor.

Neither the General nor anyone else ever persuaded Mary Walker to give up her "garmenture of dual form," as a contemporary journalist euphemistically referred to the trousers she wore during her military service and, indeed, to the end of her life after World War I. In that half century she became, largely owing to her garb, almost as much a Washington landmark as the Capitol itself.

A century before the label's invention, Dr. Walker was a "women's liberationist," an activist in every sense of the word, who devoted the energies of a lifetime to emancipating herself and her "sisters," as she called them, "from the bondage of all that is oppressive." According to her, and other reformers of the period, female bondage in the 19th century took two main forms: constricting, "unhygienic" clothing which called for dress reform, and denial of the right to vote. At one point the two causes were united in a single organization, "The Mutual Dress Reform and Equal Rights Association."

Active in both movements, Dr. Walker stood out from all her associates because of her costume. The genteel, gathered-at-the-ankle pantaloons recommended by Amelia Bloomer in the 1850s were too tame for the little doctor who adopted straight, tailored, masculine-style trousers which infuriated her contemporaries, especially the males. For half a century American readers were entertained by newspaper accounts of the arrests and other encounters stemming from Mary Walker's pants. Humorist "Bill" Nye labeled her America's "self-made man."

Dr. Walker's eminently practical war uniform consisted of trousers topped by a neat, military-style tunic ending in a modest knee-length overskirt. At the close of the war she was arrested in New York for "impersonating a man." She defended herself briskly, calling the female corset she abhorred a "coffin" contrived of "iron bands." The swaying, leg-revealing hoopskirt she termed an invention of "the prostitutes of Paris." She concluded her defense by claiming the right "to dress as I please in free America on whose tented fields I have served four years in the cause of human freedom." The judge advised New York policemen "never to arrest her again," and Mary Walker, according to the *New York Times,* departed "under a storm of applause."

She hit the papers again as the result of a dog bite. "That curious anthropoid, Dr. Mary Walker," as a *Times* reporter referred to her, was blamed for the incident by having willfully exposed her legs in her "best Summer trousers," and sympathy was expressed for the dog! "With skirts, the Doctor would have been safe."

Except for a few curls she retained so "everybody would know that I was a woman," Dr. Walker by the 1870s had given up virtually all concessions to female dress and appeared in frock coat and trousers by day and in full male evening dress on the lecture platform and at evening social affairs.

It was this insistence on wearing masculine-type clothing, while expecting to be accepted and treated as a lady, that so riled Mary Walker's contemporaries. "Clad in the majesty of trousers and the splendor of a frock coat," fumed an editorial writer, half seriously, "while Dr. Walker represents herself outwardly to be a man, she claims to be a woman whenever she can thereby appropriate any of the rights of the female sex. . . . What must be demanded by all who have the interests of the Republic at heart is the refeminization of Dr. Walker. Her trousers must be taken from her—where and how is, of course, a matter of detail."

Dr. Walker took plenty of abuse over the years. She could also dish it out. As an 80-year-old woman she was introduced to the Assistant Secretary of the Navy, Franklin Roosevelt. Promptly she informed him of her low regard for his cousin "Teddy," whom she detested.

Dr. Walker's restless life began sedately enough in 1832 at Oswego, New York, where her Yankee parents, both descended from Pilgrim stock, conducted a school. At first she herself was teaching, but left this to overcome the many obstacles then in the path of a woman bent on a career in medicine. In 1855 she emerged from the Syracuse Medical College holding a medical degree, the only woman in her class. (Elizabeth Blackwell, the first woman physician in America, received her medical degree in 1849 from Geneva College of Medicine.) Primitive by our standards, Mary Walker's training was par for the time, but her first practice, in Rome, N.Y., with her husband, Albert Miller, was small. The American public was not yet ready for women doctors, and neither was the army, as she discovered when she arrived in Washington at the start of the Civil War seeking a commission as an army surgeon.

Many dedicated American women were to serve in hospitals throughout the conflict, under atrocious conditions and sometimes close to the battle zones, but as nurses—not as physicians. Denied a surgeon's contract, Dr. Walker went to work in whatever medical capacity she could be useful. A stint in the makeshift hospital set up in the corridors of the old U.S. Patent Office Building, during the early war days, was followed by service at Warrenton, Virginia. Disgusted by the care some of the men received in field hospitals, she had many of them packed off to Washington by train.

A "Man for Man" Exchange

Ordered in 1863 to Chattanooga, Dr. Walker actually replaced a male medical officer in an Ohio infantry regiment. On one of her missions, she was captured by a Confederate patrol and packed off to Richmond where she languished, along with other Federal officers, in a prison known to its inmates as "Castle Thunder," a converted warehouse on the banks of the James River. During her four-month stay the *Richmond Examiner* ran a story of their female POW, complaining, among other things, that she refused to assume garb "more becoming to her sex." It was always a source of pride to Dr. Walker that she was exchanged in 1864, "man for man," for a Confederate officer.

The Medal of Honor was awarded to Dr. Mary Walker by President Andrew Johnson at the end of the war, and she wore it proudly all her life. In 1917, when she was 85 and nearing the end, a government review board withdrew her medal, along with those of 900 other Civil War veterans, claiming they had been improperly awarded—in her case, on a question of her status as a member of the army or a contract doctor. Dr. Walker not only refused to relinquish her original medal or the later design given her in 1907, but vowed she would continue to wear one everyday, "and the other I will wear on occasions."

Dr. Walker's opinion on how to free 19th-century women from the bondage imposed by their clothing and by tradition she expressed in two books with unusual titles: *Hit* (1871) and *Unmasked; or the Science of Immorality* (1878). She railed against the cruel corsets, tight garters and other underpinnings that "shackled and enfeebled" the female.

As her own practical contribution to dress reform, Mary designed what she called her "Dress Reform Undersuit," calculated not only to improve female health generally but also to discourage both seduction and rape. "The linen," she wrote, "is made with a high neck and loose waist, and whole drawers, and long sleeves with wristbands attached; thus making a complete undersuit in one garment. The drawers are folded over the ankles and the stockings adjusted over the drawers, thus keeping the ankles warm and also keeping the stockings arranged without elastic or other bands, or any troublesome or injurious arrangement, most of which impede the circulation and produce varicose veins, and weariness in walking." Over this undersuit was to be worn a sensible suit consisting of "pants made like men's, either buttoned to the waist of the undershirt or arranged with the usual suspenders. The dress is made to hang free of the body, the waist and skirt of one piece like a sack coat and falling to the knees; thus preventing it being stepped upon while descending stairs, or of becoming soiled in rainy days—but principally because of a needed relief to women from its shortness."

Education for women was advocated by Mary Walker on the most practical ground and one with which she herself was quite familiar—the need to earn a living. "Not only every son but every daughter should be given a practical knowledge of some business whereby they can support themselves," she wrote, adding, moreover, that they should receive equal pay for equal work instead of "the pittance paid for woman's work."

As for marriage, Mary believed "there should be perfect freedom for woman to select a partner for life in a straightforward, honest, and honorable manner." As do feminists of today, she observed that in American homes the work of women was not only never finished but also undervalued. "One, and I may say the great reason why the mass of women are so dissatisfied with their domestic duties," wrote Dr. Walker, "is because they are painfully conscious of the inability of men to duly appreciate the thousand cares, thoughts and anxieties of their position. Too well do women know the great mass of men feel that if they earn the money, they have performed the nine-tenths part of living, and whatever a woman does is only of minor consideration. . . ."

And what if this social contract called marriage failed to work? Why, divorce was the answer—the one she chose when her own marriage failed. "If it is right to be legally married, it is right to be legally divorced. . . . To be deprived of a Divorce is like being shut up in prison because someone attempted to kill you. It is just as honorable to get out of matrimonial trouble legally, as to be freed from any other wrong."

From the end of the Civil War through the 1870s Dr. Walker was part of the dedicated band of suffragettes headquartered in Washington, D.C., that included Susan B. Anthony, Lucy Stone, Mary Livermore and the attorney, Belva Lockwood, second woman to run for President, Victoria Woodhull being the first. The women worked ceaselessly, delivering speeches to whoever would listen, collecting signatures on petitions, besieging Congressmen in their offices, and staging demonstrations out of their national headquarters, the Central Women's Suffrage Bureau.

Frederick Douglass, the great black abolitionist, himself marched with the little group when they tried to register to vote in the nation's capital in 1871, basing their hopes on the passage of the 15th Amendment which the previous year had guaranteed that right to the emancipated blacks.

When the suffragettes lost their faith in an Act of Congress as their means of achieving the vote, redirecting their energies to the passage of a Constitutional Amendment, maverick Mary Walker decided to go it alone. She had made up her mind that it was merely illegal state and local laws that denied women the vote. This theory she termed her "Crowning Constitutional Argument," had copies printed up, and proclaimed it the rest of her life.

As the years marched on, Dr. Walker had to scratch hard to make a living. She fought hard for a government clerkship which failed to work out, each side blaming the other, but there are enough references to her unusual mode of dress to indicate she may have been discriminated against because of it. In 1898 she won a $20 monthly pension based on disabilities she charged to her wartime imprisonment in Richmond. She spent more time, as she grew older, at the old family farm at Oswego where, like many old ladies, she was the butt of cruel pranks. At 81 she outwitted an apparent attempt to tar and feather her.

Near the end of her long life, Dr. Mary Walker herself remembered those years when her youthful daring, strength and brains had captured the nation's attention. "Presidents, cabinet ministers and great generals were glad to meet and listen to me," she recalled, adding wistfully, "I was younger then."

At long last and late—she would be 145 this year—Congressional action has been initiated to restore Mary Walker's Medal of Honor.

HAIR—A LABEL WE
HAVE WORN FROM CAVE TO COMMUNE

K.C. Tessendorf

Pompadour, peroxide or Piccadilly weeper, we'll try any style to 'be ourselves.' Hers's the long and the short of it all.

Hair has always been a hang-up. Early scratchings on cave surfaces depict hunters sporting carefully shaped beards, their heads shaved to emphasize a tufted forelock. Our hirsute preoccupation persists in the annals of social history.

The reason is as plain as the hair on your face. Hair has high visibility and is easy to manage. Who of us can modify or improve our various weak chins, bony Adam's apples, jug-handle ears, knobby knees or feet shod in 13E? But our hair can be long or short, combed or matted, lank or curled, dyed or powdered and easily counterfeited. It serves all purposes for all men; at once badge, shield, romantic invitation. Our hair is the most facile advertisement for ourselves—after our smiles.

Baldness, some believe, is caused by a cueball hard-headedness. Thus women escape through being comparatively softheaded, or fatheaded with better nourished hair roots. The most outrageous view, recorded in pre-Lib days, posited that men inadvertently burned out the roots of their hair through heavy use of brainpower; in other words, grass doesn't grow on a busy street.

The physical dimensions of hair have been precisely measured, and the very hairs of our head have been numbered. A German accomplished this tedious task: on a blond, 140,400 hairs; a brown, 109,440; a black, 102,962; a redhead, 88,740. Hair is curly in proportion to its flat-bladedness. It is mildly elastic. What may hang by a hair? Approximately two pounds.

The empirical resources of science once determined the clinical preciseness of Pope Julius's remark that his beard was "a forest grown populous with troublesome little animals." The experiment took place in Paris in *fin de siècle* times. A young lady agreed, solely in the interest of science, to be kissed by two strange gentlemen—one clean-shaven, the other moustached. Following a normal business day in the city, the gentlemen repaired to the laboratory, where:

"The shaven young man applied his lips to hers in the customary manner. The professor then passed a sterilized brush over the young lady's lips, dipped it into a test tube containing a sterile solution of agar-agar and quickly sealed the top. The girl's lips, and face even, having been . . . sterilized a second time, the bearded man followed the example of his shaven companion and the sterilized brush and the test tube were again called into play in the same manner. During each of the operations the young woman held her breath in order that no accidental germ might be drawn upon her lips from the atmosphere."

"After four days the tubes were opened. The first, taken from the shaven man, was speckled with dots, each of which was a colony of yeast germs, such as cause mould but are practically harmless. The second, from the moustached man, literally swarmed with malignant microbes.

The long, thin tubercle bacillus was the first found, followed by diphtheria and putrefactive germs, minute bits of food, a hair from a spider's leg and goodness knows what all—so great a variety in any case that nobody had the hardihood to reveal the results of the experiment to the lady."

One Symbol of Maleness

Hirsute appearance was long associated with the wellsprings of virility. On the island of Delos in ancient times, boys and girls in an apparent puberty rite anointed favored tombs with "first full fruits of beard," and virgin lock. A pogonophile of that day declaimed: "The beard is nature's symbol of the male just as is the crest of the cock and the mane of the lion." Undue cutting of this heritage was for "womanish creatures."

An abundant growth of hair on women, especially on the upper lip, has traditionally been the tip-off of robust sexual resources. On the other hand, St. Modeste was revered for having escaped an untoward marriage by awakening on her wedding day miraculously decked out in a full beard. Throughout the Age of Faith pious women concealed their locks beneath chaste if elaborate headdresses.

The medieval English clergy was particularly vociferous on hair. St. Wulfstan, Bishop of Worcester, continually carried a small knife in his pocket, and whenever anybody offending in this respect knelt before him to receive his blessing, he would whip it out slyly and cut off a handful, and then throwing it in his face, tell him to cut off all the rest, or he would go to hell. We are told a weeping Henry I had his long beard scissored by a chaplain, following a sulfurous sermon upon St. Paul's text.

Facial hair escaped this severe dictum. Pope Julius II grew a mighty beard to enhance the majesty of his appearance. Certainly the stereotype of the wise, bearded patriarch endures. Could Michelangelo have been convincing in the Sistine chapel had his Jehovah been as hairless as his Adam? Can we relate to a shorn Santa Claus, Uncle Sam (originally beardless) or Christ in a crewcut?

Hair has a familiar role in differentiating the stranger from our own kind, visibly setting off master from slave, youth from age. Greeks generally favored natural growth, but Romans settled upon short hair and shaven cheeks. For some centuries in France, the Establishment was bearded, the peasantry shaven. When the latter gradually became as hairy as their lords short hair returned to high fashion.

Styles occasionally had whimsical origins. When a king too young to support a beard ascended the throne his courtiers had to shed theirs. The reign of Francis I was shorthaired because he wished to display a head wound valorously received.

When fashion had banished the beard from the rest of Europe, Peter the Great sought to westernize the Russian masses by decreeing them beardless (peasants excepted). There was great consternation; those who were able began to flee Russia. Peter ameliorated the decree by imposing a stiff tax on beards. Some of the devout, too poor to pay, reluctantly cut theirs to be piously preserved and reunited with their owners in the grave. They feared to stand beardless at heaven's portal before an outraged St. Peter.

The rare blond of the classical era in the eastern Mediterranean was considered the scum of the earth, until light-haired northern barbarians began to score military successes against the Roman Empire. Thereafter, blond and red-haired barbarian women were sheared as regularly and profitably as sheep, to provide wigs for fashionable ladies who could not afford to shade their raven braids with gold dust.

Queen Bess Owned 80 Wigs

By 1550 women's hair had emerged publicly from outdated headdresses, and within a few decades cosmetics appeared on the European scene. Hair was frizzed, powdered pale violet, false curls and ringlets crafted, the whole mass held in place by sticky pastes. Bogged down in goo, women soon shaved it all away, and resorted to periwigs of great variety and splendor.

Queen Elizabeth, a natural blond, preferred an auburn tint in her wig—she owned about 80. These were often festooned with jewels, flowers and feathers. Sometimes when raw material was in short supply unwary children were grabbed and sheared.

Natural hair was back in by the mid-17th century, fashioned over wire nets, sometimes peaking like a rooster's comb, sometimes "wired-out" into curls with strands of pearls. Romance was served by small curls at the nape of the neck called *crève-coeurs* (heartbreakers); others hung near the ear, *confidants.*

Wigs were popular again toward the end of the 18th century. A great emancipation occurred about 1830 when hair began to be styled to fit individual personality instead of merely the rigid dictates of fashion.

Powdered wigs, as we know from early American presidential portraiture, were as popular among men as among ladies. A concession to amour was the 17th-century lovelock, a much longer braid of strands hanging in front of the left shoulder.

Men possessed one fashionable advantage; they could experiment endlessly with their whiskers. Beards at various times were braided, twined with ribbons, ornamented with precious stones, powdered with gold dust, colored "a vivid green, a fine orange, and a deep rich blue." The fantail beard was "three inches long in the shape of a fan, rounded and set off with two long stiff whiskers, catlike in appearance. At night the fan-beard had a wadded bag to sleep in, and for the good reason that the scented wax with which the beard was colored and stiffened took some time to manipulate, and was easily cracked."

The moustache had its finest hour in the late 19th century when it curled, drooped, bristled and pointed like waxen daggers. There were moustache strainers and moustache trainers. Sideburns had outlandish designs: muttonchops and "Piccadilly weepers"—full-blown swathes hanging at the ears and framing a smooth-shaven face like dusty side curtains.

Long a Mark of Protest

It is an easy step to convert hair fashion into a banner of protest. Subjugated by short-haired, smooth-visaged Normans, the original Britons bristled ferociously to signify their discontent. The "roundheads" of Cromwell were in visible reaction against the mannered tresses of Charles I. An era of elegant wigs was literally cut short in the French Revolution. Dissidents of our day, polarizing upon the point that cropped crowns and hairless cheeks are unalterably the badge of puritanical meanness, have forgotten this style was initiated by libertine souls, among them Oscar Wilde, in revulsion against the shaggy insufferability of late Victorians.

Richard Corson in his excellent compendium *Fashions in Hair* recalls that 17th-century Harvard boys were forbidden "long haire, locks, foretops, curlings, crispings, partings, or powdering of ye haire."

An American lady writing at the beginning of this century got exercised over the implications of whiskers: "There are opinionated whiskers . . . long and narrow. They announce as plainly as possible 'I am it. All else is dirt.' I never saw a man wearing a Van Dyke beard who was not selfish, sinister, and pompous as a peacock. . . . There are unctuous whiskers—long, broad, sweeping, plethoric. . . . They usually fringe full, sensual, smug, hypocritical lips. Never trust such whiskers. . . . There are the whiskers of the anarchist—unkempt, matted, a ferocious setting for a savage face."

Do shaggy, shoulder-length locks inform us of contemptuously rebellious nihilists or dangerous revolutionaries? In relative numbers there are a very few who relate their thorough revulsion against society by their unkempt appearance. Vast publicity, and a natural, kindred distaste for authority, have stirred the current of imitative fashion. Yet the mod gentleman who supports a habit of $20 to $50 a month at his hairdresser is scarcely seen as a surly anarchist.

Hair costuming—wigs and paste-on sideburns, beards, moustaches—has suddenly come on as a business of promise. Short-haired musicians don shaggy wigs to perform at rock concerts, and hirsute youths remove lovebeads and produce crewcut wigs at National Guard armories.

For just a few dollars, you can now change your whole personality.

THE FASHIONABLE TOOTH

Dr. Charles I. Stoloff

*Before sparkling white became an oral fetish, gold was glamorous,
black was beautiful, and a jewel or two supplied dental dazzle.*

A huge gold molar suspended from the front of an office building in Union Square, New York, told Terence McGrover that he had reached his destination. He was a large, burly man, and the cut of his clothes and the angle at which he wore his pearl gray derby gave some indication of his business and position in life. McGrover was the proud and prosperous owner of one of the largest cafes on the Bowery. The year was 1901.

Ascending a staircase, McGrover found himself in a room typical of the elaborate dental parlors of the time, a room heavy with carved furniture and velvet portieres. But if Terence McGrover took any notice of the room or of the dozen waiting occupants, he gave no sign of it. He quickly made his way to the adjoining chamber and buttonholed the dentist.

"Doc, you don't know me, but I'm a person of some importance in my part of town," he said. "I want some teeth, the classiest set of teeth you can make. The price doesn't matter; just make 'em rich looking, and make 'em all gold!"

It is a pity that no picture or pattern exists of the set of teeth that that Cellini of Union Square installed in the mouth of Terence McGrover. We have only the word of his contemporaries that it was the most spectacular job to be seen in the city in those days. When the great Terry smiled at his customers from behind his bar, it was a sight to be pointed out to the slumming visitors from "uptown," for the dentist had taken McGrover at his word—and his pocketbook. The new teeth were 22-karat gold; and from the central incisors, two finely cut diamonds glittered, adding to the brilliance of McGrover's smile.

The esthetic appeal of gold teeth reached a zenith in this country at about the turn of the century. The lady of fashion would stand before her mirror and primp her pompadoured coiffure, smooth her tight-waisted, full-skirted gown, and note with approval the faintly golden richness that her dentist had added to her already charming smile. Her husband, no less vain, was as proud of his two or more gold teeth as he was of his custom-made, high-buttoned shoes.

Even the youth of the nation took their pennies to the candy shop to purchase brass caps, which they jammed over their teeth in imitation of their elders' dental elegance. What was a little gum soreness when one could make a swaggering entrance into the schoolyard with a sensational grin?

In the nineties and the early 1900s, gold teeth were as much a part of the fashion scene as peg-top trousers, choker collars, and chatelaine watches. There were, of course, certain practical reasons for this popularity. From the viewpoint of the average dentist, gold-shell crowns provided a simple method of securely anchoring artificial teeth; at the same time they covered ugly, broken-down, and discolored natural teeth, as well as much inferior dental work. And to the patient, gold seemed to represent the most in value received.

Gold has always been a popular, valuable, and sought-after metal, desired for its color, workability, and rarity. It was used in fine jewelry and coinage and, for almost as long, in dentistry. For some people, gold in their mouths not only created a magic and mysterious spell, it also had the added dash of elegance.

Ancient records indicate that gold was used in dental appliances more than 4,500 years ago. A simple Egyptian device made about 2500 B.C., and consisting of gold wires designed to hold a loose tooth, was found at Gizeh, Egypt, some years ago. The Egyptian artisans of this period were very knowledgeable and clever about manipulating the metal, and were constantly called upon to create exquisite jewelry for the embellishment of their patrons.

It would seem logical that the Egyptians of antiquity, who possessed a love of color and glitter, and who went to great lengths to beautify themselves with the expert use of balms, lotions, colorful cosmetics, and sparkling jewels, would give some attention to ornamenting their teeth. The mummies of persons of high rank were decorated with gilt liberally applied to the eyebrows, nose, lips, and teeth, between which a gold coin was placed. A thin gold plate placed on the tongue completed the toilette and permitted the deceased to enter the new kingdom with a suitably gleaming facade, which might improve his chances of a cordial welcome.

Beauty aids and dental techniques were later developed by the Etruscans, Greeks, Romans, and other Mediterranean civilizations. The Etruscans further refined the art of dentistry, banding natural teeth to hold artificial ones, and sometimes covering portions of the supporting teeth with broad strips of pure gold. Basically utilitarian, the practice also became a status symbol—a luxury accessible only to persons of rank.

Archeologists have uncovered other ancient dental appliances, some dating back to the seventh century B.C., that were made to hold loose or artificial teeth for utility and improved appearance. A few were similar to Egyptian and Etruscan appliances; others, of Greek and Roman origin, were of a more advanced design. The devices consisted of gold and silver wires, and flat bands of pure gold, which were attached to the remaining natural teeth. One unusual Roman dental bridge of the first century B.C. utilized the first known gold-shell crown. It completely covered the top of the anchorage tooth, assuring a firm hold. In union with a series of additional gold ribbon loops, it held several artificial teeth, probably carved from ivory or ox bone. As far as is known, it is the prototype of all gold-shell crowns.

After such a promising beginning, a hiatus in Western dental technology set in, which lingered throughout most of the medieval period. During this time very little in the way of new or improved restorative and esthetic devices was created.

Charlatanry, such as the bizarre treatment recommended by an English doctor at Oxford in 1400, became prevalent. For those who were unhappy about the appearance of their teeth he offered two formulas: the first one to make teeth fall out, the second to make them grow again.

The first: "Dried cow's dung or the fat of a green frog would positively cause teeth to fall out when applied to them. . . . If an ox, peradventure, chewed a little frog with the grass, its teeth would fall out on the spot." The second: "The brains of a hare rubbed on the gums . . . will make teeth grow again where they have been lost."

In other areas of the world, however, developments in dental techniques and concepts of oral beauty continued to grow from earlier traditions. From Marco Polo's *Travels,* written about A.D. 1280, we learn that in China dental adornment was being pursued on a somewhat higher level. He tells of the "interesting Chinese custom of both men and women covering their teeth with thin plates of gold, which are fitted with great nicety to the shape of the teeth and remain on them constantly."

The invasion of Mexico in 1518 by the Spanish conquistadores revealed a Maya culture in which tooth mutilation was performed on sound, decay-free teeth. This custom—notching, grooving, and filing the biting edges of the front teeth—may have been rooted in religion, but it was also practiced for ornamental purposes. At an earlier point in their history, the Maya and their subjects had developed the art of inlaying frontal teeth with gold and precious and semiprecious stones to a high level, but by the time the Spaniards arrived, this custom had faded out.

To enhance their appearance, the Yucatan Maya filed their teeth until they were sawlike in appearance. The dental operations involved are believed to have been performed by old women who used stones and water to file the teeth. As to the ability of the patients to bear the discomfort and pain of such dental work, it is possible that they were addicted to chewing coca leaves mixed with lime, and had discovered its anesthetic properties.

Other, more primitive peoples also notched, cut down, reshaped, or pointed their teeth. Knocking out, or ablating, sound teeth to deliberately create gaps in the dentition was another widespread custom in these cultures. Throughout the ages, such practices have been traditional in many civilizations for health, religious, ceremonial, and esthetic reasons. To those to whom such dental distortion was the norm, people with natural dentition were looked upon with suspicion or were often the subjects of disdain and ridicule.

The custom of knocking out sound, healthy teeth is probably Neolithic in origin. Ample evidence in fossil craniological collections indicates that it occurred during that period in Spain, England, Africa, Asia Minor, and Japan. Ablation was also practiced by people of the California coast, the Pueblo region, Florida, Alaska, and the Aleutian Islands, but much later than in other areas of the world. Studies have been made of ancient skulls to distinguish purposeful ablation from accidental or disease-induced removal. As a rule, the upper two incisors were the teeth most frequently knocked out, but other incisors, canines, and, rarely, molars were also removed in this manner.

Why ablation was practiced during the Neolithic age is obscure, but anthropological studies of more recent cultures have shed some light upon its origins and purposes. In many cultures the noncurative removal of a specific tooth was carried out as a trial of endurance and bore religious significance as a protection from death: evil spirits residing in the body could exit through the gap.

The willful removal of one or more front teeth was also motivated partly by esthetic reasons. To some people it was the highest concept of beauty to disclose a gaping hole when the lips were parted.

As recently as the nineteenth century, tooth removal was an important custom among the Kilao people living in the vicinity of Kweichow, southwest China. Girls were taken out of the house on their wedding day and two of their incisors were literally broken out. At first this act, called "damaging the husband's house," was done to identify them as married women. The custom eventually took on a connotation of beauty.

The Masai of East Africa also knocked out their teeth, but the practice has diminished greatly with the present generation. Until recently, most adult men and women had their two lower front incisors removed, considering their absence a distinctive identifying and beautifying feature. It is believed, however, that this custom had other origins. The story persists that sometime in the past a clever Masai medicine man conceived the idea of creating a gap in the lower jaw as a lifesaving device for those stricken with lockjaw, a disease to which the Masai were highly susceptible. The gap permitted the victims to be fed.

From earliest times, filing teeth to a point was widely practiced in Africa, Southeast Asia, and Central, North, and South America. As recently as 1934 it was reported that Negrito pygmies in the Philippines sharpened and pointed their front teeth to resemble those of a carnivorous animal. The Niam-Niam tribe of the Congo region of Africa also filed their teeth, claiming it improved their efficiency in piercing an enemy's flesh during fights. They have continued the practice, now deeming it ornamental.

Perhaps the most widespread dental decoration was the deliberate coloring of teeth. Symbolic ceremony, vanity, and status were the most important factors in the use of color as dental ornamentation. Black and red were the favorite extranatural colorations. Blue, yellow, and green, were also used occasionally.

Prior to the middle of the nineteenth century, men of high rank in Sumatra flaunted their station by dyeing their upper teeth black and covering their lower ones with fine gold plate, which, in full light, afforded a fine contrast. This practice was no doubt influenced by the Chinese custom of covering their front teeth with gold plate. On other islands in that area, coloration and alteration were reversed; gold plate was used on the upper teeth and the lowers were blackened.

The skillful Lampong craftswomen of Sumatra filed the enamel from their teeth, thus roughening them to obtain better adhesion before rubbing in color.

As a beauty aid, the Bontok women of Luzon in the Philippines burned a resinous wood, then mixed the ashes with sugar cane juice to make a paste with which they blackened their teeth. Asiatic Papuans of the Nicobar Islands in the Bay of Bengal, who blackened their teeth at the age of puberty, derisively compared white teeth to those of a dog or a pig.

Among the tribes on the African continent who dyed their teeth for ornamental reasons, red was the preferred color. Regardless of how this practice originated, these people were so accustomed to the coloration that its use as a cosmetic became *de rigueur*.

In Japan the staining of teeth black, known as *ohaguro*, had esthetic importance in all social strata. Ancient Chinese records about "the black teeth people" indicate *ohaguro* was practiced some 4,000 years ago, originally only by women. In 1233 the custom was adopted by a royal family, and its use spread thereafter. Since geishas, professional entertainers who were expected to be perfect beauties, also practiced this custom, we can assume that it was regarded as beautifying. Among women it served as an indication of marriage. Many princes, nobles, and aristocrats embellished their smiles with black-stained natural teeth and Stygian artificial teeth carved of wood and ivory. The custom waned after America established commercial relations with Japan in the nineteenth century, no doubt a consequence of the Japanese desire to conform to a Western life-style.

It was in early eighteenth-century France that dentistry became a learned profession, with its own literature and qualifying restrictions for its practice. Methods for replacing missing teeth improved gradually. The gold-shell crown *(calotte d'or)*, initially used by the Romans in the first century B.C., was revived, but used in a new way. Where exposed to view, a fairly natural appearance could be achieved by enameling the bright gold with a pale tint. A similar enameling process was employed to cover shiny gold areas on bridges and full sets of teeth. Unfortunately, the enameling had no permanence. The artistic objective was worthwhile, the artisans skillful, but the process was doomed because of lack of proper materials and technology.

The early eighteenth-century dental restorative efforts then reverted to the materials previously favored—animal ivories, hippopotamus teeth, ox bone, and occasionally gilded or painted wood carved into artificial teeth—despite the tendency of these materials to deteriorate because of mouth fluids.

The problems George Washington had with his teeth illustrate the situation well. His ivory teeth were a source of anxiety because they were uncomfortable, generated foul odors by rotting in the mouth, and had a depressing effect on his appearance due to lack of support for his sagging mouth and surrounding tissues. The result was that at times his lips had a pouting and swelled appearance; at other times they were abnormally fallen, depending upon how successfully his latest dentures had been made.

The false teeth he began wearing after 1798—a full upper and lower set carved from hippopotamus tusks—were also not satisfactory. They were inadequate because dentists lacked the proper materials and because it was difficult to keep the teeth securely in place.

In the correspondence between Washington and his dentist, Dr. Greenwood, there were serious discussions about the discoloration caused by port wine, which turned his ivory teeth black. On December 28, 1798, in reply to a query by the President, Dr. Greenwood wrote: "If you want your teeth more yellow soak them in broth or pot liquor, but not in tea or acids. Porter is a good thing to color them."

The search continued for better-looking artificial teeth that would not rot in the mouth. A Parisian apothecary, Duchateau, hit upon a major improvement in 1774. He was continually nauseated by the accumulated malodors absorbed by his carved hippopotamus teeth, which also sponged up the unpleasant tastes from the many prescriptions he sampled. He conceived a brilliant idea to rid himself of his misery and, at the same time, to make teeth that looked more beautiful and stayed that way. Looking at the mortars in which he customarily ground his medications, he thought, "Why not use the same nonabsorbent porcelain?" This significant advance was carried to practical fruition in the 1790s by Nicholas de Chemant, a Paris-trained dentist, who made "incorruptible teeth of mineral paste" and by Fonzi, an Italian-Parisian dentist, who provided platinum hooks in the porcelain teeth for connection to the base that held them in position.

Samples of these early porcelain teeth did not reach the United States until 1817, too late to relieve Washington's discomfort. The early 1800s marked a turning point, however, as American ingenuity developed fair-looking teeth that could be made widely available. By 1844 enough improvements had been made in porcelain artificial teeth to permit their manufacture on a commercial scale.

The average citizens of most societies had, until then, only the brutal instruments of the marketplace, barnyard, and kitchen for the removal of their aching teeth, while esthetic restoration was but a dream. All previous dental treatment and replacement procedures had been the province of a select few—those of rank and well-filled purse. It was, perhaps ironically, only in the so-called primitive cultures that dental practices were widespread.

The Goodyear process of rubber vulcanization, developed in the mid-nineteenth century, further aided the availability of more attractive artificial teeth. Dental plates of moderate cost could now be manufactured, but the great mass of rubber used to cover the palate was cumbersome. The time was right for the reintroduction of an ancient dental device: the gold-shell crown. Since it could be used to hold false teeth to the remaining ones, thereby eliminating the necessity for using large amounts of rubber, the popularity of gold crowns spurted, ushering in the American gold tooth era of which Terence Mc-Grover and his contemporaries were such shining examples.

This popularity was short-lived however, and began to decline in the years after 1910. A new fashion in teeth began evolving in the United States: an image based on natural, wholesome, well-shaped teeth was becoming the norm.

The expansion of oral and visual communication through radio, movies, and television kept pace with technical dental improvements.

The increasingly large audiences of millions of listeners and viewers were made aware of the mouth, lips, and teeth as a basis of beauty. Words such as tempting, ravishing, alluring, and, of course, sexy impregnated the airwaves and appeared in bold type in magazines and newspapers. Their objective was to sell beauty aids—facial conditioners, lipsticks, eye makeup, tooth whiteners—by building an idealized picture of what was beautiful. Where teeth were the subject, the health aspect was only secondarily alluded to.

One could not, and cannot, escape this new image, which was appropriately called "Hollywood teeth." It sprang up on billboards along the highways in the multicolored beauty, personality, and sex periodicals, and on movie and television screens. Closeup techniques in movies and television created new visual hazards for the stars, who were setting universal concepts of beauty. The magnification of the screen's close-ups disclosed even minute tooth defects, initiating a vast amount of dental restorative activity to eliminate them.

Plastic cosmetic caps, dubbed "Hollywood veneers," were first experimented with, but the slippage of veneers at the wrong moment, perhaps during an amorous scene or speaking passage, made more practical and permanent replacements imperative. Crowns made of porcelain and

plastic came into wide cosmetic use. Carefully fitted and matched to the shades of surrounding teeth, these caps cover the entire tooth and all manner of dental defects, as well. Even close exposure does not reveal their presence. Now widely available, they have added a new dimension to the pursuit of oral charm.

With the increasing impact of global communications, even people living in the remotest areas of the world are no longer immune to the blandishments of Western culture. The allure of sparkling white teeth, carefully created by the advertising wizards of modern business, is penetrating into settlements formerly isolated from extracultural contact. Some peoples still resist and cling to the old ways, staining and reshaping their teeth to suit their ancient concepts of what is tantalizing and captivating. But it is a losing battle; the inexorable trend is toward diminution, and eventual abandonment, of native folkways and customs. Because Western standards—based on advanced technology and material wealth and proselyted by the pervasive media—are effecting a world wide conformity in dress, food, and shelter, pearly whites will soon become the universal concept of oral beauty. Compared to the colorful past, it will be a duller world.

THE SONG OF THE SHIRT

Judith Hennessee and Joan Nicholson

The invention of the sewing machine was called "a blessing to mankind, and especially to the female." But did it really work out that way?

"During the 19th century the Singer Sewing Machine has added countless hours to women's leisure for rest and refinement, it has opened new avenues for her employment, and it has brought comforts which were formerly attainable to few within the reach of all."—*Early Singer Advertisement*

Women always have been stuck with the sewing. The connection is there in Greek myth and legend—the Three Fates are women, and one of them, Atropos, cuts the thread of life. Ariadne used thread to save Theseus from the Labyrinth; in Homer, Penelope, famous for her patience, used weaving to put off her unwelcome suitors. Primitive Indian women chewed hides and sewed them with bone needles. American farm women, weighed down with huge families and no servants, spent hours stitching— *after* all the other household work was done. Even in their leisure time they quilted while they socialized. James Fenimore Cooper read novels to his wife in the evening while she sewed. Fenimore Cooper went on to write the "Leather-stocking Saga"; we don't know what Mrs. Cooper did with herself.

"Oh! teach the orphan boy to read, or teach the orphan girl to sew," Tennyson's Lady Clara Vere de Vere said, but the daughter of a thousand earls was never burdened, as the working-class woman was, with the boring and fatiguing labor of sewing clothes. Through the centuries, needlework was thought of as an accomplishment for the highborn, not an act of labor. A lady was an ornament, like her needlework. It is significant that the only woman connected with the American Revolution that anyone remembers is known for her sewing—Betsy Ross.

Before the Industrial Revolution and labor-saving machinery, a woman's home was her factory. Working 12 or more hours a day, Colonial women manufactured household products from the raw materials the men brought in. They were domestic slaves, old at 30. In a divorce-less age, some men used up as many as three wives; they just wore out. Men's drudgery was relieved by their sitting down to a meal cooked by women, and by wearing clothes

From "The Song of the Shirt." *Ms.* Magazine, October 1972, pp. 65–70, Pictures are omitted. Reprinted by permission of the publisher.

that had been sewed by women. There were few jobs for spinsters, and the normal route out of a father's house was through marriage or prostitution. Possessing neither money nor an education, many looked forward to the state of widowhood as an ideal one.

When the poorer women left their homes to earn a few extra pennies, they merely extended their sphere of domesticity. They did bits of sewing and knitting, made hats, shoes, or cloth. This piecework, done in the home, became the forerunner of the "sweated" system.

An English import, the system hinged on a middleman, called the sweater, who contracted with the manufacturer for a certain number of finished garments and employed five or more operators (the sweated) to sew them. The operators went to the dealer's workroom and staggered back carrying bundles of cut material on which they worked for 12 to 16 hours a day, shut up together in airless, sunless rooms. They could earn about 30 cents a day, while the sweater, or "slop shop" contractor, picked up $1.50 a day for doing nothing. Those who sweated never knew exactly what their wages would be, and if they thought the price of piecework too small, the sweater could easily find others to replace them. Men and women did it; children did it; whole familes did it. But, for the women, it was the only skill they had.

An essay published in 1790 by Judith Sargent Murray discussed the distribution of brains between men and women and concluded that women required, as men did, more mental activity than that derived from "the mechanism of a pudding, or the sewing of the seams of a garment." It was an idea whose time had not come. Instead the factory came, and women leaped at the chance to get out of the house. Low wages and independence were better than unpaid labor at home.

In the factory they did exactly the same work they had done at home. They sewed. They made cloth, clothes, hats, and shoes, and because the work could also be done at home, the trade was always overcrowded and underpaid. Then—as now—the wage differential was enormous. Sarah Grimke wrote in 1837, ". . .in tailoring, a man has twice or three times as much for making a waistcoat or pantaloons as a woman, although the work done by each may be equally good. In those employments which are peculiar to women, their time is estimated at half the value of that of men."

In an age that exalted motherhood to a state next to divinity, the mother herself was of little importance. Again, then—as now—the children bogged her down and cost her dearly. A working mother who sewed at home averaged about $36.40 a year. Without children she averaged $58.60 a year. If she sewed without stopping from sunrise to 10 or 11 o'clock at night without any interruptions for sickness or family care or anything else, her reward was $1.50 a week, or $78 a year. (A journeyman machinist made $9 a week.) In the factory, she and her children worked 12 to 16 hours a day with time off for two meals—breakfast and dinner.

The Civil War removed the main source of income from thousands of families and pushed more women into the factories. With only their sewing to offer, they were desperate for work and their desperation was taken full advantage of. Through the system of subcontracting, a variation of the sweatshop, they earned enough to starve. In 1865, a group of them petitioned President Lincoln: "We are unable to sustain life for the price offered by contractors, who fatten on their contracts by grinding immense profits out of the labor of their operatives. As an example, these contractors are paid one dollar and seventy-five cents each for making gray woolen shirts, and they require us to make them for one dollar per dozen. . . ." At that time, calico was going for 50 cents a yard, coffee for a dollar a pound, and a pair of gloves at Macy's cost a dollar.

Leisured ladies also sewed for the soldiers, but in a significantly different way. They found the task romantic and exciting. Interspersed among gossip of engagements and flirtations, parties, and trips, letters of the period invariably mention sewing:

> Has it been very gay in New York this winter? It has been tolerably so here. Mrs. C — — — had a small party, and Mrs. E — — — P — — — both were very pleasant indeed. Mrs. D — — — P — — — has a sewing circle every week for the soldiers, the hour of meeting is half past seven, and if you are a minute late you have to pay a small sum I have forgotten how much—rather a queer rule don't you think so? I do not belong, but Mrs. S — — — has had a very pleasant one, only young ladies, about thirty or forty, and all creatures of the masculine order have been entirely banished so that the females, not being distracted by their presence, have sewed quite steadily and accomplished a great deal—next Tuesday is the last meeting.

But the ladies had their problems, too. One of them wrote:

> I am dreading the fall months, for I am to spend them here, and devote myself entirely to sewing. Abby intends going to Miss H — — — 's in January, and I have promised to assist her in her preparations which are not inconsiderable, in view of the fact that she has to make up a set of new underclothes.

At about the time Scarlett O'Hara was converting her mother's green velvet drapes into a new dress, a lady of fashion in Salem, Massachusetts, was acquiring a sewing machine. "Dear P — — —," she writes to her friend in New York,

> I have been occupied lately in purchasing a sewing machine. I finally decided upon the Florence which I think I shall like very much. Abby A — — —bought one at the same time and we both expect to do wonders with them. It really seems as if there were nothing they couldn't do. They gather, hem, quilt, braid, cord, and fell besides making four different

stitches and joining off at the end of a seam. In fact, they promise so much that I feel somewhat doubtful about their performance, but every one who has tried them likes them.

The sewing machine—"woman's best friend"—was invented in 1790, but it didn't come into popular use until shortly before the Civil War when Isaac Singer, who designed the foot treadle and added to the practicality of the machine, marketed it. Although half the human race had been occupied chiefly in making clothes for the other half, there was no great outcry for the mechanical stitcher which was ultimately named (along with the steam engine, the telegraph, and the plow) one of the great laborsaving inventions of civilization. An almost moralistic belief that it would be wrong to threaten the jobs of the thousands of poor tailors and seamstresses, and an amazing lack of understanding about the value of machines to society had prevented its earlier development. In 1841, in France, an angry mob of tailors had destroyed one of the first machines.

Although he was not the first to build a sewing machine, Singer seems to have been the first man to become aware of the lot of the "weary seamstress." His machine, which he called a "servant in the house," was the first of the laborsaving devices for women and could do the work of 12 of them. John Scott was later to write, "Steam and telegraph deal mainly with creation's Lord; the sewing machine with his lowlier sister." Men congratulated themselves on the coming liberation of womankind through the machine—and no man blamed himself for past abuses of those same women. Socialists believed that the proletariat would be freed by the new technology of machines; and women, part of that downtrodden class, would also gain. The rampant idealism of the time prompted men to greet the machine as an "advance agent of civilization." They said it "manumitted the white slave." They said women would be free for "cultural activities"—and at the same time they discussed in glowing terms the benefits of the new leisure on a growing male child.

To some male minds, the sewing machine was practically an elixir, capable of curing all ills. (There was some fear that its vibrations might cause abortions, but the medical research of the period was unable to substantiate this notion.) It was "a healthy substitute for the degrading, exhausting, debilitating. . . needle, with its. . . accompaniments of poverty, misery, and vice." It was a reforming agent, active in "the prevention of pauperism, the reformation of the Magdalen, the support of the widow, and care of the orphan." It could also prevent disease "as an agent antagonistic to the tendency of the times, the sedentary, inactive, enervating, unmuscular habits of the women of the world." After six months of intensive investigation, during which he questioned male munufacturers but not female sweatshop employees, the author of these stirring phrases, one J.P. Stambaugh, concluded, "The sewing machine is a blessing to mankind, and especially to the female." It didn't quite happen that way.

Middle-class women certainly did benefit from the machine, and so did their sewing girls, and eventually cheap factory-made clothes were available to everyone. Singer, who called the machine a "boon to womankind," proceeded to invent the installment plan to promote sales. By 1879, the company had sold 6 million machines. Many young single women signed their own contracts (a privilege we seem to have lost) to buy $100 machines for $5 down and payments of one, two, or three dollars a month. Each purchaser was given a book and coupons, and when the payment was made every month, a coupon was pasted in the appropriate space. According to the records, the Singer Company had little trouble with deadbeats. The honesty and goodwill of his customers were instrumental in making Singer a millionaire.

But thousands of working women were living in poverty while the men who owned the factories fought all efforts at reform. Some shops locked their doors, probably to keep the women from going on strike. Hundreds of them, jammed together in stifling rooms, were divided into small competing sewing teams under the control of the male sweater, who haggled with the manufacturer for work. They were subjected to petty humiliations, such as having to file singly past a guard with their pocketbooks open as they left. If they didn't come to work on Sunday they were told, they needn't bother to show up on Monday. Foremen moved back the hands of the clock when they weren't watching so that when it was 6, the clock said 5. Shops were housed in filthy old buildings, crusted with years of grime, their windows nailed shut. It was always dark. Many of these "huddled masses yearning to breathe free" ended up choking and coughing themselves to death. Tuberculosis was the disease of the age, and the air in the sweatshops, a deadly mixture of dust and moisture, encouraged its growth and spread.

The women, who had the choice of sewing or walking the streets (and many of them chose the latter), were forced to accept whatever treatment was handed out to them. Sometimes their wages were withheld, and they had no redress. They were fined if their stitches were crooked, or if they stained the goods with machine oil, or if they talked or laughed or sang. As late as 1906 they were charged 50 cents a week for the use of the machines and electricity, 5 cents a week for the use of a mirror and towel, and 5 cents a week for drinking water.

With this kind of economic leverage, the foremen had unlimited power over them, and the women were prey to all sorts of unwelcome attentions. In 1912, women striking a corset company outraged the city of Kalamazoo, Michigan, by charging the company with immoral behavior in the plant. Josephine Casey, one of the strikers, said, "The girls are compelled to pay for their own thread and this is quite an item. It is a common practice for foremen to forget to charge them for the thread for several days and then suggest to them a way which these girls might repay them for their act of 'kindness.' " The striking women were arrested.

The "boon to womankind" had left them exactly where they were before. In a burst of paternalistic idealism, Singer had guaranteed profits of five to six dollars a day to "Journeymen, Tailors, Seamstresses, Employers, and all others interested in sewing of any description," but the seamstresses and tailors never came anywhere near that figure. In 1884, bustle-makers in Boston, working from 8:30 A.M. to 6 P.M., were earning 25 cents a dozen—a day's output. Men did better. In the 1880s, a cloak-maker got one dollar for making a seal-plush cloak that sold for $75. One cloak was a full day's work for an expert male operator.

"Bertha the Sewing Machine Girl, or Death at the Wheel," was a melodramatic serial that appeared in 1871 in Street and Smith's *New York Weekly*. Bertha stood up to her boss who was paying her a "miserable pittance," but most women were too expendable to risk a confrontation. There had been sporadic efforts to organize for decades, all of them ending either in failure or in slight gains, such as knocking a half hour off a twelve-and-a-half-hour day. In 1831, 1,600 seamstresses struck, some of them staying out for as long as five weeks, but the whole weight of tradition was against them. The public attitude was clearly expressed by an indignant magistrate who roared at a striking shirtwaist-maker, "You are on strike against God and Nature."

God and Nature notwithstanding, the women had no real weapon to use against their employers. There were too many of them, hungry and uneducated, and successive waves of unskilled immigrants flooded the factories and sweatshops, driving the low wages lower. "There are not many things that an unskilled foreigner, knowing no English, can do," wrote Ray Stannard Baker, "but almost any man or woman can sew." For the most part, the men in factories saw women as a threat to their own efforts to get higher wages. Women were coolie labor. The early union organizations excluded women altogether. The shop was closed to all but qualified men.

Women were also severely hampered by their obsession with behaving in a "ladylike" manner. The Daughters of St. Crispin, a union of women who stitched shoe tops, passed a strong resolution at their annual convention in 1870, demanding "the same rate of compensation for equal skill displayed, or the same hours of toil, as is paid other laborers in the same branches of business; and we regard a denial of this right by anyone as a usurpation and a fraud." But they were too nervous to let it stand. Ladies didn't talk that way, and they weren't in a position to offend the sensibilities of potential supporters. They

added one submissive sentence which canceled out the aggressive tone of their demand: "Resolved, that we assure our fellow-citizens that we only desire to so elevate and improve our condition as to better fit us for the discharge of those high social and moral duties [devolving] upon every true woman."

This "ancient capitalistic paternalism" was the reasoning behind the first protective hour law for women, passed in Wisconsin in 1867. Women whose health was damaged by overwork couldn't serve the race properly as mothers. The protective laws were necessary ones, but they should have protected men, too. Instead they worked to keep women's wages at a minimum and women dependent on men.

The Daughters of St. Crispin, like other unions before it, fell apart. It was almost impossible for women to have strong, effective organization. With wages as skimpy as their skirts were voluminous, they were too poor to pay regular dues or contribute strike money or pay the basic expenses of a continuous organization. And always there was the bright, shining dream of a marriage that would whisk them away from the drudgery of factory work to live happily ever after. There was no way for a woman to achieve a decent standard of living except through a man, and if she was too militant, it might cost her a husband.

Leonora Barry, an organizer for the Knights of Labor, the first nationwide union for both men and women, met with little success in her efforts to get women to join. Apathy was too ingrained, she said, as was "the habit of submission and acceptance without question of any terms offered them, with the pessimistic view of life in which they see no ray of hope. . . . Again, many women are deterred from joining labor organizations by foolish pride, prudish modesty, and religious scruples; and a prevailing hope and expectancy that in the near future marriage will lift them out of the industrial life to the quiet and comfort of a home. . . ."

All this time Susan B. Anthony and other women were traveling up and down the country fighting for the vote, but a number of things had kept them apart from factory workers. Class was important, more important than sex. How could a woman of leisure have anything in common with a poor, dirty, ignorant, disease-ridden seamstress? It was scarcely thinkable. Middle-class women had traditionally allied themselves with men. It was easier, and it was the only way they could stay on top of the heap. They preferred to exchange the dangers of freedom and independence for pirvileges effortlessly acquired through marriage. The sweatshop women themselves, who had never understood how to defend themselves against their employers, saw no connection between their own degraded position and their lack of political power. When the suffragists tried to form a coalition with them, it failed.

The idea of political power, or voting, was remote to green immigrants whose knowledge of English was so limited that strike posters had to be printed in three languages—English, Yiddish, and Italian. They saw the vote, if at all, as a luxury, and they were in need of necessities. Their attention was focused on wages, on job security, and on better working conditions. In addition to the general Victorian repression of all women, the immigrants were doubly inhibited, saddled with the heavy European patriarchal mores they had brought with them. And they were exhausted. Their 12-hour day was only the beginning. On them devolved the entire load of housekeeping and child care—and sewing for their families. The vision of suffrage had no bearing on their daily lives. There had been isolated instances of sexual solidarity in the past—in some of the short-lived unions, for instance—but it had been largely confined within one class. It wasn't until the early 1900s, when the pall of Victorianism began to dissolve and social consciousness invaded elegant Fifth Avenue mansions, that rich women saw that they had a common cause with the sweated class.

The strike that finally made a dent in the Establishment and built up the International Ladies' Garment Workers' Union was the 14-week Shirtwaist Strike of 1909, which is significant less for its labor reforms (the small shops capitulated but the larger ones, like the Triangle Shirtwaist Company, held out), than for the solidarity of women as a sex.

In the past, women who got better wage and therefore had less reason to complain had stayed aloof from their less fortunate sisters, and this lack of cohesiveness had been one reason for the women's defeat. This time, the intellectuals, the women who attended classes and lectures, who counted their pennies to buy theater tickets to see Ibsen, led and inspired the others and kept them on the picket line despite police clubbings, threats by neighborhood thugs, fines, and workhouse sentences. "The girls" dressed in their best for the picket line and were applauded by *Survey* magazine for being "entirely orderly" while being harassed.

It was very important for respectable girls to be orderly. Twenty-one days after the strike began, Mrs. O.H.P. Belmont, a social leader and suffragist, brought to bear not only her social clout but her economic power. She offered her half-million-dollar Madison Avenue mansion as security for the release of three of the strikers. She was followed by Carola Woerlshoffer, who persuaded her mother to convert family real estate into bonds, posted herself at the door of the Jefferson Market Court, and entered it with every group of arrested women to offer the bonds as security for their release.

These upper-class women also held a rally in Carnegie Hall and spent an estimated $60,000—a fortune in 1909—on strike benefits. One society woman, Mary Dreier, allowed herself to be arrested on the picket line and was taken to the station house before identifying herself. *Survey* wrote that the embarrassed officer "upbraided her for not having told him she was 'the rich working-girls' friend,' had he known which, of course, he would not have arrested her ."

The alliance didn't last much beyond the strike, but the ILGWU was on its way. The Triangle Shirtwaist Company fire in 1911, in which 146 women died, helped to consolidate its position. The labor reforms that followed the fire protected women from the worst excesses of the sweatshop. Some sweatshops remain today for those who are not unionized (mainly outside New York), populated by black and Puerto Rican women who are in the same sort of position the immigrant were in. Organized in 1900 by men, the union remains male dominated even though its membership and that of its offshoot, the Amalgamated Clothing Workers of America, are each 80 percent women.

Patriarchal from its inception, the same traditional sex hierarchy still prevails in the industry. Today the most skilled occupation and the best paid is that of the cutter, and most of the cutters are men. The next-best-paid is the presser, and the most of the pressers are men. Then come the sewing-machine operators. Most of them are women. Among those who sew, more men than women work on coats and suits, garments that require more skill than petticoats or dresses. The industry is fluid, and the low representation of women in higher-paying jobs does not seem to have been a policy of deliberate exclusion.

In the early 1900s, U.S. Labor Commissioner Carroll Wright said, "The lack of direct political influence constitutes a powerful reason why women's wages have been kept at a minimum." Women have had the vote for 52 years—the suffragists thought its mere possession would make miracles—but they have never used it for themselves, to gain their own ends as women. And they have behaved the same way in their unions. Not enough women pay attention to the Equal Pay Act of 1963 or to Title VII of the Civil Rights Act of 1964, which prohibits job discrimination because of sex. It is one of those unfortunate facts of life that weapons are necessary to enforce the law. Women have the weapon—the union—but they aren't active enough in its leadership to force compliance. They are still letting the men take care of them. The sewing machine did not emancipate women after all. No machine can do that, because it is not a lack of machinery that oppresses women.

When the sewing machine became popular, an odd thing happened. In discovering that they could sew 10 stitches in the time it used to take to sew one, women began to put 10 times as many stitches in everything they made. Even now, most women don't buy the attachments—they do the fancywork by hand. To date, the Singer company has sold more than a hundred million machines in every part of the world. Down in the Everglades, they changed the dress of the Seminole Indians, who used to be drably and scantily dressed. The women of the tribe loved the machine, and Seminole costumes are now designed with hundreds of pieces of elaborate and colorful material: The time that could have been saved is used to create more work.

Most American women are free of the terrible drudgery that shortened the Colonial woman's life. Only the packaging has improved. Very little has changed since 1867. The date 1867 is important. That was the year a man invented the typewriter.

CHAPTER 4

Clothing Behavior: Social and Psychological Viewpoints

INTRODUCTION

Lois M. Gurel

Many forces are responsible for individual clothing choices. Attitudes toward clothing, interest in clothing, and the importance of clothing to an individual are the results of many deliberate actions, environmental conditions, conscious acts, and unconscious motivations. The processes involved in daily clothing selection and the societal forces that influence this selection may not always be easily indentifiable, but there are underlying causes. "Clothing behavior is not the random and purposeless activity it is so often presumed to be. In most cases it is influenced by the same forces—social, psychological and economic—that affect other aspects of human activity."[1]

Clothing behavior may be explained by studying the social and psychological aspects of dress: why we as individuals dress as we do; why we are interested in particular clothing items; the effect of clothing on human behavior; the way we see each other's clothing; the impressions we make on other people because of the clothing we wear. If people did not live in social situations, it would not make any difference what was worn; clothing would be far less important in our lives; fashion would be irrelevant.

Psychology is the study of people and their behavior as individuals. *Sociology* is the study of people and their behavior in groups. The sociopsychological aspects of dress can be divided into these two categories. Many sociological and psychological theories are used by researchers in an attempt to explain clothing behavior: the effect of the self-concept; the influence of reference groups; the role and status of an individual; the degree of conformity and/or individuality; the relative security and insecurity of people; the priority of needs, especially those related to self-actualization; the force and effect of the authoritarian type of personality; and the life (or sex) and death drives of psychoanalytic theory. In many cases a division of these theories between the two disciplines is artificial, sometimes impossible, and often results in overlap.

Social psychology is the study of individual behavior and how it is affected by groups. Those theories listed above which concern both individual and group behavior

best fit into the field of social psychology. Clothing behavioral studies utilizing these theories are also best classified as social psychological in nature.

The first four articles in this chapter are about groups similar in some ways to those described in Chapter 2. The alternate life styles found in the "back to nature" communes and among the poor have much in common with peoples separated from society because of religious beliefs. So, too, age groups either segregate themselves or are segregated by society. All are subcultural groups within the larger American culture and as such may be studied from an anthropological perspective. But they also serve as illustrations of the profound effect of group belongingness on individual clothing behavior and are, therefore, sociological in nature, also. Group structure is used to influence individual members in regard to the type, style, and even in some cases amount of clothing owned. The conforming influence of group action on adolescent clothing illustrates the power that peer groups exert on these young people to dress like the other members of their age group. So, too, society sets apart the aging population and many other special needs groups, forcing conformity where it may not be necessarily desirable or desired.

Blumer's now classic article on fashion sets the stage for numerous theories concerning why individuals dress the way they do, fashion being just one among many. The pervasiveness of fashion is stressed along with an admonition to think of fashion in terms other than those traditionally reserved for costume and adornment. The selection by Horn explains role theory—the *use* of clothing by individuals to portray a role as well as the converse, the roles *assumed* by individuals because of the clothing they wear. The uniform, often offered as an alternative to fashion, is diametrically opposite the use of clothing for self-expression, particularly in role portrayal. The purpose of the uniform is to suppress individuality not to foster it. This concept is discussed by Joseph and Alex in "The Uniform: A Sociological Perspective." And a plausible explanation for the widespread interest in dress as a tool for economic success can be attributed to role theory. Beeson describes this phenomenon that occurred in the late 70s in a commentary on the many books and articles purporting "recipes" for success through dress.

1. Horn, M.J., *The Second Skin.* Boston: Houghton Mifflin Co., 1968, p. 2.

The age old theory, that clothing is primarily used as a sexual lure, was investigated by McCullough, Miller, and Ford. Although the results of their research, that sexual attraction was not the primary motive that influenced clothing usage, is of interest in itself, the major purpose for the inclusion of this article was as an illustration of social science research in the field of clothing.

The effects of individual action on group behavior are discussed by Zalaznick. "Fashion from the Streets" illustrates the influence of collective individual behavior on fashion and the availability of styles.

Clothing plays a double role in society. It affects the behavior and actions of the wearer, and it plays a part in how we see and understand others. This dual nature of clothes can be seen through many articles in this section, such as "Body Decoration and Camouflage." Often our initial impressions of others are erroneous, seldom are they accurate, and yet they are continually made with great speed and firm determination in their accuracy. Clothing plays an important role in these first impressions, in how we see and understand someone else, as demonstrated by "T-shirts for Tea."

Conversely, we are greatly affected by the clothes we wear. The roles we choose, the moods we reflect are all part and parcel of a total personality. Clothing affects how we behave and how others see and understand us. Clothing is a "silent language"; we express our inner most traits of personality through our selection of clothing. As a form of nonverbal communication, the language of clothing is read by others and interpreted in forming their impressions of us.

ADDITIONAL READINGS

On fashion:

Simmel, George. "Fashion," *International Quarterly,* Vol. 10, October 1904, pp. 137–140; also in *American Journal of Sociology,* Vol. 62, May 1957, pp. 541–558.

A classic analysis.

"Is Sex Killing Fashion?" *Clothes,* March 1, 1974, pp. 36–43.

On clothing as communication:

Argyle, Michael. *Bodily Communication.* N.Y.: International Universities Press, Inc., 1975.

Chapter 17 (pp. 323–344) is "Clothes, Physique, and Other Aspects of Appearance."

Rosenfeld, L.B. and Plax, T.G. "Clothing As Communication," *Journal of Communication,* Vol. 27, spring, 1977, pp. 24–31."

Thurman, Judith. "How to Get Dressed and Still Be Yourself," *Ms.* Magazine, Vol. 7, No. 10, April, 1979, pp. 50–53+.

On clothing as expression of deviant lifestyles:

"The Commune Comes to America," *Life,* Vol. 67, July 18, 1969, pp. 16–23.

Photographs in color.

Howard, J. "Flowering of the Hippie Movment," in *Collective Behavior,* second edition, by R. Turner and L. Killian. Englewood Cliffs, N.J.: Prentice-Hall, 1972, pp. 321–331.

Sabol, Blair, and Truscott, Lucian. "The Politics of the Costume," *Esquire,* Vol. 79, May 1971, pp. 123–134.

Photographs in color show examples of clothes used to create a political statement.

Kirkham, George L. and Sagarin, Edward. "Cross-dressing," *Sexual Behavior,* Vol 2, No. 4, April 1972, pp. 53–59.

Many aspects of transvestism discussed, including possible causes, legal problems, and social dictates.

On clothing of the adolescent subculture and influences on the larger society:

Creekmore, Anna M. and Young, Mary Jane. "The Generation Gap in Clothing," *Illinois Teacher,* Vol. XIV, No. 6, July-August 1971, pp. 289–294.

Gurel, Lois M., Wilbur, June C., and Gurel, Lee. "Personality Correlates of Adolescent Clothing Styles," *Journal of Home Economics,* Vol. 64, No. 3, March 1972, pp. 42–47.

"The Class of '74: the Way They Are." *Clothes,* Vol. 8, No. 20, January 1, 1974, pp. 58–67.

"Consciousness III," *American Fabrics* Magazine, Issue 89, Winter 1971, pp. 47–50.

Comments by professionals in the textiles and apparel industries on the views of Charles Reich, author of *The Greening of America.*

Kneitel, Ken, Maloney, Bill and Quinn, Andrea. *The Great American T-Shirt.* N.Y.: A Push Pin Press Book for the New American Library, Inc., 1976.

Primarily photographs of people wearing an enormous variety of T-shirts.

Owens, Richard M. and Lane, Tony. *American Denim.* N.Y.: Harry N. Abrams, 1975.

On clothing for special needs:

Galbreaith, Patricia. *What You Can Do for Yourself: Hints for the Handicapped.* N.Y.: Drake Publishers, Inc., 1974.

Chapter 1 is "Clothing—Shoes," pp. 3–29.

May, Elizabeth Eckhardt, Waggoner, Neva R., and Boettke, Eleanor M. *Homemaking for the Handicapped.* N.Y.: Dodd, Mead & Co., 1966.

Chapter 7 is "The Selection and Adaptation of Clothing to Suit Particular Needs," pp. 68–79; Chapter 8 is "Self-Help Clothing for Adults, pp. 80–92; and, Chapter 9 is "Self-Help Clothing for Children," pp. 93–112.

Allon, Natalie. "Group-Dieting Rituals," in *Deviant Life-Styles,* edited by James M. Henslin. New Brunswick, New Jersey: Transaction Books, 1977, pp. 101–121.

Pressures to be thin are described.

Norment, Lynn. "Big Can Be Beautiful," *Ebony,* October 1978, pp. 82–88.

Photographs show women wearing clothes suitable for large figures.

CLOTHING IN THE COMMUNE

Marianne S. Beeson

Clothing as a visible manifestation of philosophy and principles is important to many groups who choose to set themselves apart from the mainstream of society. Individual clothing behavior which is outside of generally accepted norms may be regarded as merely eccentric, but on a larger scale, "unusual" dress may call attention to the underlying purposes of such behavior. Within the group, adherence to new clothing norms which are expressive of the group's reason for being contribute unity and solidarity.

In the American past "set apart" communities, sometimes called intentional communities in the current literature, have often been of religious intent. Dictates regarding dress have been consistent with religious beliefs. The prosperous Amana colonies were thus described by a visitor in 1874.

> The women and girls wear dingy colored stuffs, mostly of the society's own make, cut in the plainest style, and often short gowns, in the German peasant way. All even to the very small girls, wear their hair in a kind of black cowl or cap, which covers only the back of the head, and is tied under the chin by a black ribbon. Also all, young as well as old, wear a small dark-colored shawl or handkerchief over the shoulders, and pinned very plainly across the breast. This peculiar uniform adroitly conceals the marks of sex, and gives a singularly monotonous appearance to the women.
>
> The sex, I believe, is not highly esteemed by these people, who think it dangerous to the Christian's peace of mind. One of their most esteemed writers advises men to 'fly from intercourse with women, as a very highly dangerous magnet and magical fire.' Their women work hard and dress soberly; all ornaments are forbidden. To wear the hair loose is prohibited. Great care is used to keep the sexes apart (1, pp. 95–96).

According to Fogarty, "The range of communitarian activity throughout the 19th century was extraordinary: It included free lovers, celibates, anarchists, socialists, and spiritualists (1, p. x)." Dress of communal members was often voluntarily chosen or imposed by rule so as to parallel specific utopian ideals.

Veysey enumerates several themes in American cultural radicalism

> . . . opposition to established agencies of social authority, such as governments and churches; the ideal of uncompromising social brotherhood; economic decentralization and self-sufficiency; inner self-development and the search for mental clarity; the pursuit of a guru or other enlightened leader; religious free thought; mysticism and spiritualism; the quest for individual and collective states of ecstasy; pacificism; racial and sexual equality; abolition or modification of the nuclear family; belief in a simpler, more natural way of life, for instance in matters of clothing and diet; and extreme progressivism in education (2, p. 55).

Intentional communities or communes today are seeking a more "perfect" life through a style of living evolved around such themes. Very rough estimates of the number of communes in America at present range from 1,000 to 3,000 (2, p. 457). The desire to return to the land, to subsist on it, to grow, raise, and create with one's own hands the necessities of life form a central focus of many communes. Natural foods and fibers, hand spun yarns, hand woven fabrics, and hand made clothing are part of the scene.

Deliberate isolation, usually rural, is geographical and philosophical. Communes tend to treasure their privacy. Rejection of the mass culture may include doing without electricity, indoor plumbing, modern medicine in all but the most severe situations, formal education for the children, and commitment to antimaterialism in almost every sense.

Fashion is also alien, although the functional and some aesthetic aspects of clothing may be highly regarded. Work clothing that is durable, warm winter clothing, protective boots, and the like are desirable and sought. Hand embroidered and appliqued decorations may be applied to clothes in leisure hours. Pretty colors and loose-fitting, comfortable styles are likely to be preferred in the agrarian communes with which this author is familiar.

B.F. Skinner's novel *Walden Two* illustrates how the wastefulness of fashion may be rejected in a utopian society without also rejecting style and taste. Perhaps the compromise position regarding dress so described is explained by the continued contacts between this fictional commune and the outside world, along with a rather sophisticated life style. The following are excerpts from conversations in which the *Walden Two* characters explain their experiments in living to visitors.

> "Here we are not so much at the mercy of commercial designers, and many of our women manage to appear quite beautiful simply because they are not required to dress within strict limits."
>
> "Going out of style isn't a natural process, but a manipulated change which destroys the beauty of last year's dress in order to make it worthless. We opposed this by broadening our tastes. Little touches which now seem out of style . . . will then appear natural and pleasing . . . a line or feature is never in itself dated. . . ."
>
> "We want to avoid the waste which is imposed by changing styles, but we don't want to be wholly out of fashion. So we simply change styles more slowly, just slowly enough so we needn't throw away clothing which is still in good condition."
>
> "We simply chose the kind of clothes which suffer the slowest change—suits, sweaters and skirts, or blouses and skirts, and so on. You won't find half a dozen 'party dresses' among us—and those aren't from the community supply. Yet each of us has something that would be in good taste except at very formal functions."

"Full dress . . . is a form of conspicuous consumption which doesn't amuse us—except when we see it in others."[1]

In defense of even this degree of style consciousness, the *Walden Two* conversants continue.

"It isn't that we mind being thought queer, I'm sure. Perhaps we don't want to think ourselves queer."

". . . we aren't really cut off from the world and don't want to be. Our art and literature, our movies, our radio, and our occasional excursions outside the community keep us in constant touch with American life. A complete break would be more trouble than it's worth. Also, it would be unfair to our children to make them feel out of place or ill at ease among outsiders. It might suggest that life at Walden Two was somehow odd or even inferior."[2]

The time and effort for dressing up are viewed positively.

"We have plenty of time for everything. We like a break between the active part of the day and the quieter social hours at dinner and in the evening. A bath and a change are an important point in the day's schedule. They are psychologically refreshing."[3]

In the real world a fear of the future and a desire to avoid the awesome responsibilities of participation in a complex, techno-industrial society have led some to the commune as an escape route. Veysey relates this kind of immaturity to a new phenomenon of the counter-culture, a situation sharply contrasting to the serenely organized Walden Two.

The loss of faith in the long-range future perhaps explains another striking characteristic of the recent counter-culture, the previously unknown willingness to let one's body stay physically dirty for long periods. Washing is a form of planning, a way of making oneself ready for future occasions. In a world which is believed to have no future, it becomes senseless. Going dirty reduces the need for devoting time to upkeep and makes one's life far more flexible. The mind is freed for immediate experience (2, pp. 470–471).

If success of communes is measured by overall stability and continuous existence even though individuals may leave and be replaced by newcomers, then successful communes of today seem to be characterized by long-range planning, structure, and serious dedication to purpose. Twin Oaks, near Louisa, Virginia, has endured since 1967 on these bases plus a system of "labor credits" to insure equality in the distribution of tasks. Communally owned clothing is an interesting aspect of the shared living experience at Twin Oaks.

Our institution of community use of clothing has grown entirely without any rules or planning. We never sat around discussing whether using the same clothing would make us feel "closer" or whether it was more "equal," or even whether it would save us money. We left the subject alone and did as we pleased. What many people pleased was fullscale community clothing from a central closet, and that is what we have now.

This is how it works. Every member has clothing he or she doesn't particularly care about. Most of us simply have too much clothing. So we all take our surplus clothes to the big Community closet, the clothing manager sorts it out, puts it on hangers or in labeled boxes. Then anybody who needs something to wear goes and gets it. After wearing, things go to Community laundry, and from there back to the big closet.

One of the things that makes this system work is that it is not compulsory. We all know that Community clothing often suffers from carelessness or ignorance (witness that big box of wool sweaters that have been shrunk in the dryer over the years). If members have things they are particularly fond of, they are more than welcome to mark them with their names and have them delivered to their rooms from the laundry. This option is a completely acceptable norm; you are not considered "less communitarian than we" if you choose it. There are perhaps six people in the Community who do; the rest of us literally prefer communal use.

There are good reasons for that. The big one is that one need not use one's precious bedroom space for clothing storage. One drawer for the next two days' changes is adequate. Next in importance is the fun of having an immense wardrobe and the satisfaction of seeing something you brought being enjoyed by someone else. Maybe it just confirms your taste, or perhaps it makes you feel that you contribute something of worth. A less positive but very real reason for preferring Community clothing is that it is always difficult to get one's own things back from the laundry. You forget to mark them, or the laundry person did not find your mark, or it washed out. This is particularly true of socks. You have to care a lot about socks to take the time to sew name tags on them—most of us don't. For years now it has been a Community style norm to wear unmatched socks.

What makes communal clothing work is affluence. We have been told that the Israeli kibbutzim long ago gave up the concept because it caused more difficulties than it was worth. Our experience is that in most cases it is private clothing that is more difficult than it is worth. The difference is probably not that we are more radical than the kibbutzim, but that we have more clothing. America has got to be the world's most superfluously dressed nation! Here at Twin Oaks, with an annual income per capita of about $700, we have more clothing than we can possibly use. We have a box in storage marked "shirts with rips and stains," another labeled "out-of-style shirts we could wear if we had to," and another called "perfectly good shirts we haven't room to hang up." Then there are the shirts that *are* hanging up, most of which hang there from month to month without being used, while a handful of light-blue denim workshirts get worn to shreds by the proletarian style conscious.

There are three boxes of women's dresses that are slightly out of style, plus sixty or seventy acceptable ones in several sizes. There are three cardboard cartons that contain long-sleeved turtle-neck shirts, one for short-sleeved turtle-necks, two for colored T-shirts, three for white T-shirts, and two other miscellaneous knit-top boxes. And so forth. A few days ago we ripped up a dozen whole shirts to make rags out of

---

1. Excerpted from *Walden Two* by B.F. Skinner. N.Y.: The Macmillan Company, 1948 (Macmillan Paperbacks Edition, 1962, pp. 33–35). Reprinted by permission of the publisher.
2. *Ibid.*, p. 36.
3. *Ibid.*

them. We have a surplus of clothing, but a shortage of rags for the garage and print shop.

Visitors probably notice that communitarians don't dress very well, in spite of this tremendous overflow of available clothing. That is because the visitor's eye is not attuned to inside culture. They cannot possibly know that we feel dressed up in a pair of jeans with a patch on the knee and a clean T-shirt. They certainly do not know that they look rather funny to us in their brilliant, shiny clothing, rather like actors in costume. (When our outside workers change into acceptable town clothing for their outside jobs, they refer to it as "putting on their costumes.")

The keynote for style is tolerance. You can wear absolutely anything. On the same day you will see jeans, short dresses, long dresses, pant-suits, and shorts. Not long ago some of us were discussing Twin Oaks' unconscious dress codes, and we realized that it would probably not be acceptable for a member to set her hair or wear a shirt-waist dress. Now that we recognize it as a taboo, we will probably hasten to violate it as soon as the weather is warm enough to permit the shirt-waist. I don't know about setting our hair, though—it's such a lot of trouble for a pretty small Cause.

Community clothing is not without its drawbacks. Everything you would suspect might happen does indeed happen. There have been times when someone made a perfectly good pair of jeans into cutoffs, or did a printing job in a new blouse, or wore something too small for him and ripped it. But our style norms and enormous surplus prevent these things being a serious problem. So you lost your yellow blouse to someone else's carelessness—take a blue blouse instead. Put your name on it if you want, and take it to your room—there are lots more.[4]

Two other statements about clothing at Twin Oaks indicate some inconsistencies: an abundance of clothes with no worry about style, then a surplus of clothes with low demand ("perfectly good," but out of style?), and a shortage of certain types of clothing.

In case this issue is being read by anyone who has a mile-high pile of ironing waiting to be done, you may be interested to know that Twin Oaks' ironing is always up to date, and that we spend little more than an hour and a half a week on it. It may surprise you that twelve people have so little ironing, but the reason is fairly simple. Most of the members do not want their clothes ironed. Blue jeans and sweat shirts take remarkably little care. Ironing is done for people who go to school or to town, or for any member who requests it.

Mending is another matter. At least two hours a week are spent on mending. Suddenly it *is* worth our while to darn socks (eight minutes per hole) and patch jeans. We draw the line, however, at patching the elbows of cotton shirts. We tried that one day—it took four hours to patch one shirt that had only cost $3 to begin with and had already been worn for over three years. It was a relaxing job, and the person who did it didn't mind it. But the group knows that for every hour of unnecessary work one member does, the other members do

an hour of work to match it. With that in mind, silly mending jobs like shirt elbows are now classed "recreation," and no labor credits are given.

We have so far bought almost no clothing. Exceptions have been winter boots for some members who had none. Ordinary clothes, though, we have in surplus. We have a tendency to wear the things we like best, that are most comfortable, and we wear them until they wear out, which is a long time with mending service available. For that reason, the clothes that we brought are really more than we need. Since we have no fear of their going out of style, we simply save them for future use.[5]

"Look," says Linda, the clothing manager, "any new members who want to join Twin Oaks have got to come in nude. I cannot deal with any more clothes!"

Community clothes is indeed flourishing, and there are still boxes of excess clothing that is perfectly good (or was, in another era); but we haven't room to hang it up. Nevertheless, some articles of clothing are much in demand, and we don't have enough of them. Especially scarce are loose, pretty cotton dresses for hot weather. They are very simple to make, and we have already made several. Linda says we would make more if we had more cotton materials, and suggests that there might be readers who have some around the house that they would send. Appeals like this have been very successful in the past, when we wanted rug wool. So we try again. What we need are yard goods, big enough to make a garment—not scraps (we have lots of those).[6]

Apparently a new clothing norm has been established, and there is some degree of conformity to it. If an objective of Twin Oaks was to avoid the wastefulness of fashion and to follow the pattern set by the fictional characters in *Walden Two,* then excesses of unworn, serviceable clothing reveal a lack of success in this area.

In summary, clothing in the commune may be somewhat different from the usual clothing of society at large, at least for the present. However, patterns of conformity in dress may not be very different from those in the mass society.

Congruity in the clothing worn, even in the source of clothing and ownership, with philosophical aims and ideals of the commune may contribute to the communal experience. Consistency may enhance the self-concept of communal members, bringing ideals and actual practice into alignment.

REFERENCES CITED

1. Fogarty, Robert S. *American Utopianism.* Itasca, Ill.: F.E. Peacock Publishers, Inc., 1972.
2. Veysey, Laurence, *The Communal Experience: Anarchist and Mystical Counter-Cultures in America.* N.Y.: Harper & Row, 1973.

4. From *Journal of a Walden Two Commune: The Collected Leaves of Twin Oaks,* Vol. 1, pp. 98–99. Louisa, Virginia: Twin Oaks Community, 1972. Reprinted with permission of Twin Oaks Community.

5. *Ibid.,* p. 28.
6. *Ibid.,* p. 109.

CLOTHING, CULTURE, AND POVERTY

Lois M. Gurel

The Culture of Poverty

Does growing up poor contribute to socially unacceptable behavior? lowered educational achievement? poor mental health? Do the poor pay more for goods and services? Does lack of adequate clothing contribute to the maladaptive behavior that is characteristic of the cultures of poverty? truancy and school dropouts? crime? lack of social participation? Unfortunately, affirmative answers may be given to all these questions, ". . . since children of the very poor families are apt to contribute, in time, a disproportionate share of their numbers to the mentally ill, the delinquent, the broken family, and the socially rejected, as well as to the undereducated and unemployed (1, p. 2)." Commonalities among the various cultures of poverty separate the hard core poor from the rest of society. There are fewer differences among poverty groups than there are between the poor as a whole and those living higher up the economic ladder.

The *cycle of poverty* (poverty that extends from generation to generation) and the *cultures of poverty* (the distinguishing folkways of the very poor) define and describe the core of common problems and concerns raised in the questions above. Andrew Young said that there are no longer "specifically black problems," that they are just the problems of the poor (2, p. C 1). The concerns of the very poor are not a result of race, ethnicity, age, religion, or region. The problems do not belong exclusively to the White, the Black, the Chicano, the Puerto Rican, the Indian, the elderly, the rural or the urban poor (3, p. vii). There are commonalities among the poor whether they live in the black ghettos of the city, the migrant camps or Indian reservations of the southwest, or the mountains of Appalachia. Primarily economic in origin, the poor are locked into a culture based on economic impoverishment.

If culture is a general pattern of living transmitted to future generations by past and present ones, then aren't the behaviors generated by these patterns similar among the poor of many races and regions? Oscar Lewis, at a conference of social workers in 1961, suggested the term "subcultures of poverty (4)." As a culture, he stated that poverty had its positive and negative aspects. Social and psychological deprivations and handicaps held negative connotations for all the poor. On the positive side were the strengths used by the poor for survival—rationalization and defense mechanisms (3, p. 5) as well as "the fortitude with which they face the many frustrations which threaten to engulf them (5)." "Poverty in America is a culture, an institution, a way of life. . . . In short, being poor is not one aspect of a person's life, it is his life (6)."

The Poor—Who Are They?

When we speak of the poor we refer to an indefinite group of people who are not as well off as most. They generally reside (we think) in an undesirable part of town, in run-down houses or tenements; perhaps they live in rural shacks only partially hidden from the highway or in the piney-woods regions of the South. Poverty is an unpainted shack, monotony, wishing, a stream of promises, and a trickle of opportunities (7, p. 2). Defining the poor is difficult. It is difficult for professionals, even more so for the layman. Those near the top of the income spectrum will have a different conception of how poor is poor than will those from the middle or lower levels. Minimum levels of living, those which are essential for meaningful participation in community and economic activities, define poverty. Family income, used by the Federal government to delineate the poverty line, is justified by the belief that a number of the consequences of poverty are a function of income deprivation relative to the rest of society. Government agencies answer the question, "What is poverty?" statistically. If a person earns so much income he is poor. If he earns more than the established amount he is either near-poor or non-poor.

Statistics on the American poor are obtained by the Bureau of the Census and published in *Current Population Surveys*. The latest was conducted in March, 1975. "The poverty definition used in this report is based on an index developed at the Social Security Administration in 1964 . . . and revised in 1969 (8, p. 2)." This is the standard formula used now by all federal agencies. This concept of poverty was first established by the Department of Agriculture and was based on nutritionally adequate food consumption requirements of families as related to size, composition, sex, age, and location of residence (farm or non-farm). According to this economy plan,

. . . families of three or more persons spend approximately one-third of their income on food; the poverty level for these families is, therefore, set at three times the cost of the economy food plan. For smaller families and persons living alone, the cost of the economy food plan was multiplied by factors that were slightly higher in order to compensate for the relatively larger fixed expenses of these smaller households. Annual revisions of these SSA poverty cutoffs were based on price changes of the items in the economy food budget (8, p. 143).

The poverty line index is adjusted each year to reflect the increases in the cost of living and the CPI (Consumer Price Index).

The last Consumer Price Survey indicated that there are over 24 million people living below the poverty level

($5,038 for a non-farm family of four), 12% of the United States population. This figure represents about 16% of the nation's elderly (those over 65 years of age); over 10 million children or 15.5% of all the children in the United States; 31% of all blacks; 9% of all whites; and 23% of all peoples of Spanish origin. Thirty-three percent of those living below the poverty level are in households headed by women. Sixty-six percent of the nations poor are either black, of Spanish origin, elderly, or in families headed by women (or combinations of these) (8, pp. 1–2).

There are millions of families in the United States who do not have enough money to buy an adequate life and have little chance to better themselves. "The United States is the richest nation on Earth . . . yet, one out of every ten people in America does not have enough of the right kind of food to eat to maintain health; a dwelling that is warm or large enough to house the family; clothing suitable for the climate; and medical care necessary to prevent disease and maintain life. (9)."

From an article entitled "If You Were on Welfare," the following paragraph helps to illustrate some of the problems of the poor.

The poor suffer from our complete incapacity to imagine them. They are not us. Who are they? One might presume to answer that they are ourselves with $1,600 a year or less. Imagine yourself living in a family with an income of $3,200. You will, of course, buy few books and records. You do not take vacations. The great questions of our time do not interest you. A good part of your time is spent worrying. You have been afflicted with this terrible blight, and you wish to survive. Then you worry if there is enough food, if your children have the right clothing, or about the rent. You worry about the mail and if your check will arrive on time. Perhaps you worry what your children will be like ten years from now, or what you will be like (10).

The Poor—Their Clothing

Michael Harrington, in *The Other America* says that,

Clothes make the poor invisible too; American has best dressed poverty the world has ever known. For a variety of reasons, the benefits of mass production have been spread much more evenly in this area than in many others. It is much easier in the United States to be decently dressed than it is to be decently housed, fed, or doctored. Even people with terribly depressed incomes can look prosperous.

This is an extremely important factor in defining our emotional and existential ignorance of poverty. In Detroit the existence of social class became much more difficult to discern the day the companies put lockers in the plants. From that moment on, one did not see men in work clothes on the way to the factory, but citizens in slacks and white shirts. This process has been magnified with the poor throughout the country. There are tens of thousands of Americans in big cities who are wearing shoes, perhaps even a stylishly cut suit or dress, and yet are hungry. It is not a matter of planning, although it almost seems as if the affluent society had given out costumes to the poor so that they would not offend the rest of society with the sight of rags (6, pp. 5–6).

Though the poor have less money to spend on the basic essentials of life, they are most often forced to pay more than others around them. This fact is especially true in the purchase of apparel items. The poor are constantly faced with high mark-ups, poor quality, shady sales practices, high interest rates, and poor selection of merchandise. There are many reasons why the poor are often put in this position of paying more for their consumer goods. Transportation out of the neighborhood, the farm, the reservation, the migrant camp, or the mountains to the town, the shopping center, or the discount store may be non-existent or costly. Automobiles, gasoline, and fares for public transportation add to the price of purchases. When the nearest town is 40 miles away, the general store may be all that is available.

Since the poor tend to lack the education necessary to be effective consumers, they are also more susceptible to high pressure sales techniques and an inability to use the tools necessary for efficient decision making when it comes to their clothing dollars. Not recognizing quality they do not miss its advantages directly, but their ability to use labeling information is extremely limited and as a group they are not aware of wise buying techniques. Comparison shopping requires a level of sophistication as well as education that is probably beyond the experiences of many poor individuals and families.

Poor families generally cannot think of future clothing needs. End of season clothing sales are not utilized very often; money is not available and existing needs are pressing while long range ones have to wait. It is hard for the poor to conceive of buying a sale coat in April to be put away until mid-November.

There is an old Arabian proverb that states, "eat whatever thou likest, but dress as others do." It has been repeatedly shown that the "proper clothes" or being dressed like others in a group is very important to a person's social acceptance as well as to a feeling of belongingness. Clothing is important to people of all ages in adding to one's self-confidence and impressing others with one's worth. Even as early as first grade, appropriate clothing, that which is like others in the groups, is important (11). Clothing has an even greater role to play in adolescence. Clothing, and the various uses made of it, is one of the primary motivators of adolescent behavior. Social roles are portrayed, high school positions obtained, and rewards for expected behavior within the subculture are all dependent, with varying degrees, on quality and quantity of clothing available for use. To most adolescent girls, proper clothing is essential for popularity (12) and related to high school position (13). Ryan (14) found that teenage girls who were poorly dressed were worried, cross, ill-at-ease, and less confident. ". . . clothing can serve as an essential 'prop' for the teenager . . ." in his or her immediate relationship with peers and popularity in high school as well as successful future adult role identification

(12, p. 171). Obviously, then, clothes can help the poor to feel more secure in situations outside the family. Social leaders are found among the best dressed students, thus putting even more pressure on the poor. Often the parents of very poor children blame themselves for the problems that lack of appropriate clothing create for their children.

A Culture of Poverty—Appalachia

One of the poorest sections of the United States, in terms of per capita and per family income, is the mountainous regions of the southeastern states known collectively as Appalachia. Because many parts of Appalachia are high enough in elevation to be cold in the winter, lack of adequate clothing is a common problem, particularly for school-aged children. Most have no socks, few have shoes. Clothing as an insulation aids in the conservation of body energy both by keeping body heat in and cold air out. Energy reserves, fat in the form of excess caloric intake, must be used by those who do not have sufficient clothing to keep warm in cold weather. "Poor people . . . often become thin because their supply of food is apt to be limited, and it is necessary for them to burn their own tissues to keep their bodies warm (15, p. 68)."

Many students drop out of school early, both because of the irrelevant nature of school to their lives and their lack of proper clothing. Many adults will not participate in public meetings, social or otherwise, because they feel poorly dressed. Many of the children of the mountains rely on hand-me-down, used clothing, clothing banks or other charitable sources from outside of Appalachia itself.

In a clothing survey conducted in rural Kentucky, families indicated that clothing was the most important group of expenditures. Quantity was related to income and age. That is the larger amounts of clothing were found in those with slightly more income. Younger adults in the family tended to have more clothing than did the older adults. Only half of the clothing was purchased, the rest came from gifts, relatives, neighbors, and school teachers. Most of the boys, eight out of ten, had only one pair of shoes, while half of the girls had only one pair. About half of the children in the survey had no raincoats or boots.

Illustrative of the importance of clothing in the lives of the poor is the following conversation with a mother who was receiving an ADC (Aid to Dependent Children) check when the appropriated funds ran out. Asked where it "hurt the most, what did you stop buying?" she said,

No more clothes, fruit, milk. Clothes hurt the most because mostly for school. Borrowed clothes to go to church. Needed school clothes. . . . They are ashamed of their ragged clothing. No spending money in school. This makes my children want to get out. Boy dropped out of Boy Scouts, no shoes, no getting away from the house.

In our world a lack of buying power leads to social starvation and social death. It costs money to go to school, money for clothes, ice cream with other kids, notebooks and paper. It costs money to go to church, money for the offering, Sunday clothes. It costs money for Scouts, money for dues, uniforms, and activities.

In Summary

Although many generalizations have been made here in reference to the cultures of poverty, caution is necessary lest one conclude that the problems of *all* the poor are *all* the same. This, of course, is far from the truth. Whether we look at nutritional needs, shelter, interpersonal relationships, child rearing practices, or clothing, the issues and answers vary. With clothing, at least, the urban poor can perhaps be more invisible than individuals at a Chicano camp in South Florida. On the other hand, the traditional dress of Mexican Americans or American Indians may also mask the true family economic status. But one is still impressed with the similarities: the hand-me-downs and secondhands; the lack of home sewing skills; the poor quality at high cost; the lack of consumer education; few shoes or warm clothing, fad items for peer approval; and the social consequences of these—school dropouts, delinquency, shop-lifting, social withdrawal, and nonparticipation.

Following the decade of the 60s and President Lyndon Johnson's much acclaimed "war on poverty," the poor may once again become invisible. Although some progress has been made to help the poor, students, churches, and the mass media have all been involved in social actions aimed at eliminating poverty. ". . . the United States provides its worse-off citizens only a percentage of what they desperately need. And since half of the poor are young people destined to enter a sophisticated economy at enormous disadvantage, unless countermeasures are taken the children of this generation's impoverished will become the parents of an even larger generation of the other America (6, p. ix)."

REFERENCES CITED

1. Chilman, C.S. *Growing Up Poor*. Washington: U.S. Government Printing Office, 1966.
2. Fairlie, H. "Stripping Pride of Its Prejudice." *The Washington Post*, August 22, 1976.
3. Gottlieb, D. and Heinsohn, A.L. *America's Other Youth*. Englewood Cliffs, N.J.: Prentice-Hall, Inc., 1971.
4. Lewis, O. *Children of Sanchez*. New York: Random House, 1961.
5. Handel, G. and Rainwater, L. "Working Class People and Family Planning," *Social Work*, April 1961, Vol. 6, No. 2.
6. Harrington, M. *The Other America*. Baltimore: Penguin Books, Inc., 1972.

7. Struchen, J. *This is the Puzzle of Poverty.* New York: Friendship Press, 1966.

8. *Characteristics of the Population Below the Poverty Level: 1974.* Washington: United States Government Printing Office, January 1976.

9. Liston, R.A. *The American Poor.* New York: Delacorte Press, 1970.

10. Elman, R.M. "If You Were on Welfare," *Saturday Review,* May 23, 1970.

11. Kelley, E.A. and Turner, D.N. "Clothing Awareness," *Journal of Home Economics,* June 1970, Vol. 62, No. 6, pp. 396–400.

12. Hendricks, S.H., Kelley, E.A., and Eicher, J.B. "Senior Girl's Appearance and Social Acceptance," *Journal of Home Economics,* March 1968, Vol. 60, No. 3, pp. 167–173.

13. Kuehne, S.H. and Creekmore, A.M. "Relationships Among Social Class, School Position, and Clothing of Adolescents," *Journal of Home Economics,* October 1971, Vol. 63, No. 7, pp. 555–556.

14. Ryan, M.S. *Clothing: A Study of Human Behavior.* New York: Holt, Rinehart, and Winston, Inc., 1966.

15. Bogert, L.J., Briggs, G.M., Calloway, D.H. *Nutrition and Physical Fitness.* Philadelphia: W.B. Saunders Co., 1966.

CLOTHING FOR PEOPLE WITH SPECIAL NEEDS

Lois M. Gurel

For those who are fortunate enough to be part of the mass society as far as size, shape, age, energy, and other physical attributes are concerned, attention to those who are not may seem startling and unnecessary. Deviance, in any form, not only surprises us but makes us slightly uncomfortable. Recently many public action groups have forced such attention on us in behalf of those in society who *are* different and who, therefore, have special needs. The elderly and the physically handicapped are groups of people who have been singled out in an attempt to arouse public interest in their civil and legal rights. However, defined in its broadest sense, people with special needs include those who are very short or very tall, very fat or very thin, the mentally handicapped, the chronically ill, and even those engaged in some occupational and recreational activities.

Focusing primarily on the clothing problems of people with special needs the following broad definition will be used. Any individual or group of people whose clothing needs cannot be met on the standard American mass clothing market have special clothing needs. These unmet needs may arise from size, shape, and other physical limitations, from personal or emotional problems, or from specialized working or playing conditions. Although there may be psychological barriers to the production of clothing for special groups, the elderly, for example, the major reason why clothing purchase problems exist for those whose needs lie outside the normative patterns of society is one of economics. It just doesn't pay. Since the major purpose of the apparel and related industries, like any other business, is to make a profit, many types of target audiences for clothing are not large enough or are too diverse to receive the attention of the large industrial firms that produce clothing or the retail establishments that sell to the ultimate consumer.

* * * * * * * * *

A deviant is one who differs, voluntarily or otherwise, from the prescribed norms or the accepted cultural standards of a society. Almost any characteristic, physical or behavioral, can be considered deviant if not shared by the majority. Everyone has felt different in some way at some time, particularly since the borderline between what is accepted behavior or appearance and what is not, not only is slight but varies continually within and between cultures. Until fairly recent times all forms of deviance were stigmatized and individuals were subject to, if not outright persecution, then at least deprived of the basic civil and human rights accorded the rest of society. A city ordinance in at least one major American city read:

> It shall be unlawful for any person who is diseased, maimed, mutilated or deformed as to be an unsightly person to be allowed in or on public streets . . . thoroughfares or public places, to expose himself/herself, or his/her injury to public view (1).

Being "odd man out" in a conforming world is uncomfortable for all of us. And even if being different is simply a temporary physical limitation it is awkward and frustrating. Have you, perhaps, broken an arm, leg, or even toe or finger? Mobility itself presents problems not encountered before. Dressing ranges from awkward to impossible. The choice of clothing becomes restricted; not only, in the case of a foot or leg, must slippers or socks be substituted for shoes, but with an arm cast even the circumference of a sleeve must be considered. When you remind yourself that it is only for six weeks do you stop and think about those who must live all their lives with these or similar physical limitations that affect the selection and maintenance of clothing?

There are also individuals with clothing problems who, although not considered physically handicapped nonetheless have physical dimensions that differ from the norm.

Think about the tall and the short, the fat and the thin. Since clothing fulfills many functions for an individual beyond the simple physical need for protection, those who have difficulty finding clothes that fit suffer psychologically and socially as well. Just the sheer existential pleasure of wearing something "pretty" is often denied them. Remember that obesity can be as great a limitation in the acquisition of ready-to-wear clothing as many physical disabilities.

Those who are short, considerably shorter that is than the average American heights of 5 feet 10 inches for men and 5 feet 6 inches for women, have trouble finding clothes. Children's departments may be helpful. Alterations are necessary, and at least for women, often expensive. Flare bottom pants are out. By the time they are shortened the bell is gone and straight leg or stovepipe becomes the style, like it or not. Miss America 1978 was a welcomed change for the "not too tall." At 5 feet 4 inches, Kylene Barker was the shortest winner of the pageant since 1926. Those who have "to chop 14 inches of material off every dress, skirt, or coat . . ." that they buy were pleased to see that "the long-legged beauties who can braid their legs and still have them touch the floor are out of style" (2).

Midgets and dwarfs, differentiated by growth patterns, have an even harder time adjusting to a world geared for tall people. The physical causes of their abnormal growth patterns are not the same, however, their clothing problems are similar. When children's clothing does not meet their needs, custom made clothes are often the only alternative. They have organized the Little People of America (LPA) in order to provide a voice for their more than 2,000 members. The only requirement for membership is height—4 feet 10 inches or shorter. This organization has aligned itself with those who are seeking barrier-free access for the physically handicapped, since many problems are similar, if not in degree than in kind. The LPA assists its members with some of the practical everyday problems of coping in a world geared for taller people as well as the social and psychological aspects of dealing with their physical differences (3).

And when you think of others whose physical make up is different, have you thought about left-handers? Consider their looking glass approach to life. Whether genetically left-handed from birth, or functionally left-handed due to disease or injury, they are forced to live in a world designed by and for right-handed people. Although their problems are less clothing oriented and more related to the design of utensils and equipment, theirs is definitely a case of people with special needs. They do daily battle with things that right-handed people take for granted. It is estimated that approximately 10% of the population is left-handed, and we have yet to devise good methods for teaching them as children to tie shoes and fasten openings; to handle needles, scissors, or pencils; to dial a telephone.

Researchers have designed special clothing items for many occupational and recreational groups. The problem is that because only a limited market would purchase these items, the highly individualized requirements for each one makes mass production not feasible. Therefore, as a specialized product costs would be high. Watkins at Cornell University has developed and adapted clothing to meet the needs of a specific occupational group, coal miners (4) and for a specific athletic activity, ice-hockey (5). Based on the principle that form follows function, in depth analyses of specific activities were made and clothing designed to meet the resulting needs. Functional design involved a study of thermal qualities of fabrics, body movements, and need for protection and safety. Relationships between disciplines not customarily associated with clothing—physics, anatomy, and physiology—were combined with aesthetics and psychology to produce garments with user acceptability.

Other examples of special clothing items to serve specific needs have been on the market for many years. Corrective shoes for children are readily available and at very slightly higher prices than regular shoes. The careful shopper can also find overalls for toddlers with reinforced knees, socks with reinforced toes, and clothing in chubby and huskie sizes. At least one large retail chain has been marketing clothing for large women for a long time. Nurses uniforms and other career apparel are available in wide selections of styles and fabrics. Recreational clothing is not only designed and available for the sports man and woman, but for the non-sports enthusiast as well, and more jogging and tennis outfits are bought by sedentary on-lookers than by those running along the roads or filling the courts. Trade, professional, hobby, and sports periodicals often carry advertisements for clothing specifically for their readers. These serve as examples of clothing for people with special needs.

* * * * * * * * * *

The clothing needs of the elderly and the physically handicapped are still largely undefined and unmet. Therefore, the remaining pages of this article will focus on these groups specifically and serve as examples of needs, the reasons that these needs exist, and some possible solutions to the problem of fulfilling them. The reader should remember, however, that although the problems of these two groups are pressing and that public awareness has been drawn to them by powerful pressure and lobby groups, they are not the only people who have special needs, particularly special clothing needs. Deviance is common. Differences are relative. Midgets are as unusual as giants. Enlightenment is indeed recent.

If a person is different in any way from surrounding norms, regardless of whether this difference is evaluated positively or negatively, he will consider himself deviant . . . every person who feels deviant will in some extent be affected (1).

People who are different have many commonalities: behavior, treatment by society in general, needs, unresolved problems having to do with all aspects of daily living. This is why such vastly different, in some ways, societal groups as the elderly and the physically handicapped are so often considered together. They are different, but they are also alike. They are to a more or less degree dependent upon the mass society and its marketplace for basic needs of food, clothing, and shelter. They are also anxious and willing to be independent if given the chance by this mass society. In the case of the physically handicapped solutions to many clothing problems have been found through functional design, but since the solutions are so highly individualized, they are often costly. In most cases physical handicaps are so specialized that no market purchase is feasible and all clothing must be custom made. And the aging population, while relatively homogeneous, has an image problem. Who wants to buy their clothing in an "old woman's boutique!"

The Elderly

The last third of life, for everyone lucky enough to live that long, is that of the senior citizen. Referred to as the golden years by some, the land of aging is, to the younger generation, just plain old. *Gerentology,* the social, psychological, and economic study of aging is a new word for an ancient subject. (*Geriatrics* refers to the physical and medical aspects of aging.) Awareness of the problems faced by this segment of our population is very current; the problems were not, however, invented in the 20th century. Perhaps more so than any other age or subcultural group, it is not possible to separate the clothing problems and needs of the elderly from their other problems and needs.

There are definite physical changes that occur with advancing years. These changes do contribute to the difficulty experienced by many older people in finding suitable clothing. But in a very real sense, they are peripheral. General problems associated with age are far more important causes of clothing problems than physical change.

The Aging Population

The greatest problem that society now faces in regard to the elderly is the size of this increasingly older population. The number of people over 65 has doubled twice in the 20th century. It is the fastest growing age group, not in numbers, but in proportion to the rest of society. In 1890, 2% of the population was over 65. By 1975, 10.4% were in that age group. The prediction for the year 2000 is for 20% of the population of Americans to be past the age of 65. There are now 22.5 million senior citizens; in 2000 the prediction is that there will be 52 million in the United States alone, or one out of six people (6).

Primary reason for this increase is, of course, the advances in medicine and technology that have eliminated many killing diseases. Life threatening a few years ago, many are now chronic due to new drugs, and prognoses of the number of years left to live for many with serious disorders has lengthened appreciably. Not only are diseases controlled, if not cured, by drug therapy, but many chronically ill are living extended and normal life spans. A cure for cancer will add five years to statistical life expectancies. Control of heart disease will add 10 years, and advances in bio-genetics that can halt the aging process could increase average life spans by 15–30 more years (6).

Another reason for the prediction of an older population in the next century is the post war baby boom that occurred between 1947 and 1957. Forty-three million babies were born in that decade. They are now in their 20's and flooding the job market. By 2000 A.D. they will be over 50 and early in the next century they will reach retirement age. This bulge in the world's population has been likened to a goat swallowed whole by a boa constrictor. At each stage of life this cohort group will sizeably affect all population statistics. Many young people, not overly concerned about the future, are not very interested in gerentological issues. However, not only will those people in college today have to deal with the societal problems that accompany any imbalance in population, they will be part of that problem.

Body Changes

The physical changes that come with age are very real even though they need not be incapacitating or result in problems associated with the acquisition of clothes. The body does change, but it does so gradually throughout a life time. Most people are aware of these changes long before the magic age of 65. If compensations are made early in life as changes take place retirement need put little additional strain on the physical process of aging. More has been written about the body changes of women, perhaps because women have traditionally been more concerned about physical appearance and the aging process than have men. However, the changes know no sex bias and older men are increasingly interested in their appearance, too.

As one gets older there is usually an increase in weight and a general downward shift in body fat. Breasts elongate and flatten, the trunk becomes fuller and arms and legs thinner. Waistlines thicken and often disappear (more of a problem for men than for women because of the need to hold trousers up with belts). Stomach muscles lose firmness and there is less control. Therefore, the abdomen becomes more prominent. Arthritis, bursitis, and heart or circulatory disorders can result in less ease of motion. Shoulders tend to become rounder. Thermal comfort becomes a problem as the built-in temperature regulating mechanisms cease to function as efficiently. The body in general is more sensitive to hot and cold. Changes in personal coloring occur as the hair greys and the skin tends to yellow, become thin, dry, and inelastic. Facial features often become harsh and prominent as facial fat deposits disappear.

These physical changes gradually increase over time, the rate and degree varying of course with the individual. The time may come when standard ready-to-wear clothing no longer fits. However, this is the exception, rather than the rule. The problem is not one of unavailability, but of finding appropriate styles and sizes to accommodate these changes. And time, money, patience, and energy as well as transportation are often in short supply for the extensive shopping necessary to find suitable clothing.

Clothing Selection

To compensate for the physical changes that result from the aging process, the following ideas, compiled from many sources, are made for clothing selections. Readily apparent is the fact that all of these suggestions involve apparel items available in the mass market and do not require extra expense or special design. That is not to imply that such accommodations to the needs of the elderly are not important. Some of the methods use in functional design by Watkins at Cornell, applied to specific clothing needs of the elderly, would fill a void, provided that the psychological image problems could also be addressed. However, until this happens, appropriate clothing *is* available. The problem may be one of communication rather than design *per se*. That is to say, the clothing is there. What is needed is a way to improve the negative image associated with aging, and then to bring these clothing items suitable for the changing elderly figure to the attention of not only those who need them, but to their families' attention as well.

Clothing Suggestions for the Elderly Woman

1. Soft collars and casual necklines reduce the prominence of facial features.
2. Garments without waistlines and belts fit better and are more comfortable.
3. Soft fabrics are more comfortable on dry skin while rough textures and heavy fabrics may be irritating.
4. Dresses with jackets or coordinated sweaters make temperature adjustments possible.
5. Three-quarter length sleeves, V-neck dresses, and garments which zip or button down the front are easier to put on and fit wider figure fluctuations.
6. Raglan sleeves provide greater ease in movement and tend to fit rounded shoulders better than set in sleeves.
7. Blue, a widely preferred color by elderly people, is flattering to skin with a yellowish cast.
8. Stretch nylon stockings, slightly opaque, cover varicose veins and still appear sheer.
9. Garments that can be stepped into help those with less agile arm and shoulder joints due to arthritis.
10. Shoes of a slip on style that do not require lacing make dressing easier.
11. Protection from icy winter streets and sidewalks could be achieved with boots or overshoes with rippled or other types of slip-proof soles.
12. Garments with vertical princess seams as dart equivalents are easy to adjust to individual requirements.
13. No iron, permanent press fabrics of knit construction aid fit as well as simplify care.

Clothing Suggestions for Elderly Men

Many of the above suggestions made for the elderly woman can be applied equally well to men. However, men have a few additional physical changes. Old age seems to accentuate the basic body build. If a man has been short and stout most of his life he tends to put on additional weight with age. Tall thin men, on the other hand, usually get even thinner. Since basic build cannot be changed, clothing can be used to create an illusion that makes the man seem taller or shorter, slimmer, and better proportioned.

1. To create an illusion of height, the short, stout man should choose:
   a. one color scheme for pants and shirt.
   b. vertically striped shirts.
   c. flared leg pants.
2. To create an illusion of width, the tall, thin man should choose:
   a. shirt and trousers in contrasting colors.
   b. horizontal lines in seams, pockets, stripes, or belts.
   c. straight leg, but loose fitting pants.
   d. light colors.

In recent years the increased use of casual styles and of color in men's clothing has enabled men to employ more of the foregoing suggestions than would have been possible a few years ago. . . . Vertical stripes may be used to create a slimming effect and loose casual clothes which do not hug the figure will provide a useful disguise and are smarter than tailored garments which are several sizes too small (7, p. 3).

3. Bulky knit cardigans and light weight blazers tend to be more comfortable than conventional tailored suit jackets.
4. Raglan sleeve shirts and jackets give more freedom of movement.
5. Shoulder and back pleats in shirts and jackets give more room across the back.
6. Clip on ties, both bow and four-in-hand can be fastened easier by an arthritic hand.

The Physically Limited Elderly

An area of very great concern is that where the problems of age interface with those of the physically handicapped. There is a difference of opinion among professionals working with both groups as to whether these problems should be considered part of the aging syndrome or rather as a general problem faced by those that are physically limited regardless of age.

Perhaps the greatest single contributor to the physical problems of age and the clothing difficulties of elderly people is the crippling disease—arthritis. Lack of dexterity of hands, fingers, arms, and legs create dressing problems in old and young alike. And although arthritis is not an old people's disease, it is more prevalent in later years. Fingers that cannot manipulate buttons and other fasteners, arms that can no longer manage center back zippers, joints that can't bend to put on and tie shoes are typical of the problems faced by the arthritic senior citizen. The trend now is toward a problem oriented solution to the difficulties of the handicapped, that is to treat people with similar physical limitations together, regardless of age or original cause of the disability. Physical limitations stem from many sources and solutions to clothing oriented problems tend to be similar, depending upon the disability and not the disease. That is the opinion of the author and the position that will be taken here. Therefore, the problems of physically disabled elderly people will be included in the next section.

* * * * * * * * * *

The clothing problems of the elderly are *not* mainly due to physical changes that occur with age. However, there are problems and unmet needs. Obtaining appropriate clothes and adequately caring for them is difficult for most people past 65. Fixed incomes in an inflationary time mean that many elderly people have less discretionary money to spend on non-essentials. Unfortunately clothing falls in this category. Food, housing, and medical expenses take ever increasing percentages of income, and as important as clothing may be to one's self-concept, self-image, and social participation, there just is not enough to cover all needs. People in general, and elderly people especially, sometimes see clothing expenditures as frivolous, and this may be one of the first places that they attempt to cut expenses. Old, out-dated, and poorly fitting clothing left from previous years have an additive effect on the general problems of the elderly. The elderly often cut themselves off from much needed outside activities because they are ashamed of their appearance and at a time when appearance is even more important to maintain self-respect and overcome the physical process of aging. Other reasons that make the acquisition of clothing difficult are decreased energy to shop, lack of transportation to stores, little social life to provide the motivations and desires for new and stylish clothing.

Psychological Needs

The psychological needs of the elderly remain essentially the same as for a younger group—affection, attention, approval, personal dignity, a sense of usefulness, and

social contacts and participation. If in good physical health, active involvement with people outside the home is important for mental health. Research has shown that pride in personal appearance and the means to maintain it are an essential ingredient of social participation at any age. Friends are also important, even more so for those whose lifestyles and long term friendship patterns have changed due to age.

Adequate quantities of suitable clothing increase self-confidence, self-respect, and an interest in personal appearance that can help the senior citizen make and keep the social contacts so important at this stage of life. Discouraged by changing body dimensions, fading hair and skin, and a realization that one is getting old can lead to a poor self-image and emotionally manifested problems. Clothing can, for the elderly, create an illusion, not of youth, but of an attractive, well-groomed man or woman and thus improve self-image and a feeling of being in step with the times.

The Physically Handicapped

Consider how much of what you do each day is done automatically, at a barely conscious level. Consider only the physical process of getting out of bed, washed, combed, and dressed for the day. There are many people, of all ages, who see these simple tasks, taken for granted by so many, as major hurdles to be overcome. These are the physically handicapped. Public awareness of their problems can contribute greatly to their living independent and productive lives. No matter what the nature of the physical disability, *having* a handicap does not mean that a person *is* handicapped. Physical handicaps are not related to age, sex, social class, or intelligence. They may be congenital—present at birth—or caused by disease, accident, or drugs. Thirty million Americans have some form of physical limitation (8). The emphasis, however, is increasingly on what they *can* do and not on what they *can't* do.

The handicapped person wanting to be a part of society, encounters many barriers, sometimes the least of which are the currently publicized physical barriers imposed by an unaware and uncaring society—stairs, curbs, doors, etc. Maybe even more important are the internal barriers imposed by the handicapped person, personal attitudes toward the disability and the resulting conflict and frustration.

Physical defects are unique and personal and in a society that values the "body whole" and the "body beautiful" a tremendous burden is placed upon the individual to reconcile ones own problems with the ideal societal image. Body image is a complicated idea but can be generalized as the way we see ourselves and/or describe ourselves to others. It is a basic part of the total personality and cannot be separated from one's whole being. It does however, play a large part in determining our reactions to our environment and particularly to the people that we come in contact with at all levels of interaction, from chance meetings with strangers to our closest friends and relatives.

The two basic aspects of the self-image can be called ideal self-image, or how we would like to look ideally or appear to ourselves and others, and the actual or perceived self-image, that which actually exists, at least in our own perceptions of ourselves. The greater the congruity between these two, the better the psychological adjustment. In order to adjust to the impact of a disability that is disfiguring in any way, the body image has to change from the image of a previously non-handicapped, non-deformed, near normal body, to one that is physically defective. Psychological disturbances often accompany somatic distortions. We do not have an image of our bodies, a picture in our minds of what we look like.

Usually there is a parallel change between actual body distortion and self-image. When there is a change in body structure with no change in body image, frustration and anxiety are the general result because a person is then unable to carry out behavior associated with the changed body.

Clothing can play an important role in this process of self acceptance and also in society's acceptance of those who are physically limited. Clothing enhances self-esteem; clothing creates an image; possibilities for communication through clothing are boundless; clothing can help to draw attention away from the handicap to the person.

Dependency on the part of the handicapped person, and its counterpart, over protection of family and friends, are important sources of maladjustment. Often a handicapped person *is* unable to care for himself. This is unwanted dependency and generally demoralizing. However, with careful planning many people with even severe physical limitations are able to achieve varying degrees of independence. Again, clothing can be an important ingredient in the success or failure of such a venture. Self-help clothing, designed specifically to aid in the process of self-dressing, can be an important assist and often the mainspring for other independent actions.

The handicapped are a complex, heterogeneous group of individuals with a wide variety of sizes, shapes, psyches, ages, and physical limitations. They include children and adults, the young and the elderly, those with single and those with multiple handicaps, persons who are institutionalized and those who can live independent lives as well as all stages in between. Even within this wide diversity some categorization is possible. The following is one attempt to classify physically handicapped individuals in order to provide some systematic means of addressing their clothing needs.

1. Clothing for adults and adolescents able to at least partially dress themselves.
2. Clothing for young children, other than babies, who can partially dress themselves.
3. Clothing for those who have to be dressed by others (babies, children, or adults).
4. Clothing made to resist wear from crutches, braces, prosthesis, etc.
5. Clothing for babies and toddlers of handicapped parents.
6. Clothing for those who are incontinent.
7. Clothing for those confined to wheelchairs or beds.

This method of classifying clothing related needs seems more appropriate and useful than the former method of classification that was based on disease. Incontinence may be the result of many disorders, senility, accident, paralysis, neurological or emotional disorder, but it is the incontinence that is the problem. The same is true for other handicaps. Problems associated with arthritis have more to do with where the arthritis is than with the nature of the disease itself. These types of categories are especially helpful to the clothing designer where knowledge of the physical aspects of a disease are less important than insight into what the clothing has to do for the handicapped person.

Of the above categories, there are two major classifications that really outweigh all the rest. Can the handicapped persons dress themselves or do they have to be dressed? Those who must be dressed may be babies of handicapped mothers or fathers, extremely handicapped children, and helpless adults. The second category would include those who could dress themselves if self-help clothing were available. This group includes toddlers and small children of handicapped parents, most handicapped children, and most handicapped adults.

Depending upon the nature of the physical limitations, clothing for the handicapped needs to (1) fit bodies that are not standard in size or shape, (2) be strong enough to withstand abrasion from appliances or mechanical aids, (3) allow for easy movement for persons in wheelchairs, (4) have openings that can be reached and fasteners that can be operated by persons with limited arm movements or poorly controlled hand movements, and (5) be attractive and in fashion. Additionally, fabric should be easy to care for and comfortable in terms of texture and absorbency.

Because of the tremendous diversity in physical limitations a generalized list of clothing suggestions, similar to that offered for the elderly man and woman, cannot be made. Traditional mass production of garments is not practical and even small commercial operations are severely limited in the garments they are able to offer for sale. There are several publications directed toward those who have the skills necessary to adapt ready-to-wear clothing or commercial patterns for home sewing (9, 10, 11, 12, 13). However, in some cases even this is not possible, the only solution may be custom designed and made garments.

The following list of suggestions are just a few among many things that can be looked for when attempting to find ready-to-wear garments suitable for use with and by the physically limited.

Clothing Suggestions

For infants and toddlers that must be dressed by handicapped parents:

1. Prefolded and disposable diapers save time and energy.
2. Protective pants that open flat and snap shut are easier to put on.
3. With shirts, gowns, and outerwear that open flat and then close down the front, babies can be placed on the garment rather than pulled into it.
4. Garments with ties, bows, drawstrings, and small buttons at best complicate dressing and may be unmanageable for the handicapped parent.

For handicapped children and adults who can dress themselves:

1. Look for garments with large openings. These are much easier to slip into than small necklines and narrow sleeves.
2. If armcyes and waists are cut full they can be pulled on more readily.
3. Raglan sleeves are not only easier to put on but allow more freedom of movement than set in sleeves.
4. Fasteners should be large and easy to reach and manipulate.
5. Fabrics that stretch, have absorbency, and are sturdy will withstand the strain of dressing as well as the accommodation of braces and crutches.

* * * * * * * * * *

Clothing should enhance one's self-esteem and be personally satisfying. For people with disabilities, attention to their clothes offers an opportunity to:

–attain peer approval
–enhance family acceptance
–alleviate any uneasiness about who they are
–provide for increased mobility and ease of mobility

–face the harsh reality that clothes matter in the market-place for skills and talents.

A disability is no hindrance to fashion. You have choice through:

–custom designed clothing
–self-constructed garments with special features
–commercially produced clothing which can be adapted with special features
–fabrics that lend themselves to better serviceability and easier care
–features which can disguise the disability and provide greater comfort and ease of dressing (14, p. 1).

Adequate, functional, attractive clothing, along with good grooming, is important to everyone. For the physically limited it is an essential ingredient in their adjustment to life. Not only can clothing stimulate physical and mental well-being, but it can enhance the self-concept, develop a positive body image, assist in gaining independence, and increase social interaction.

REFERENCES CITED

1. Doob, A.N. "Deviance: Society's Side Show." *Psychology Today,* 5, No. 5 (Oct. 1971), p. 47.
2. Bombeck, Erma. "Kylene Stands Up for Short People." *Roanoke Times and World News,* October 1, 1978.
3. Kleinfield, S. "Our Smallest Minority—Dwarfs." *Reader's Digest,* 1976 (Jan.), pp. 151–156.
4. Watkins, Susan M. "Designing Clothing for Coal Miners." *Journal of Home Economics,* Vol. 69, No. 1, January 1977, pp. 24–27.
5. Watkins, Susan M. "Designing Functional Clothing." *Journal of Home Economics,* Vol. 66, No. 7, November 1974, pp. 33–38.
6. "The Graying of America." *Newsweek,* February 28, 1977.
7. McCartney, P. *Clothes Sense for Handicapped Adults of All Ages.* London: The Disabled Living Foundation, 1973.
8. *Newsletter.* National Society for Crippled Children and Adults, Inc., Chicago, Illinois.
9. *Clothes for the Physically Handicapped Homemaker.* Agricultural Research Service, U.S. Department of Agriculture, Home Economics Report No. 12. U.S. Government Printing Office, Washington, D.C. June 1961.
10. *Clothes to fit Your Needs.* Cooperative Extension Service, Iowa State University, Ames, Iowa, September 1974.
11. *Clothing for the Handicapped.* Sister Kenny Institute Rehabilitation Publication 737, Sister Kenny Institute, Minneapolis, Minnesota, 1977.
12. *Convenience Clothing and Closures.* Talon Consumer Education and Velcro Corporation, New York, N.Y.
13. *Flexible Fashions.* Public Health Service Publication No. 1814. U.S. Department of Health, Education, and Welfare, U.S. Government Printing Office, Washington, D.C.
14. Beasley, M.C.; Beems, D. and Weiss, J. *Adapt Your Own.* The University of Alabama: Division of Continuing Education, July 1977.

HIGH SCHOOL AS MEETING PLACE

Joanne B. Eicher and Eleanor A. Kelley

Now that the function of dress is no longer simply moral or thermal, certain other of its attributes are becoming apparent. One of these, the possibility of relationship between adolescent dress and social behavior, presented itself rather ideally from the sociologist's point of view when, in a local election, a small economically deprived area was annexed to an erstwhile upper middle-class school district. We chose to examine the significance of attitude towards appearance and social acceptance as expressed by a group of girls followed from ninth grade through twelfth.

Our sources of data were a questionnaire and an interview, including a rating of personal appearance by an interviewer. The questionnaire was to reveal information about personal background and choice of friends, and the interview sought each girl's opinion of others, her self, and her group. All information was processed each year by the same team according to methods developed in the initial phase of the project. A detailed description of both methodology and result has already been published. [1, 2]

A sociometric question asking the girls to name their best friends was used to reveal their acceptance by, or isolation from, other girls. Analysis of the answers showed that during the four years, four friendship groups persisted. For purposes of identification, we named the groups Social Elite, Melting Pot, Coalition, Green Meadows. Most of the girls of the lower social class formed their own groups or remained isolates. By twelfth grade the few who had not dropped out of school were still either isolates or part of their own single clique. It was the Social Elite, composed of both upper and middle social class members who were recognized as the leading crowd, the most popular, the best-dressed. The Melting Pot and Coalition girls were infrequently recognized as most popular or best dressed, nor were they recognized as "not dressed right" as were the Green Meadows girls.

The girls of the lower social class who were identified by their classmates as residents of Green Meadows were characterized as "all dressed alike" and "not dressed right." They wore inappropriate clothing such as summer skirts in winter-time; they tried to wear the latest fashions but did not quite know how; they "over-did" hair and make-up. Actually analysis showed that even when these girls scored high in clothing-awareness, they still scored low in clothing-satisfaction and clothing-confidence. But while money is usually cited as the reason for "poor" dressing, our findings suggest that a misunderstanding of how to put together the fashion package is equally responsible.

Perceptual understanding of what is acceptable to the social group to which the girl aspires is also important.

While there is a range of permissible deviation, too broad a deviation is socially deadening; the measure of individuality must operate within conformity to group norms. Incidentally, we discovered that while isolates most often consulted their parents about dress, members of the social elite sought the approval of their boyfriends.

We have been asked as we have analyzed our data whether the data continue to be relevant as time passes. In the opinion of our research team, the critical aspect of its study is the phenomenon of conformity to style, not the significance of any specific style. The young strain within their own lines of conformity against the conformity of their elders. Crucial to their acceptance of each other is knowing what constitutes acceptable appearance. According to the girls interviewed in this study, it is dress first, then personality, then common interests that lead to the pursual of friendships.

Actually, this is not as superficial a characteristic of adolescence as some parents and teachers like to call it. Since adolescents are searching for suitable adult identities, they are not only unsure of how persons of their kind are expected to act, but they are also unsure at times of what kind of persons *are* their kind. Thus we see during their continued jockeying for position, that appearance serves as an initial identification medium from two perspectives. It serves as an easily identifiable "prop" as the adolescent experiment with roles that might be "his kind," and it also serves as an identifying badge of others in the same pursuit.

Goffman summarizes the apparent over-emphasis on appearance that adults seem to perceive as they view adolescents:

> When an individual is unsure of himself in a new social situation he may attempt to compensate for his alienation by wearing exactly the right clothes, employing exactly the right equipment or assuming exactly the right stance. Those around him may say that he is "over-involved in the situation." In fact, however, it might be more accurate to say that he is insufficiently involved in the occasioned main involvement and overdependent on selected signs of being at one with this activity. [3]

An adolescent who is trying to assume the attributes of the main role may use dress as a sign of being "at one" with the main role requirements when he is unsure of the appropriate norms of total behavior.

From "High School as Meeting Place." *Michigan Journal of Secondary Education.* Vol. 13, No. 2, Winter 1972, pp. 12–16. Reprinted by permission of the publisher.

The adult world continuously makes value judgments about physical size, beauty, and appropriate clothing. Thus, the adolescent evaluation of appearance as an important aspect in our daily lives is not superficial, but instead a realistic appraisal of the key communication function which appearance has in our society today. Again, we believe the adolescent is not different from his adult role models. The so-called "hippies" acknowledge the importance of appearance as a key variable in communication by flouting the conventions of middle-class dress. By rejecting the expected attire, they indicate their rejection of the expected in thinking and behaving. In fact, this strategy of rejection seems to be spilling over into the larger adolescent population in the early 1970's as the "poverty look." [4]

Perhaps one of the more important observations which can be drawn from our study concerns the relationship of friendship to social class background. As we assess the attitudes of the girls in the Social Elite versus the girls from Green Meadows, we must guard against judging harshly. The snobbish or "snopular" attitude attributed to the Social Elite by peers cannot be blamed on the teenagers themselves. They reflect the values of their parents as well as those they share with their peers. Friendship groups reflect certain sociological facts.

Most adults as adults prefer to choose friends whom they like and who like them, feelings of friendship usually resting on similarity of interests, experience and background. A radical does not ordinarily seek a liberal for his closest friend. As a matter of fact, most of us do not usually seek out someone different from us except as an exercise in tolerance or observation.

What then are the implications of our study for the changing educational and employment situations into which we thrust our children? Integrated schools and occupational situations may accomplish physical proximity of those who differ in ethnic, racial or social backgrounds, but there is no guarantee that social proximity and friendship will follow. Our data provides evidence that in a situation where physical proximity of girls from different social classes occurred, social proximity did not follow. Coleman pointed out in the early sixties the responsibility of adults when he said "the norms of the system are created in large part by the activities to which it is subject."[5] The adult community determines the adolescent community's activities most frequently by using the school activities for community purposes:

> . . . for example, by using high school sports as community entertainment, and as contests between communities—and by restricting adolescent activities outside of school. The adolescent has little or no possibility of responsibility today; adults have shut him out of the job market—have told him in effect, to go off to school and not bother them. Seldom are adoles-

cents allowed any sort of responsibility in modern society. If the adult community regularly created responsibilities for adolescents, then the status system of the adolescent culture would hardly be what it presently is. As things now stand, however, it is the adult community, in its role, not as parents, but as community members and designers of school policy, who must be held to account for the values of adolescent culture. [6]

Perhaps we do not or should not expect friendship to follow from integrated schools, jobs, or neighborhoods; instead we should focus on the question of fostering tolerance. If we accept this as our goal, the responsibility is back with the adults. It is we as parents and educators who must teach or demonstrate by example the importance of tolerance. This is our challenge. It might well shape the future of our nation. Let us hope it is not too late![7]

REFERENCES

1. M.C. Williams and J.B. Eicher, "Teen-agers' Appearance and Social Acceptance," *Journal of Home Economics,* Vol. 58, No. 6 (June, 1966), pp. 457–461.
2. S.H. Hendricks; E.A. Kelley; and J.B. Eicher, "Senior Girls' Appearance and Social Acceptance," *Journal of Home Economics,* Vol, 60, No. 3 (March, 1968), pp. 167–172.
3. Erving Goffman, *Behavior in Public Places* (London: Collier Macmillan, Ltd., Free Press of Glencoe, 1963), p. 51.
4. See the discussion of the "new generation" clothing in *The Greening of America* by Charles Reich (New York: Random House, 1970), pp. 209–213. Designer's reactions and other implications for consumer behavior are found in *American Fabrics Magazine,* Winter, 1971, pp. 47–56. Much of the rest of the issue is devoted to the sociological implications of current clothing trends. On page 50 in the issue, researchers of Analytical Research Institute reinforce the point we are making in our report: "While in some respects the new clothes express 'democratic values', there is sufficient evidence to show that peer group influences and pressures are resulting in a conformity which is often as rigid as that demonstrated by 'squares' in or close to the Establishment. Under the circumstances, jeans, too, become a uniform." We would add, regarding the long term implications of establishing principles of behavior related to clothing, that the current "uniform" of jeans was the uniform of their parents during World War II and shortly after. Thus, in this instance not only do we see the principle of a clothing uniform for acceptance continued as relevant, but also we see a full cycle return to the *same* uniform of World War II—with a few new embellishments by the " now generation."
5. James S. Coleman, *The Adolescent Society* (New York: The Free Press of Glencoe, 1961), p. 305.
6. *Ibid,* pp. 305–306.
7. The reader interested in more details of the research findings may consult the following articles: Wass, B.M., and Eicher, J.B. "Clothing as Related to Role Behavior of Teen-Age Girls," *Quarterly Bulletin* of the Michigan Agricultural Experiment Station, Michigan State University, Vol 47, No. 2 (November, 1964), pp. 206–213. Ostermeier, A.B., and Eicher, J.B. "Clothing and Appear-

ance as Related to Social Class and Social Acceptance of Adolescent Girls," *Quarterly Bulletin* of the Michigan Agricultural Experiment Station, Michigan State University, Vol. 48, No. 3 (February, 1966), PP. 431– 436.

Kelley, E.A., and Eicher, J.B. "A Longitudinal Analysis of Popularity, Group Membership, and Dress," *Journal of Home Economics,* Vol. 62, No. 5 (May, 1970), pp. 246–250.

Kelley, E.A., and Eicher, J.B. "Communication Via Clothing: Implications for Home Economics Teaching," *Forum* (J.C. Penney Co.), (Spring/Summer, 1970), p. 23.

ADOLESCENT DRESS

Understanding the Issues

Mary Ellen Roach

Adolescent dress and undress today provokes criticism, confusion, and conflict; perhaps it always has. This article looks at the question of appropriateness of dress historically—showing that the concern dates back at least to Biblical times—and analyzes current social, economic, and cultural factors influencing adolescent dress.

From the East coast to the West rages a controversy into which some Americans venture bravely while others stand disdainfully on the sidelines and label the whole affair a tempest in a teapot. Complete detachment is not easy to achieve, however. For, no matter how diligently a person tries to avoid or ignore it, the winds of the controversy waft over him, and he becomes aware that sides are drawn up one more time in the never-ending battle over what is "proper" display of the human body.

How old is the battle? We do not know for sure, but probably as old as mankind himself. We do know that as early as 700 B.C. the prophet Isaiah (1) was denouncing the women of Israel for hankering after fine linen and veils, tinkling ankle bracelets, and nose jewels of which he did not approve. We know that today numbers of his spiritual descendants carry on the good work. For with almost predictable regularity the popular press spreads the gospel of what is wrong—and what is right—in dress and adornment. But a number of sects have arisen which support different points of view. Therefore, determining what is the true gospel becomes increasingly difficult and things have gone so far that judges in our courts are asked to make decisions concerning conflicts which arise.

Whatever its antiquity, the most prominent present day manifestation of the perennial dispute is the considerable amount of press notice given to conflicts concerning the clothing and personal care of adolescents. Why do the teenagers capture the spotlight? Because their legs are so much exposed—or their faces so little exposed? Because they wear bright colors—or overall basic black? Because their dress is so different from that of ten years ago—or ten minutes ago?

Superficially, these may appear to be some of the reasons. However, comprehension of the full meaning of current debates concerning adolescent dress requires attention to more than its external form. It demands examination of a number of interdependent factors which relate to the issues involved. Understanding of these issues will be enhanced by consideration of four questions: Who invented the teenager and his dress? What motivates his manner of personal display? How have sociocultural factors contributed to the kind of personal display which he exhibits? What sometimes causes social tensions concerning the kind of display which he effects?

Who Invented the Teenager and His Dress?

Compilers of Western costume history inform us that the Roman fathers were dismayed when young dandies of the fourth century A.D. began to wear barbarian bracco (trousers) despite public censure and interdict (2,3). Otherwise we have little reference to dress of young people until the eighteenth century. Indeed, an Englishman by the name of Musgrove says that special concern for the adolescent and his personal needs, such as costume, began in Western society late in the eighteenth century. According to him:

The adolescent was invented at the same time as the steam engine. The principal architect of the latter was Watt in 1765, of the former Rousseau in 1762. . . .The tailor, the publisher, the social reformer, and the educator came to Rousseau's assistance: they began in the later 18th and early 19th centuries to cater for a specific age group of "young persons," neither children nor adults. Instead of wearing imitation-adult clothing, young people at the end of the 18th century had their distinctive uniform, including "long trousers," which

From "Adolescent Dress." *Journal of Home Economics,* Vol. 61, No. 9, November 1969, pp. 693–697. Footnotes are omitted. Reprinted by permission of the publisher.

actually anticipated the grown-up fashions of the future. School stories such as *Tom Brown* (1856) and *Eric, or Little by Little* (1858), *The Boys' Own Paper* (from 1879), and *Stalky and Co.* (1903), addressed themselves to and helped to create, a specifically (middle-class) adolescent world (4).

One may argue that Musgrove oversimplifies when he credits Rousseau with the invention of the teenager. Less debatable is a suggestion that the late eighteenth and the nineteenth centuries brought socioeconomic changes which encouraged the setting apart within society of an age group which had previously been caught either in the dependency of childhood or the responsibilities of adulthood.

Motivations for Personal Display

Once invented, what motivates the adolescent's manner of personal display? One simple way to handle this question is to sum up the adolescent's motives under the rubric "survival" and to add that, whereas his motives may differ in emphasis or intensity, they do not differ in kind from those of other age groups. Clothing use, by people of all ages, is related to two kinds of survival: survival of the species and survival of the individual human being.

When clothing contributes to attraction between the sexes, its use is closely related to the sex drives which promote survival of the species. Thus, to the extent that clothing encourages sexual interest, it can be instrumental in the biological act of mating. However, whereas some clothing may serve as a stimulant to sexual interest, other may be a means of controlling sex urges. Still other clothing may be both stimulant and control. The use of clothing to stimulate sexual interest may be especially manifested in adolescence; as Heller says:

> . . .the teen-ager is caught up in new and powerful aspects of sexuality. The problem of achieving a sexual identity is not easy for teen-agers. What is easy is the opportunity to grab hold of a stylized, superficial sexual identity found all around them. They may dress "sexy," they may act "sexy," even defiantly so, but very often they are very frightened and insecure underneath the pseudosexual exterior (5).

Survival of the individual human being depends on his survival as a biological organism, as a psychic entity, and as a socially acceptable being. To insure their survival as biological organisms, people use clothing as a defense against extremes of heat and cold, as a guard against contact injuries, and sometimes as protection against magical forces which may bring disease or disaster. If dangers of the physical and magical environment do not impinge too closely, or if science and technology provide alternate means of protection, such as medicine, heated houses, and air-conditioned vehicles for travel, clothing may lose some of its significance as a protective cultural product; and the importance of its role in biological survival is lessened. However, as we push our frontiers to the arctic regions, high altitudes, and outer space, hostile features of the environment are magnified and our interest in the close protective environment of clothing is increased.

Since space travel is still for only a select few, American adolescents, as well as other age groups, are relatively little concerned about the protective aspects of clothing. They let medicine and sanitary practices rather than magic shirts protect their health. They are aware that changes in the season signal changes in kind or amount of clothing worn, but they give consideration to protective utility ordinarily as afterthought rather than forethought.

The expression "survival as a psychic entity" identifies our human strain to verify that we exist—that we make some sort of impact on our world. One way we may try to verify our existence is through body decoration. Hoebel (6) suggests that body decoration helps us make an impression on our social world by intensifying our presence as individuals—it sets each of us apart, makes us noticed and distinguished from others. Clothing, as decoration, thus helps to establish our individualism, our separateness from others.

Establishing identity is especially crucial for teenagers. Neither children nor adults, they reach out for experiences which will help clarify who they are. A mature older person knows himself fairly well and has usually found a self-image compatible with roles to be fulfilled and with which he can be comfortable. This is not the case with teenagers. In their search for self they are adventuring into and trying out new modes of behavior within a society which offers many alternatives. Not surprising, therefore, is their susceptibility to fads as they cast about among the many alternatives. Also not surprising is their frequent concern with appearance. Clothes, cosmetics, and grooming aids allow each to experiment with the image he wishes to present. Positive and negative responses elicited from others are the tests of the effectiveness or quality of each experimentation.

At the same time that it may help establish the uniqueness of an individual, somewhat paradoxically, clothing also may deemphasize the individual. To the extent that we conform to the clothing customs of others, we acknowledge the influence of a group force on our behavior and our willingness to jeopardize our individualism to some degree for the security which comes from establishing our connectedness with other people. The security derived from identifying with others and gaining their acceptance and approval promises *social survival*. Since, as Coleman (7) suggests, the teenager is a member of a small peer society within which many or most of his social interactions occur and which maintains relatively limited connections with the outside adult society, his survival as a socially acceptable being is likely to depend to a great extent on approval by peers rather than adults. Therefore, dressing ways that insure social comfort in the presence of his peers may contribute significantly to his social survival.

Influence of Sociocultural Factors

During the last three centuries a number of sociocultural factors have worked together to shape the world of the American adolescent and the kind of personal display which he exhibits. Influential early in this time were the eighteenth century European philosophers who, like the previously mentioned Rousseau, emphasized individualism and encouraged regarding children as persons entitled to their own rights and considerations. These philosophies were easily transferred to the frontiers of the new world where an attitude of individual self-reliance was a great advantage, if not a necessity, and each child, a valuable economic asset. Indeed, the rural family in early America desperately needed all the hands it could get in order to wrest a living from the soil and maintain the household. But even as America industrialized, children maintained economic importance as whole families sometimes went to work in the factory (8). Employment in the nineteenth century factory did not allow adolescents much time of their own nor any book learning; but it did put them in a place of responsibility and recognized economic importance. For those from the country, jobs away from their isolated country homes even provided opportunities for expanded social horizons.

In the twentieth century the work ways of family members have separated. Older members, especially men, are occupied in jobs away from home. Younger family members, in the teen years, have been excluded more and more from employment in jobs of responsibility, and have been set apart in a stage of life which is so distinct from either childhood or adulthood that we not only give it a special name, adolescence, but also assoicate it with something called an adolescent society or culture. This segregation of young people appears to have grown mainly out of social and economic necessity for delaying the entry of young people into the labor market, and has the effect of giving them uncommitted time which to some extent is taken up by lengthened periods of schooling.

But what is the nature of the delaying action which keeps young people out of the labor force? Musgrove (9), in observations which apply in America as well as in England, points out first that improved medical care and sanitation have meant that more children survive to adulthood and more adults to old age. Therefore, social and economic positions of responsibility are vacated less quickly and opportunities for young people are reduced. Second, technical changes in industrial and agricultural production have brought a decline in need for great numbers of untrained laborers on the farm or in the factory.

Young people who had supplied this much-needed labor early in the nineteenth century have, therefore, gradually lost a position of central importance in the economy. Third, unions tend to protect semiskilled and skilled labor from competition of new recruits to the labor force; and fourth, entrance into white-collar jobs is based on a high level of education that adolescents have not yet had a chance to achieve. With these forces working together—inability of the economy to absorb the young, barriers built up by vested interests, and an increase in jobs requiring relatively high levels of education—maintenance of a general philosophy that encourages greater and greater lengths of schooling and hence a delay of adulthood is facilitated.

What happens then to teenagers? Cut adrift from any strong relationship with the economic system and hence any strong functional identification with adults, teenagers have become segregated into a small subculture with its own cultural patterns, including a value system and even a language and dress all its own. The subsystem itself is relatively stable but its personnel and cultural patterns are not. Stability of personnel is lacking because the adolescent soon ages and moves into adult responsibilities of child-rearing and productive occupational work. Instability of cultural patterns is related to the inability of a changing personnel to establish continuity and traditions as well as to the vagueness with which the role of a teenager is defined.

Young people are aware of their situation and give evidence of trying to live up to their reputation for subcultural clannishness and instability. One Wisconsin high school senior made this comment on a questionnaire. "Many so-called 'fads' have come and gone. Some I have contributed to but most I haven't, but it's all part of being a teenager and growing up." In another situation a fifteen-year-old boy ended an argument with his mother in this way: "Don't tell me you aren't concerned about what *your* peer group thinks." The eighteenth century philosophers were correct. These young people are indeed intelligent human beings. They are knowledgeable about how the system works, and, as it is necessary and convenient, will endeavor to live up to what adults have come to expect of them.

Historically, of course, the cultural patterns and sanctions of an older generation rarely have coincided with that of the younger. Presently, however, with an accelerated rate of change, the possibility of conflicts is greatly enhanced, and the degree of separateness encouraged—perhaps necessarily. At least Coleman (10) says that American parents cannot afford to shape their children in their own image. He says that the parents come to be "out of touch with the times" and unable to understand, much less inculcate, the standards of a social order that has changed so much since they were young. He also comments that the setting apart of children in schools for longer and longer periods of time cuts a child off from the rest of society and forces him toward carrying out most of his social life with others of his own age.

Adolescents, caught within social and economic conditions that split them off into a separate society, understandably develop modes of dress which symbolically reinforce their separateness. In effect, their clothing wins for them the social approval of their peer group at the same time that it sets them apart from other age groups. Contributing to the development of an exclusively teenage costume is the availability to teenagers of both time and money. Freed of responsibilities of a job, the teenager has time to spend dressing and grooming himself if he so wishes. In addition, the average American teenager is well provided for financially and is granted a great deal of independence in spending his share of the family clothing budget. According to Jackendoff (11), "Family budgetary limitations place a ceiling only on the quantity or quality of teen-age dress, not on its character."

Causes of Social Tensions

Social and economic conditions have worked together, therefore, to bind contemporary teenagers into a distinct contingent within the social structure, a contingent which, not unlike many previous generations of the young, challenges the old and embraces the new. Even those societies which are highly geared to change may feel threatened by breaks with traditions. Therefore, as adolescents adopt new standards for behavior that represent their adjustments to the situations of their own generation, they often meet resistance from the establishment. Even though adults within their own life times have observed many vacillations in standards for behavior, including those for appearance and personal display, they are not always ready to meet changes in mode of dress with equanimity. Many of them do; but others, rightly or wrongly, associate deviance in dress with the antisocial act. The individual who adopts sharply differing dress is felt to be preparing for undesirable and potentially disrupting behavior.

Within the schools, conflicts over appropriate appearance often come to a head. The school is to an extent a self-contained "little society" with limited functions—educational ones to be exact. Since students represent many kinds of backgrounds, especially at the elementary and secondary levels, the stage is set as in the larger society for tensions to grow. One way administrators sometimes attempt to ease tensions and facilitate students' understanding and getting along with each other is by encouraging some conformity in dress. The implied hope is that some uniformity in appearance will reduce the distractions of differences and also serve as a means for controlling behavior so that energies may be turned to the important job at hand—the accumulation of knowledge and

skills that will prepare students for effective performance of adult roles. Such a course of action, the encouraging of conformity in dress, is supported in many ways by values which help American people adjust to a pluralistic society. For example, conformity in externals such as housing, recreation, speech, manners, and dress, helps bridge the gap between individuals holding widely varying attitudes and beliefs (12). And value comes to be placed on conformity in these externals since they represent a sort of social currency or basis of social exchange among people of very different backgrounds.

However, since cultural values which support opposing points of view may also exist, controversies often arise in the schools. Parents sometimes protest the "inalienable right" of a teenage son to wear a haircut not approved by school administrators. They thereby defend a time-honored American value placed on individual freedom and independence.

Debates concerning haircuts of the male have puzzling aspects. Obviously, there is nothing inherently evil in any haircut per se. In addition, throughout history many gentlemen with long hair have been honored and respected. Therefore, the physical fact of a haircut must not count as much as its symbolism. If a certain haircut is interpreted to symbolize irresponsibility where responsibility is required, or femininity where masculinity is demanded, protests may be registered. Most societies not only expect responsibility of their members but also clear symbolic separation of men from women on the basis of dress. As a consequence appropriation by a member of one sex of dress and grooming practices commonly assigned to the opposite sex may stir up feelings of irritation, discomfort, and bewilderment. Easily noted in American society is a greater permissiveness with women than with men concerning exchange of clothing symbols. Women may wear trousers and men's tailored shirts, but a similar appropriation of "women's clothing" by men—except for costume purposes—is not readily tolerated.

Summary

A comprehensive review of factors related to the development of the dress of American adolescents reveals that this dress is indeed socially meaningful. In the first place, it is for these adolescents a tool which may be manipulated in their struggle for social survival, especially within the peer group which provides the environment for much of their significant interaction. Additionally, their dress symbolizes that adolescents of today reside within a long period of social and economic dependence marking time until they can emerge as fully productive, participating units within adult society. During their period of "incubation" adolescents may experiment with a succession of unique arrangements of their personal appearance. That they may achieve great vituosity in their personal display is attributable to their intelligence, their creativeness, and to the fact that they not only have time to devote to sartorial pursuits but also money in their pockets. To the extent that their appearance differs greatly from traditional ways and demonstrates their separateness from adult society, it will continue to inspire confusion, comment, and conflict.

REFERENCES

1. Isaiah 3:18–24.
2. Bradley, C.G. *Western World Costume* New York: Appleton-Century-Crofts, Inc., 1954, p. 70.
3. Davenport, M. *The Book of Costume* Vol. I, New York: Crown Publishers, 1948, p. 75.
4. Musgrove, F. *Youth and the Social Order* Bloomington, Ind.: Indiana University Press, 1965, p. 33.
5. Heller, M.S. What we know about today's teen-agers. In *Educating the Teen-Ager in Human Relations and Management of Resources* Washington, D.C.: American Home Economics Association, 1965 , p. 5.
6. Hoebel, E.A. *Man in the Primitive World* New York: McGraw-Hill Book Co., Inc., 1958, p. 247.
7. Coleman, J.S., *et al. The Adolescent Society* New York: The Free Press of Glencoe, Inc., 1961, p. 2.
8. Speare, E.G. *Child Life in New England 1790–1840.* Sturbridge, Mass.: Old Sturbridge Village Booklet Series, No. 12, 1961, p. 13.
9. Musgrove, *op. cit.* pp. xiii– xiv.
10. Coleman, *op cit* pp. 2–3.
11. Jackendoff, R. The teen-age market—Ill. In *Educating the Teen-Ager in Human Relations and Management of Resources.* Washington, D.C.: American Home Economics Association, 1965, p. 97.
12. Williams, R.M. *American Society.* New York: Alfred A. Knopf, Inc., 1960, pp. 450–454.

FASHION: FROM CLASS DIFFERENTIATION TO COLLECTIVE SELECTION

Herbert Blumer

Deficiencies of Fashion as a Sociological Concept

This paper is an invitation to sociologists to take seriously the topic of fashion. Only a handful of scholars, such as Simmel (1904), Sapir (1931), and the Langs (1961), have given more than casual concern to the topic. Their individual analyses of it, while illuminating in several respects, have been limited in scope, and within the chosen limits very sketchy. The treatment of the topic by sociologists in general, such as we find it in textbooks and in occasional pieces of scholarly writing, is even more lacking in substance. The major deficiencies in the conventional sociological treatment are easily noted—a failure to observe and appreciate the wide range of operation of fashion; a false assumption that fashion has only trivial or peripheral significance; a mistaken idea that fashion falls in the area of the abnormal and irrational and thus is out of the mainstream of human group life; and, finally, a misunderstanding of the nature of fashion.

Fashion Restricted to Adornment

Similar to scholars in general who have shown some concern with the topic, sociologists are disposed to identify fashion exclusively or primarily with the area of costume and adornment. While occasional references may be made to its play in other areas, such casual references do not give a proper picture of the extent of its operation. Yet, to a discerning eye fashion is readily seen to operate in many diverse areas of human group life, especially so in modern times. It is easily observable in the realm of the pure and applied arts, such as painting, sculpture, music, drama, architecture, dancing, and household decoration.

Its presence is very obvious in the area of entertainment and amusement. There is plenty of evidence to show its play in the field of medicine. Many of us are familiar with its operation in fields of industry, especially that of business management. It even touches such a relative sacred area as that of mortuary practice. Many scholars have noted its operation in the field of literature. Its presence can be seen in the history of modern philosophy. It can be observed at work in the realm of political doctrine. And—perhaps to the surprise of many—it is unquestionably at work in the field of science. That this is true of the social and psychological sciences is perhaps more readily apparent. But we have also to note, as several reputable and qualified scholars have done, that fashion appears in redoubtable areas as physical and biological science and mathematics. The domain in which fashion operates is very extensive, indeed. To limit it to, or to center it in, the field of costume and adornment is to have a very inadequate idea of the scope of its occurrence.

Fashion as Socially Inconsequential

This extensive range of fashion should, in itself, lead scholars to question their implicit belief that fashion is a peripheral and relatively inconsequential social happening. To the contrary, fashion may influence vitally the central content of any field in which it operates. For example, the styles in art, the themes and styles in literature, the forms and themes in entertainment, the perspectives in philosophy, the practices in business, and the preoc-

From *The Sociological Quarterly,* Vol. 10, No. 3 (Summer 1969). Reprinted by permission of the publisher.

cupations in science may be affected profoundly by fashion. These are not peripheral matters. In addition, the nature of the control wielded by fashion shows that its touch is not light. Where fashion operates it assumes an imperative position. It sets sanctions of what is to be done, it is conspicuously indifferent to criticism, it demands adherence, and it by-passes as oddities and misfits those who fail to abide by it. This grip which it exercises over its area of operation does not bespeak an inconsequential mechanism.

Fashion as Aberrant and Irrational

The third deficiency, as mentioned, is to view fashion as an aberrant and irrational social happening, akin to a craze or mania. Presumably, this ill-considered view of fashion has arisen from considerations which suggest that fashion is bizarre and frivolous, that it is fickle, that it arises in response to irrational status anxieties, and that people are swept into conforming to it despite their better judgment. It is easy to form such impressions. For one thing, past fashions usually seem odd and frequently ludicrous to the contemporary eye. Next, they rarely seem to make sense in terms of utility or rational purpose; they seem much more to express the play of fancy and caprice. Further, following the classic analysis made by Simmel, fashion seems to represent a kind of anxious effort of elite groups to set themselves apart by introducing trivial and ephemeral demarcating insignia, with a corresponding strained effort by non-elite classes to make a spurious identification of themselves with upper classes by adopting these insignia. Finally, since fashion despite its seeming frivolous content sweeps multitudes of people into its fold, it is regarded as a form of collective craziness.

Nevertheless, to view fashion as an irrational, aberrant, and craze-like social happening is to grievously misunderstand it. On the *individual side,* the adoption of what is fashionable is by and large a very calculating act. The fashion conscious person is usually quite careful and discerning in his effort to identify the fashion in order to make sure that he is "in style"; the fashion does not appear to him as frivolous. In turn, the person who is coerced into adopting the fashion contrary to his wishes does so deliberately and not irrationally. Finally, the person who unwittingly follows a fashion does so because of a limitation of choice rather than as an impulsive expression of aroused emotions or inner anxiety. The bulk of evidence gives no support to the contention that individuals who adopt fashion are caught up in the spirit of a craze. Their behavior is no more irrational or excited—and probably less so—than that of voters casting political ballots. On its *collective side,* fashion does not fit any better the pattern of craze. The mechanisms of interaction are not those of circular transmission of aroused feelings, or of heightened suggestibility, or of fixed preoccupation with a gripping event. While people may become excited over a fashion they respond primarily to its character of propriety and social distinction; these are tempering guides. Fashion has respectability; it carries the stamp of approval of an elite—an elite that is recognized to be sophisticated and believed to be wise in the given area of endeavor. It is this endorsement which undergirds fashion—rather than the emotional interaction which is typical of crazes. Fashion has, to be true, an irrational, or better "non-rational," dimension which we shall consider later, but this dimension does not make it into a craze or mania.

The observations that fashion operates over wide areas of human endeavor, that it is not aberrant and craze-like, and that it is not peripheral and inconsequential merely correct false pictures of it. They do little to identify its nature and mode of operation. It is to this identification that I now wish to turn.

Simmel: Fashion as Class Differentiation

Let me use as the starting point of the discussion the analysis of fashion made some sixty years ago by Georg Simmel. His analysis, without question, has set the character of what little solid sociological thought is to be found on the topic. His thesis was essentially simple. For him, fashion arose as a form of class differentiation in a relatively open class society. In such a society the elite class seeks to set itself apart by observable marks or insignia, such as distinctive forms of dress. However, members of immediately subjacent classes adopt these insignia as a means of satisfying their striving to identify with a superior status. They, in turn, are copied by members of classes beneath them. In this way, the distinguishing insignia of the elite class filter down through the class pyramid. In this process, however, the elite class loses these marks of separate identity. It is led, accordingly, to devise new distinguishing insignia which, again, are copied by the classes below, thus repeating the cycle. This, for Simmel, was the nature of fashion and the mechanism of its operation. Fashion was thought to arise in the form of styles which demarcate an elite group. These styles automatically acquire prestige in the eyes of those who wish to emulate the elite group and are copied by them, thus forcing the elite group to devise new distinctive marks of their superior status. Fashion is thus caught up in an incessant and recurrent process of innovation and emulation. A fashion, once started, marches relentlessly to its doom; on its heels treads a new fashion destined to the same fate; and so on ad infinitum. This sets the fundamental character of the fashion process.

There are several features of Simmel's analysis which are admittedly of high merit. One of them was to point out that fashion requires a certain type of society in which to take place. Another was to highlight the importance of prestige in the operation of fashion. And another, of particular significance, was to stress that the essence of fashion lies in a process of change—a process that is natural and indigenous and not unusual and aberrant. Yet, despite the fact that his analysis still remains the best in the published literature, it failed to catch the character of fashion as a social happening. It is largely a parochial treatment, quite well suited to fashion in dress in the seventeenth, eighteenth, and nineteenth century Europe with its particular class structure. But it does not fit the operation of fashion in our contemporary epoch with its many diverse fields and its emphasis on modernity. Its shortcomings will be apparent, I think, in the light of the following analysis.

Modernity and the Selection Process

Some years ago I had the opportunity to study rather extensively and at first hand the women's fashion industry in Paris. There were three matters in particular which I observed which seem to me to provide the clues for an understanding of fashion in general. I wish to discuss each of them briefly and indicate their significance.

First, I was forcibly impressed by the fact that the setting or determination of fashion takes place actually through an intense process of selection. At a seasonal opening of a major Parisian fashion house there may be presented a hundred or more designs of women's evening wear before an audience of from one to two hundred buyers. The managerial corps of the fashion house is able to indicate a group of about thirty designs of the entire lot, inside of which will fall the small number, usually about six to eight designs, that are chosen by the buyers; but the managerial staff is typically unable to predict this small number on which the choices converge. Now, these choices are made by the buyers—a highly competitive and secretive lot—independently of each other and without knowledge of each other's selections. Why should their choices converge on a few designs as they do? When the buyers were asked why they chose one dress in preference to another—between which my inexperienced eye could see no appreciable difference—the typical, honest, yet largely uninformative answer was that the dress was "stunning."

Inquiry into the reasons for the similarity in the buyers' choices led me to a second observation, namely, that the buyers were immersed in and preoccupied with a remarkably common world of intense stimulation. It was a world of lively discussion of what was happening in women's fashion, of fervent reading of fashion publications, and of close observation of one another's lines of products. And, above all, it was a world of close concern with the women's dress market, with the prevailing tastes and prospective tastes of the consuming public in the area of dress. It became vividly clear to me that by virtue of their intense immersion in this world the buyers came to develop common sensitivities and similar appreciations. To use an old but valuable psychological term, they developed a common "apperception mass" which sharpened and directed their feelings of discrimination, which guided and sensi-

tized their perceptions, and which channeled their judgments and choices. This explains, I am convinced, why the buyers, independently of each other, made such amazingly identical choices at the fashion openings. This observation also underlines a point of the greatest importance, namely, that the buyers became the unwitting surrogates of the fashion public. Their success, indeed their vocational fate, depended on their ability to sense the direction of taste in this public.

The third observation which I made pertained to the dress designers—those who created the new styles. They devised the various designs between which the buyers were ultimately to make the choices, and their natural concern was to be successful in gaining adoption of their creations. There were three lines of preoccupation from which they derived their ideas. One was to pour over old plates of former fashions and depictions of costumes of far-off peoples. A second was to brood and reflect over current and recent styles. The third, and most important, was to develop an intimate familiarity with the most recent expressions of modernity as these were to be seen in such areas as the fine arts, recent literature, political debates and happenings, and discourse in the sophisticated world. The dress designers were engaged in translating themes from these areas and media into dress designs. The designers were attuned to an impressive degree to modern developments and were seeking to capture and express in dress design the spirit of such developments. I think that this explains why the dress designers—again a competitive and secretive group, working apart from each other in a large number of different fashion houses—create independently of each other such remarkably similar designs. They pick up ideas of the past, but always through the filter of the present; they are guided and constrained by the immediate styles in dress, particularly the direction of such styles over the recent span of a few years; but above all, they are seeking to catch the proximate future as it is revealed in modern developments.

Taken together, these three observations which I have sketched in a most minimal form outline what is significant in the case of fashion in the women's dress industry. They indicate that the fashion is set through a process of free selection from among a large number of competing models; that the creators of the models are seeking to catch and give expression to what we may call the direction of modernity; and that the buyers, who through their choices set the fashion, are acting as the unwitting agents of a fashion consuming public whose incipient tastes the buyers are seeking to anticipate. In this paper I shall not deal with what is probably the most interesting and certainly the most obscure aspect of the entire relationship, namely, the relation between, on one hand, the expressions of modernity to which the dress designers are so responsive and, on the other hand, the incipient and inarticulate tastes which are taking shape in the fashion consuming public. Certainly, the two come together in the styles which are chosen and, in so doing, lay down the lines along which modern life in this area moves. I regard this line of relationship as constituting one of the most significant mechanisms in the shaping of our modern world, but I shall not undertake analysis of it in this paper.

Fashion and the Elite

The brief account which I have given of the setting of fashion in the women's wear industry permits one to return to Simmel's classic analysis and pinpoint more precisely its shortcomings. His scheme elevates the prestige of the elite to the position of major importance in the operation of fashion—styles come into fashion because of the stamp of distinction conferred on them by the elite. I think this view misses almost completely what is central to fashion, namely, *to be in fashion.* It is not the prestige of the elite which makes the design fashionable but, instead, it is the suitability of potential fashionableness of the design which allows the prestige of the elite to be attached to it. The design has to correspond to the direction of incipient taste of the fashion consuming public. The prestige of the elite affects but does not control the direction of this incipient taste. We have here a case of the fashion mechanism transcending and embracing the prestige of the elite group rather than stemming from that prestige.

There are a number of lines of evidence which I think clearly establish this to be the case. First, we should note that members of the elite—and I am still speaking of the elite in the realm of women's dress—are themselves as interested as anyone to be in fashion. Anyone familiar with them is acutely aware of their sensitivity in this regard, their wish not to be out of step with fashion, and indeed their wish to be in the vanguard of proper fashion. They are caught in the need of responding to the direction of fashion rather than of occupying the privileged position of setting that direction. Second, as explained, the fashion-adopting actions of the elite take place in a context of competing models, each with its own source of prestige. Not all prestigeful persons are innovators—and innovators are not necessarily persons with the highest prestige. The elite, itself, has to select between models proposed by innovators; and their choice is not determined by the relative prestige of the innovators. As history shows abundantly in the competitive process fashion readily ignores persons with the highest prestige and, indeed, by-passes acknowledged "leaders" time after time. A further line of evidence is just as telling, namely, the interesting instances of failure to control the direction of fashion despite effective marshalling of the sources of prestige. An outstanding example was the effort in 1922 to check and reverse the trend toward shorter skirts which had started in 1919 to the dismay of clothing manufacturers. These manufacturers enlisted the cooperation of the heads of

fashion houses, fashion magazines, fashion commentators, actresses, and acknowledged fashion leaders in an extensive, well organized and amply financed campaign to reverse the trend. The important oracles of fashion declared that long dresses were returning, models of long dresses were presented in numbers at the seasonal openings, actresses wore them on the stage, and manikins paraded them at the fashionable meeting places. Yet, despite this effective marshalling of all significant sources of prestige, the campaign was a marked failure; the trend toward shorter skirts, after a slight interruption, continued until 1929 when a rather abrupt change to long dresses took place. Such instances—and there have been others—provide further indication that there is much more to the fashion mechanism than the exercise of prestige. Fashion appears much more as a collective groping for the proximate future than a channeled movement laid down by prestigeful figures.

Collective Selection Replaces Class Differentiation

These observations require us to put Simmel's treatment in a markedly different perspective, certainly as applied to fashion in our modern epoch. The efforts of an elite class to set itself apart in appearance takes place inside of the movement of fashion instead of being its cause. The prestige of elite groups, in place of setting the direction of the fashion movement, is effective only to the extent to which they are recognized as representing and portraying the movement. The people in other classes who consciously follow the fashion do so because it is the fashion and not because of the separate prestige of the elite group. The fashion dies not because it has been discarded by the elite group but because it gives way to a new model more consonant with developing taste. *The fashion mechanism appears not in response to a need of class differentiation and class emulation but in response to a wish to be in fashion, to be abreast of what has good standing, to express new tastes which are emerging in a changing world.* These are the changes that seem to be called for in Simmel's formulation. They are fundamental changes. They shift fashion *from* the fields of *class differentiation to* the area of *collective selection* and center its mechanism in the process of such selection. This process of collective selection represents an effort to choose from among competing styles or models those which match developing tastes, those which "click," or those which—to revert to my friends, the buyers—"are stunning." The fact that this process of collective selection is mysterious—it is mysterious because we do not understand it—does not contradict in any way that it takes place.

Features of the Fashion Mechanism

To view the fashion mechanism as a continuing process of collective selection from among competing models yields a markedly different picture from that given by conventional sociological analysis of fashion. It calls attention to the fact that those implicated in fashion—innovators, "leaders," followers, and participants—are parts of a collective process that responds to changes in taste and sensitivity. In a legitimate sense, the movement of fashion represents a reaching out for new models which will answer to as yet indistinct and inarticulate newer tastes. The transformation of taste, of collective taste, results without question from the diversity of experience that occurs in social interaction in a complex moving world. It leads, in turn, to an unwitting groping for suitable forms of expression, in an effort to move in a direction which is consonant with the movement of modern life in general. It is perhaps unnecessary to add that we know very little indeed about this area of transformation of collective taste. Despite its unquestioned importance it has been scarcely noted, much less studied. Sociologists are conspicuously ignorant of it and indifferent to it.

Before leaving the discussion of fashion in the area of conspicuous appearance (such as dress, adornment, or mannerism), it is desirable to note and consider briefly several important features of the fashion mechanism, namely, its historical continuity, its modernity, the role of collective taste in its operation, and the psychological motives which are alleged to account for it.

Historical Continuity

The history of fashion shows clearly that new fashions are related to, and grow out of, their immediate predecessors. This is one of the fundamental ways in which fashion differs from fads. Fads have no line of historical continuity; each springs up independently of a forerunner and gives rise to no successor. In the case of fashion, fashion innovators always have to consider the prevailing fashion, if for no other reason than to depart from it or to elaborate on it. The result is a line of continuity. Typically, although not universally, the line of continuity has the character of a cultural drift, expressing itself in what we customarily term a "fashion trend." Fashion trends are a highly important yet a much neglected object of study. They signify a convergence and marshalling of collective taste in a given direction and thus pertain to one of the most significant yet obscure features in group life. The terminal points of fashion trends are of special interest. Sometimes they are set by the nature of the medium (there is a point beyond which the skirt cannot be lengthened or shortened [see Richardson and Koreber, 1947; Young, 1937]); sometimes they seem to represent an exhaustion of the logical possibilities of the medium; but frequently they signify a relatively abrupt shift in interests and taste. The terminal points are marked particularly by a much wider latitude of experimentation in the new fashion models that are advanced for adoption; at such points the fashion mechanism particularly reveals the groping character of collective choice to set itself on a new course.

If it be true, as I propose to explain later, that the fashion mechanism is woven deeply into the texture of modern life, the study of fashion in its aspects of continuity, trends, and cycles would be highly important and rewarding.

Modernity

The feature of "modernity" in fashion is especially significant. Fashion is always modern; it always seeks to keep abreast of the times. It is sensitive to the movement of current developments as they take place in its own field, in adjacent fields, and in the larger social world. Thus, in women's dress, fashion is responsive to its own trend, to developments in fabrics and ornamentation, to developments in the fine arts, to exciting events that catch public attention such as the discovery of the tomb of Tutankhamen, to political happenings, and to major social shifts such as the emancipation of women or the rise of the cult of youth. Fashion seems to sift out of these diverse sources of happenings a set of obscure guides which bring it into line with the general or over-all direction of modernity itself. This responsiveness in its more extended form seems to be the chief factor in formation of what we speak of as a "spirit of the times" or a *zeitgeist*.

Collective Taste

Since the idea of "collective taste" is given such an important position in my analysis of the fashion mechanism, the idea warrants further clarification and explanation. I am taking the liberty of quoting my remarks as they appear in the article on "Fashion" in the new International Encyclopedia of the Social Sciences V (1968:341–345).

> . . . It represents an organic sensitivity to objects of social experience, as when we say that 'vulgar comedy does not suit our taste' or that 'they have a taste for orderly procedure.' Taste has a tri-fold character—it is like an appetite in seeking positive satisfaction; it operates as a sensitive selector, giving a basis for acceptance or rejection; and it is a formative agent, guiding the development of lines of action and shaping objects to meet its demands. Thus, it appears as a subjective mechanism, giving orientation to individuals, structuring activity and moulding the world of experience. Tastes are themselves a product of experience; they usually develop from an initial state of vagueness to a state of refinement and stability, but once formed they may decay and disintegrate. They are formed in the context of social interaction, responding to the definitions and affirmations given by others. People thrown into areas of common interaction and having similar runs of experience develop common tastes. The fashion process involves both a formation and an expression of collective taste in the given area of fashion. Initially, the taste is a loose fusion of vague inclinations and dissatisfactions that are aroused by new experiences in the field of fashion and in the larger surrounding world. In this initial state, collective taste is amorphous, inarticulate, vaguely posed, and awaiting specific direction. Through models and proposals, fashion innovators sketch out possible lines along which the incipient taste may gain objective expression and take definite form. Collective

taste is an active force in the ensuing process of selection, setting limits and providing guidance; yet, at the same time it undergoes refinement and organization through its attachment to, and embodiment in, specific social forms. The origin, formation, and careers of collective taste constitute the huge problematic area in fashion. Major advancement in our knowledge of the fashion mechanism depends on the charting of this area. . . .

Psychological Motives

Now, a word with regard to psychological interpretations of fashion. Scholars, by and large, have sought to account for fashion in terms of psychological motives. A perusal of the literature will show an assortment of different feelings and impulses which have been picked out to explain the occurrence of fashion. Some students ascribe fashion to efforts to escape from boredom or ennui, especially among members of the leisure class. Some treat fashion as arising from playful and whimsical impulses to enliven the routines of life with zest. Some regard it as due to a spirit of adventure which impels individuals to rebel against the confinement of prevailing social forms. Some see fashion as a symbolic expression of hidden sexual interests. Most striking is the view expressed by Sapir in his article on "Fashion" in the first edition of the Encyclopedia of the Social Sciences VI (1931:139–141); Sapir held that fashion results from an effort to increase the attractiveness of the self, especially under conditions which impair the integrity of the ego; the sense of oneself is regained and heightened through novel yet socially sanctioned departures from prevailing social forms. Finally, some scholars trace fashion to desires for personal prestige or notoriety.

Such psychological explanations, either singly or collectively, fail to account for fashion; they do not explain why or how the various feelings or motives give rise to a fashion process. Such feelings are presumably present and in operation in all human societies; yet there are many societies in which fashion is not to be found. Further, such feelings may take various forms of expression which have no relation to a fashion process. We are given no explanation of why the feelings should lead to the formation of fashion in place of taking other channels of expression available to them. The psychological schemes fail to come to grip with the collective process which constitutes fashion—the emergence of new models in an area of changing experience, the differential attention given them, the interaction which leads to a focusing of collective choice on one of them, the social endorsement of it as proper, and the powerful control which this endorsement yields. Undoubtedly, the various feelings and impulses specified by psychologists operate within the fashion process—just as they operate within non-fashion areas of group life. But their operation within fashion does not account for fashion. Instead, their operation presupposes the existence of the fashion process as one of the media for their play.

The foregoing discussion indicates, I trust, the inadequacy of conventional sociological and psychological schemes to explain the nature of fashion. Both sets of schemes fail to perceive fashion as the process of collective selection that it is. The schemes do not identify the nature of the social setting in which fashion arises nor do they catch or treat the mechanism by which fashion operates. The result is that students fail to see the scope and manner of its operation and to appreciate the vital role which it plays in modern group life. In the interest of presenting a clearer picture of these matters, I wish to amplify the sketch of fashion as given above in order to show more clearly its broad generic character.

Generic Character of Fashion

It is necessary, first of all, to insist that fashion is not confined to those areas, such as women's apparel, in which fashion is institutionalized and professionally exploited under conditions of intense competition. As mentioned earlier, it is found in operation in a wide variety and increasing number of fields which shun deliberate or intentional concern with fashion. In such fields, fashion occurs almost always without awareness on the part of those who are caught in its operation. What may be primarily response to fashion is seen and interpreted in other ways—chiefly as doing what is believed to be superior practice. The prevalence of such unwitting deception can be considerable. The basic mechanism of fashion which comes to such a clear, almost pure, form in women's dress is clouded or concealed in other fields but is none the less operative. Let me approach a consideration of this matter by outlining the six essential conditions under which fashion presumably comes into play.

Essential Conditions of Its Appearance

First, the area in which fashion operates must be one that is involved in a movement of change, with people ready to revise or discard old practices, beliefs, and attachments, and poised to adopt new social forms; there must be this thrust into the future. If the area is securely established, as in the domain of the sacred, there will be no fashion. Fashion presupposes that the area is in passage, responding to changes taking place in a surrounding world, and oriented to keeping abreast of new developments. The area is marked by a new psychological perspective which places a premium on being "up to date" and which implies a readiness to denigrate given older forms of life as being outmoded. Above all, the changing character of the area must gain expression or reflection in changes in that subjective orientation which I have spoken of under the term, "taste."

A *second* condition is that the area must be open to the recurrent presentation of models or proposals of new social forms. These models, depending on the given areas of fashion, may cover such diverse things as points of view, doctrines, lines of preoccupation, themes, practices, and use of artifacts. In a given area of fashion, these models differ from each other and of course from the prevailing social forms. Each of them is metaphorically a claimant for adoption. Thus their presence introduces a competitive situation and sets the stage for selection between them.

Third, there must be a relatively free opportunity for choice between the models. This implies that the models must be open, so to speak, to observation and that facilities and means must be available for their adoption. If the presentation of new models is prevented the fashion process will not get under way. Further, a severe limitation in the wherewithal needed to adopt models (such as necessary wealth, intellectual sophistication, refined skill, or esthetic sensitivity) curtails the initiation of the fashion process.

Fashion is not guided by utilitarian or rational considerations. This points to a *fourth* condition essential to its operation, namely, that the pretended merit or value of the competing models cannot be demonstrated through open and decisive test. Where choices can be made between rival models on the basis of objective and effective test, there is no place for fashion. It is for this reason that fashion does not take root in those areas of utility, technology, or science where asserted claims can be brought before the bar of demonstrable proof. In contrast, the absence of means for testing effectively the relative merit of competing models opens the door to other considerations in making choices between them. This kind of situation is essential to the play of fashion.

A *fifth* condition for fashion is the presence of prestige figures who espouse one or another of the competing models. The prestige of such persons must be such that they are acknowledged as qualified to pass judgment on the value or suitability of the rival models. If they are so regarded their choice carries weight as an assurance or endorsement of the superiority or propriety of a given model. A combination of such prestigeful figures, espousing the same model, enhances the likelihood of adoption of the model.

A *sixth* and final condition is that the area must be open to the emergence of new interests and dispositions in response to (a) the impact of outside events, (b) the introduction of new participants into the area, and (c) changes in inner social interaction. This condition is chiefly responsible for the shifting of taste and the redirection of collective choice which together constitute the lifeline of fashion.

If the above six conditions are met, I believe that one will always find fashion to be in play. People in the area will be found to be converging their choices on models and shifting this convergence over time. The convergence of choice occurs not because of the intrinsic merit or demonstrated validity of the selected models but because of the appearance of high standing which the chosen models carry. Unquestionably, such high standing is given in major measure by the endorsement and espousal of models of prestigeful persons. But it must be stressed again that it is not prestige, *per se,* which imparts this sanction; a prestigeful person, despite his eminence, may be easily felt to be "out-of-date." To carry weight, the person of prestige must be believed or sensed to be voicing the proper perspective that is called for by developments in the area. To recognize this is to take note of the importance of the disposition to keep abreast of what is collectively judged to be up-to-date practice. The formation of this collective judgment takes place through an interesting but ill-understood interaction between prestige and incipient taste, between eminent endorsement and congenial interest. Collective choice of models is forged in this process of interaction, leading to a focusing of selection at a given time on one model and at a different time on another model.

Fashion and Contemporary Society

If we view modern life in terms of the analytical scheme which I have sketched, there is no difficulty in seeing the play of fashion in many diverse areas. Close scrutiny of such areas will show the features which we have discussed—a turning away from old forms that are thought to be out-of-date, the introduction of new models which compete for adoption; a selection between them that is made not on the basis of demonstrated merit or utility but in response to an interplay of prestige-endorsement and incipient taste; and a course of development in which a given type of model becomes solidified, socially elevated, and imperative in its demands for acceptance for a period of time. While this process is revealed most vividly in the area of women's fashion it can be noted in play here and there across the board in modern life and may, indeed, be confidently expected to increase in scope under the conditions of modern life. These conditions—the pressure to change, the open doors to innovation, the inadequacy or the unavailability of decisive tests of the merit of proposed models, the effort of prestigeful figures to gain or maintain standing in the face of developments to which they must respond, and the groping of people for a satisfactory expression of new and vague tastes—entrench fashion as a basic and widespread process in modern life.

The Expanding Domain of Fashion

This characterization may repel scholars who believe that fashion is an abnormal and irrational happening and that it gives way before enlightenment, sophistication, and increased knowledge. Such scholars would reject the thought that fashion is becoming increasingly embedded in a society which is presumably moving toward a high level of intelligence and rational perspective. Yet, the facts are clear that fashion is an outstanding mark of modern civilization and that its domain is expanding rather than diminishing. As areas of life come to be caught in the vortex of movement and as proposed innovations multiply in them, a process of collective choice in the nature of fashion is naturally and inevitably brought into play. The absence or inadequacy of compelling tests of the merit of proposals opens the door to prestige-endorsement and taste as determinants of collective choice. The compelling role of these two factors as they interact easily escapes notice by those who participate in the process of collective choice; the model which emerges with a high sanction and approval is almost always believed by them as being intrinsically and demonstrably correct. This belief is fortified by the impressive arguments and arrays of specious facts that may frequently be marshalled on behalf of the model. Consequently, it is not surprising that participants may fail completely to recognize a fashion process in which they are sharing. The identification of the process as fashion occurs usually only after it is gone—when it can be viewed from the detached vantage point of later time. The fashions which we can now detect in the past history of philosophy, medicine, science, technological use and industrial practice did not appear as fashions to those who shared in them. The fashions merely appeared to them as up-to-date achievements! The fact that participants in fashion movements in different areas of contemporary life do not recognize such movements should not mislead perceptive scholars. The application of this observation to the domain of social science is particularly in order; contemporary social science is rife with the play of fashion.

The Societal Role of Fashion

I turn finally to a series of concluding remarks on what seems to be the societal role of fashion. As I have sought to explain, the key to the understanding of fashion is given in the simple words, "being in fashion." These words signify an area of life which is caught in movement—movement from an out-moded past toward a dim, uncertain, but exploitable immediate future. In this passage, the need of the present is to be in march with the time. The fashion mechanism is the response to this need. These simple observations point to the social role of fashion—a role which I would state abstractly to be that of enabling and aiding collective adjustment to and in a moving world of divergent possibilities. In spelling out this abstract statement I wish to call attention to three matters.

The *first* is a matter which is rather obvious, namely, that fashion introduces a conspicuous measure of unanimity and uniformity in what would otherwise be a mark-

edly fragmented arrangement. If all competing models enjoyed similar acceptance the situation would be one of disorder and disarray. In the field of dress, for example, if people were to freely adopt the hundreds of styles proposed professionally each year and the other thousands which the absence of competition would allow, there would be a veritable "Tower of Babel" consequence. *Fashion introduces order in a potentially anarchic and moving present.* By establishing suitable models which carry the stamp of propriety and compel adherence, fashion narrowly limits the range of variability and so fosters uniformity and order, even though it be passing uniformity and order. In this respect fashion performs in a moving society a function which custom performs in a settled society.

Second, fashion serves to detach the grip of the past in a moving world. By placing a premium on being in the mode and derogating what developments have left behind, it frees actions for new movement. The significance of this release from the restraint of the past should not be minimized. To meet a moving and changing world requires freedom to move in new directions. Detachment from the hold of the past is no small contribution to the achievement of such freedom. In the areas of its operation fashion facilitates that contribution. In this sense there is virtue in applying the derogatory accusations of being "old-fashioned," "outmoded," "backward," and "out-of-date."

Third, fashion operates as an orderly preparation for the immediate future. By allowing the presentation of new models but by forcing them through the gauntlet of competition and collective selection the fashion mechanism offers a continuous means of adjusting to what is on the horizon.* On the one hand, it offers to innovators and creators the opportunity to present through their models their ideas of what the immediate future should be in the given area of fashion. On the other hand, the adoption of the models which survive the gauntlet of collective selection gives expression to nascent dispositions that represents an accommodation or orientation to the immediate future. Through this process, fashion nurtures and shapes a body of common sensitivity and taste, as is suggested by the congeniality and naturalness of present fashions in contrast to the oddness and incongruity of past fashions. This body of common sensitivity and taste is analogous on the subjective side to a "universe of discourse." Like the latter, it provides a basis for a common approach to a world and for handling and digesting the experiences which the world yields. The value of a pliable and reforming body of common taste to meet a shifting and developing world should be apparent.

---

*The recognition that fashion is continuously at work is, in my judgment, the major although unintended contribution of Simmel's analysis. However, his thesis that the function of fashion is the oscillating differentiation and unification of social classes seems to me to miss what is most important.

Conclusion

In these three ways, fashion is a very adept mechanism for enabling people to adjust in an orderly and unified way to a moving and changing world which is potentially full of anarchic possibilities. It is suited, *par excellence,* to the demands of life in such a moving world since it facilitates detachment from a receding past, opens the doors to proposals to the future, but subjects such proposals to the test of collective selection, thus bringing them in line with the direction of awakened interest and disposition. In areas of life—and they are many—in which the merit of the proposals cannot be demonstrated, it permits orderly movement and development.

In closing, let me renew the invitation to sociologists to take fashion seriously and give it the attention and study which it deserves and which are so sorely lacking. Fashion should be recognized as a central mechanism in forming social order in a modern type of world, a mechanism whose operation will increase. It needs to be lifted out of the area of the bizarre, the irrational and the inconse-quential in which sociologists have so misguidingly lodged it. When sociologists respond to the need of developing a scheme of analysis suited to a moving or modern world they will be required to assign the fashion process to a position of central importance.

REFERENCES

Blumer, Herbert. 1968. "Fashion." Pp. 341–345 in International Encyclopedia of the Social Sciences V. New York: Macmillan.

Lang, Kurt and Gladys Lang. 1961. Collective Dynamics. New York: Crowell.

Richardson, J., and A.L. Kroeber. 1947. "Three centuries of women's dress fashions: a quantitative analysis." Anthropological Records 5:111–153.

Sapir, Edward. 1931. "Fashion." Pp. 139–141 in Encyclopedia of the Social Sciences VI. New York: Macmillan.

Simmel, G. 1904. 'Fashion." International Quarterly 10. 1957. "Fashion." American Journal of Sociology 62:541–558. (reprint).

Young, A.B. 1937. Recurring Cycles of Fashion: 1760–1937. New York: Harper & Brothers.

CARRYING IT OFF IN STYLE

The Role of Clothing

Marilyn J. Horn

Clothing vividly reflects one's values and life style. An individual's clothes serve as a kind of "sign language" that transmits a variety of information which usually becomes the basis of our initial impressions of a person.

It doesn't matter if the perceptions are accurate or fair. Whether we like it or not, people make these kinds of judgments about us. And although we may not admit it, we make such judgments about them.

These first impressions are sometimes false, but often amazingly accurate. Thus we should understand the role clothing plays in order to achieve the kind of image that family members desire.

For most people, clothing satisfies the need to be warm and comfortable. But if chosen wisely, it can also make them more attractive, help them feel part of a group, provide social status or prestige, give them individuality, or satisfy the need for creative self-expression.

Such needs will not only vary from individual to individual, but some may even be in conflict. Adolescents in particular—although this is not restricted to youth by any means—will sacrifice comfort, beauty, economy, and even health in order to gain the social approval that comes from conformity to peer group fads and fashions.

Clothing is probably one of the greatest sources of disagreement between parents and children. A conscientious father tries to instill in his son the importance of a neat and well-groomed appearance. The son's preference for patched jeans, sandals, and a wild head of hair not only baffles but outrages the father. He regards such behavior as a blatant violation of values the family holds important: respect for authority, cleanliness, and an appearance of success. The father becomes convinced that young people are against anything traditional, just for the sake of being against it.

For some youth, style of dress does in fact symbolize both a rejection of the middle-class culture and assertion of a counterculture. No doubt the new generation has been strongly influenced by the appearance and lifestyle of those who espouse an antimaterialistic ethic. However, the majority of young people adopted the "look" not for ideological reasons, but for reasons of fashion.

Fashion is a powerful force in human nature. We can't afford to ignore it, nor should we rationalize our fashion motives in the direction of more "logical" reasons. The basic character of human life is expressed in what we call "normal behavior"—a "norm" meaning the typical or

Reprinted from *The 1973 Yearbook of Agriculture: Handbook for the Home,* U.S. Department of Agriculture. Washington, D.C.: U.S. Government Printing Office, 1973, pp. 316–319.

common way of responding. Nowhere can such behavior be seen more visually than in the whole fashion process.

We live in an age of volatile fads and rapidly shifting fashions. New styles are quickly diffused via the mass media. This, in turn, encourages the avant-garde to introduce newer styles at an even faster pace.

Changing fashions often makes one's clothes old hat before the wear life of a garment is over. An understanding of the fashion cycle—the gradual rise, peaking, and eventual decline in the popular acceptance of a style—will help you be a wise consumer. It may prevent you from investing in quality that will long outlast the fashion value of your clothing.

Remember that a fashion, on its way in, is accepted and worn by the relatively few people who have the resources and the desire to be conspicuously different. As the popularity of a style spreads, more and more people hop on the bandwagon until the style finally snowballs to the peak of acceptance. But once everyone has it, the attraction is past. There is no place left for the style to go but to slide into obsolescence.

Forces that give vent to the rise and fall of fashion are identical with the tensions that exist between the need for conformity and individuality in dress. Conformity, particularly within small social groups, is widespread, and the desire to be like others, to "fit in with the crowd," is strongly reinforced in human interaction.

Beginning at a very early age, most of our social behavior is imitative. As children, we learn a great deal by copying the actions of older persons. Especially at a time when the child becomes concerned about changing body proportions, it is important to make him feel he is no different from others of similar age.

The parent who insists on frilly dresses when all the other little girls are wearing denim pants and cotton T-shirts may unknowingly alienate the child from the group. Undue emphasis placed on the importance of clothes early in life can contribute as much to later personality maladjustments as feelings of clothing deprivation.

While conformity to a given set of clothing norms thus provides for social approval and group belongingness, we all feel the need to achieve some distinction for ourselves as unique individuals. The search for individuality appears to be somewhat more crucial in today's world because of what the economists have termed "the homogenization of the consumer market." The steady growth of our economy and the accompanying diffusion of affluence has made it possible for many, many more people to enjoy the luxuries which only a few decades earlier had been limited to a few.

As a result of the economies of mass production, coupled with increased spending power among the middle income groups, lower income families now have access to the same kinds of fashionable clothes as the families of successful businessmen or professionals.

Out of this homogeneous-looking society comes a deep-seated psychological need for people to differentiate themselves from others. This need for self-expression is one of the things at the base of the boom in the home sewing market. We can assess this trend not only in terms of increased sales in yardgoods and sewing machines, but in the accessory field as well, e.g., belts, buckles, hand-tooled leather goods and stitcheries of all kinds.

More and more men's wear patterns are available, and people have taken to sewing their own thing simply because it gives them an opportunity for expressing their individuality.

The decision to make rather than buy much of the family clothing thus has a stronger psychological base than an economic one. If you sew at home, chances are you have a more extensive wardrobe of better quality and fit than the person who spends the same amount for ready-to-wear. But if you value your time, you may want to ask yourself if it is economically worthwhile to make your own garments.

At every stage of development, clothes can help establish one's identity for himself and for those with whom he interacts. The childhood game of "dressing up" in parents' clothes provides the opportunity for the child to practice the roles that he will be expected to play in adult life.

Many "roles" in life can't be carried off successfully without the aid of the "props" of costume. The banker who looks like a rock singer may have considerable difficulty convincing his associates of his financial acumen. The degree to which a person chooses clothes that "fit" the role—whether it's a salesman, a teacher, a cowboy or a college president—will affect the cogency of his performance in that role.

Clothes are, moreover, an important factor in developing feelings of self-confidence and self-respect. When you look good, you feel good. For most people, clothes are often a source of positive reaction from others, since in our culture we are more apt to compliment a person on his appearance than on other aspects of the "self."

Most Americans also recognize that a "proper" appearance and "proper" dress are the keys to association with the "right crowd," which in turn opens the door to job advancement, increased income, and greater prestige.

At this point it should be clear that our clothing needs are influenced by a multitude of circumstances. Buying motives are seldom simple, and rarely is the final selection made on completely rational terms. Every day we are faced with a number of choices regarding the selection of apparel.

The first step in the decision-making process is to make a conscious ordering of the things that are important to us. If a person recognizes and accepts the priorities of his values—e.g., that his status and prestige may be more important than his physical comfort or his individuality—

his choice of clothing is not only simplified, but more likely to bring him greater satisfaction.

Quality and good workmanship are still important economic considerations. But if we evaluate clothing solely in terms of its economic worth, we may deny ourselves the psychological satisfaction that a seemingly "worthless" garment may provide. No costume or item of clothing will ever meet all our needs, but we might check some of our purchases against the following list of criteria:

Is the outfit compatible with my self-image and style of life?

Does it contribute to my feelings of self-worth and self-esteem?

Will it make me more effective in the performance of my business or social roles?

Will it bring approval from the group I want to belong to?

Does it enhance my physical characteristics and make me more attractive?

Does it provide an outlet for creative expression or a personal identity?

Is it comfortable and functionally designed?

Is the quality and workmanship in keeping with its anticipated fashion life?

Is the cost within the limitations of my income and other financial obligations?

Is it easy to care for?

THE UNIFORM: A SOCIOLOGICAL PERSPECTIVE[1]

Nathan Joseph and Nicholas Alex

The uniform is viewed as a device to resolve certain dilemmas of complex organizations—namely, to define their boundaries, to assure that members will conform to their goals, and to eliminate conflicts in the status sets of their members. The uniform serves several functions: it acts as a totem, reveals and conceals statuses, certifies legitimacy, and suppresses individuality. The interaction of these components and the acceptance or rejection of the uniform and its associated status by the wearer are described.

Why the Uniform?

The survival of a group rests in its ability to exert some degree of control over its members who must carry out the goals of their organization. Both their colleagues and the public must be certain that the activities of the policeman on duty, for example, will be consistent with the needs and functions of the department instead of the result of personal whim or affiliation with a political party, social class, or other group. At the same time, the individual must reconcile the multiple and often conflicting demands imposed by his numerous affiliations and statuses.

The uniform identifies group members, helps insure that organizational goals will be attained, and orders priorities of group and status demands for the individual.

In the first section of this paper, we shall isolate the components of the uniform.[2] In the second section, attention will shift to the dynamics of the uniform as a dramaturgical device which provides the symbolic framework for interaction and thus permits group control.[3] Finally, we shall indicate the degree of acceptance or rejection of the uniform by the individual and the implications for the group.

The Uniform as a Sociological Concept

The Uniform as a Group Emblem

The uniform designates a group. One does not simply wear blue, white, or khaki; instead one's dress indicates membership in a police force, medical group, or military service.[4]

From *American Journal of Sociology,* Vol. 77, No. 4 (January 1972), pp. 719–730. Copyright © 1972 by the University of Chicago Press. Reprinted by permission of the University of Chicago Press and the author.

2. These components will form the basis of a future comparative study of uniforms and other forms of apparel, such as ordinary dress and costume. Uniforms are seen as only one type of clothing in a continuum, each shaping social interaction in a distinctive manner. "Dress" pertains to ordinary apparel not as formal or prescribed as uniforms, on the one hand, or as autonomous of status as costumes. "Costume" is that form of apparel not customary within one's own group; it represents rebellion, rejection, or a lack of concern with the standards of one's group. Although not of equal importance with dress or uniform, costume is of heuristic value, especially in the examination of contemporary youth.

3. In this paper, we shall assume as a constant certain characteristics of Western urban society—i.e., the prevalence of bureaucratic organization, the distribution of apparel and other goods by a market economy, a widespread division of labor, and urban anonymity.

4. A uniform is a modality of dress whose standardization is based either upon legal sanctions (the "formal uniform") or upon convention (the "quasi uniform"). The former designates standard dress which legitimates a group and is consequently protected by law—e.g., military or police dress. (For descriptions of formal uniforms, see Barnes n.d.; Carman 1957; Lewis 1948; Martin 1963; Todd 1941.) The proliferation of formal uniforms in modern society stems from their eminent suitability for bureaucratic organizations (Davis 1952). Quasi uniforms refer to standardized clothing which does not possess such legitimating functions, which often arises informally, and is regulated by convention (e.g., work uniforms). Our discussion is based upon both types of uniforms.

1. We should like to express our appreciation to Murray Hausknecht for his encouragement and assistance throughout the writing of this article. We are particularly indebted to Florence Levinsohn, managing editor of this *Journal,* for giving clarity and order to an earlier draft, and for her many invaluable suggestions for its improvement.

Because of its identification with a group, the uniform assumes the properties of a totemic emblem and embodies the attributes of a group. In a sense, the uniform becomes the group, and it rather than the group is often the focus of thought and affect. Thus, an individual's behavior may reflect favorably or unfavorably upon his uniform rather than upon his group and, in extreme instances, one may "disgrace the uniform." Reciprocally, the uniform may enhance or denigrate the honor of its wearer.

Perhaps the epitome of the identification of uniform and group is that of the *ehrenkleid* of Germany before World War I—the honor garment which transfers to the individual the accrued glory of a uniform and group, usually military (Vagts 1959, p. 444). On the other hand, the police uniform in the black ghetto signifies all the hated manifestations of "white power" and overcomes even the common bond of color (Alex 1969). Black policemen in their own communities complain that they are not considered "human beings" by the local inhabitants. The effect of the uniform depends therefore upon the relative degree of prestige accorded its group. Where the prestige granted a uniform is low, it may represent a source of embarrassment rather than pride.

Within a society, uniforms and groups vary in legitimacy and prestige, conferring different degrees of honor upon members and influencing their willingness to enter and serve the group. In municipal services, the uniforms of police and fire departments, and the organizations themselves, generally have higher levels of prestige than the sanitation department or other groups.

Legitimacy and prestige of uniforms and groups also vary with the components of the population. Minorities usually accord lower esteem to the police departments; southerners in the United States usually grant higher prestige to the military services.

The uniform provides the symbol of a group toward which the public may demonstrate its attitudes. Military uniforms have often been abused to indicate rejection of the military service or of political institutions. Revolutionaries in Germany and Russia after World War I frequently singled out for attack military uniforms, especially those of officers who represented hated class distinctions. The focuses of such attacks on many occasions were officers' epaulets, the embodiment of rank.

In our own time, the use of military uniforms as ordinary dress by youth—the "anti-uniform"—is a mode of mocking the military services and, since the military are viewed as a key institution of our society, ultimately an expression of rebellion or rejection of society itself. That the uniform is not worn by the young solely for utilitarian reasons of warmth, comfort, or inexpensiveness is indicated by the use of inverted stripes, incongruous insignia or emblems sewn on the uniform, and other items which suggest a language of mockery.

In a similar manner, the vocabulary of religion often serves, when suitably distorted, as the vocabulary of profanity. But just as the latter calls attention to religion and its crucial place in the culture, so the contemporary anti-uniform calls attention to and may sustain the existence of the uniform it mocks (Durkheim 1961, pp. 51–63).

Admission to a group may be symbolically indicated by the ceremonious conferring of the uniform or salient parts of it (e.g., the items representing legal authority, such as the policeman's shield, the officer's bars, the nurse's cap or pin) upon the newly initiated. These routinized changes in status afford a basis for change in the individual's self-conception from postulant to initiated, and later, upon promotion, to "old hand." Within the New York City Police Department, promotion from the probationary gray to the standard blue uniform is accompanied by the right to wear a gun, to make arrests, and to perform duties other than those of traffic regulation. The change in status is described by policemen as moving up to "the blues."

Similarly, expulsion from the group has been accompanied at times by the destruction or removal of parts of the uniform during degradation ceremonies (e.g., the sword which is an indicator of honor, the bars which designate rank, or the buttons which denote legitimacy).

The Uniform Reveals and Conceals Status

The uniform makes the wearer's status much more visible than other types of dress; it minimizes the possiblity of confusing members with nonmembers. Its importance as a differentiating device is indicated by the sometimes severe sanctions against imposters. Ironically, the explicit symbolism of the uniform facilitates its counterfeiting. It was much easier for the cobbler from Koepenick to assume the status of captain in the Kaiser's army than for Liza Doolittle to simulate membership in the English upper class. The cobbler's claim to status was legitimated by his appearance in easily identifiable and guaranteed symbols, while for Liza status had to be legitimated by appropriate behavior as well as appearance.[5]

The explicitness of the uniform as a status indicator depends upon its monopolization. While he is in uniform, indicators of all other statuses of a citizen are suppressed. As an extreme example, army regulations discourage officers in uniform from carrying packages—the ultimate indication of domesticity. The wearer of a uniform is

5. In sharp contrast, costumes reveal status least of all and indeed are often used to obfuscate social position. The costume designates a status under creation by its wearer, either in a transient fashion as in a dress ball, masquerade, or a "moral holiday" (e.g., Halloween, Saturnalia) or in a more permanent fashion as in the hippie communes. The basis for the new status may be past statuses (e.g., historical costumes), regional statuses (e.g., Mao or Nehru jackets), or a social class (e.g., adoption of proletarian dress by new radical groups). All of these costumes represent attempts to create a new status and identity for the wearer.

therefore not normally permitted the means used by ordinary citizens to express attitudes: dramatization of political allegiances through buttons and the like, religious adherence through insignia, and symbols of individual esthetic or ludenic preferences are prohibited to the wearer of a uniform.

The basis for recruitment into uniformed civilian and military services has broadened to include racial minorities and women in recent years. These groups offer unmistakable evidence of statuses which cannot be disguised by uniforms. Organizations may deal with the incongruity of symbols in several ways—by denial, as exemplified by the masculinity of women's uniforms in World War I; or by co-optation, as seen in the assignment of black uniformed policemen to black communities.

The Uniform Is a Certificate of Legitimacy

The very existence of a uniform implies a group structure—at least a two-step hierarchy, the wearer and a superior individual(s)—which has granted the right to wear its uniform, which supervises conformity to group regulations and standard definitions of behavior, and to which one can resort with complaints. The uniform acts as a guarantee that an upper level in the group will control the members and, in turn, that members will conform. By permitting the use of its uniform, a group certifies an individual as its representative and assumes responsibility for his activities. The uniform is a symbolic statement that an individual will adhere to group norms and standardized roles and has mastered the essential group skills and values. Gross derelictions of duty will result, at an extreme, in discharge from the group and deprivation of the uniform.

For the uniform to function as a certificate of legitimacy for its representatives, the public must learn to recognize it as an indicator of a special status. The current proliferation of uniforms may, however, result in public confusion.

In a social version of Gresham's Law, New York City policemen complain about the lessening of the significance of their uniform as a certificate of legitimacy due to its adoption by other municipal services such as Transit Authority and Department of Sanitation patrolmen, and by private agencies. Evidently, the public's recognition of the uniform and its associated status tends to find the lowest common denominator. Thus, many policemen complain of fixed posts because they are very often confused with private guards while occupying them.[6]

6. The adoption of the police uniform by other municipal agencies is tantamount to counterfeiting certificates of legitimacy since the uniform is restricted by law to the New York City Police Department. The illegal spread of this uniform may indicate the great drive to establish legitimacy by borrowing established symbols.

The Uniform Suppresses Individuality

The uniform suppresses individual idiosyncrasies in behavior and appearance. Since the conformity imposed by a uniform stems from its symbolization, deviations are much more visible when the individual is in uniform. A detective asleep in a car arouses far less notice than a uniformed patrolman engaged in the same practice of "cooping." In the latter instance, relevant standards are known to others, making deviations much more apparent and more readily censured. A sleeping policeman is incompatible with our expectations of vigilance and alertness. On the other hand, what are the appropriate standards for an apparent civilian, the sleeping detective?

Standardization of apparel is another source of group-imposed conformity. Were uniforms to deviate from standards, their utility to demarcate members and as certificates of legitimacy would be diminished. The range of permissible variation in uniforms differs with the existence of functional equivalents of certificates of legitimacy. We more readily accept a police officer in shirtsleeves if he occupies a desk in a precinct house; his presence in headquarters implies awareness and acceptance by other police officers. Furthermore, deviation in the uniform entails tampering with the legitimacy of symbols. One is impugning the sacredness of group totems and ultimately of the group itself. One is also implying that the group is not controlling its own process of certification.

Variation from uniform standards stems in part from the ludenic element in man which finds expression through many media, not the least of which is personal adornment or self-enhancing modes of dress (Huizinga 1950, pp. 183, 192–94; Sapir 1931, pp. 140–41; Simmel 1957, pp. 541–58). It is a basic element guiding the selection of ordinary dress and especially costume. (Note the scorn attached to the uniform-like quality of ordinary dress in periods when the ludenic value was deemed suppressed—for example, the gray flannel suit of Madison Avenue about two decades ago.)[7] However, the successful maintenance of the uniform as a device for group regulation requires the suppression of these individual variations. Although resistance to conformity is a universal feature of existence in groups, the problem looms larger for uniformed groups because uniform regulations can be much more precise than other types of norms. The distance between chevrons and shoulders can be defined and enforced more precisely than the procedures of academic grading or teaching. The slightest deviation from prescribed wear may be defined as being "out of uniform."

7. A striking example of the ludenic element is the current attempt to play with sex statuses by the adoption of "unisex" dress—clothing that is interchangeable between the sexes and thus implies a homogenization of sex statuses. With the widespread use of such dress, it has probably lost its ludenic quality for the individual and become the new norm for groups. In sum, there seems to be a dialectical interplay between group norms and the ludenic element.

The Uniform and Its Function in the Control of Social Interaction

Our task in this section is twofold, to demonstrate how the components of the uniform shape interaction and how interaction in turn enables the uniform to solve the problems outlined in the introduction—the definition of group boundaries, the achievement of organizational goals, and the ordering of an individual's status set.

Although it undoubtedly structures interaction in all stages, the impact of the uniform can be most readily seen in social placement. On first encounter, a stranger is categorized on the basis of external characteristics, such as dress, accent, and posture (Stone 1962). Only after the initial question, With whom am I dealing? is answered, does the discursive process of interaction described by Mead (1934) occur.

The first aspect of social placement is that of recognition: Whom does the other purport to be? For the uniformed stranger, the question is answered clearly and almost instantaneously. Socially, he is a one-dimensional man who announces only the status he wears on his sleeve. The ambiguity ordinarily attached to the stranger in modern urban society is absent for the uniform-wearer, whose group membership, and perhaps his rank, seniority, and prior achievements, are proclaimed by his apparel.

A second process in social placement is the assessment of the status claimed by the stranger. We know who he purports to be, but can his assertion be verified? Again, the uniform provides a ready answer. It validates the claim, this time as group emblem and certificate of legitimacy.

One of the authors noted that, during a door-to-door search by the police for a missing child, a plainclothes officer was accompanied by a uniformed policeman who served to reassure the resident of the identity of the detective. The reluctance to admit a stranger to one's apartment in the early morning hours was obviated by the sight of a uniform; the uniformed patrolman was wearing credentials for both.

In contrast, when an individual asserts membership in an upper social class by expensive attire, no comparable procedure of validation exists. In an anonymous urban society, his self-definition has to be accepted at face value in lieu of detailed knowledge of his background. We are much less likely to doubt the legitimacy of a man in a police uniform, regardless of our attitudes toward the police. Correlatively, the exposure of an imposter in uniform is usually much more devastating, to the wearer and to the other, than the exposure of one in mink and pearls.

As a result of the two processes of placement, which may occur simultaneously, the problem of group boundaries is met. We know the identity of the stranger at the door; we can recognize our peers in a uniformed group, thus settling one of our problems. But, how do we know

that the uniform-wearer will conform to group norms? How does he solve his own dilemma of multiple status membership? The answer to the latter two problems requires the examination of the dynamics of interaction in more detail.

Interaction with a uniform-wearer has certain consequences for the viewer who must become an other for a specific status, and second, must view the uniform-wearer as either peer or outsider.

Everyone who recognizes the uniform to any extent becomes an other who has some expectation of how the uniform-wearer will fulfill his position, and manifests these expectations in interaction.[8] Everyone becomes an other and reacts primarily in terms of the wearer's key status, the principal clue he offers to his social identity.

Only one set of norms is applicable in evaluating the uniform-wearer. With strangers in ordinary dress, several sets may be applicable, none of which may be as explicit as the single set pertaining to the policeman, for example. This is to say that the wearer does not have the protection of the status anonymity of the modern urban stranger. He becomes closely identified with his uniformed status and only with this status. Often he must remove his uniform to escape his obligations as a member of the group. Policemen will frequently wear civilian dress to and from work to avoid being on call by the public at all times. Similarly, a uniformed individual may remove his uniform while engaging in pursuits which might disgrace his group, such as frequenting bars off duty.

The uniform influences the wearer himself, for everyone is an other who proffers the same mirror. Since no other statuses, or any touch of individuality, are recognized in the uniformed individual by others, he is encouraged to act primarily as an occupant of his uniformed status. The definition of his status and of his duties may vary between colleagues and public, but both groups will agree on his key social position. For his peers, on the other hand, the uniform underscores a common membership, allegiance to the same set of rules, and the probability of similar life experiences. If he is an outsider, the uniform stresses the differences in status, norms, and way of life. It serves, then, to bind the wearer to his peers and to separate him from outsiders. (For a similar and earlier distinction, see Simmel 1957, esp. pp. 544–47, on the function of clothing in uniting and separating groups.)

Two sources of ego-gratification for the uniformed wearer are therefore available by virtue of his dress: from his own group, he will obtain self-esteem through con-

---

8. Obviously, although others may recognize a uniform, they may not be completely accurate in their knowledge of the duties or behavior of the concomitant status. At an extreme, even though they may not be aware of the type of occupation performed by the individual in a work uniform, they are aware of his membership in a service occupation and have formed some conception of his status and duties.

formity; from other groups, he may obtain self-prestige by conflict. (See Gouldner 1970, pp. 221–22, for the distinction between consensual and conflictual identity validation.) Although these processes of identity validation are available to all groups, the relevant groups are much less subject to doubt for the man in uniform.

While the uniform-wearer is encouraged to order the priorities of his statuses and the demands made upon him in accordance with the group perspective, he may very often flee to the safety of his uniform to avoid the anomie of ordinary life. (See Lyman and Scott 1970, pp. 210–11, on the panic suffered by those separated from their uniform.) For these individuals, the multiplicity of the demands imposed by modern society is simplified by collapsing the status set to a single dimension, and to the extent that the uniform wearer has internalized the norms of his group, organizational efficiency is assured. Even where it has not been fully accomplished, the uniformed individual is subject to external constraint by peers and outsiders aware of the norms to which he is expected to adhere.

Acceptance and Rejection of the Uniform

A status is often only partially accepted by all its participants. Deviations in uniformed statuses are more apparent because of the standardization of norms and are more readily interpreted as a rejection of group control because of the close identification of the uniform and the group. This section will look at the conditions of rejection within the group.

Several distinctions are useful. First, what is the target of rejection? Is it opposition to the uniform itself, to the uniformed position as the key status, or to the group represented by the uniform? Another distinction—the source of rejection—needs to be specified because the relationship between other groups and the uniformed group is very often the cause of rejection. Finally, how the group reacts to the rejection of its uniform will provide insight into group control.[9]

Members may accept a group's status but reject the premise that control is best exercised through uniforms. One of the objections may be that uniforms create obstacles to performance. An outstanding example is the attempt by contemporary Roman Catholic priests and nuns and European worker-priests to alter or even abandon the clerical uniform. The separation of members, one of the results of the uniform, is felt to be a handicap to fulfillment of clerical obligations as redefined by some members. They advocate blurring the distinction between clergy and laity as a means of reaching the unchurched masses. They also prefer to use other means to control

their members. Thus, as redefinition of clerical status arises, bringing an altered relationship to superiors and the public, it tends to be manifested partly in the language of uniforms.

Another objection to uniforms may be their denial of individuality. Policemen may want to escape from the "bag" or the uniform to attain the greater autonomy of nonuniformed status. Similarly, in World War II, many irregular units were manned by those who liked military life but not the restrictions of rigid uniform regulations. Smaller elites within larger uniformed groups attempted to distinguish themselves from the run-of-the-mill member by introducing unofficial modifications of the uniform (e.g., the "twenty-mission" crushed hat of American pilots). "Pink" trousers of overseas officers in World War I served the same purpose. The relevant reference group in such cases is not the entire organization nor the governing body, but rather a segment deemed superior because of experience, expertise, or other characteristics.

Another form of rejection may be an expression of discontent, not with the uniformed status itself, but with it as the key status. For instance, soldiers in occupying armies often discard their uniforms in off-duty hours, often against regulations, to gain better relationships with the civilian population. Thus, while control of the uniformed status by the institution may be completely acceptable, there is often a countereffort to resist total control.

Finally, the rejection of the uniform may represent opposition to the group itself. The altered uniform is worn, in this instance, to express dislike of the group and constitutes an interesting effort to oppose the group short of leaving or destroying it. The most recent and striking example is found in the report from Vietnam of the drastic modification of the uniform by love beads, peace slogans, etc. (Emerson 1970). Like the worker-priests, the protesting soldier still retains some ties to the organization. Unlike the worker-priests, the protesting soldier doubts the basic purpose or legitimacy of the group.

To summarize, the rejection of the uniform may be explained by the same components and processes used to examine interaction in the preceding section where acceptance was assumed. Worker-priests object to their strong identification with a group and the clear visibility of their status. The detective and irregular soldier object to the repression of individuality by the uniform. The soldier in the occupying army objects to the top priority of his uniformed status. Finally, the rebellious soldier objects to the uniform as a symbol of the basic institution which he rejects.

What is the source of rejection of the uniform? In the preceding discussion, rejection stemmed from a perception of the uniformed status which differed from the standardized one within the uniformed group. Redefinition of the status may also stem from alternative reference groups which suggest other models for the uniformed position.

---

9. We shall not consider all sources of change in the uniform and its status—only those stemming from its rejection by members. Therefore, we shall not include changes instituted by the heads of uniformed groups.

One frequent source of resistance to uniforms is social class. An aristocracy may insist upon the primacy of its class membership even while in the armed services, and may manifest its resistance to institutional control by departure from uniform regulations. As an example of the unpopularity· of the uniform among some aristocratic groups, the Duke of Cambridge, commander-in-chief during the latter part of the nineteenth century, punished a subaltern by ordering him to wear his uniform in London for a prescribed period (Turner 1956, p. 239).

Professionals may be subject to conflicting demands by their professional groups and the uniformed organizations to which they also belong. To resist complete control by the uniformed services, chaplains of the British and Commonwealth military forces retained some of the symbols of their profession even while on active duty. "Unlike the practice in the American armed forces, RAF chaplains wear the clerical collar as part of their uniform. . . . The basic regulation identifies the chaplain as a military officer while the collar is a constant reminder that he is, after all, a clergyman" (Zahn 1969, p. 100). Similar efforts to assert the superiority of professional status may be displayed by independent medical practitioners who resist wearing medical uniforms in hospitals.

Prior racial and ethnic affiliations may present another source of status reinterpretation. In the United States army, a recent attempt to incorporate racial symbols into uniforms was successfully made by black soldiers who received permission to wear "Afro" hairstyles while on duty.

A "public" in the social psychological sense, or a "climate of the times," may also provide alternative definitions of uniformed status. At the present time, there is a pervasive wave of dissatisfaction with contemporary institutions which cannot be attributed to any single group.

What are the reactions of the group to rejection of their uniform? The group has two options: to suppress deviations, or to accept and incorporate them into the uniform and status. In the latter instance, the validity of alternative definitions of the status is acknowledged and the influence of other organizations upon the uniformed group is accepted. The British Army in India and elsewhere recognized the importance of religious and ethnic groups by using distinctive symbols for native units, adopting some indigenous weapons, accepting some caste restrictions, and in many other ways incorporating local culture into its procedures.

The outcome, suppression or co-optation, is determined by at least two factors. First, the relative power of the uniformed and of the alternative reference groups, inside or outside the organization, is important. The views of powerful reference groups cannot be ignored. Power may stem from the social position of these groups—for example, the high prestige of a profession or an elite officer's corps—or from their size and importance for recruitment—for example, the blacks in the United States vis-à-vis the armed forces.

Second, the uniformed groups may recognize the function of rejection as a safety valve, since it is a less drastic alternative to desertion or mutiny. The rejection may be accepted by tactful official silence or by explicit incorporation into a redefinition of the uniform or status. In the examples described above, the uniformed group fails to be totally encompassing because it is unable to ignore other reference groups.

Whereas the relationship of member and group had been previously described as one of control by the latter, we have now seen that members can introduce changes and influence officials of the group. The uniform at any one time may therefore embody the compromise resulting from a multiplicity of forces—some stemming from the directors of a group, some from below, and some from outside the group.

In this paper, we have attempted to describe the components of the uniform that may be used to solve the problems of organizational control, differentiation between members and nonmembers, and articulation of individual status sets. These components shape interaction by providing immediate recognition and validation of the uniformed status, by making uniformed positions key statuses, and by compelling all viewers to become others who identify themselves as peers or outsiders. The result is to remind the uniform wearer of his position and to structure the sources of his ego gratification. Finally, the causes of rejection of the uniform and its status were examined.

REFERENCES

Alex, Nicholas. 1969. *Black in Blue: A Study of the Negro Policeman.* New York: Appleton-Century-Crofts.

Barnes, R.M. n.d. *A History of Regiments and Uniforms of the British Army.* London: Seeley Service.

Carman, W.Y. 1957. *British Military Uniforms from Contemporary Pictures: Henry VII to the Present Day.* London: Leonard Hill.

Davis, Arthur K. 1952. "Bureaucratic Patterns in the Navy Officer Corps." In *Reader in Bureaucracy,* edited by Robert K. Merton et al. Glencoe, Ill.: Free Press.

Durkheim, Emile. 1961. *The Elementary Forms of the Religious Life.* New York: Collier.

Emerson, Gloria. "G.I.'s Now Wear a Lot the Army Didn't Issue." *New York Times,* August 28, 1970, p. 37.

Gouldner, Alvin W. 1970. *The Coming Crisis of Western Sociology.* New York: Basic.

Huizinga, J. 1950. *Homo Ludens: A Study of the Play-Element in Culture.* New York: Roy.

Lewis, Michael. 1948. *England's Sea-Officers.* London: Allen & Unwin.

Lyman, Stanford M., and Marvin B. Scott. 1970. *A Sociology of the Absurd.* New York: Appleton-Century-Crofts.

Martin, Paul. 1963. *European Military Uniforms: A Short History.* London: Spring.

Mead, George H. 1934. *Mind, Self, and Society*. Chicago: University of Chicago Press.

Sapir, Edward. 1931. "Fashion." In *Encyclopedia of the Social Sciences*. Vol. 6. New York: Macmillan.

Simmel, Georg. 1957. "Fashion." *American Journal of Sociology* 62 (May): 541–58.

Stone, Gregory P. 1962. "Appearance and the Self." In *Human Behavior and Social Processes*, edited by Arnold M. Rose. Boston: Houghton Mifflin.

Todd, Frederick. 1941. *Soldiers of the American Army: 1775–1941*. New York: Bittner.

Turner, E.S. 1956. *Gallant Gentlemen: A Portrait of the British Officer*. London: Joseph.

Vagts, Alfred. 1959. *A History of Militarism*. New York: Meridian.

Zahn, Gordon. 1969. *The Military Chaplaincy: A Study of Role Tensions in the Royal Air Force*. Buffalo, N.Y.: University of Toronto Press.

IN THE GRAY FLANNEL MOLD

Marianne S. Beeson

In October, 1978, the Associated Press carried a story about a young man who had represented himself as the holder of three degrees in psychology, including the doctorate. Using phony credentials, he had obtained a summer teaching position at Old Dominion University in Norfolk, Virginia. After the close of the summer session, in checking out his application for full-time employment, embarrassed University administrators discovered that the impostor had earned no more than a bachelor's degree in psychology (4).

The psychology department chairman was quoted in the newspaper account.

> I still can't believe it . . . He looked the role of a young clinical psychologist—suit, tie, the whole thing (4).

While "looking the part" is not endorsed as a means to dishonest ends, the relationship between dress and success in the job situation has been the theme of a number of recent books and articles. The "how to" emphasis in selection of clothing cues to manipulate the reactions of others is reflected in these words from two of the current writings:

> In business you are not dressing to express personal taste; you are dressing in a costume which should be designed to have an impact on your bosses and teammates. If your clothes don't convey the message that you are competent, able, ambitious, self-confident, reliable, and authoritative, nothing you say or do will overcome the negative signals emanating from your apparel (7, p. 277).

Or, dress not to please yourself, but ". . . dress to impress (5, p. 66)."

The titles of some of these books and articles are revealing—"Power Dressing: a Report on Combat Gear for the Trip to the Top (6)," "How Clothes Shape Your Future (17)," "Which Look Cinched the Job? Dressing for a Management-Level Job (18)," "The Sweet Look of Success," a chapter in Michael Korda's book *Success!* (12), "The Uniform—What to Wear as an Active Game

Player," in Betty L. Harragan's book *Games Mother Never Taught You: Corporate Gamesmanship for Women* (7), and two books by John T. Molloy, *Dress for Success* (13) and *The Woman's Dress for Success Book* (14).

The reader appeal of such hard-driving titles was apparently the rationale behind the naming of Prince Egon von Furstenberg's guide to dress for men. *The Power Look* was chosen ". . . more for its sales potential than its contents (11)."

In a period of tight jobs and an oversupply of trained people in some occupational areas, guarantees implied by a formula approach, which is espoused in most of these books and articles, seem particularly attractive to a person entering the job market or to someone feeling trapped in a job dead end. In other words, A (you) plus B (the success looks in dress and accessories) equals C (securing the job or the promotion), and ultimately, or preferably instantly, come success, power, leadership, fame and fortune. It's a lot easier to change one's clothes and acquire a few symbols of status and authority than it is to earn another degree, to serve another apprenticeship, or otherwise to improve one's real qualifications or level of expertise.

There is another factor, common to the background of most of today's young people who are seeking to make their way in business careers—that is the absence of dress regulations in the education experience. Dress codes in colleges and universities are almost entirely past history. A student today would be outraged, or at least baffled, if the student handbook contained a rule requiring him or her to "dress for dinner" in the dining hall, or to wear coats and ties, for the men, or skirts, for the women, to such a casual occasion as a class! Such rules were very common on campuses 20 years ago.

This generation of graduates is leaving the most permissive college environment ever, where blue-jean-sloppy is expected and revered, and trying to enter a business world where there are indeed rules. And shockingly enough there are rules for what was formerly a personal and private matter, namely *dress*. Then, adding insult to injury, *disregard of or failure to comply with these dress rules brings about undesirable consequences.*

> Those who do not dress according to the unwritten laws of the business world are limiting their future, offers Luciane Franzoni, fashion designer for Hart Schaffner & Marx. . . . "I personally feel this is wrong, but it's there," he says. "In our industry, we're always talking about nonverbal communication. People are judged by what they're wearing (17, p. 52)."

Molloy says that in a survey he made of the dress code in business, "Ninety-seven out of 100 top executives of major corporations stated they have a written or unwritten but *understood* dress code [italics added] (10)." To understand fully a dress code, even if it is written, is the nature of the problem. Stated in a written dress code that male executives will wear suits and ties is superficially understood by anyone with a third grade level of reading comprehension. But, understanding the nuances of messages conveyed by the choices of color, fabric, style, and fit of a particular suit and tie is what is being offered in this current series of books and articles on how to dress. The promise to decipher the code is selling not only the printed word, but consulting services[1] and banquet speakers as well.

From the raft of prescriptions and proscriptions on dress put forth in these books and articles, a few principles emerge. For the job interview, "Dress for the job you're hoping to get (1, p. 107)." For recognition, promotion, advancement, ". . . dress for the job you want, not the job you have (14, p. 125)," or, stated another way, adopt the dress standards of ". . . the more senior and successful people in your own organization (12, p. 153)."

Even outside of the business milieu, in the halls of academia, similar advice is offered. Jane Chance Nitzsche writes about "what every young professor needs to know to make it up the academic ladder (15, p. 40)."

> . . . there is another element to achieving success: Your colleagues must like you to want to keep you. While you may feel powerless to sway their opinion, it is possible to try. It will help if you are pleasant, hard-working, well groomed, and dress as other faculty dress. (If they wear jeans, wear jeans; if suits, suits. Choose an image based on the success and effectiveness of the professorial type.) Again, observe your seniors closely to discern those personal qualities admired in a professor (15, p. 41).

For a *woman* aspiring to climb the executive ladder, observations of her successful superiors are complicated by the likelihood that her potential models are all, or mostly, men. Male business attire as such is not the appropriate look for women; Molloy says the "imitation man look" gives the same impression on women as it does when worn by small boys, ". . . cute, not authoritative (8, p. 38)." He places on his "never wear" list the man's fedora, shirt and tie, and the pin-striped or chalk-striped, man-tailored pants suit (14, p. 29).

However, there seems to be consensus that the male executive's compulsive attention to status-laden details of dress is just what should be emulated by females wanting to make their way up in the ranks.

> Seemingly innocuous details in a suit, such as a fractional narrowing of lapel width, a minute indentation in seam or dart tapering, an inch difference in vent height, a smidgen less shoulder padding, the stitching on buttonholes, a finger-breadth variation in jacket or trouser length are enormously significant. Tremendous import is conveyed by color and fabric, each of which trumpet signals through almost imperceptible gradations of hue or shadowy suggestions of stripe or plaid designs. Proper fit is crucial, and men's suit manufacturers are graded for "quality" according to the amount of hand-tailoring they put into the finished garment which insures that the shaping will hold up. In effect, quality workmanship consists of sewing as many sacred hieroglyphs as possible into the business uniform. The suit is the master power symbol, but the rank message can be distorted if the caste marks are not painstakingly reinforced by matching emblems in shirts, ties, shoes, and socks. All five elements must be expertly coordinated to achieve the total symbolic effect. The wrong shirt or tie can make a disastrous mess of a perfect suit.[2]

Michael Korda describes the selection of the appropriate man's business suit.

> . . . make sure it is simple, single-breasted and either dark-blue (the darker, the better) or dark-gray. The cloth should not have any fancy textured pattern. It is also important to avoid contrasting stitching or piping, pockets with buttons on them and lapels so wide that they come out to your shoulders . . .
>
> When you have found it, be ruthless about alterations. It is not all that important how much the suit costs, *but it must fit*. Nothing makes a man look more like a failure than a poorly fitted suit . . .
>
> The left lapel of your suit should have a buttonhole. It is correct, it is traditional and it belongs there. There should be at least three buttons on the sleeve cuffs of a suit, and if possible four. If the suit only has two, ask for a third one to be sewn on, or get it done yourself. Ideally, the sleeve buttons should be real—i.e., you should be able to button and unbutton them—but to get this small, correct touch, you have to go to a tailor.[3]

---

1. For example, Emily Cho is an "image consultant" in the business of advising women in their selection of clothing and accessories (Source: NBC-TV *Today Show*, November 7, 1978). She is also co-author with Linda Grover of *Looking Terrific: Express Yourself Through the Language of Clothing.* N.Y.: G.P. Putnam's Sons, 1978.

2. From *Games Mother Never Taught You: Corporate Gamesmanship for Women* by Betty Lehan Harragan. Copyright © 1977 by Betty Lehan Harragan. Reprinted by permission of Rawson Associates Publishers, Inc., p. 271.

3. Excerpted from *Success!* by Michael Korda. New York: Ballantine Books, Division of Random House, Inc., 1977. Reprinted by permission of Random House, Inc., pp. 156–157.

With some of these same male suit "caste marks," the female business suit "uniform" is proposed by Molloy, Harragan, and others as essential to success. Some have described the appropriate look as deliberately dowdy, functioning as a camouflage (6, p. 214). A litigation lawyer's view is quoted.

> Looking terrific is a minus for a woman because then it's assumed you spend a lot of time thinking about what you should wear, which in turn discredits your seriousness and your case (6, p. 214).

Molloy, in his ". . . tackily written how-to manual for professional women (19, p. 97)," is firm in his proposal for the woman's business uniform consisting of a skirted suit, usually dark, and a contrasting blouse. Harragan speaks with equal favor for skirts or pants for the business uniform—skirts which are "pleated or flared enough to allow a free stride (7, p. 279)," and long enough not to ride above the wearer's knees when she sits (7, pp. 279–280). If pants are chosen for the suit, they should fit perfectly, that is with a fitted waistband (not elastic), creases which fall straight to the floor, and at the same length, in relation to shoes, that successful men wear their trousers (7, p. 280). The "high water" look of too short pants and the baggy effect produced by pants which are too long should be scrupulously avoided by both men and women according to several writers on the subject.

Harragan and Molloy have different opinions as to what colors each considers appropriate for this uniform. Harragan regards navy, black, dull grays, and subdued solids in general as lacking strength for women, ". . . to much . . . 'blending with the wallpaper (7, 282).' " She sees women in strong colors, such as red, carrying an air of "confidence and assurance (7, p. 282)." Molloy, on the other hand, says "Deep red is a sexual turn-on color. Women should not wear red to work (5, p. 64)."

Sexuality as a factor in choosing business clothes will harm a woman's career according to Molloy (14, p. 21). He explains, ". . . dressing to succeed in business and dressing to be sexually attractive are almost mutually exclusive (14, p. 21)."

Molloy preaches to women, "bedroom or boardroom—your choice (14, p. 21)." "Flaunted femininity," says a designer of tailored business suits for women, can make the boss think ". . . he's dealing with a lover or a secretary (2, p. 77)."

Accessories with sexual associations should also be avoided by women in business. For example, Korda advocates a "good, solid brief case (12, p. 169)" rather than a handbag. He elaborates,

> I have the distinct impression that in a working situation men are made nervous by a woman's handbag when it is placed on their desk or in the immediate vicinity. Perhaps it's because the handbag is, in men's mind, a symbol of femininity, and

contains God knows what intimate feminine possessions (12, p. 169).

Korda says that the successful woman may carry a handbag *or* a brief case, but *not both* (12, p. 168).

Harragan suggests that the handbag is needed basically because women's clothes lack pockets. That is, women use their handbags to transport between home and work the numerous items which men can carry in pockets—keys, money, checkbooks, glasses, credit cards, etc., but she says

> . . . there are powerful reasons not to drag such an encumbrance all over a business office, especially to meetings. A purse or handbag is so uniquely a female article that it arouses a host of subconscious connotations among men (7, p. 284).

Molloy says it is ". . . better for a businesswoman not to carry a handbag (14, p. 94)." He considers the plain, good quality *leather* attaché case indispensable and a symbol of authority (14, p. 93).

The position of John T. Molloy himself as a "symbol of authority" on business dress for men and women appears to be widely accepted in the popular media. His exposure on television talk shows has been considerable, and he writes a syndicated newspaper column entitled "Dress for Success (9)." Mr. Molloy is head of his own company, Dress for Success, Inc., in New York City. His background includes school teaching, insurance underwriting (2, p. 77), and haberdashery (5, p. 63).

Mr. Molloy calls himself a "wardrobe engineer," specifically, "America's first wardrobe engineer (14, p. 187)." He has served as "a clothing consultant for General Motors, American Telephone and Telegraph, United States Steel, and Merrill Lynch, Pierce, Fenner & Smith (9)." His dictates on dress are based, he says, on 17 years of "behavioral testing and interviewing of thousands of business and professional people (5, p. 63)."

The type of research conducted by Molloy and his staff includes such techniques as to show subjects "two pictures of the same woman with one variable—the suit, or the blouse, or whatever—and ask them such questions as 'Which woman has the better job?' (14, p. 50)."

From these kinds of data, Molloy evidently feels confident to state absolutes like,

> Wear a bow tie, and no one will take you seriously.
>
> Women in peasant dresses are usually treated like peasants (5, p. 64).
>
> Never
> •be the first in your office to wear a fashion . . .
> •wear anything sexy to the office . . .
> •wear the knit polyester pantsuit . . .
> •wear pants when you're dealing with men in business . . .
> •take off your jacket in the office . . .
> •make an emotional decision about a piece of clothing when an intellectual decision is possible (14, pp. 185–186).

A feature of *The Woman's Dress for Success Book* is a coupon in the back which can be mailed to Molloy's firm along with $23.00 for a Personal Dress for Success Profile for man or woman. The coupon clipper provides information such as height, weight, age, etc., business/profession, education and career target, and so forth (14, p. 187). Facts and ambitions are presumably reconciled with data previously collected and stored in a computerized information bank, producing for the client a formula for the appropriate authority symbols and success looks in dress.

Molloy's writing on women's dress has attracted more attention than his earlier (1975) *Dress for Success* on the subject of men's clothing. A contribution of the men's dress book is to inform the reader of the status value of beige raincoats. "Black raincoats give the impression the wearer cannot afford to keep a beige coat clean (5, p. 65)."

A special interest in women and their business dress at this time is probably attributable to the three following factors:

(1) "Women are in the ascendancy (3, p. 18)," and any element claimed to have a causal connection to success or failure of women in business and the professions is of real interest to women seeking success, business and professions desiring to hire and promote successful women, and the government enforcers of the anti-sex discrimination clause of the Civil Rights Act.

(2) If large numbers of women in white collar[4] jobs were to adopt a "uniform," that is, a classic, slow to change style, for their working hours, it would represent a serious threat to the fashion industry. The sale of fashion depends upon continually shifting desires for something new and different.

(3) The "uniform" business suit has been the norm for men since industrialization in the 19th century.[5] For women it is a radical departure from the norm.

A fashion magazine reacts predictably to the business uniform for women.

> . . . is it boring? We think so. Is it bland? Do you have to ask us? Of course it's bland. Is it irritating and frustrating that women executives are following suit just like their male counterparts? We find it so (6, p. 188).

Molloy predicts that the fashion industry's probable war against the uniform might be waged on one of two fronts.

4. Consider that there are several occupations traditionally dominated by women in which a uniform *per se* is a custom: waitress, beautician, and nurse, for example. Another work category of interest is the growing number of women in blue collar jobs; the availability of appropriately sized work clothing, some of which may be uniforms, could be a problem for women plumbers, electricians, and the like.
5. See "What Will Happen to the Gray Flannel Suit?" pp. 62–66.

First, they can use the industry's favorite ploy—the disappearing act. . . . If the fashion industry tries to take the skirted suit off the market, women should let out a loud, collective howl . . . and close their pocketbooks (14, pp. 36–37).

The other method the fashion industry might use . . . is to start creating nothing but suits for women to wear on social occasions. . . . Their objective would be to undermine the effect of the skirted suit as the business uniform (14, p. 37).

Molloy makes concessions to fashion for two groups of businesswomen. For women in sales,

> A saleswoman must dress to match her product. This means she must look as if she is able to use it well. For a woman selling almost any business-oriented product, this would mean the standard skirted suit. *But for a woman selling fashion, it would mean the latest look* [italics added] (8, p. 37).

In cases where women need to get across to *other women* that they are important, they might consider that

> Most women feel that certain elements of fashion are an essential ingredient for being well dressed. Therefore, if you are dealing only with women, your outfit should include something that would be considered high fashion. For example, in the early 1970s, when the fashion industry was pushing hardest on the midi, a midi-length skirted suit would have been the ideal uniform for a woman in charge of women (8, p. 37).

The possible conflicts brought about by business dealings in the same day with a group of men, who reject fashion orientation, and then a group of women, who expect it, can be resolved, according to Molloy, by wearing the current year's fashion color in a nonfashion style.

> A blouse in the right color can be authoritative and chic. But if the "in" color turns out to be purple, green, or gold, don't wear it. Any positive fashion impact would be offset by people's negative reactions to those colors (8, p. 37).

With all this advice being heaped upon women at the present time, what will be the actual clothing choices of business and professional women? Will there be a mass adoption of the business suit, tailored of medium gray or blue wool or linen, with a nonfrilly blouse of silk or cotton (or silk or cotton-looking), dark colored, plain pumps, the woman's fedora, and a leather attaché case? Will women welcome the security of a uniform, or will they become bored with it? Will such attire continue to carry a message of authority if every businesswoman is wearing it?

What about the reaction of men to a regiment of similarly dressed executive or executive-aspiring women? Will men abandon their own "gray flannel suits" if women purloin the sacred symbols for themselves? Will men relinquish their uniform to women and then develop other ways to play the status game?

In 1946, a presumably well-intentioned guide for future secretaries, *The Successful Secretary,* stressed the importance of careful grooming and the "right" clothes in a section which begins,

The business world is a *man's* world, and every man would like his secretary to be *decorative* as well as useful [italics added] (6, p. 31).

Having thankfully moved out of this lockstep into a business and professional world which is both a man's *and* a woman's world, where a secretary can be either female *or* male whose decorative functions are of little or no importance, are we headed now into another trap?

An underlying theme of the books and articles reviewed here is the advocacy of a seemingly superficial obsession with clothes and symbols and conformity, which are purported to be the means to achieving success goals. A New York executive and *Newsweek* provide a caution:

"When the bosses find a woman can raise the company's profit line, they really don't care what she wears. . . ." There's no doubt that inappropriate clothes are an unneeded handicap to a woman in business, but the notion that "success" clothes can substitute for talent or energy on the job is just another fashion fantasy. Taken too seriously, all the "dress for success" maxims may lead a woman not to the boardroom, but only to the dressing room (2, p. 77).

REFERENCES CITED

1. Bergen, Polly. *I'd Love To, But What'll I Wear?* N.Y.: Wyden Books, 1977.
2. Cowley, Susan Cheever. "Dress for the Trip to the Top," *Newsweek,* September 26, 1977, pp. 76–77.
3. Dowling, Colette. "The Clothing Game," *Family Circle,* June, 1972, pp. 18–21.
4. " 'Dr. Rock' Decides to Roll: Fake Credentials Exposed," *Roanoke Times & World News,* October 27, 1978, p. B–1.
5. "Dress to Succeed," *Nation's Business,* August, 1977, pp. 63–66.
6. Gross, Amy and Comer, Nancy Alexrad. "Power Dressing: A Report on Combat Gear for the Trip to the Top," *Mademoiselle,* September, 1977, pp. 188–189 +.
7. Harragan, Betty Lehan. *Games Mother Never Taught You: Corporate Gamesmanship for Women.* N.Y.: Rawson Associates Publishers, Inc., 1977.
8. "John Molloy Takes the Dare: He Tells Women How to Dress for Sales," *Sales and Marketing Management,* November 14, 1977, pp. 36–38.
9. Klemesrud, J. (ed.). "Behind the Best Sellers: Dress for Businesswomen," *New York Times Book Review,* March 12, 1978, 83:44.
10. Koehn, Hank E. "Return of the Dress Code," *Journal of Systems Management,* August, 1977, p. 18.
11. Koelln, Georgann. "The Prince No Pauper As Fashion Designer," *Roanoke Times & World News,* October 24, 1978, p. C–3.
12. Korda, Michael. *Success!* N.Y.: Ballantine Books, Division of Random House, Inc., 1977.
13. Molloy, John T. *Dress for Success.* N.Y.: Warner Books, 1975.
14. ———. *The Woman's Dress for Success Book.* Chicago: Follett Publishing Co., 1977.
15. Nitzsche, Jane Chance. "How to Save Your Own Career: the Junior Professor's Dilemma," *Change,* February, 1978, pp. 40–43.
16. Pratt, Margaret. *The Successful Secretary.* N.Y.: Lothrop, Lee & Shepard Co., 1946.
17. Sommer, Dale W. "How Clothes Shape Your Future," *Industry Week,* October 10, 1977, pp. 52–56.
18. "Which Look Cinched the Job? Dressing for a Management-Level Job," *Glamour,* February, 1978, pp. 152–153.
19. Wolf, Jamie. "Metamorphoses of the Little Black Dress," *Harper's,* September, 1978, pp. 95–99.

SEXUALLY ATTRACTIVE CLOTHING: ATTITUDES AND USAGE

Elizabeth A. McCullough, Mary Fran Miller, and Imogene M. Ford

The attitudes and clothing usage of 68 black and 163 white unmarried college females (18 to 21 years of age) enrolled in either one of two southern state universities were studied in relation to the sexual attractiveness of clothing. Subjects rated the sexual attractiveness of 20 specified clothing items and indicated the frequency with which they would wear these items for class time, leisure time, casual date, special date, and job interview. Chi-square analysis indicated that the black females and the white females differed significantly in their attitudes toward the attractiveness to males of one-third of the clothing items and on 43 of the 100 clothing usage variables. The black subjects reported that they would wear 75 percent of the clothing items more frequently and on more occasions than the white subjects. However, both groups reported infrequent use of clothing items which they perceived to be sexually attractive. It appears that sexual attraction is not the primary motive that influences a female's clothing usage.

From *Home Economics Research Journal,* Vol. 6, No. 2, December 1977, pp. 164–170. Reprinted by permission of the publisher.

An individual's body concept encompasses more than a visual image of physical attributes. Body image is based on past and present perceptions and is, therefore, continually changing. A person's body awareness is intensified during adolescence because of the radical changes that occur, the emphasis assigned to physical attributes by the peer group, and the increased tendency to compare oneself with culturally determined standards and ideals (Schonfeld, 1936, pp. 42–57).

In American society, clothing has become an integral part of each individual's body image (Gorman, 1969, p. 10). Thus, a person may change his or her body image by changing attire. In this way, clothing may be used as a means of attaining some of the desired characteristics of the ideal body image.

By late adolescence, most young people begin to become interested in selecting mates (Powell, 1963, p. 235), and many females use clothing as a method of enhancing their sexual attractiveness (Fisher, 1973, p. 97). This may be accomplished through the exposure, concealment, and emphasis of different parts of the body and through the use of erotic symbolism in clothing. The degree to which a female uses clothing to attract males varies with the occasion or with the role she is expected to play (Goffman, 1961, pp. 145–147). On certain occasions, clothing may be used as a means of emulating the cultural ideal and/or attracting the opposite sex.

Numerous authors have presented evidence to support the theory that women dress with the intention of attracting the opposite sex (Cunnington, 1941, p. 42). However, the majority of support for this premise is based on the interpretation of observations of the dress of many peoples over time rather than on empirical research (Hurlock, 1929, p. 19; Laver, 1969, pp. 1–27). An early study by Silverman did find the desire for sexual attractiveness to be a motivating factor in attention to dress for adolescents aged 12 to 18 (Silverman, 1945, p. 116).

Cultural ideals for beauty vary among societies and change over time. Subcultural ideals may exist for groups that are set apart from the general society on some basis such as differences in religion, age, ethnic background, and physical attributes (Roach and Eicher, 1973, pp. 211–212). Therefore, anthropometrical differences between black individuals and white individuals, as well as incongruities in cultural and social environments, may lead to differences in attitude toward personal body images and that of the cultural ideal. The increased coverage of blacks by the media and their renewed identification with Africa have promoted a new cultural ideal for blacks. In light of the new black cultural ideal, black females may differ from white females in their attitude toward the sexual attractiveness of clothing and how often they might wear this clothing on various occasions.

The purpose of this study was to provide insight into the attitudes and clothing usage of black and of white females in relation to females' use of clothing to attract males. It was hypothesized that there would be a significant difference between black and white college females in (1) their rating of the sexual attractiveness of specified clothing items to males and (2) the frequency with which they would wear these clothing items for each of five occasions.

Research Design

The sexual attractiveness rating and corresponding wear of specified clothing items (dependent variables) for black females or white females (independent variables) were compared. Black or white females were defined as any female belonging to either the racial and cultural group of Afro-Americans or American Caucasoids as noted by the researcher. The sexual attractiveness variable was defined as the females' rating of specified clothing items in terms of their degree of sexual attractiveness to males. The clothing usage variable was defined as the frequency with which females would wear specified clothing items for five different occasions if such items were in their wardrobes.

Instruments

An adaptation of the Sensuous Clothing Measure originally developed by Cressman (1972) was used to determine female attitudes toward the sexual attractiveness of specified clothing items. Whether or not these items were actually sexually appealing to males was not tested because although females' perceptions may be incorrect, they are utilized as information in selecting clothing for wear. Modifications made for this study included examples of clothing styles currently in fashion, different fabrics, various degrees of body exposure, and ways of wearing garments (i.e., unbuttoned). The subjects rated the 20 clothing items listed in the instrument in terms of sexual attractiveness by using the numerical values of 1 to 5 in the following attitudinal scale: (1) *Not* attractive to the opposite sex, (2) *Slightly* attractive to the opposite sex, (3) *Moderately* attractive to the opposite sex, (4) *Quite* attractive to the opposite sex, and (5) *Very* attractive to the opposite sex.

The Sensuous Clothing Usage Measure developed by McCullough (1975) was employed to determine the frequency with which a female would wear specified clothing items for five different occasions if such items were in her wardrobe. The subjects indicated how often they would wear each clothing item for class time, leisure time, casual date, special date, and job interview by using the numerical values of 1 to 5 in the following wear frequency scale: (1) Would *never* wear it, (2) Would wear it *once* in a blue moon, (3) Would wear it *occasionally,* (4) Would wear it *often,* and (5) Would wear it *most of the time.*

The Sample

The subjects were selected on the basis of sex, race, marital status, and age. Unmarried females were chosen because of their relative accessibility in a university setting and because their attitude toward and use of clothing to attract the opposite sex might differ from that of married females. The median age for the marriage of females was 21.1 in 1974 (United States Bureau of the Census, 1975, p. 67). Therefore, it was assumed for the purpose of this study that a female might be more desirous of attracting males when she was approximately 18 to 21 years of age rather than at another age. The sample consisted of 68 black and 163 white unmarried females between 18 and 21 years of age who were majoring in either home economics or business at two southern state universities. The black sample was taken from one institution and the white sample from the other. The rationale behind this separation was twofold. First of all, the ratio of blacks to whites at one university was nine to one and at the other university, one to nine. Consequently, sufficient data could not be collected in a classroom situation for both groups at either school. In addition, a more homogeneous black sample with respect to clothing attitudes and usage was thought to be possible in an environment populated primarily by members of that particular group. The data were collected during the winter of 1975.

Statistical Analysis

Chi-square analysis was selected to measure differences in response patterns between the black and the white groups on the 20 sexual attractiveness variables and the 100 clothing usage variables in the questionnaire. The means were calculated for each variable by race, but not statistically tested for significance. The reliability of internal consistency was computed for the two instruments using split-half analysis (Downie and Heath, 1974, pp. 188–203, 237–238). Each instrument yielded high reliability coefficients (over .80) for the black subjects, the white subjects, and the total sample, thus increasing the credibility of the findings.

Results and Discussion

Clothing items in the Sensuous Clothing Measure that yielded mean ratings over 3.0 were considered sexually attractive, whereas, those items with means below 3.0 were considered unattractive to males. Fifteen (75 percent) and 16 (80 percent) of the clothing items were rated sexually attractive by the black and the white subjects respectively (Table 1).

The black group had higher mean ratings on 10 of the 20 clothing items, including revealing holes or "cutouts," and the white group had higher means on the other 10 items, including garments of shiny, lustrous fabric. However, the percentage of responses from the black females that were in the highest sexual attractiveness rating category (5) was greater than that for the white females on 13 of the 20 clothing items. The white subjects had the higher percentage of responses in the moderately attractive rating category (3) on 16 of the clothing items. The

chi-square analysis illustrated this difference in response patterns by indicating significant differences on seven (33 percent) of the clothing items (Table 1).

Chi-square was utilized to analyze each of the 20 clothing items for each of the five occasions of wear listed in the Sensuous Clothing Usage Measure (i.e., 100 clothing usage variables, see Table 2). Significant differences were indicated for the subjects' reported wear of eight (40 percent) of the clothing items such as plunging front and back necklines during class time; 16 (80 percent) of the items including revealing holes or "cutouts" during leisure time; nine (45 percent) of the items such as knit body shirts for a casual date; six (30 percent) of the items including midriff tops for a special date; and four (20 percent) of the items such as going braless during a job interview. The black females indicated a higher wear frequency than did the white females on all of those clothing usage variables on which significant differences occurred with the exception of three items: going braless during leisure time, going braless on a special date, and exposing bare shoulders on a special date. The white group reported a higher usage of these clothing items than did the black group.

Differences in attitude toward the sexual attractiveness of clothing often are reflected in corresponding dissimilarity in the frequency of wear. The black subjects reported that they would wear five of the significant items in Table 1 more frequently than would the white subjects on all occasions where a significant difference in use was found. *Knit body shirt* was the only clothing item that yielded significant differences on the sexual attractiveness variable and on the clothing usage variables for all five occasions. The black females reported higher usage for knit body shirts on all occasions, but the white females gave the item a higher sexual attractiveness rating than did the black females

The subjects did not differ in their use of garments of clingy knit fabric and short shorts or "hot pants" on any occasion even though differences in attitude toward the sexual attractiveness of the items were found. Black and white persons use some clothing similarly on various occasions even when their attitudes toward the clothing are dissimilar.

Buttons partially unfastened was the only item on clothing that did not yield any significant differences on either the sexual attractiveness variable or the frequency of wear for any of the occasions. Although the subjects rated the item sexually attractive, perhaps this method of wearing clothes is so common in daily dress that both groups use it similarly on different occasions.

The black females and the white females rated some of the clothing items as sexually unattractive (with no significant differences), and yet the two groups differed significantly in their use of these items on various occasions. On occasions for which a significant difference occurred on the usage of a clothing item, the blacks indicated that

TABLE 1
Mean ratings and *chi*-square tests for differences in the rating of sexually attractive clothing items by race[a]

Clothing Items	*Chi* Square	Mean Ratings[b] Blacks	Whites
Midriff top	15.13**	3.95	3.72
Knit body shirt	14.74**	3.38	3.39
Garments of velvet or velour fabric	2.36	2.64	2.66
Sheer stockings	2.94	3.26	3.38
Short dresses and skirts	14.64**	4.06	3.66
Halter style garments	7.94	4.40	4.20
Garments of clingy knit fabric	10.07*	3.80	3.95
Flared, flippy skirts	3.00	2.98	2.93
Plunging back necklines	10.85*	3.17	3.44
Plunging front necklines	4.01	4.01	4.10
Going braless	6.26	3.40	3.14
Short shorts, "hot pants"	18.41**	4.11	3.61
Garments of shiny, lustrous fabric	4.03	2.89	3.13
Buttons partially unfastened	3.73	3.32	3.39
Garments of sheer fabric	5.97	3.55	3.33
Bare shoulders	7.62	3.43	3.74
Garments belted at the waist	2.22	2.85	2.72
Revealing slits	2.23	3.55	3.53
Garments of plush fabric	3.65	2.80	2.82
Revealing holes or "cutouts"	10.67*	3.59	3.14

[a]Based on sample size of 68 black and 163 white females.
[b]Sexually attractive clothing items were those which received mean ratings over 3.0 on a scale from 1 (sexually unattractive) to 5 (very sexually attractive) on the Sensuous Clothing Measure from the black or the white groups.
*Indicates significance at the 5 percent level.
**Indicates significance at the 1 percent level.

TABLE 2
Chi-square tests for differences in clothing usage for five occasions by race.[a]

Clothing Items	Class Time	Leisure Time	Casual Date	Special Date	Job Interview
Midriff top	6.26	14.01**	12.43**	15.49**	5.30
Knit body shirt	20.49**	15.57**	17.24**	18.62**	13.49**
Garments of velvet or velour fabric	23.59**	14.48**	22.34**	2.86	23.03**
Sheer stockings	7.62	12.31**	3.72	6.72	4.77
Short dresses and skirts	1.61	27.87**	5.34	5.95	3.63
Halter style garments	2.83	13.91**	1.53	3.76	0.46
Garments of clingy knit fabric	1.41	0.63	4.03	4.06	2.57
Flared, flippy skirts	5.11	13.24**	8.69	1.48	5.83
Plunging back necklines	22.21**	42.84**	28.01**	6.66	1.95
Plunging front necklines	17.80**	26.66**	12.05**	1.47	11.00*
Going braless	12.09**	11.60**	4.39	11.42*	8.21*
Short shorts, "hot pants"	4.69	5.35	2.75	6.88	0.83
Garments of shiny, lustrous fabric	7.69	10.09*	11.34*	12.87**	1.84
Buttons partially unfastened	3.43	8.73	5.63	4.35	1.95
Garments of sheer fabric	5.07	14.99**	6.91	5.49	1.40
Bare shoulders	9.85*	24.97**	9.84*	10.46*	4.76
Garments belted at the waist	9.07*	16.88**	5.49	2.75	8.16
Revealing slits	4.33	23.57**	9.90*	8.59	2.59
Garments of plush fabric	19.18**	3.53	21.14**	4.30	3.55
Revealing holes or "cutouts"	8.85	24.56**	7.95	10.90*	0.88

[a]Based on sample size of 68 black and 163 white females.
*Indicates significance at the 5 percent level.
**Indicates significance at the 1 percent level.

they would wear all of the items more often than the whites. For example, the blacks reported that they would wear the sexually unattractive item, garments of velvet or velour fabric, more frequently than the whites for class time, leisure time, casual date, and job interview. Thus, the two groups differed in their clothing usage for some clothing items for reasons other than their attitude toward the sexual attractiveness of the clothing.

The black subjects reported that they would wear 75 percent of the clothing items more often and on more occasions than the white subjects. However, both groups did wear sexually attractive clothing on all occasions, but to a low degree. For example, plunging back necklines and revealing slits were rated sexually attractive to males, but the subjects indicated infrequent use of the items. These findings support those of Stanford, who found that women preferred to dress modestly by concealing their bodies, even though men preferred immodesty in women and revealing apparel (Stanford, 1975, p. 169).

The clothing items listed in the measures, however, were not exhaustive of the sexually attractive items available for wear. In addition, low usage of sexually attractive clothing was expected for a job interview. Many of the clothing items that the females rated as attractive to the opposite sex were more commonly worn in the spring and summer seasons also, and the data were collected in the winter.

The clothing item, *garments belted at the waist,* was one of the few items rated sexually unattractive by the black and the white subjects. Both groups reported that they would wear the item often on every occasion of wear, even though they did not consider it attractive to males. This is in agreement with Snyder (1975, p. 56), who noted that an individual's attitude toward sexually attractive clothing was not necessarily reflected by the actual use of that clothing. Many authors, however, have stated that women dress with the intention of attracting the opposite sex (Laver, 1969, pp. 1–27). According to the results of the present study, sexual attraction is not the primary motive that influences a female's clothing usage.

The sexual attractiveness of a garment is based partly on its ability to draw attention to specific parts of the body. If a garment such as a midriff top were worn by the majority of women most of the time, the "attention-getting-effect" of the garment would decrease, and the garment would lose some of its appeal. Perhaps this is why the subjects reported limited use of sexually attractive clothing items. The current popularity of unisex clothing also might contribute to the females' infrequent use of clothing to attract males.

It is recognized that there are certain occasions when a woman wants to "play down" her sexuality and consequently dresses accordingly (Fisher, 1973, p. 98). A job interview is indicated in this study as one of these occasions. For example, sexually attractive clothing items were worn less frequently during a job interview and most frequently during leisure time. Thus, these unmarried females are interested in attracting the opposite sex during leisure time; however, they may wear these clothing items for other purposes such as recreational activities.

The black females and the white females differed more extensively in their clothing usage on occasions during which behavioral expectations were less defined and more types of activity were socially acceptable. Specifically, the groups differed in their reported use of 80 percent of the clothing items during leisure time. In addition, differences in clothing usage occurred for five of the items on this occasion only (Table 2). Conversely, the concept of a job interview was more definitive in terms of acceptable and unacceptable behavior. The black and the white groups shared similar behavioral expectations for this occasion in that they differed on only 20 percent of the clothing usage items for a job interview.

Black persons often are stereotyped as a group who wear garments of plush, shiny, velvet, and velour fabrics frequently. Clothing items of these fabrics were included in the measures to determine whether black females would rate them sexually attractive and report frequent wear. According to the results of the Sensuous Clothing Usage Measure, the blacks did report more frequent use of the items than did the whites on almost all occasions. However, garments of plush, shiny, velvet, and velour fabrics were among the five clothing items that the black subjects rated as sexually unattractive (Table 1).

The black and the white groups responded similarly on over half of the sexual attractiveness and clothing usage variables. However, differences in the cultural and social environments of the black and the white populations may have been reflected in the dissimilarity in clothing attitudes and usage indicated by this study. The identification of many black persons with a new black ideal body image that differs somewhat from the white ideal also is suggested. Although the black and the white groups differed in their use of many sexually attractive clothing items on various occasions, they also differed in their use of some sexually unattractive items. It appears that the subjects' attitude toward the sexual attractiveness of clothing is not the only factor contributing to differences in clothing usage. Therefore, more research is needed to elucidate the motives behind the clothing usage of various ethnic groups.

REFERENCES

Cressman, J.L. Instruments for assessing attitudes of black and white female adolescents toward selected clothing behaviors and specified body parts. Unpublished master's thesis, University of Tennessee, 1972.

Cunnington, C.W. *Why Women Wear Clothes.* London: Faber and Faber, Limited, 1941.

Downie, M.N., and Heath, R.W. *Basic Statistical Methods.* New York: Harper and Row, 1974.

Fisher, S. *Body Consciousness: You Are What You Feel.* Englewood Cliffs, NJ: Prentice-Hall, 1973.

Goffman, E. *Encounters.* Indianapolis: Bobbs-Merrill, 1961.

Gorman, W. *Body Image and the Image of the Brain.* St. Louis: Warren H. Green, 1969.

Hurlock, E.B. *The Psychology of Dress.* New York: Ronald Press, 1929.

Laver, J. *Modesty in Dress.* Boston: Houghton Mifflin, 1969.

McCullough, E.A. Attitudes of black and white college females toward sensuous clothing, selected body attributes, and the use of sensuous clothing. Unpublished master's thesis, University of Tennessee, 1975.

Powell, M. *The Psychology of Adolescence.* New York: Bobbs-Merrill, 1963.

Roach, M.E., and Eicher, J.B. *The Visible Self: Perspectives on Dress.* Englewood Cliffs, NJ: Prentice-Hall, 1973.

Schonfeld, W.A. The body and body image in adolescents. In G. Caplan and S. Lebovici (Eds.), *Adolescence: Psychosocial Perspectives.* New York: Basic Books, 1963.

Silverman, S.S. *Clothing and Appearance. Their Psychological Implications for Teen-Age Girls.* New York: Bureau of Publications, Teachers College, Columbia University, No. 912, 1945.

Snyder, A.E. Sensuous clothing in relation to self-esteem and body satisfaction. Unpublished master's thesis, University of Tennessee, 1975.

Stanford, D.H. *Sex Appeal of Women's Clothing as Evaluated by Young Adult Women and Men.* (Doctoral dissertation, Texas Woman's University) Ann Arbor, MI: University Microfilms, 1975, No. 9076

United States Bureau of the Census. *Statistical Abstract of the United States: 1975.* Washington, D.C.: Government Printing Office, 1975.

FASHION FROM THE STREETS

January 1969

Sheldon Zalaznick

In clothes, it has been clear for some time that the traditional process by which fashions are declared and then popularized has been overthrown. As *Fortune* has reported ("The Great Fashion Explosion," October, 1967), fashion now filters up, not down. "Haute couture," says designer Rudi Gernreich, "doesn't have the same meaning any more because money, status, and power no longer have the same meaning. Now fashion starts in the streets. What I do is watch what kids are putting together for themselves. I formalize it, give it something of my own, perhaps, and that is fashion. But St. Laurent and other designers must pick it up at the same time I do. No one person invents anything today and then sends it out to the rest of the world. It's got to be in the air. That's why I watch the kids."

Fashion filters up, moreover, not merely from youth to age, but from lower economic class to upper. The boot kick started with motorcycle gangs, if it can be said to have started anywhere, and it was picked up by Negroes and Puerto Ricans in New York and Los Angeles patronizing Thom McAn long before it reached Florsheim. The elegance men seem increasingly ready for can be traced to London's Teddy Boys of the late 1940s and early 1950s. Carnaby Street is far more powerful than Savile Row in setting upper-class men's fashions. As for hair styles, Elvis Presley now seems rather restrained, and the old Beatles would look almost ordinary.

Rudi Gernreich is struck by the enthusiasm with which boys and girls wear the same outfits. "One of the reasons some older people cannot stand what's happening," he says, "is that it threatens their confidence in their own sexuality. That's why so many older people retain such a fierce interest in clothes." But Gernreich also thinks an even more fundamental change has occurred—a new sense of the body in general, a new idea of total body freedom. "It has to do with the kids' re-examination of values, with their striving for honesty," he says. "Honesty is almost a hang-up today. A bra-less woman at a party or dancing at a discotheque is not a shock anymore. I think this new awareness of the body is no fad. I think it is a permanent change." Such a change cannot be entirely welcome to a considerable number of older folks who in the past could corset and strap and power-net themselves into shape. As Gypsy Rose Lee said recently as she approached her fifty-fifth birthday, "I have everything now I had twenty years ago, except it's all lower."

Today, though their bodies may sag a bit, a lot of older folks are apparently finding fun in looking and acting young, or trying to. The Stork Club and other once celebrated outposts of café society—which provided cachet for people born outside the older, tradition-oriented high society—are dead. But discothèques like Nepentha in New York and the Factory in Los Angeles are thriving—places that provide settings in which all ages and conditions may affect youthful tastes in music, dance, and costume.

Political leaders, popular artists of a kind, find that kissing babies won't do any more. It is no longer enough to be well disposed and tolerant toward youth. Instead,

From "The Youthquake in Pop Culture." *Fortune,* January 1969, pp. 85–87. Reprinted by permission. © 1968 Time Inc.

one must *be* youthful. Richard Nixon promised the Republican convention that he would "tell it like it is." Both Nixon and Hubert Humphrey touched up their hair at the temples. Both spent valuable time speaking to students not old enough to vote. Both took turns through the long presidential campaign promising to "sock it to . . ."

A letter to the New York *Times* recently pointed out that a character in Mark Twain's *A Connecticut Yankee in King Arthur's Court* had "socked it to" the Round Table. Another letter to the *Times* noted that Ralph Waldo Emerson, no less, said, "Do your own thing." Implicit in the letters is the sensible caution that some part of the impact of today's youth upon the culture at large may not be new and that much of it may be exaggerated.

BODY DECORATION AND CAMOUFLAGE

Seymour Fisher

When Cinderella went to the ball disguised as an elegant, high-status figure, she was really not behaving terribly differently from most people as they don their costumes each morning in preparation for their round of daily contacts. Each of us has an elaborate ritual of grooming and putting on of clothes that is intended to slant the impression we make. You can't reconstruct your body but you can, by means of clothes, exercise choice in the type of facade you attach to it. There is no doubt that we are all fascinated by the process of clothing ourselves. There are few things that involve us so continuously. In our clothing choices we reveal our values and life intentions. Anatole France wrote:

> If I were allowed to choose from the pile of books which will be published one hundred years after my death, do you know what I would take? I would simply take a fashion magazine so that I could see how women dress one century from my departure. And these rags would tell me more about the humanity of the future than all the philosophers, novelists, prophets, and scholars. (Rudofsky, 1947, pp. 17–18.)

As we decorate and clothe ourselves, we are, in a sense, doing a self-portrait. The layers of camouflage that we apply are intended to fill out an image that we have in mind. By the time we are adults we have had a chance to experiment with many different facades or "fronts." We have learned to dramatize certain aspects of our appearance and conceal others. Our use of clothes might fancifully be compared to that of camouflage experts who have been given the job of concealing certain facts from observation—and perhaps even creating a few illusory ones. Actually, it is an oversimplification to imply that there are only one or two major factors that determine how a person chooses to dress. Even aside from the fact that you may want to look a certain way, your clothing choices could be influenced by economic considerations or fashion standards. Because of limited income you may have to buy cheap clothes that create a special image by virtue of their cheapness (Roach and Eicher, 1965). Or you may fit your-

self into the latest fashion costume because you want to conform, in spite of the fact that this costume is discrepant with how you want people to see you. But I would add that factors like wealth and socioeconomic status were once of much greater importance in determining how a person dresses than they are today. As mass production of quality clothing has progressed, persons of low income can look quite well dressed.* It is more and more difficult to identify a person's social class from his clothes.** Also, the range of competing fashions on the current scene makes it less likely that anyone will get locked into a style of attire that is grossly different from his true preference. There is plenty of opportunity in Western culture for each individual to put on his camouflage according to his own unique wants.

Several investigators have tried to understand the major motives that enter into clothing choices. If you question women about their choices they specify a number of different intents. Some say they are primarily interested in wearing things that are "comfortable"—not restraining, inhibiting, or difficult to put on. Others indicate that they want clothes that make them look attractive and elicit admiration from men. Still others emphasize winning social approval or being conservatively modest or creating an aesthetic impression. Whatever the general definition each individual gives about why he dresses as he does, I would speculate that his overall purpose is to tell himself and others that he is a certain kind of person. One researcher has shown that women and men differ in their basic dressing motivations. Women seem to be more concerned with winning approval with their clothing strategies. Men were found to be largely interested in avoiding disapproval of the way they clothe themselves. The majority just want to get by without their clothes drawing

Excerpted from Seymour Fisher, *Body Consciousness: You Are What You Feel,* © 1973, pp. 85–92. Reprinted by permission of Prentice-Hall, Inc., Englewood Cliffs, New Jersey.
*See "A Democracy of Clothing," p. 203.
**See "Clothing, Culture, and Poverty," p. 97.

criticism. Of course, more recent developments suggest a growing inclination for young men and women to dress in a way that will not avoid but rather provoke disapproval by the Establishment at the same time that they are looking for approval from their peers. Clothes have taken on new importance as a way of protesting and expressing opposition. There are many precedents for the use of clothes to convey political and ideological messages. The black shirts of the Fascists and the robes of the Ku Klux Klan are examples.

It is interesting, also, to note that the absence of clothes—nudity—has often been used as a weapon of protest. There are religious sects that have dramatized their opposition to particular laws by parading naked in the streets. Nudity is also a popular means for adolescents in Western societies to demonstrate their contempt for the constraints of the Establishment. Some schizophrenics announce their withdrawal from what they consider to be an unbearable world by dramatically throwing off their clothes and running out into the street. The implications of nudity as a way of declaring one's complete freedom have often elicited strong countermeaures from those in authority. Nudity is punishable by death in some cultures. The Roman Catholic church has taught in convent schools that it is sinful to expose your body even to your own eyes. The wearing of clothes represents a form of submission to prevailing mores. It is like putting on a "citizen's uniform" and agreeing to play the game.

Nudity may be used in a magical way to negate the world as it is. It may be used as a way of declaring that one wants to see a major change in nature. It can become a vehicle for asserting that all of the usual rules are cancelled and that a dramatic new state of affairs prevails. There are nudity ceremonies that illustrate this point. In one culture the women strip themselves naked at times of drought as part of a plea for rain. In another a woman whose child is seriously ill removes all of her clothing and goes to the goddess's temple at night as a way of appealing for help. An Eskimo feels that he must strip naked when he eats venison and walrus on the same day—otherwise he will cause serious pain for the soul of the walrus. There is implicit in such behavior the idea that violent change in the state of one's body may help to instigate or cushion the effect of what is considered to be a radical state of affairs in nature. Goffman (1963) has noted that body exposure may be used as a way of expressing trust or security. He points out that a woman may wear a dress at a ceremonial ball that reveals much more of her body than she allows to be seen in everyday circumstances. He goes on to say that this may be a declaration on her part that she feels so secure in that social circle and trustful of the good conduct of its members that she can expose herself without fear of being exploited. It is well-known that strong elements of temptation and counterbalanced control are built into the framework of the conventional

nudist camp. Puritanical codes of male-female interaction often prevail. The exposure of the nude body, with the obvious sexual temptations involved, is carefully balanced by a network of restraining rules of conduct.

What do we really know about the impact of clothing? If I dress in a certain fashion, will this perceptibly influence the way others evaluate me? Attempts have been made to explore these questions. In one experiment audiences were asked to give their impressions of people who posed in different types of clothing. In another, raters evaluated people who were represented only by pictures of their heads and then again when they were depicted full-length in various costumes. Evidence has emerged from such studies that clothes do, indeed, affect the impression you make on others. But the strength of the effect depends upon how well-known you are to them. If another person is not personally acquainted with you, he is more likely to let his opinion of you be influenced by the character of your clothes than if you are well-known to him. It is when you are the anonymous stranger that people are especially dependent upon the appearance of your clothes to cue them about what sort of person you are. Those who are close personal friends are only slightly affected in their opinions of each other by the clothes they happen to wear on any one particular occasion. This suggests, of course, that those who have intimate, long-term relationships, like husbands and wives, are somewhat immune to being influenced by each other's costume changes.

To what extent is a person's feeling about himself influenced by what he wears? Since we are all presumably well acquainted with ourselves one might not expect much change in self-feelings as the result of clothing change. But the analogy may not be reasonable. After all, when we change clothing it is the appearance of our own body that we alter, and in that sense we are much more ego-involved with the alteration than with one we perceive in another person. Furthermore, costume shifts may actually involve tactual and kinesthetic shifts that are not apparent to the outside observer. One set of clothes may feel smoother or rougher than another. One set of clothes may be experienced as tighter or looser than another and therefore affect how free or inhibited we feel. It is also possible that each of us has learned through long trial and error that putting on certain clothes does affect our mood or level of anxiety. Perhaps specific clothes duplicate specific childhood experiences or help to defend against particular forms of uncertainty. It will be recalled that one experimenter found that schizophrenic women may choose clothes with loud patterns as a way of making their body boundaries more visible and therefore more psychologically substantial. Some people might find that the caressing smoothness of a costume reinstates pleasurable contacts with mother's body remembered from early life. A bright, cheerful outfit might serve as a repeated reminder to oneself that life need not be sad or bad. In other words, it is possible that the clothing we wear delivers more powerful messages to ourselves than it does to others.

A person may choose a style of dress because it helps him to control his own conduct. This is obviously true in religious circles. To cover the body fully and to conceal its sexual qualities may "help" the individual to avoid the temptations of the flesh. Hasidic Jews believe strongly in the power of clothes to regulate behavior.* They wear distinctive costumes that set them off from surrounding communities and that also identify the strata within their own ranks. Those who are most religiously devoted wear such articles as a black, large-brimmed hat, a long black coat, and white knee socks. The members of the sect feel that by wearing distinctive garb they are helped to avoid sin. One is quoted (Poll, 1962) as saying: "With my appearance I cannot attend a theater or movie or any other place where a religious Jew is not supposed to go. Thus, my beard and my sidelocks and my Hasidic clothing serve as a guard and a shield from sin and obscenity." Within the Hasidic community the greater the religious devotion of any member the greater the number of special garments he may wear as a badge of his virtue. But once a member begins to wear the garments symbolizing his higher status, he has to show religious behavior consistent with it. He has to keep justifying his superior garments by the frequency and intensity of his religious acts (which are carefully monitored by those who know him). In a sense we all use clothing in a manner analogous to the Hasidic Jew. We put on costumes that remind us that we are supposed to behave in certain ways in certain situations. The man who dons his expensive business suit and goes off to the office is partially cueing himself about the role he is about to fill. The act of putting on the suit and feel of it on his body tell him that he is supposed to display certain patterns of behavior. When the judge wraps himself in his robes he is reminded that he represents the law. He knows that he is framed by his garments and that people expect him to fit his actions to that frame. The pressure of a tie that is correctly tight may be a persistent reminder to someone at a formal affair that he has to be on his best behavior. The release from the constriction of the tie may help to arouse images of taking it easy and doing as he pleases. Paradoxically, the person who cultivates an appearance of uncontrolled disarray confines himself to the expectation that he creates in both himself and others that he will behave unconventionally. He defines his intent by his clothes and he would feel that he had failed unless he publicly fulfilled this intent.

The basic style of dress in any culture partially recollects the attitudes that culture has historically taken to-ward the body. Quite a number of standard decorative details in clothes represent traces of past customs. The cuffs on men's trousers, the nick on men's suit collars that divides the collars from the lapels, the differential right-left placement of buttons on women's, as compared to men's, garments—all represent survivals of past clothing styles that are no longer functional but have stayed on out of inertia and also as a symbolic bridge to the past. When one looks at the clothing configurations of Western society, certain obvious and yet provocative facts emerge:

1. They have assigned considerable significance to distinguishing between the sexes. The distinction has primarily involved the difference between the trouser, which enclosed the lower part of the body, and the dress, which leaves the lower body sector open.
2. Usually, they have required that the body be completely covered (except for the hands and head) and, in addition, have called for more than one layer of clothing.
3. Generally, they have called for points of constriction or careful fastening. The neck and the waist have been favorite sites for applying constricting pressures.
4. They dictate that the color and design schemes of garments will have a certain minimum harmony or relation.
5. They usually avoid gross right-left asymmetries. The right side usually looks exactly like the left, although recent styles have experimented more with right-left differences. Upper-lower asymmetries are considerably more common.
6. Directly or indirectly, they have typically been designed to draw the eyes of the beholder to body areas with sexual significance. This is done either by exaggerating the size of the area or by concealing it in an overdetermined manner.
7. They have, with rare exceptions, built in definitions of worth or status in terms of the quality or financial worth of the garment.
8. They seek to distinguish age levels (although this is less and less true).

Some of the fundamental values of Western society with respect to the body are obviously reflected in these clothing patterns. The fact that we so carefully assign different clothes to the two sexes reflects our chronic anxiety about matters of sexual identity—whether one's body is unequivocally in the right sexual category. The closed versus open attributes of the garments covering the lower part of the body in men and women probably also reflect a strong need to make it clear that the male body is not penetrable whereas that of the female is.

The concern about proper matching of design and color in one's clothing, which was mentioned above, may have important aesthetic roots, but it probably also derives

---

*See "The Pious Ones," pp. 50–51.

from the need to experience one's body as properly integrated—all the parts working together. It is further true that the individual is constantly searching for ways to unite his body with his life role. He wants his body to mirror, and to be sensibly related to, what he has achieved in life. It is no wonder, then, that people try endlessly to cloak themselves in impressive clothing. The person who is proud of his social attainment (for example, as the result of accumulating wealth or power) tries to impart these same qualities to his body by covering it with "rich," high-status garments.

What do we know about the personalities of people who wear different types of clothing? There are all sorts of stereotyped ideas about what you can judge to be true of a person from his clothing. For example, those who wear dark conservative clothing are supposed to be conservative and well controlled. Those who wear sexy-looking clothes are supposed to be sexy. Those who wear bright colors have been said to be emotionally expressive, and so forth. Few of such formulations have been scientifically tested, and we do not know how valid they are. One difficulty that I see with most of them is that they are too simplistic. They assume that a person's traits are directly and visibly transmuted into his style of behavior. But the process is much more complex. People may express a trait in one area of behavior but not in another. Or they may defensively express the opposite of how they really feel. Someone who is chronically a bit depressed may try to fight this feeling by wearing bright colors; it would be wide of the mark in his case to assume that his bright attire meant he was cheerful and light-hearted. In a study carried out in my laboratory we found that you could not distinguish sexually responsive women from the non-sexually responsive on the basis of their appearance or clothing. We asked judges to pick out from a series of women's pictures those who were most sexually active and arousable. The sexual attitudes and behavior of these women had been thoroughly studied. There was only a chance relationship between the judges' evaluations of sexiness and what was actually true of the women. The sexual responsiveness of a woman could not be determined from how colorful or feminine or frilly or revealing her clothes were.

In fact, as you scan the published research concerned with whether people who wear certain styles of clothes have specified personality traits, the yield is sparse. Several attempts have been made to show that secure and insecure people differ in how they dress, but no consistent results have emerged. The dimension of dominance-submission has also been studied. But there is no convincing evidence that dominant people dress in an obviously different fashion from submissive people. It has been demonstrated (Roach and Eicher, 1965) that people with high self-esteem say that they are less concerned about whether their clothes are modest and socially acceptable than are those with low self-esteem. There is an interesting trend

(Roach and Eicher, 1965) for persons in the higher socioeconomic classes to be more aware of clothing cues and differences than are those in lower classes. In the higher classes there was a greater tendency to draw conclusions about others on the basis of their attire. Relatedly, another study (Bethke, 1968) detected a tendency for Anglo-American women in Texas to be more sensitive to clothing differences than Mexican-American women living in Texas. These findings suggest that those who are of relatively dominant social status and who would presumably have more resources to spend on clothes, are especially likely to use clothing cues in making judgments about others. Is this a form of snobbery? Those with superior clothing resources can afford to use clothing criteria to classify others on an inferior-superior continuum. Note, by the way, that the middle classes seem to be most responsive to the successive waves of new clothing fashions. In contrast to the upper and lower classes, they are the ones who shift most radically from very short to very long and back again to very short skirts, and so forth (Roach and Eicher, 1965).

A surprising result has been reported by Compton (1962). She could detect no relationship between a woman's clothing preferences and her actual physical attributes. Preferences were not correlated with eye color, hair color, height, and weight. At a more psychological level, Compton did find that women who prefer small rather than large designs in their dress fabrics are particularly feminine and interested in making a good impression on others. She also found that those who prefer deep shades and saturated colors in their dresses are more sociable and less submissive than those who reject such shades and colors.

Attempts to find consistent changes in clothing preferences with age have not been very successful. A few trends have been spotted. For example, there is a decreasing preference for bright, saturated colors with increasing age. But the findings are really minor in character. Differences between the sexes during the developing years resolve themselves primarily to the fact that girls are more conscious of and interested in clothes than boys. Girls also seem to exceed boys in the extent to which they perceive clothes as a way of establishing that they are mature and grownup. Girls regard the putting on of makeup and certain articles of clothes (the brassiere, for example) as definite badges of their grownup status. But age differentiations in clothing styles for men have all but disappeared, and this is an interesting phenomenon in itself. At one time, the male went through definite clothing stages—for example, from short to long pants—in the process of growing up. However, it is now accepted practice for little boys to wear long pants. Of course, it is generally true that the male makes use of a much smaller range of clothes than the female and is also less likely to wear special garments to match specific social occasions.

More needs to be said about the use of clothes to muffle the body. It is possible to cover your frame with layers of cloth that render your body almost invisible to yourself. The average middle-class man wears a costume during working hours that conceals every inch of his skin except for his hands and head. He cannot with ease directly touch the major parts of his trunk. His skin sensations result primarily from the pressure and movement of his clothes, and there is not too much of that. Since his clothes also help to maintain rather constant temperatures, he has few temperature sensations. It is true that he can quite directly experience the sensations from the interior of his body, but even they seem distant, as if they were being picked up through the thickness of enfolding cloth. The feet, in their heavy leather casings, are well insulated from the ground and there are only the dull pressure variations that accompany each successive step. Even the eyes are increasingly screened from direct contact with the world by glasses of various kinds. The impact of the sun on the eyes is muted by dark filters. In fact, such filters are being used more and more to attenuate the sensory impact of ordinary indoor illumination. What all of this adds up to is an attempt to reduce the possibility of variation in body experience. It is a way of declaring that it is unpleasant to have to cope with unexpected changes in patterns of body sensation. The avoidance of such changes may be comfortable but it removes some of the adventure of relating to your own body. One might say that it results in boredom with one's body. Nothing ever happens.

REFERENCES CITED

Bethke, C.S. "Ethnic Responses to a Modified Clothing TAT." *Journal of Home Economics* 60 (1968): 350–355.

Compton, N.J. "Personal Attributes of Color and Design Preferences of Clothing Fabrics." *Journal of Psychology* 54 (1962): 191–195.

Goffman, E. *Behavior in Public Places.* Glencoe, Illinois: The Free Press, 1963.

Poll, S. *The Hasidic Community of Williamsburg.* New York: Free Press of Glencoe, 1962.

Roach, E., and Eicher, J.B. *Dress, Adornment, and the Social Order.* New York: Wiley, 1965.

Rudofsky, B. *Are Clothes Modern?* Chicago: Paul Theobald, 1947.

WHY YOU WEAR WHAT YOU DO

Liz Smith

Understanding the Psychology of Fashion

On blue Monday, Linda wore a pale yellow mini dress to work. Tuesday, the 23-year-old management trainee showed up at the departmental meeting in a knee-length, gray, pin-striped shirtwaist with white cuffs and collar. She'd planned to wear another dress on Wednesday, but the rain made her change to a denim smock top and cotton slacks. On the way home, Linda stopped at the dry cleaners to pick up the flowered silk pallazzo outfit she planned to wear to the theater on Saturday; and later, she changed into a pair of comfortable jeans, tank top, and floppy suede hat for an informal supper party. Linda doesn't know it, but her clothes are talking—about her.

"Linda obviously has a rich personality and a good self-image," says Jean Rosenbaum, M.D., a Colorado psychiatrist. "She's flexible and has options in her social situations. She takes advantage of the dress options available to her."

Clothes say a lot about Linda—just as they do of everyone. Clothes are a deeply needed, strongly motivated psychological statement—an expression of self. In what people wear and don't wear, in how they wear what they do, in what they do to make their clothes seem unique while still remaining safely part of the group, people are telling the world what they think of themselves.

"We have an image of ourselves, of our bodies. Our clothing is an extension of this image," says Dr. Rosenbaum, secretary of the Southwest Association for Psychoanalysis, and author of *Is Your Volkswagen a Sex Symbol?* "You make your clothes a part of your body. They are your second skin. They are *you.*"

The story of clothes begins—at the beginning, of course—in Genesis, on the bare heels of man and woman as they leave the Garden of Eden. And while Adam and Eve didn't have a Bloomingdale's or Saks to go to, mankind, theoretically, has been "shopping around" ever since—searching for better, more durable, and more attractive fig leaves.

Change in clothing styles, however, has not followed a consistent pattern. The Egyptians, for example, did not substantially change their styles for 3,000 years, and until the fourteenth century, clothing fashions were fairly static. Then, during the Renaissance, man discovered that clothes could be used as a compromise between exhibitionism and modesty, and "fashion" was created.

James Laver,* British costume historian, believes that the mystique of clothes may be unexplainable. "Fashion

From "Why You Wear What You Do." *Today's Health,* published by the American Medical Association. October, 1973. Reprinted by permission of the publisher and the author.
*See "What Will Fashion Uncover Next?" pp. 159–161.

is a very much bigger thing than individual taste or personal convenience. There is something in the story of the clothes we wear which is beyond our comprehension and certainly beyond the control of our conscious minds," he explains. "That is the reason of its importance and the secret of its perennial fascination."

But there are people who dress basically for utility or comfort or style. "The utilitarian dresser is usually a very secure person," says Dr. Rosenbaum. "In California, where dress seems to be less formal, you see people working the cameras for the top shows, clad in trousers and shirts; in New York, they're wearing suit-coats and ties.

"The same goes for those who dress for comfort," he continues. "These people have a secure sense of identity." People who wear loose, comfortable clothes can usually relate well to others, and they're comfortable about themselves. They tend to be cooperative, optimistic, and adaptable. But—according to the psychiatrist—tight an uncomfortable clothing often indicates feelings of anxiety, tension, and even inferiority.

The clothes hog—the lady with 60 pairs of shoes in her closet, the man who throws out his old wardrobe and buys everything new when a fashion change is announced—thinks his or her individual personality is worthless, says the doctor. This person has to depend on others for a sense of identity, and could be suffering from hidden depression. "But no matter what this person does, no matter how many hats or purses or suits he or she buys, the bad self-feeling remains." The opposite, on the other hand, is not necessarily the sign of a good self-image. The person who refuses to buy new clothes and continues to wear the noticeably out-of-date, tattered clothing of years back is demonstrating a personal rigidity and inflexibility.

Except for Rudi Gernreich, inventor of the topless bathing suit, who feels that clothes are becoming "really a very superficial thing," most fashion people agree that clothes are one of the ultimate means of self-expression and self-image. Expression through dress has long been used as a symbol of status, religion, education, occupation, and even rebellion. After the French Revolution, peasant-type costumes were "in," and the new American woman of the mid-nineteenth century celebrated her independence by adopting the bloomer look.

More recently, blacks, Chicanos, the young, and members of the counterculture have expressed their discontent—and often contempt—through their dress. The onslaught of psychedelic clothes, "costumes," ethnic dress, drug culture and hippie fringe attire, and jeans are what *Village Voice* fashion writer Blair Sabol calls "street fashion." Ms. Sabol claims that all *real* fashion trends originate in the street. Even designers are influenced by their models, "the first ones to bring street fashion into the salon," says film costume designer Eli Schumacher. A model comes to work in rolled anklets one day, and a fashion is born. (It happened to Yves St. Laurent.)

Not long ago, fashion sophisticates announced fashion as something that originated with blacks, was then taken up by daring homosexuals, copied in turn by Madison Avenue media people, and, finally, passed through communications to the masses.

Today, says Ms. Sabol, the fashion route has changed; the homosexual middle man is no more. He has been absorbed by the youth culture, the hippie culture, and the increasing respectability accorded Gay Liberation. "There are now just two big street forces for fashion—the Shaft-TNT-Cleopatra Jones thing out of Harlem and the transvestites who have proliferated via Rock'n'Rouge weirdos like David Bowie and Alice Cooper," she explains. "You don't need homosexuals to filter fashion anymore. Now, big tough football players leap right out of locker room showers into clunky platform shoes and Lurex T-shirts originated by the black culture."

No matter where it comes from, fashion, according to Mr. Laver, is "what the eye becomes accustomed to." But there's more to it than that. "Fashion is an endless game of 'follow the leader,'" said the late Lawrence Langer [Langner], theatrical producer and author of *The Importance of Wearing Clothes,* "with the leader constantly changing her clothes as they no longer distinguish her from those who are following. Fashion enables people to achieve, and then maintain, the goal of superiority which is one of the chief reasons we wear clothes."

"Although clothes cannot actually change a person's personality," says Dr. Rosenbaum, "they can, to an extent, make him feel better. If a person sees himself as socially inept, for example, he might force himself to dress up to shore up his confidence, to make himself feel superior." A tennis outfit does not make a tennis player, says the psychiatrist, but it might have a positive effect and make the person *feel* he can play better.

Clothes can help, too, to get one out of a bad mood or a mild depression, according to the doctor. It's the old story of the man who's been kicked around by the boss all week and feels like he's at the bottom of the world—he goes out and buys a new suit, and finds he has a new perspective on life.

"Color is important, also," explains Dr. Rosenbaum. "If you're feeling sad and find yourself wearing something neutral or dark colored, change to something brighter. If you want to make a positive impression, wear something blue or green, colors that indicate cooperativeness and awareness."

The "costume" approach often involves both style and color and is an example of dressing to feel important, says the psychiatrist. It's seen most often in large cities—the wild, loud, incredibly outlandish outfit that is sure to draw everyone's attention. "The person wearing the costume is really feeling insignificant because of the fragmentation of society," he explains. "But what he is saying, through his clothing, is, 'I'm not insignificant—look at me, please.'

And of course, one can hardly help but look." This person, however, is not really wearing his clothes; they are wearing him.

"And, in fashion," says Eve Orton, one of America's "Best Dressed" women, "the woman must wear the clothes, the clothes must not wear the woman." Ms. Orton, a public relations representative for Wolf Brothers, Revlon, Revillon Furs, and Ralph Lauren of Polo, says she couldn't care less what's in or out. "I felt it was a joke when I got on the 'Best Dressed' list. I dress to please myself."

Another woman who doesn't let clothes wear her is Jacqueline Onassis, known as one of fashion's great "shoppers." She not only will buy a polo shirt at Madison Avenue's Veneziana boutique—but will buy it in every one of its 28 colors. Yet, she is apt to get herself up, day after day, in the same sweater, slacks, and shoes, causing *Women's Wear Daily* to say "tch, tch." Mrs. Onassis also buys expensive designer clothes and wears them frequently, even after they've been seen by everyone.

What does this prove? Merely that the former First Lady has the money to ignore convention, the courage to ignore what people say, and the conviction to dress as she pleases. Flouting fashion dictates may be Mrs. Onassis's own little rebellion, the nose-thumbing of a woman who is so rich and famous she can literally do as she pleases.

This is a trend that may be part of the future for everyone, too. "Even the traditionally conservative business world is loosening up on dress codes, and in many places people can wear whatever they want to work," says Dr. Rosenbaum. "It used to be that everyone had to look the same. It was part of the work ethic. You had to show, partially by the way you were dressed, that you knew that life was serious and hard. You also had to show, again by your dress, that you could be dominated. The person who was different was considered a threat to the business."

This unwillingness to do as one is told to because someone gave the order will continue to affect the fashion world—and it's a healthy sign, according to Dr. Rosenbaum. It worked once already, in the great midi disaster of several seasons back. Despite the fact that designers, manufacturers, and the media all promoted the midi, it was a big flop. The women said no, they didn't want it.

"Often the designers who create the less flattering fashions for women are homosexuals who dislike women," says the doctor. "They try to make women look as ugly as possible. They use them as dolls." But women finally refused to be used.

The trend away from dictated fashion is in evidence elsewhere, also. Valentino, the Roman high priest of fashion, for example, recently decreed that "jeans are out." But his dictated word means nothing. Jeans are *not* out. In fact, they're more in than ever. Last year, Americans spent nearly $1.5 billion for an estimated 175 million pairs of denim jeans. In Russia, black-market jeans go for as high as $75 a pair; and in Paris, "used" jeans, embellished with embroidery, are selling for $25 a pair.

"People will stick with things they love—like blue jeans—although you'll see more dresses for variety," says Ms. Sabol. "But the future of fashion is in technology." She predicts that new synthetic fibers will result in innovations—for example, a "wired" coat that warms itself up. She also predicts that architecture will be the next true fashion influence.

"Our apartments or homes, what we live inside of, how we decorate them will influence what we wear," she explains. "Look at how men are now wearing caftans at home. We are all going to be more influenced by our personal surroundings than by freak fashions like these dangerous, ugly platform shoes."

Another influence on the future of fashion is the past itself—harking back to another time that appears, somehow, more peaceful, romantic, and adventurous. James Laver advanced the famous "Law of Fashion" which states that the same dress is indecent 10 years before its time, daring 1 year before its time, chic in its time, dowdy 3 years after its time, hideous 20 years after its time, amusing 30 years after its time, romantic 100 years after its time, and beautiful 150 years after its time.

But, says Rudi Gernreich, nostalgia is "sick." It is a denial of the present and a fear of the future. "I foresee something in clothes that is much more related to a real need, a very logical need to garb yourself in a purely functional way," he explains. "I think people are going to have more of a desire to disappear than to attract attention."

Gernreich believes that the further emancipation of women will continue to make the sexes dress more and more alike. But if the women have something to say about it, he might be wrong. "There's no question—unisex in clothes is here to stay, to some extent," says Ms. Sabol. "But I was taken for a boy so often last year, I began to feel neuterized." So Ms. Sabol stopped wearing jeans and has gone back to dresses. "I'm into more feminine clothes now," she explains. "Just to please myself and attract men. I consider myself liberated, but I *like* the reaction of hard hats on the street."

Perhaps the glamorous lady is due for a comeback. "I think the way women go around is awful," says model-actress Marisa Berenson. "They used to be so glamorous and there is none of that anymore. I like imagination in clothes; putting odd colors together, using very aggressive jewelry. I think I like glamour most of all." And when Ms. Berenson, the granddaughter of dress designer Schiaparelli, accepted an Oscar for *Cabaret* cinematographer, Geoffrey Unsworth, last spring, she demonstrated—on national television—her conception of glamour. Although her poison-green satin dress with a Depression-era flower evoked cries of "tacky" from some reporters, Marisa wore it with the courage of her fashion conviction, her clothes speaking for herself.

No matter what becomes the fashion tomorrow, clothes will continue to say a lot about the people who are wearing them. They'll continue to serve as advertisements for one's self-image. "When you're selecting clothes, you're choos- ing a kind of substitute body," says Dr. Rosenbaum, who believes people should choose clothing that emphasizes their positive features and hides their bad points. "You can tell the person who thinks well of himself," he says, "by the way he dresses."

And just what did your orange sneakers say about your self-image today?

IN DEFENSE OF MODESTY

Alexander Lowen

People ordinarily assume that clothes are worn as a means of protection against the elements of nature. Though such protection is obviously needed in arctic cli- mates, it does not explain the use of clothes in tropic regions or heated homes. Clothes serve two other impor- tant functions, they draw attention to a person's individ- uality at the same time that they hide the secret core of his personality. To understand the complex role that clothes play in our lives we need to study the antithetical tendencies of bodily display on the one hand and bodily modesty on the other.

The desire to draw attention to the body and to display its charms reflects an exhibitionistic impulse that is found in all people. Among primitives there is an almost uni- versal tendency to decorate the body with such devices as paints, ornaments, garlands, etc. This feeling for display- ing the body is common to many animals and man. Among the animals it is closely related to the sexual drive and follows an instinctive pattern. Nature has endowed many animals, especially the males, with decorative fea- tures which serve this display function. Among human beings, display is a more conscious activity which employs many external agents to enhance the appeal of the indi- vidual. Psychologists and anthropologists generally agree that the primary function of clothes is to serve this display function.

Display emphasizes the uniqueness and superiority of the individual over the rest of the group. It often takes the form of physical exhibition as in the display of dancing ability or athletic prowess but in daily life the main reli- ance is upon decorative devices or clothes. In all primitive societies, the ruler or tribal leader is more elaborately decorated than his subjects or followers. In civilized so- cieties, organized on a class basis, status and rank are expressed by the costliness and elaboration of dress. The king's royal robes and the courtiers' ornate costumes dis- tinguished them from the common man. These distinc- tions of dress tend to disappear in democratic societies, where they are displaced by fashion, which serves as a status symbol. To be dressed in the height of fashion is some indication of social superiority for it often requires more money and time than the average working person can afford to devote to clothes. Clothes serve, therefore, to accent the differences between people, socially and sex- ually.

Nakedness is the great leveler of social distinctions for it reduces all persons to the common bodily or animal level on which they came into this world. Nudity strips the individual of his ego pretensions and, sometimes, of his ego defenses. Punishment has frequently taken the form of the public exposure of the naked body. People who are paraded nude through the streets before the gaze of others who are dressed experience a deep humiliation. When, however, everyone is undressed, the feelings of shame and embarrassment tend to disappear and one often experiences a sense of release and freedom in nudity. The need to maintain an appearance or support an ego image is a restraint that inhibits the joy and spontaneity of the body. In the privacy of our homes, we all welcome the opportunity to relieve ourselves of this ego burden by removing some of our clothing.

In human beings, the tendency to exhibit and display the body is coupled with a feeling of modesty about it which derives from an ego consciousness of the body. Man is conscious of his body, especially of its sexual nature, in a way the animal or the young child isn't. Man has de- veloped an ego which views the body as an object and is aware of its sexual function. The animal is fully identified with its body and lacks this awareness and ego develop- ment. Man, as opposed to the animal and the young child, has become self-conscious. Modesty is an expression of this self-awareness, a mark of personality, and a sign of individuality.

Covering part of the body, particularly the genital area, reflects a sense of privacy which is the basis of modesty. Among primitive people, the genital area is often the only

From "In Defense of Modesty." *Journal of Sex Research*, Vol. 4, No. 1, February 1968, pp. 51–56. Reprinted by permission of The Society for the Scientific Study of Sex.

part of the body that is covered. In the Trobriand Islands, as reported by Malinowski, when a girl begins to have sexual relations she puts on a fibre skirt. The skirt, like the palm leaf or loincloth of the man, denotes a feeling of privacy about the genital organs. We express a similar feeling about the genital organs when we speak of them as "the privates" or the "private parts." Privacy is connected with personality, which masks an individual's innermost feelings and enables one to hide certain bodily expressions that are considered personal not public. The genital organs are covered because their reactions are least subject to voluntary control. While we can mask certain feelings or prevent them from showing in our faces, we can be betrayed by a genital excitation that cannot be controlled. Pride informs a man that his sense of privacy requires that his sexual feelings be kept hidden from public view.

Pride, privacy, and adult genitality go hand in hand. At the other end of this scale is infantile or childhood behavior in which there is neither pride, privacy, nor, of course, genital satisfaction. Natural pride is an expression of the degree of one's self-feeling or self-respect. It denotes the ability of an individual to contain his feelings and represents, therefore, the ability of a person to hold a strong sexual charge. The lack of pride is an indication of a lack of self-esteem, self-containment, and strong feeling. Correspondingly, the individual without pride is unable to hold a strong sexual charge and his release will fail to yield the pleasure or satisfaction it should provide. Pride cannot be divorced from a sense of privacy or a feeling of modesty.

Nudity removes all privacy and reduces all pride. Contrary to popular imagination, social nudity has a restricting effect upon sexual feeling. In his interesting study, *The Psychology of Clothes,* J.C. Flugel writes: "Nakedness tends to diminish 'sexuality' (i.e., the more directly genital impulses of sexuality). The by now extensive experience of the Friends of Nature [a nudist organization] would seem to show that this contention is correct, the chief reason probably being that the increased pleasure of exhibitionism and of skin and muscle erotism have drained off a certain quantity of sexual energy that might otherwise have found a purely genital channel."

I believe that Flugel's explanation has some validity. When the erotic feeling is transferred to the total body, the focus upon the genitals diminishes. The situation of nudists parallels that of children where sexuality is diffused as skin and muscle erotism without the strong genital charge that demands release. In other words, nudity is a regressive experience that brings one back to the pleasures of childhood at the expense of the stronger adult genital excitation. This psychological regression accounts in large part for the decrease of sexual feeling in nudist gatherings. Having regressed to the level of children, nudists forsake their sexual maturity.

Adult sexuality is a combined function of the ego and the body. The ego increases the genital excitation (1) by focusing erotic feeling on the genital apparatus, (2) by directing this feeling to a specific individual, (3) by containing the excitation, thereby allowing it to build to a higher peak. The stronger the ego the greater the orgasm or sexual satisfaction. The ego is like the arm that draws the bow for the flight of the arrow. The stronger the arm, the greater the tension that can be supported and the further the flight of the arrow. The weak ego "lets go" more easily, but since the build-up of tension is minor the pleasure of release is minimal.

Since both the tendency to display and the feeling of modesty are ego manifestations, they further the ego aim of adult sexual satisfaction, i.e., orgasm. Clothes can be considered, therefore, as a mechanism of genital arousal, and modesty promotes this aim, for by hiding the prize, its allure is intensified. The young child knows no modesty since it has no genital aim. The sexually mature individual who is conscious of his body is necessarily modest. Modesty, however, must not be confused with prudery or shame.

The distinction between modesty and shame is the difference between claiming a sense of privacy and fearing self-exposure. A modest person is not afraid of exposure; he can choose when or where to express his feelings and he will expose them in appropriate situations. The person who is ashamed cannot express his feelings even in appropriate situations. He is afraid to expose himself even when the situation calls for such exposure. In therapy we deal with people who who are ashamed of their feelings. They cannot express them even in the privacy and intimacy of the therapeutic situation. Shame is pathological whereas modesty is normal. Prudery may be defined as the shame of the body.

We are witnessing a reduction in the shame of the body that we inherited from Victorian days. The sexual revolution of the past fifty years will lead naturally to an even greater acceptance of bodily exposure. The question that arises is—what are the limits to this exposure? In San Francisco some of the night clubs are featuring "topless waitresses." It is quite conceivable that before long, if the present trend continues, nude waitresses may appear in some night clubs. There are magazines and films in which the nude or almost nude body is exposed without any sense of modesty. Such a development, it seems to me, is not in the interest of mental health. The girls who are so exposed are degraded since their privacy is stripped from them. The effect of such disregard for modesty is to reduce the respect for the body and to diminish the excitement and mystery of sex.

One simple principle, I believe, explains the behavior of organisms—the search for excitement and pleasure. Excitement is life. The lack of excitement is boredom and death. Since Adam and Eve, the excitement of life has centered around the mystery of sex. Clothing intensifies this mystery. It cloaks the biological response with the aura of personality (persona = mask) and adorns it with the unique characteristics of the individual ego. Sex is elevated from a generic response to a personal one. This response is the basis of love; from it derives all romance, the elixir that transforms mundane existence into enchantment and ecstasy. This transformation does not exist on the animal level, where sex is a purely biological function. The specifically human quality that raises sex from its animal level is the sense of awe that grows out of the awareness of the surrender of individuality and the fusion of the self with the universal. The mystery of consciousness resides in the dialectic whereby the individual self arises out of the universal by an act of love (mother love) and returns to the universal by another act of love (sexual love).

This dual aspect of man's consciousness, the sense of self and the feeling of unity with the universal, is reflected in the antithetical tendencies of display and modesty. Exhibitionism accents the self or the individual, modesty expresses the feeling that the individual self is an aspect of the universal. A self without modesty is a thing, an object, an uprooted tree that has lost its vital connection to the earth and has become wood. How can one compare the excitement of a piece of wood with that of a living tree?

The loss of modesty in our time is a manifestation of a cultural tendency, the scientific attitude that tends to strip the mystery from all aspects of life. Without this mystery, the body loses its individuality and becomes an object of commerce to be exploited like other articles of commerce. By the same token, the excitement that resides in the human body is lost. One outstanding result of the current tendency to expose the female body in magazine and film is the lack of romance and excitement in the story or the film.

There is an excitement in nakedness. We derive an elementary pleasure in the exposure of the skin to sun, air, and water. When conditions are right, we feel vibrantly alive in this exposure. We sense more keenly the biological roots of our nature and we gain an identification with the body that is not possible when the body is fully clothed. However, the pleasure of public nudity is achieved by regression to the level of the young child whose innocence parallels that state of existence in the Garden of Eden before man became conscious of his individuality. Like every regressive phenomenon it can have a place in mature living. It is possible to retain a sense of modesty in nude gatherings when nudity is socially approved, as in the age-old custom of nude bathing in many countries. Divorced from a sense of modesty, however, public nudity reduces man to the level of a barnyard creature. Such a development would lead to the loss of the mystery and romance of life and force people to adopt desperate measures to seek some excitement in life.

T-SHIRTS FOR TEA

Maria Josephy Schoolman

Clothes make the man, they say. Sure—clothes make him comfortable, unrestricted, and conveniently equipped with breast pockets, vest pockets, patch pockets, and watch pockets. Men's clothes, particularly work clothes, allow men a kind of psychological and functional freedom that is impossible for the "well-dressed" woman to enjoy. Her clothes are not only visually symbolic of femininity but force her to behave in a particular "feminine" way.

An awareness of this is growing among women. One sign is that pants, boots and flat-heeled shoes have become commonplace for city wear. Women are wearing work shirts to work and T-shirts to tea. We are taking our functional clothes out of the house.

Like many women my age, 38, I have worn jeans and sneakers at home or in my neighborhood but have made it a point to get dressed up to go downtown—whether here in Washington, D.C., or in Chicago and New York where I've lived before. Going downtown for me usually involves business appointments (I am a free-lance graphic designer), shopping, museums, restaurants, etc.

Not long ago, while working on a stone carving, I broke two chisels. They had to be replaced in order for my work to continue. A hardware store in the middle of Washington's downtown shopping district was the only place such chisels could be purchased. Too rushed to change clothes, I simply left the house in my jeans. I found the store had closed for an hour so I decided to get some lunch in the meantime. I bought a hot dog and walked down the street eating it until I found a tiny park with an almost virgin newspaper on a bench. There I sat reading and finishing my lunch. I was wearing a pair of corduroy jeans with pockets big enough to get my hands in, a sweat shirt, a loose coat with large pockets, socks, and boots. Several

From "T-shirts for Tea." *Ms.* magazine, Vol. 1, No. 8, February 1973, pp. 42–43. Pictures and footnotes are omitted. Reprinted by permission of the publisher.

people stopped to talk to me, including the inevitable propositioner. I found that instead of freezing up or moving away, I answered naturally, without embarrassment; eventually the man on the make moved on good-humoredly. During this little episode I felt an unfamiliar sense of freedom and absence of vulnerability. I realized it was related solely to the "I don't care" way I was dressed.

Later, in trying to analyze how a simple change of costume could create such an overall relaxation, I contrived the following fantasy:

Imagine a woman of any age between 20 and 70 who has just had her hair done; it is sprayed or teased or elaborately pinned up. She is wearing a dress with a tight short skirt, short sleeves, and no pockets. Over the dress she wears a fitted coat with tiny pockets or none at all. (Under the dress, most women in this costume would also be wearing a girdle and bra.) High-heeled shoes, stockings, white gloves, screw-on earrings, pearls, full makeup, and a purse complete the ensemble. Call her the Lady.

Now imagine a second woman who has either uncurled short hair, or long hair worn loose or pulled back simply with a clip. She is wearing a shirt and a sweater, jeans or loose pants with pockets, a duffel coat with large pockets and a practical, warm hood. On her feet are socks and sneakers or flat-heeled sturdy boots. She wears no makeup or jewelry. Call her the Slob.

Both women live in the suburbs and are going downtown for the day. Once in their cars each woman realizes she needs gas. At the gas station, the attendant says the car needs two quarts of oil. The Lady accepts his judgment because it is too difficult to get out of the car in her tight skirt. The Slob gets out, looks under the hood at the oil gauge, sees the guy is exaggerating, and tells him one quart will do.

Both women arrive late at the parking lot of the railroad station. The Lady hurries, but her fitted skirt and high heels impede her progress. With mincing steps she tries to run around a guardrail between the parking lot and the tracks. Unfortunately, she misses the train.

The Slob (assuming she has the energy) is dressed in such a way that she can jump the rail, take the steps two at a time, run down the platform, and leap on the train at the last second.

The Lady has to wait 25 minutes for the next train. She has nothing to read because she couldn't fit a book or magazine in her purse (the one that matches her shoes). She doesn't sit down on the sooty bench because her coat would have to go right to the cleaners. She paces the platform studying the posters. Her feet are already beginning to hurt.

Meanwhile, the Slob is on her way to the city. She has taken a book out of her roomy coat pocket and is reading on the nearly empty train with her feet up on the opposite seat.

Once in town, they each go to a museum. The Slob checks her coat at the door. The Lady keeps hers. She is afraid the checkroom clerk might get confused and give it to someone else. Also, because of the short sleeves on her dress, the Lady is afraid of being cold. It turns out that the more distant galleries are, in fact, very hot. The Slob removes her sweater, ties it around her waist and rolls up her shirt sleeves. The Lady carries her coat on the same arm as her purse. By this time her feet really hurt.

Both women are hungry when they leave the museum. At a crowded little lunchroom nearby, the only available seats are at the counter. The Lady waits for a table; she's sure her coat will drag on the floor since there are no backrests on the stools. She won't hang her coat on a hook because it is inviting enough to steal since it has a mink collar, and besides the neckline has no hanging loop. Moreover, the counter has no place for her purse or the little box of notepaper she bought at the museum. The Slob hangs her duffel coat on a hook, pops her package in the pocket, and sits down at the counter right away. After eating, she digs some money out of her pants pocket, puts on her coat, and leaves. The Lady finally gets seated and has lunch (with her coat, gloves, purse, and package piled up across from her, taking up a seat). At the cashier's desk the Lady goes through a familiar juggling act with coat and package while searching through her purse. She finds the change and bills in separate compartments and pays the cashier while struggling to keep everything from tumbling to the floor.

It has begun to drizzle outside. The Lady is worried about her hair. To protect her $20 investment at the hairdresser's, she puts on an unattractive, uncomfortable plastic scarf. The Slob puts up the hood on her coat and shoves her hands in her pockets. The Lady takes care not to grip wet handles or banisters with her white gloves. The Slob sloshes through puddles that the Lady must walk around, and ties her shoe by putting her foot on a fireplug.

Each of them has to make a phone call. The Slob goes into the nearest place, a rather seedy-looking bar, uses the phone, and leaves, largely ignored. The Lady avoids the bar and walks until she finds a drugstore. The phone receiver pushes her earring off while she's phoning. She knocks her bag and gloves to the floor as she bends to retrieve the earring. She skips buying a candy bar she'd like because it might mess up her makeup and gloves.

Back on the street, the women reach a construction site where the sidewalk is torn up. The Lady crosses the street to avoid the mud. She looks down demurely to avoid the hardhats' comments. The Slob stops and watches the digging through a break in the fence. A few workers notice her and whistle. She grins and shakes her fist at them.

We can go on imagining endless situations of the same sort. But the point has been made: the Lady will usually find herself uncomfortable, embarrassed, or inconvenienced, physically and psychologically. The Slob is comfortable because her clothes are utilitarian. Her movement isn't restricted nor are her clothes fragile or easily soiled. Her shoes are sturdy and comfortable. Her pants allow her to move naturally. With lots of pockets for her belongings, her hands are left free. She wears a sweater or jacket which can be removed and has sleeves which she can roll up. Her coat pockets can accommodate larger objects. The coat is made of a durable fabric with a loop for hanging. Her hairstyle is simple and nonperishable.

To be sure, if the Slob went into Tiffany's, an opera house, or an elegant restaurant, she might feel out of place—or might even be denied entry. There are still places which demand that both men and women conform to standard dress. For men, the adjustment is a matter of style—trade a faded work shirt for a white dress shirt, change from a dungaree jacket and jeans to a suit. Only the necktie restricts. On the other hand, to look acceptable, it seems a woman must give up some of her physical and more of her psychological freedom. That's why women are (and must continue) demanding clothes that are practical and nonrestrictive. It should be possible to achieve personal style and freedom of movement and still look neat.

As an example, I have a pair of men's tennis shorts that by sheer luck fit me as well as any tennis gear made in women's sizes. They have two deep side pockets big enough to hold the second ball while serving. (This is a necessity if you use a two-handed backhand: witness poor Chris Evert at Wimbledon repeatedly dropping the second ball behind her when she got her first serve in.) No women's tennis clothes I have seen have deep side pockets—most have none. Women's ski pants also have no pockets. (Try to carry a purse on skis!) Pockets, then, are one essential for active women.

Long, full skirts might work almost as well as pants. They keep you cool and mobile and feeling graceful if you like that feeling. Frontier women managed in the mud by hiking them up. However, lifting long skirts to go upstairs can be a trial, especially if you're carrying something in both hands.

Whether based on trousers or the long skirt, women's clothes will require considerable rethinking. It may take some desk-pounding and consciousness-raising on Seventh Avenue and in the fashion magazine editorial offices to get designers to produce a range of comfortable, attractive clothes that truly liberated women can wear. It shouldn't be necessary to look like an advertisement for Sunny's Surplus Store to feel comfortable and competent. But the dictates of arbitrary *fashion* must be replaced by an individual aesthetic based on the real needs and desires of active women. Colors, fabrics, fit, and design can be handsome without hampering. I have heard that Margaret Bourke-White somewhat grandly commissioned Jacques Fath to design clothes for her that were suitable for photographing battles. They probably worked well and looked terrific.

Women aren't throwing their bras and girdles away because they want it all to hang out, but because most underclothes *hurt*. Our children sit on curbs and read on the floor because they are more interested in comfort than in keeping themselves presentable. They don't care if their blue jeans get dirty. In the same sense, the millions of women who now wear pants in public places are not captives of changing fashion—they simply want to feel at ease in their bodies and unhampered in their activities.

We can only pity the poor guys who have given up the conveniences of men's traditional clothes for tight, pocketless pants, fancy, perishable fabrics, high-heeled boots, and all the rest. They are becoming as stupid and slavish as we have been. The peacock may have a spectacular tail when it's fully spread but it's a hell of a burden to carry around just for a few moments of splendor.

CHAPTER 5

Apparel as an Economic Good

INTRODUCTION

Marianne S. Beeson

Economics involves the study and analysis of how people use their resources in order to maximize their welfare. Economics explains the process in which people engage in specialized production (a particular job, profession) so that they can obtain the goods and services they need and want through money as a medium of exchange.

Clothing is among the goods and services people need and want. When the individual enters the clothing market, he assays the numerous items offered for sale—the supply—what sellers are willing and able to sell. His purchasing decision in his demand—what he is willing and able to buy.

The factors affecting supply and demand for clothing are important determinants of what people wear. Consumers of clothing cannot buy what is not offered for sale regardless of wants or needs. Clothing retailers cannot sell items that consumers do not want or need, although they may attempt to manipulate tastes or create wants through advertising.

Fashion is defined as the style of clothing that large numbers of people are wearing at a given time and place. Fashion tends to influence tastes and preferences which in turn affect demand. Most people want to wear clothes that are at least somewhat within the range of prevailing fashion.

Fashion implies wastefulness because some items of clothing may be discarded when they are judged to be out of fashion, even though they are not worn out. Veblen, the controversial economist who wrote about dress at the turn of the century, described this aspect of fashion as the "principle of novelty," a corollary to his "principle of conspicuous waste." It is the desire of people to conform to fashion that is the major stimulus to the textiles and apparel industries. It is fashion change which causes people to want new clothes, even though they may already have a closet full.

James Laver offers the "theory of shifting erogenous zones" to explain the way women's fashions change. His theory is based on the idea that a primary function of clothes is to attract the opposite sex.

Those who are the first to adopt a new style are described as *fashion leaders*. They may be regarded as bold or daring at first, but if they are in the public eye, well-known or admired, others will follow, and a new style becomes a fashion. *High fashion* refers to new styles worn by wealthy fashion leaders who can afford these expensive designer clothes. The process by which high fashion becomes *mass fashion* is traditionally described in terms of the *trickle down theory*. In recent years this theory has not been an accurate explanation for many current fashions. In the previous chapter *Fashion from the Streets* states, "Fashion filters up, moreover, not merely from youth to age, but from lower economic class to upper."[1] In this chapter one article discusses new ways in which styles become mass fashions. "Who Killed High Fashion?" points out several conditions in society which are changing the patterns of fashion acceptance.

An article from *Family Economics Review* surveys business and consumer trends affecting textiles and apparel and provides the 1977 dollar value of per capita expenditures on clothing and shoes. In 1974 Virginia Britton wrote in the same government publication about the effects of oil and natural gas shortages on the textiles industry, an analysis that is repeated here since the oil situation is not yet stabilized.

A Shell Chemical manager was quoted in September 1973 as saying that the United States will be short of petrochemical products for years to come because of problems with feedstock supplies, fuel shortages, and construction, and because the prices of petrochemicals are bound to soar. A general energy shortage would affect all industries, and the textile industry is energy intensive. Furthermore, the textile-dyeing-and-finishing-plant operators need natural gas, propane, and heating oil as raw materials and say there is no point in the mills producing gray goods if finishing plants cannot operate. In addition, the shortage of petroleum as a raw material feedstock would affect clothing and textiles through curtailment of production of important manmade fibers for fabrics, threads, and zippers. Examples of such fibers are polyester (the major manmade fiber), arcylics, and nylon 66 (from products derived from coal, gas, and seawater). Cuts in petroleum feedstocks would affect plastics such as vinyl for shoe uppers and products for nonleather shoe soles, and synthetic rubber for footwear and foam for coats and furniture. Also of im-

1. Zalaznick, Sheldon, "Fashion from the Streets," p. 137.

portance to consumers of clothing and textiles are the uses of petroleum feedstocks for detergents and drycleaning fluids, as well as for fertilizers important in cotton production. [2]

In fact, shortages and therefore higher prices may be the most significant factors leading consumers to reject a fast pace of fashion change. *If* the U.S. is moving away from an economy of abundance, a "throw away" society—exemplified in the extreme by disposable paper dresses of the late 1960s—toward an economy of scarcity, then people may no longer be willing to discard clothing that is not worn out just because it is out of fashion. There are present signs that consumers are seeking high quality clothing, durable fabrics and construction, in classic styles that will last a long time. Ways to achieve economy in acquiring clothing are described in an article by Virginia Britton.

The marketing strategies involved in promotions for women's shoes and scent are subjects for two articles from a trade publication, *RetailWeek*. The same periodical offers the results of a survey of college men and women regarding their clothing preferences and shopping habits. The results of this survey may be compared to an earlier report on college students, "The Class of '74: The Way They Are." (See Additional Readings, Chapter 4, p. 92.)

The research report entitled "What Consumers of Fashion Want to Know" indicates what priorities consumers place on the various types of information available at the point of sale. The article on labeling of apparel and household textiles reviews the information required by law or other government regulation, as well as voluntary and promotional labeling.

If the desire for quality and durability in apparel becomes an established trend, then consumers *may* want to know more about the performance they can expect from comparable items as they make purchasing decisions. Performance labeling refers to information based on laboratory tests and wear studies as to how a particular fabric or garment will perform in actual use. How many launderings or dry cleanings it will withstand and technical information, such as abrasion resistance or tear strength, are examples of performance labeling. The standards specified under the Flammable Fabrics Act are a kind of performance labeling in a sense. Incidentally, the Flammable Fabrics Act is also an example of sumptuary legislation.

There is a great deal of useful information that can be offered to consumers to assist in the purchase, use, and care of clothing. The implications of an information program such as performance labeling are worthy of consideration from an economic point of view. Is the consumer

willing to pay a higher price to cover the cost of extensive testing and labeling? Should such a program be voluntary or mandatory, imposed by legislation and enforced by a government regulatory agency? If the latter alternative is preferred, is the taxpayer willing to pay additional taxes to support an elaborate government policing and record-keeping agency? Simply because of the time and cost required by the testing program, a degree of style standardization would be the result of performance labeling. This situation has already been observed in the case of the children's sleepwear standard under the Flammable Fabrics Act. Since every fabric, every color, every print design, and every garment style must be tested for flammability, the variety of styles and fabrics in children's sleepwear has been severely narrowed. Thus, the ultimate questions regarding desirability of additional information on labels relate to economics. Is the consumer willing and able to pay?

The effects of fashion demand on the environment and the role of government regulation in the area of ecology are represented by two articles, one reporting the fur trade situation and the other showing how fake fur fabrics can substitute for the skins of endangered species. There have been several examples in the history of fashion where popularity of certain furs, feathers, fibers, and hides has been a threat to the survival of the species. The use of egret feathers on ladies' hats, alligator and crocodile shoes and handbags, and Alaskan seal skin coats are just a few examples. It is also curious to observe cultural restrictions determining which dead animals are appropriate to wear in a fur coat, or even to eat. A recent article in a local newspaper reported the furor raised by a young South African's plan to raise pedigreed dogs for their skins and flesh.

Pollution is of course a major contributor to problems of ecology. The production of most man-made fibers and some textile dyeing and finishing operations can result in air and water pollution. Treatment of effluents and control of emissions, whether regulated by government or voluntary, involve costs which must be passed on to the consumer in the form of higher prices for clothing and other textile products. Current economic analysis of industrial pollution proposes that pollution is an example of externalization of costs of production, that is requiring people who do not necessarily buy a particular good to bear some of the costs of producing it. For example, having to paint a house frequently because the paint is damaged by air pollution is partially bearing the production costs of the polluting industry.

Other economic-related issues which ultimately affect supply and demand for clothing are not fully covered in the following selection of readings, but they are pertinent areas of investigation. The question of import quotas on textiles, leather, and the products made from these materials is a matter requiring the periodic attention of Con-

2. Britton, Virginia, "Clothing and Textiles: Supplies, Prices, and Outlook for 1974," *Family Economics Review,* Consumer and Food Economics Institute, Agricultural Research Service, U.S. Department of Agriculture, Spring, 1974, pp. 19–20.

gress, partly in response to lobbying by industry, which naturally favors such quotas. Conversely, pressures to legislate a ban on exports of some scarce U.S. raw materials, notably cotton, may make such a restriction a reality in the future.

The labor supply to textile and apparel industries, the movement toward more widespread unionization of labor, and working conditions within these industries are areas of concern. Absenteeism, boredom on the job, and lack of pride in workmanship are current labor problems faced by all industries in the U.S. based on assembly line and repetitive job assignments. The health of workers is also a consideration. Brown lung is a respiratory condition resulting from accumulation of cotton lint in the lungs, comparable to the miner's black lung. Industry has made astounding progress, however, in improving working conditions since the days of the sweat shops described in "The Song of the Shirt."

The selection entitled "A Democracy of Clothing" is a chapter in the book, *Suiting Everyone: The Democratization of Clothing in America.* This well-illustrated publication from the Smithsonian Institution surveys the development of clothing manufacture in America, a topic which was also the subject of a major Smithsonian exhibition in 1974.

The concluding article traces the flow of raw materials and intermediate products from textile and apparel producers to consumers. Textile and apparel producers play a significant role in industrial and agricultural sectors of the economy. Consumers of textiles and apparel support a diverse complex of farmers, ranchers, chemical firms, designers, mills, manufacturers, and retailers. While the trends are towards giantism, public ownership, and conglomorates, it is the nature of this fashion-oriented industry to foster the survival and success of small, family-owned firms as well.

Economics as a social science contributes another dimension to the understanding of clothing and adornment. Why people wear what they do is determined by economic factors along with all of the cultural, historical, and behavioral influences previously discussed. In the apparel market and upon opening the clothes closet, the cumulative impact of all of these influences is expressed in a *yes* or *no* decision on the part of the individual.

ADDITIONAL READINGS

On fashion and the structure of the textiles and apparel industries:

Anspach, Karlyne. *The Why of Fashion.* Ames, Iowa: The Iowa State Univ. Press, 1967.

Laver, James. *Modesty in Dress: An Inquiry into the Fundamentals of Fashion.* Boston: Houghton Mifflin, 1969.

American Textiles Manufacturers Ins[...] *Textiles.* Charlotte, N.C.: America[...] Institute, 1972.

Priestland, Carl. *Economic Profile o[...]* Arlington, Virginia: American App[...] sociation, 1976.

On marketing of clothing and accessories:

Bender, Marylin. "Why Your Clothes Cost So Much," *McCall's* Vol. 97, May 1970, pp. 94–95 and 136–137.
    Includes the role of union contracts, fabric prices, designer prestige, etc., in determining retail price.

Brady, James. "A Matter of Dollars and Scents," *Saturday Review,* September 30, 1978, pp. 54–56.
    James Brady is the former publisher of *Women's Wear Daily.*

On government regulation affecting the market:

Morrison, Margaret. "*Cosmetics: the Substances Beneath the Form.* HEW Publication No. (FDA) 78–5007. Washington, D.C.: U.S. Government Printing Office, 1978.
    Discusses regulations affecting sale of cosmetics, including ingredient labeling and warnings required on labels. Provides information on the composition of cleansing creams, lipsticks, eye makeup, and others.

Rinzler, Carol Ann. *Cosmetics: What the Ads Don't Tell You.* N.Y.: Thomas Y. Crowell Co., 1977.
    Emphasis on cosmetic ingredients, possible side effects, and possible alternatives.

Saltford, Nancy C., Daly, Patricia A. and Rushman, Gail A. "Clothing Care Labeling," *Journal of Home Economics,* Vol 7, January 1978, pp. 42–44.

Dean, Ailene and Dolan, Elizabeth M. "Clothing Flammability Alternatives," *Journal of Home Economics,* Vol. 70, January 1978, pp. 32–33.

Crippen, Kaye. "Tris on Trial," *Journal of Home Economics* Vol. 70, January 1978, pp. 29–31.
    The case of the banned fabric finish, Tris.

On energy and the environment:

Doughty, Robin W. *Feather Fashion and Bird Preservation: a Study in Nature Protection.* Berkeley: Univ. of California Press, 1975.
    Traces the use of feathers in fashion from the court of Marie Antoinette, the effects on bird populations, and the numerous conservationist and legislative battles regarding the plumage trade.

Butler, Sara L. "Textiles and Energy," *Journal of Home Economics,* Vol. 70, May 1978, pp. 44–45.

Polyzou, Annette. "Energy Consumption for Textiles and Apparel," *Family Economics Review,* U.S. Department of Agriculture, Spring, 1979, pp. 3–10.

vanWinkle, T.L., Edeleanu, J., Prosser, E.A., and Walker, C.A. "Cotton versus Polyester," *American Scientist,* Vol. 66, May 1978, pp. 280–290.
    An engineering analysis of the energy requirements for the production and maintenance of shirts from each of the two fibers.

DRESS AS AN EXPRESSION OF THE PECUNIARY CULTURE

Thorstein Veblen

It will be in place, by way of illustration, to show in some detail how the economic principles so far set forth apply to everyday facts in some one direction of the life process. For this purpose no line of consumption affords a more apt illustration than expenditure on dress. It is especially the rule of the conspicuous waste of goods that finds expression in dress, although the other, related principles of precuniary repute are also exemplified in the same contrivances. Other methods of putting one's pecuniary standing in evidence serve their end effectually, and other methods are in vogue always and everywhere; but expenditure on dress has this advantage over most other methods, that our apparel is always in evidence and affords an indication of our pecuniary standing to all observers at the first glance. It is also true that admitted expenditure for display is more obviously present, and is, perhaps, more universally practised in the matter of dress than in any other line of consumption. No one finds difficulty in assenting to the commonplace that the greater part of the expenditure incurred by all classes for apparel is incurred for the sake of a respectable appearance rather than for the protection of the person. And probably at no other point is the sense of shabbiness so keenly felt as it is if we fall short of the standard set by social usage in this matter of dress. It is true of dress in even a higher degree than of most other items of consumption, that people will undergo a very considerable degree of privation in the comforts or the necessaries of life in order to afford what is considered a decent amount of wasteful consumption; so that it is by no means an uncommon occurrence, in an inclement climate, for people to go ill clad in order to appear well dressed. And the commercial value of the goods used for clothing in any modern community is made up to a much larger extent of the fashionableness, the reputability of the goods than of the mechanical service which they render in clothing the person of the wearer. The need of dress is eminently a "higher" or spiritual need.

This spiritual need of dress is not wholly, nor even chiefly, a naive propensity for display of expenditure. The law of conspicuous waste guides consumption in apparel, as in other things, chiefly at the second remove, by shaping the canons of taste and decency. In the common run of cases the conscious motive of the wearer or purchaser of conspicuously wasteful apparel is the need of conforming to established usage, and of living up to the accredited standard of taste and reputability. It is not only that one must be guided by the code of proprieties in dress in order to avoid the mortification that comes of unfavourable notice and comment, though that motive in itself counts for a great deal; but besides that, the requirement of expen-

siveness is so ingrained into our habits of thought in matters of dress that any other than expensive apparel is instinctively odious to us. Without reflection or analysis, we feel that what is inexpensive is unworthy. "A cheap coat makes a cheap man." "Cheap and nasty" is recognised to hold true in dress with even less mitigation than in other lines of consumption. On the ground both of taste and of serviceability, an inexpensive article of apparel is held to be inferior, under the maxim "cheap and nasty." We find things beautiful, as well as serviceable, somewhat in proportion as they are costly. With few and inconsequential exceptions, we all find a costly hand-wrought article of apparel much preferable, in point of beauty and of serviceability, to a less expensive imitation of it, however cleverly the spurious article may imitate the costly original; and what offends our sensibilities in the spurious article is not that it falls short in form of colour, or, indeed, in visual effect in any way. The offensive object may be so close an imitation as to defy any but the closest scrutiny; and yet so soon as the counterfeit is detected, its aesthetic value, and its commercial value as well, declines precipitately. Not only that, but it may be asserted with but small risk of contradiction that the aesthetic value of a detected counterfeit in dress declines somewhat in the same proportion as the counterfeit is cheaper than its original. It loses caste aesthetically because it falls to a lower pecuniary grade.

But the function of dress as an evidence of ability to pay does not end with simply showing that the wearer consumes valuable goods in excess of what is required for physical comfort. Simple conspicuous waste of goods is effective and gratifying as far as it goes; it is good *prima facie* evidence of pecuniary success, and consequently *prima facie* evidence of social worth. But dress has subtler and more far-reaching possibilities than this crude, first-hand evidence of wasteful consumption only. If, in addition to showing that the wearer can afford to consume freely and uneconomically, it can also be shown in the same stroke that he or she is not under the necessity of earning a livelihood, the evidence of social worth is enhanced in a very considerable degree. Our dress, therefore, in order to serve its purpose effectually, should not only be expensive, but it should also make plain to all observers that the wearer is not engaged in any kind of productive labour. In the evolutionary process by which our system of dress has been elaborated into its present admirably perfect adaptation to its purpose, this subsidiary line of evidence has received due attention. A detailed exami-

From *The Theory of the Leisure Class: An Economic Study of Institutions* by Thorstein Veblen. N.Y.: The Macmillan Company, 1899, pp. 167–187.

nation of what passes in popular apprehension for elegant apparel will show that it is contrived at every point to convey the impression that the wearer does not habitually put forth any useful effort. It goes without saying that no apparel can be considered elegant, or even decent, if it shows the effect of manual labour on the part of the wearer, in the way of soil or wear. The pleasing effect of neat and spotless garments is chiefly, if not altogether, due to their carrying the suggestion of leisure—exemption from personal contact with industrial processes of any kind. Much of the charm that invests the patent-leather shoe, the stainless linen, the lustrous cylindrical hat, and the walking-stick, which so greatly enhance the native dignity of a gentleman, comes of their pointedly suggesting that the wearer cannot when so attired bear a hand in any employment that is directly and immediately of any human use. Elegant dress serves its purpose of elegance not only in that it is expensive, but also because it is the insignia of leisure. It not only shows that the wearer is able to consume a relatively large value, but it argues at the same time that he consumes without producing.

The dress of women goes even farther than that of men in the way of demonstrating the wearer's abstinence from productive employment. It needs no argument to enforce the generalisation that the more elegant styles of feminine bonnets go even farther towards making work impossible than does the man's high hat. The woman's shoe adds the so-called French heel to the evidence of enforced leisure afforded by its polish; because this high heel obviously makes any, even the simplest and most necessary manual work extremely difficult. The like is true even in a higher degree of the skirt and the rest of the drapery which characterises woman's dress. The substantial reason for our tenacious attachment to the skirt is just this: it is expensive and it hampers the wearer at every turn and incapacitates her for all useful exertion. The like is true of the feminine custom of wearing the hair excessively long.

But the woman's apparel not only goes beyond that of the modern man in the degree in which it argues exemption from labour; it also adds a peculiar and highly characteristic feature which differs in kind from anything habitually practised by the men. This feature is the class of contrivances of which the corset is the typical example. The corset is, in economic theory, substantially a mutilation, undergone for the purpose of lowering the subject's vitality and rendering her permanently and obviously unfit for work. It is true, the corset impairs the personal attractions of the wearer, but the loss suffered on that score is offset by the gain in reputability which comes of her visibly increased expensiveness and infirmity. It may broadly be set down that the womanliness of woman's apparel resolves itself, in point of substantial fact, into the more effective hindrance to useful exertion offered by the garments peculiar to women. This difference between masculine and feminine apparel is here simply pointed out as a characteristic feature. The ground of its occurrence will be discussed presently.

So far, then, we have, as the great and dominant norm of dress, the broad principle of conspicuous waste. Subsidiary to this principle, and as a corollary under it, we get as a second norm the principle of conspicuous leisure. In dress construction this norm works out in the shape of divers contrivances going to show that the wearer does not and, as far as it may conveniently be shown, can not engage in productive labour. Beyond these two principles there is a third of scarcely less constraining force, which will occur to any one who reflects at all on the subject. Dress must not only be conspicuously expensive and inconvenient; it must at the same time be up to date. No explanation at all satisfactory has hitherto been offered of the phenomenon of changing fashions. The imperative requirement of dressing in the latest accredited manner, as well as the fact that this accredited fashion constantly changes from season to season, is sufficiently familiar to every one, but the theory of this flux and change has not been worked out. We may of course say, with perfect consistency and truthfulness, that this principle of novelty is another corollary under the law of conspicuous waste. Obviously, if each garment is permitted to serve for but a brief term, and if none of last season's apparel is carried over and made further use of during the present season, the wasteful expenditure on dress is greatly increased. This is good as far as it goes, but it is negative only. Pretty much all that this consideration warrants us in saying is that the norm of conspicuous waste exercises a controlling surveillance in all matters of dress, so that any change in the fashions must conform to the requirement of wastefulness; it leaves unanswered the question as to the motive for making and accepting a change in the prevailing styles, and it also fails to explain why conformity to a given style at a given time is so imperatively necessary as we know it to be.

For a creative principle, capable of serving as motive to invention and innovation in fashions, we shall have to go back to the primitive, non-economic motive with which apparel originated,—the motive of adornment. Without going into an extended discussion of how and why this motive asserts itself under the guidance of the law of expensiveness, it may be stated broadly that each successive innovation in the fashions is an effort to reach some form of display which shall be more acceptable to our sense of form and colour or of effectiveness, than that which it displaces. The changing styles are the expression of a restless search for something which shall commend itself to our aesthetic sense; but as each innovation is subject to the selective action of the norm of conspicuous waste, the range within which innovation can take place is somewhat restricted. The innovation must not only be more beautiful, or perhaps oftener less offensive, than that which it displaces, but it must also come up to the accepted standard of expensiveness.

It would seem at first sight that the result of such an unremitting struggle to attain the beautiful in dress should be a gradual approach to artistic perfection. We might naturally expect that the fashions should show a well-marked trend in the direction of some one or more types of apparel eminently becoming to the human form; and we might even feel that we have substantial ground for the hope that today, after all the ingenuity and effort which have been spent on the dress these many years, the fashions should have achieved a relative perfection and a relative stability, closely approximating to a permanently tenable artistic ideal. But such is not the case. It would be very hazardous indeed to assert that the styles of today are intrinsically more becoming then those of ten years ago, or than those of twenty, or fifty, or one hundred years ago. On the other hand, the assertion freely goes uncontradicted that styles in vogue two thousand years ago are more becoming than the most elaborate and painstaking constructions of to-day.

The explanation of the fashions just offered, then, does not fully explain, and we shall have to look farther. It is well known that certain relatively stable styles and types of costume have been worked out in various parts of the world; as, for instance, among the Japanese, Chinese, and other Oriental nations; likewise among the Greeks, Romans, and other Eastern peoples of antiquity; so also, in later times, among the peasants of nearly every country of Europe. These national or popular costumes are in most cases adjudged by competent critics to be more becoming, more artistic, than the fluctuating styles of modern civilised apparel. At the same time they are also, at least usually, less obviously wasteful; that is to say, other elements than that of a display of expense are more readily detected in their structure.

These relatively stable costumes are, commonly, pretty strictly and narrowly localised, and they vary by slight and systematic gradations from place to place. They have in every case been worked out by peoples or classes which are poorer than we, and especially they belong in countries and localities and times where the population, or at least the class to which the costume in question belongs, is relatively homogeneous, stable, and immobile. That is to say, stable costumes which will bear the test of time and perspective are worked out under circumstances where the norm of conspicuous waste asserts itself less imperatively than it does in the large modern civilised cities, whose relatively mobile, wealthy population to-day sets the pace in matters of fashion. The countries and classes which have in this way worked out stable and artistic costumes have been so placed that the pecuniary emulation among them has taken the direction of a competition in conspic-

uous leisure rather than in conspicuous consumption of goods. So that it will hold true in a general way that fashions are least stable and least becoming in those communities where the principle of a conspicuous waste of goods asserts itself most imperatively, as among ourselves. All this points to an antagonism between expensiveness and artistic apparel. In point of practical fact, the norm of conspicuous waste is incompatible with the requirement that dress should be beautiful or becoming. And this antagonism offers an explanation of that restless change in fashion which neither the canon of expensiveness nor that of beauty alone can account for.

The standard of reputability requires that dress should show wasteful expenditure; but all wastefulness is offensive to native taste. The psychological law has already been pointed out that all men—and women perhaps even in a higher degree—abhor futility, whether of effort or of expenditure,—much as Nature was once said to abhor a vacuum. But the principle of conspicuous waste requires an obviously futile expenditure; and the resulting conspicuous expensiveness of dress is therefore intrinsically ugly. Hence we find that in all innovations in dress, each added or altered detail strives to avoid instant condemnation by showing some ostensible purpose, at the same time that the requirement of conspicuous waste prevents the purposefulness of these innovations from becoming anything more than a somewhat transparent pretense. Even in its freest flights, fashion rarely if ever gets away from a simulation of some ostensible use. The ostensible usefulness of the fashionable details of dress, however, is always so transparent a make-believe, and their substantial futility presently forces itself so baldly upon our attention as to become unbearable, and then we take refuge in a new style. But the new style must conform to the requirement of reputable wastefulness and futility. Its futility presently becomes as odious as that of its predecessor; and the only remedy which the law of waste allows us is to seek relief in some new construction, equally futile and equally untenable. Hence the essential ugliness and the unceasing change of fashionable attire.

Having so explained the phenomenon of shifting fashions, the next thing is to make the explanation tally with everyday facts. Among these everyday facts is the well-known liking which all men have for the styles that are in vogue at any given time. A new style comes into vogue and remains in favour for a season, and, at least so long as it is a novelty, people very generally find the new style attractive. The prevailing fashion is felt to be beautiful. This is due partly to the relief it affords in being different from what went before it, partly to its being reputable. As indicated in the last chapter, the canon of reputability to some extent shapes our tastes, so that under its guidance anything will be accepted as becoming until its novelty wears off, or until the warrant of reputability is transferred to a new and novel structure serving the same general purpose. That the alleged beauty, or "loveliness," of the styles in vogue at any given time is transient and spurious only is attested by the fact that none of the many shifting fashions will bear the test of time. When seen in the perspective of half-a-dozen years or more, the best of our fashion strike us as grotesque, if not unsightly. Our transient attachment to whatever happens to be the latest rests on other than aesthetic grounds, and lasts only until our abiding aesthetic sense has had time to assert itself and reject this latest indigestible contrivance.*

The process of developing an aesthetic nausea takes more or less time; the length of time required in any given case being inversely as the degree of intrinsic odiousness of the style in question. This time relation between odiousness and instability in fashions affords ground for the inference that the more rapidly the styles succeed and displace one another, the more offensive they are to sound taste. The presumption, therefore, is that the farther the community, especially the wealthy classes of the community, develop in wealth and mobility and in the range of their human contact, the more imperatively will the law of conspicuous waste assert itself in matters of dress, the more will the sense of beauty tend to fall into abeyance or be overborne by the canon of pecuniary reputability, the more rapidly will fashions shift and change, and the more grotesque and intolerable will be the varying styles that successively come into vogue.

There remains at least one point in this theory of dress yet to be discussed. Most of what has been said applies to men's attire as well as to that of women; although in modern times it applies at nearly all points with greater force to that of women. But at one point the dress of women differs substantially from that of men. In women's dress there is an obviously greater insistence on such features as testify to the wearer's exemption from or incapacity for all vulgarly productive employment. This characteristic of woman's apparel is of interest, not only as completing the theory of dress, but also as confirming what has already been said of the economic status of women, both in the past and in the present.

As has been seen in the discussion of woman's status under the heads of Vicarious Leisure and Vicarious Consumption, it has in the course of economic development become the office of the woman to consume vacariously for the head of the household; and her apparel is contrived with this object in view. It has come about that obviously productive labour is in a peculiar degree derogatory to respectable women, and therefore special pains should be taken in the construction of women's dress, to impress upon the beholder the fact (often indeed a fiction) that the wearer does not and can not habitually engage in useful work. Propriety requires respectable women to abstain more consistently from useful effort and to make

*See Laver's "Law of Fashion," p. 144 in "Why You Wear What You Do."

more of a show of leisure than the men of the same social classes. It grates painfully on our nerves to contemplate the necessity of any well-bred woman's earning a livelihood by useful work. It is not "woman's sphere." Her sphere is within the household, which she should "beautify," and of which she should be the "chief ornament." The male head of the household is not currently spoken of as its ornament. This feature taken in conjunction with the other fact that propriety requires more unremitting attention to expensive display in the dress and other paraphernalia of women, goes to enforce the view already implied in what has gone before. By virtue of its descent from patriarchal past, our social system makes it the woman's function in an especial degree to put in evidence her household's ability to pay. According to the modern civilised scheme of life, the good name of the household to which she belongs should be the special care of the woman; and the system of honorific expenditure and conspicuous leisure by which this good name is chiefly sustained is therefore the woman's sphere. In the ideal scheme, as it tends to realise itself in the life of the higher pecuniary classes, this attention to conspicuous waste of substance and effort should normally be the sole economic function of the woman.

At the stage of economic development at which the women were still in the full sense the property of the men, the performance of conspicuous leisure and consumption came to be part of the services required of them. The women being not their own masters, obvious expenditure and leisure on their part would redound to the credit of their master rather than to their own credit; and therefore the more expensive and the more obviously unproductive the women of the household are, the more creditable and more effective for the purpose of the reputability of the household or its head will their life be. So much so that the women have been required not only to afford evidence of a life of leisure, but even to disable themselves for useful activity.

It is at this point that the dress of men falls short of that of women, and for a sufficient reason. Conspicuous waste and conspicuous leisure are reputable because they are evidence of pecuniary strength; pecuniary strength is reputable or honorific because, in the last analysis, it argues success and superior force; therefore the evidence of waste and leisure put forth by any individual in his own behalf cannot consistently take such a form or be carried to such a pitch as to argue incapacity or marked discomfort on his part; as the exhibition would in that case show not superior force, but inferiority, and so defeat its own purpose. So, then, wherever wasteful expenditure and the show of abstention from effort is normally, or on an average, carried to the extent of showing obvious discomfort or voluntarily induced physical disability, there the immediate inference is that the individual in question does not perform this wasteful expenditure and undergo this disability for her own personal gain in pecuniary repute, but in behalf of some one else to whom she stands in a relation of economic dependence; a relation which in the last analysis must, in economic theory, reduce itself to a relation of servitude.

To apply this generalisation to women's dress, and put the matter in concrete terms: the high heel, the skirt, the impracticable bonnet, the corset, and the general disregard of the wearer's comfort which is an obvious feature of all civilised women's apparel, are so many items of evidence to the effect that in the modern civilised scheme of life the woman is still, in theory, the economic dependent of the man—that, perhaps in a highly idealised sense, she still is the man's chattel. The homely reason for all this conspicuous leisure and attire on the part of women lies in the fact that they are servants to whom, in the differentiation of economic functions, has been delegated the office of putting in evidence their master's ability to pay.

There is a marked similarity in these respects between the apparel of women and that of domestic servants, especially liveried servants. In both there is a very elaborate show of unnecessary expensiveness, and in both cases there is also a notable disregard of the physical comfort of the wearer. But the attire of the lady goes farther in its elaborate insistence on the idleness, if not on the physical infirmity of the wearer, than does that of the domestic. And this is as it should be; for in theory, according to the ideal scheme of the pecuniary culture, the lady of the house is the chief menial of the household.

Besides servants, currently recognised as such, there is at least one other class of persons whose garb assimilates them to the class of servants and shows many of the features that go to make up the womanliness of woman's dress. This is the priestly class. Priestly vestments* show, in accentuated form, all the features that have been shown to be evidence of a servile status and a vicarious life. Even more strikingly than the everyday habit of the priest, the vestments, properly so called, are ornate, grotesque, inconvenient, and, at least ostensibly, comfortless to the point of distress. The priest is at the same time expected to refrain from useful effort and, when before the public eye, to present an impassively disconsolate countenance, very much after the manner of a well-trained domestic servant. The shaven face of the priest is a further item to the same effect. This assimilation of the priestly class to the class of body servants, in demeanour and apparel, is due to the similarity of the two classes as regards economic function. In economic theory, the priest is a body servant, constructively in attendance upon the person of the divinity whose livery he wears. His livery is of a very expensive character, as it should be in order to set forth in a beseeming manner the dignity of his exalted master;

*See "Ecclesiastical Vestments in the Modern Church," pp. 51–52.

but it is contrived to show that the wearing of it contributes little or nothing to the physical comfort of the wearer, for it is an item of vicarious consumption, and the repute which accrues from its consumption is to be imputed to the absent master, not to the servant.

The line of demarcation between the dress of women, priests, and servants, on the one hand, and of men, on the other hand, is not always consistently observed in practice, but it will scarcely be disputed that it is always present in a more or less definite way in the popular habits of thought. There are of course also free men, and not a few of them, who, in their blind zeal for faultlessly reputable attire, transgress the theoretical line between man's and woman's dress, to the extent of arraying themselves in apparel that is obviously designed to vex the mortal frame; but every one recognises without hesitation that such apparel for men is a departure from the normal. We are in the habit of saying that such dress is "effeminate"; and one sometimes hears the remark that such or such an exquisitely attired gentleman is as well dressed as a footman.

Certain apparent discrepancies under this theory of dress merit a more detailed examination, especially as they mark a more or less evident trend in the later and maturer development of dress. The vogue of the corset offers an apparent exception from the rule of which it has here been cited as an illustration. A closer examination, however, will show that this apparent exception is really a verification of the rule that the vogue of any given element or feature in dress rests on its utility as an evidence of pecuniary standing. It is well known that in the industrially more advanced communities the corset is employed only within certain fairly well defined social strata. The women of the poorer classes, especially of the rural population, do not habitually use it, except as a holiday luxury. Among these classes the women have to work hard, and it avails them little in the way of a pretense of leisure to so crucify the flesh in everyday life. The holiday use of the contrivance is due to imitation of a higher-class canon of decency. Upwards from this low level of indigence and manual labour, the corset was until within a generation or two nearly indispensable to a socially blameless standing for all women, including the wealthiest and most reputable. This rule held so long as there still was no large class of people wealthy enough to be above the imputation of any necessity for manual labour and at the same time large enough to form a self-sufficient, isolated social body whose mass would afford a foundation for special rules of conduct within the class, enforced by the current opinion of the class alone. But now there has grown up a large enough leisure class possessed of such wealth that any aspersion on the score of enforced manual employment would be idle and harmless calumny; and the corset has therefore in large measure fallen into disuse within this class.

The exceptions under this rule of exemption from the corset are more apparent than real. They are the wealthy classes of countries with a lower industrial structure—nearer the archaic, quasi-industrial type—together with the later accessions of the wealthy classes in the more advanced industrial communities. The latter have not yet had time to divest themselves of the plebeian canons of taste and of reputability carried over from their former, lower pecuniary grade. Such survival of the corset is not infrequent among the higher social classes of those American cities, for instance, which have recently and rapidly risen into opulence. If the word be used as a technical term, without any odious implication, it may be said that the corset persists in great measure through the period of snobbery—the interval of uncertainty and of transition from a lower to the upper levels of pecuniary culture. That is to say, in all countries which have inherited the corset it continues in use wherever and so long as it serves its purpose as an evidence of honorific leisure by arguing physical disability in the wearer. The same rule of course applies to other mutilations and contrivances for decreasing the visible efficiency of the individual.

Something similar should hold true with respect to divers items of conspicuous consumption, and indeed something of the kind does seem to hold to a slight degree of sundry features of dress, especially if such features involve a marked discomfort or appearance of discomfort to the wearer. During the past one hundred years there is a tendency perceptible, in the development of men's dress especially, to discontinue methods of expenditure and the use of symbols of leisure which must have been irksome, which may have served a good purpose in their time, but the continuation of which among the upper classes to-day would be a work of supererogation; as, for instance, the use of powdered wigs and of gold lace, and the practice of constantly shaving the face. There has of late years been some slight recrudescence of the shaven face in polite society, but this is probably a transient and unadvised mimicry of the fashion imposed upon body servants, and it may fairly be expected to go the way of the powdered wig of our grandfathers.

These indices, and others which resemble them in point of the boldness with which they point out to all observers the habitual uselessness of those persons who employ them, have been replaced by other, more delicate methods of expressing the same fact; methods which are no less evident to the trained eyes of that smaller, select circle whose good opinion is chiefly sought. The earlier and cruder method of advertisement held its ground so long as the public to which the exhibitor had to appeal comprised large portions of the community who were not trained to detect delicate variations in the evidences of wealth and leisure. The method of advertisement undergoes a refinement when a sufficiently large wealthy class has developed, who have the leisure for acquiring skill in interpreting the subtler signs of expenditure. "Loud" dress becomes offensive to people of taste, as evincing an undue desire to reach and impress the untrained sensibilities of the vulgar. To the individual of high breeding it is only the more honorific esteem accorded by the cultivated sense of the members of his own high class that is of material consequence. Since the wealthy leisure class has grown so large, or the contract of the leisure-class individual with members of his own class has grown so wide, as to constitute a human environment sufficient for the honorific purpose, there arises a tendency to exclude the baser elements of the population from the scheme even as spectators whose applause or mortification should be sought. The result of all this is a refinement of methods, a resort to subtler contrivances, and a spiritualisation of the scheme of symbolism in dress. And as this upper leisure class sets the pace in all matters of decency, the result for the rest of society also is a gradual amelioration of the scheme of dress. As the community advances in wealth and culture, the ability to pay is put in evidence by means which require a progressively nicer discrimination in the beholder. This nicer discrimination between advertising media is in fact a very large element of the higher pecuniary culture.

WHAT WILL FASHION UNCOVER NEXT?

James Laver

The history of women's dress: a running battle between "shifting erogenous zones" and prudery.

Toplessness—that is, the exposure of the breasts in public—has recently made several attempts to become accepted. But in every case (except perhaps in Sweden, where topless bathing suits have long been allowed on the beaches; and in a variety of California restaurants, where topless waitresses have gained a degree of publicity) it has been cracked down on by the police.

As condensed in the September 1965 *Reader's Digest,* pp. 142–145. Reprinted by permission of the publisher and David Higham Associates, Ltd. for the author.

Yet toplessness has been considered fashionable several times in history, notably at the Court of King Charles II in England and during the Directoire period in France. These two epochs are therefore labeled in the history books as immoral. Yet why should one part of the female body be more "immoral" than any other?

Fashion is essentially a game of hide-and-seek. It requires two players, prudery and style, and the game has been going on for a long time. Psychologists, who have been slow in grappling with this problem, have come forward with an explanation. They call it "the theory of the shifting erogenous zone."

The theory amounts to this: Woman as a whole is a desirable object, but man cannot take all of her in at once. He is therefore compelled to concentrate upon one particular bit of the female body. It is the object of fashion to draw attention to one bit at a time, to emphasize it in every possible way—by exposing it, or drawing the clothes tightly around it, or exaggerating its size.

Once a particular emphasis has been established, no woman feels well dressed without accepting it. In 1860, a woman who was not wearing a crinoline felt slightly indecent. The same was true of the exaggerated posterior of the bustle epoch and the flat chest of the 1920's. Today a woman whose skirts are too long feels out of place. But, after a short time, this excessive concentration on an area brings its own penalty. The portion of the body in question becomes too familiar; it becomes a bore; or, as the psychologists say, it "exhausts its erotic capital." Now the emphasis changes, the zone shifts. The new zone always seems a little indecent at first. But the emotional impact is the real reason for the change.

Occasionally there comes a time when the "zone shift" game seems to be played out, when women cover themselves up completely. We then speak of a period of prudery. But it is never quite as prudish as it pretends to be, and it never lasts long.

The shifting-zone theory does a great deal to explain the vagaries of fashion. Nowadays we take fashion for granted, and see nothing strange in women changing their styles, even their shape, every few years. Yet fashion, in our sense, hasn't always existed. In ancient Greece there was nothing recognizable as fashion. And from the fall of the Roman Empire to the middle of the 14th century, styles changed hardly at all.

Then, suddenly, in the luxurious courts of France and Burgundy, attractive women began to compete for the attention of the King or Duke by inventing, or having invented for them, the three most potent weapons in fashion's armory: tightlacing, decolletage and funny hats—or rather headdresses with elaborate veils, no longer hiding the hair and face but rising triumphantly in horns, crescents and steeples.

Of course, these developments were received with disapproval by the moralists of the period. Preachers pictured the torments of hell of those who in life had worn "immodest" clothing—that is, any "fashionable" garment. The later Puritans, both in England and America, were equally vehement. Any clothes that were more (or less) than protection against the weather were condemned. Did they not promote the lust of the eye? Of course they did. That was their object.

So fashion and prudery began the fencing match that has lasted to this day.

Most of the 15th century was, in Western Europe, a period of considerable erotic emphasis, notable for pinched-in waists and low-cut bodices. By contrast, the clothes of women in the Early Tudor period seem almost prudish. Then, a few years later, a change back: Queen Elizabeth I was extremely décolletée all her life, and the fashion persisted into the next century.

In the middle of the 17th century, the Puritan domination both in England and America brought in a more modest style of dress. But with the Restoration of Charles II, modesty was thrown to the winds. The Lely portraits at Hampton Court show us a series of "Court beauties" who certainly wear their clothes in no prudish spirit.

Curiously enough, the 18th century was prudish about shoulders. The corsage might be cut very low, but no respectable woman ever appeared in public with the point of the shoulder exposed. The period following the French Revolution had entirely different notions. Clothes were now light and flimsy. The legs, which had been hidden for so long, became discernible beneath the often semitransparent gown. And it was no longer the "cleavage" of the bosom that was visible but its rounded forms above the high, ribbon-encircled waist.

Fashion worked by suggestion in the late 19th and early 20th centuries. Skirts trailed so long that they had to be lifted when a woman walked—thus revealing a froth of frilly lace petticoats. This was a period when the suggestion of underclothes was deliberately exploited. The exploitation can be seen in its extreme form in the Toulouse-Lautrec can-can dancers.

A certain décolletage in evening dress was considered fashionable, but at other times of day the corsage was extremely proper, a neckline up to the ears being deemed essential. It is amusing to note that when this was abandoned, the so-called V-neck which resulted was denounced from the pulpit as immoral and by medical men as likely to lead to pneumonia!

All this, however, was nothing compared with the horror evoked by the postwar styles of the 1920's. Women were showing their legs! That shook contemporary moralists. Even the most "immoral" periods of the past had been content with the glimpse of an ankle.

Yet the '20's were curiously prudish about one thing: the bosom. The U.S. film censors were particularly disturbed about what they called "cleavage." It was the suggestion of duality that mattered. The "bosom" of the flapper was *one.*

If the movies had been invented a generation or so earlier, censors wouldn't have bothered about cleavage. But they would have banned immediately any film that drew attention to the female leg, which was considered highly stimulating. And of course, at the time, it *was,* for legs had been concealed for a long while and had thus accumulated considerable "erotic capital."

By the end of the '20's, legs had become a bore, however, and the emphasis shifted again, this time to the back. Evening dresses and even some daytime ones were open to the waist in back, and they stayed that way almost to the outbreak of World War II.

During the last few years there has been a deliberate return to the modes of the '20's and a new emphasis on legs. But it is possible that legs have overshot the mark. If skirts rise too far above the knee and tights are worn underneath, the effect of exposure will be lost; then the erotic emphasis will have to shift to something else.

What "something else"? If fashion progresses from copying the 1920's to aping the 1930's, attention may be switched from legs to back: no dress at all down to the waist, and the material drawn tightly over the posterior. A few years ago, there was a shift to bare midriffs, even involving exposure of the navel. And recently fashion designers have attracted attention with the "fish-net" look, which is perhaps an attempt at a kind of compromise toplessness.

As a historian, however, I am compelled to admit that the whims of fashion are never completely predictable. Who knows what it may cover—or uncover—next?

WHO KILLED HIGH FASHION?

Patricia Bosworth

"In 1959, Diana Vreeland declared the color next year would be billiard green. She wanted color samples, so I gave them to her . . . billiard green, blue green, and so on, but when she saw them, she said, 'No, no billiard green. I want billiard green of the mind.' And I said 'Oh, you mean grass green, Diana.' She smiled, 'Darling, I knew you'd understand.' And the following year everything in fashion was grass green. That's how much Vreeland could influence fashion."—Henry Wolff, Art Director/Photographer

It is fitting, perhaps, that I find Diana Vreeland in a museum. There she sits, the most splendid fashion dictator who ever lived, the former editor of *Vogue,* the woman who invented the phrase "beautiful people," the word "pizzazz," who discovered Twiggy, Suzy Parker, Penelope Tree, vinyl hairpieces; there she sits, smearing lipstick on her mouth and gulping down Mountain Valley water in her blood-red office at the Metropolitan Museum of Art, right under the Egyptian mummies. The mummies make her sneeze, but it doesn't matter. She's too busy talking about the three-month Balenciaga retrospective which she's about to organize for the Museum's Costume Institute.

"Cristobal Balenciaga was the Picasso of high fashion," she roars, between sneezes. "He was elegance personified."

I remind Mrs. Vreeland why I'm here . . . that the notion that women's high fashion is now an anachronism; that its status today is like that of the Broadway theatre. The life, the energy has gone.

She snorts. "Nothing ever dies. Not the threatre or trompe l'oeil, certainly not high fashion. High fashion will always be alive as long as certain ladies can afford to pay the price for couture clothes."

But her words betray her. Because as soon as she begins to speak of great humming workrooms, of artisans bent over their thimbles making linings one never sees, her tense inadvertently shifts into the past.

Her words recall the days when women still lunched at The Colony before spending all afternoon trying on hats at Bergdorf's. When ladies had casts made of their hands so their gloves would fit just so. When they changed clothes four times a day (for lunch, tea, dinner and dancing).

This way of life, which became associated with the term high fashion, started in the 1850's when Englishman Charles Worth began designing exquisite crinoline skirts for the Czarina of Russia. Before that, dressmakers had just followed their customers' instructions. But after that, brilliant innovators dictated fashion trends.

Even for people who did not take it seriously, this world of high fashion was synonymous with old-world perfections. And as long as such a tradition of high-priced couture excellence continued to thrive, the rich seemed happy to be rich and an intangible center in society was tremblingly preserved. There was, after all, a kind of honesty to it. Fashion sensualists understood luxury. They believed that real luxury was never vulgar . . . that luxury, fully enjoyed (like the arrogant extravagance of fur inside the hem of a coat), could provide genuine fulfillment.

Jacqueline Kennedy, of course, Americanized high fashion. Although she had a passion for Givenchy she wore only American clothes while she was First Lady.

What made them distinguished was that she accessorized her Geoffrey Beenes and Oleg Cassinis as if they were haute couture. The resulting look was elegant simplicity, which the public copied en masse, right down to her snub-nosed Vivier pumps. Millions of heretofore dowdy American women became conscious of style and taste for the first time.

But now look at what has happened. A little more than a decade later, Mrs. Kennedy, now Mrs. Onassis, organized an impromptu party at El Morocco to celebrate her fourth wedding anniversary to Ari. Nobody commented on her attire for the evening, a sweater and skirt.

Today, I think, women no longer care about Mrs. Onassis' wardrobe. . . high fashion or otherwise. Bergdorf's custom millinery salon is closed and the name Patou has long since been more famous for perfume than dresses.

Even Mrs. William Paley, one of the most fashionable women in the world, no longer buys $4,000 Givenchy originals or changes her jewels for each outfit. She buys see-through caftans and she pays $750 tops.

"You smoke a joint," a rich young Barnard student told me, "and you don't give a damn how you *look*. It's how you *feel* that counts."

I am walking through Manhattan's West Side garment district with Mayor Lindsay and a crowd of reporters and dress manufacturers. I am supposed to be helping kick off New York Fashion Week but I am actually on Seventh Ave. with another purpose in mind. Because I'm almost convinced that Diana Vreeland is wrong. I still suspect high fashion is indeed dead and I have set out to discover whether that's true, and if it is, who or what did the killing.

The top European couturiers are entering American ready-to-wear in order to survive. Now it's American ready-to-wear designers like Bill Blass who are the trend setters and American clothing dominates the world market by virtue of its diversity and relative cheapness.

Are American designers then responsible for the death of French haute couture, of high fashion?

Pauline Trigère

I decided to ask some people I know who have influence in the fashion world . . . so, I visit Pauline Trigere. She has just finished pinning up a dress for Amy Vanderbilt; to relax she is polishing her collection of jeweled turtle pins. She is glad to give me her definition of high fashion: "Elegant, very expensive clothes in luxurious fabrics that require *numerous* fittings nobody has time for anymore. That's why high fashion died. No time. Everybody wants to save time. Now we're lucky if a customer changes an outfit once a week!"

Who specifically killed high fashion?

"You wanna get me in beeg trouble, darling?" she asked in her thick French accent. "I can't put the blame on one person. In the last ten years we've had the pop look, the mod look, the hippie look, the ethnic look. Then came the midi disaster and the public became totally confused. Particularly since we don't have any fashion leaders. Not since Jacqueline Kennedy. There is nobody. In the Sixties, at least until the middle Sixties, there was always Jackie Kennedy's look to fall back on."

Vogue/Bazaar

What intrigues me is the current position of *Vogue* and *Harper's Bazaar*. Their economic state is certainly connected with the death of high fashion; in fact their arrogant editorial policies have undoubtedly helped high fashion die.

Ten years ago these two competing high-fashion bibles were rich with ads, and subscribers worshiped at the Paris couturiers' altars. Ripe copy ("will you wear a star in your hair at night? . . . or a black veiling hat?" . . . *Vogue* circa 1950) appealed to ladies of leisure. When *Bazaar* shattered taboos by running Avedon's nude photograph of socialite Christiana Paolozzi, editor Nancy White explained, "The *Bazaar* caters to our readers' off-beat taste."

Obviously *Vogue* and *Bazaar* no longer serve a function, but are they responsible for the death of high fashion? I decide to pursue the subject. In subsequent days I phone a friend of mine at *Vogue*. She agrees to see me if I give her total anonymity. We meet in a dimly lit Japanese restaurant. It's so dark I can hardly make out her emaciated turbaned figure. Did the high-fashion magazines help kill high fashion? I ask.

"Oh darling," she breathes, "of course. We humiliated women into diets and grotesque fads. 'Put peacock feathers on your eyelids,' 'stencil your body like a leopard and you'll get a man.' Sure you will." She leans forward. "The high-fashion magazines helped kill high fashion by pushing *extreme* clothes instead of classic useful ones. The midi was the last straw."

I repeat this to an art director I know. He tells me not to believe everything I hear. "I don't know why she didn't bring up the *real* reason high fashion is dead," he goes on. "We're existing in urban warfare here in New York. And in Dallas, San Francisco, L.A. and Chicago too. Nobody goes out at night anymore because they're afraid of being mugged or robbed. There's no place to wear high fashion *to*."

He then gives me James Laver's* *Modesty In Dress*. One passage is clipped. It's called "Shifting Erogenous Zone." "This is the entire basis for high-fashion styles," he has noted.

According to Laver, each fashion theme concentrates on various parts of the female body . . . breasts, waist,

*See "What Will Fashion Uncover Next?" pp. 159–161.

hips, buttocks, legs, arms. Organs "appear" and "disappear" as the theme of fashion changes. One or another part of the body is emphasized by a particular style (last season it was the back). Breasts and legs are opposites. If in one season a neckline plunges, in the next season breasts will be covered, etc.

I phone Mary Peacock, an editor of the feminist magazine *Ms.* Are there any erogenous zones left in fashion as far as you're concerned?

"Sure," she laughs. "Our heads. Our whole selves. High fashion is dead because women don't need to use clothes for seduction purposes anymore. Clothes are simple now, more utilitarian. We wear clothes that are comfortable . . . that we can move around in. Slacks, sweaters. Clothes serve no artificial purposes."

But don't you think men miss seeing women in "feminine clothes?"

"We may have *looked* feminine but we were extremely uncomfortable. I sure don't miss struggling into a girdle and a too-tight skirt. I always had a stomachache."

Blair Sabol

Around the third week of my search I come up with an important theory as to *what* killed high fashion. I hear about it from Blair Sabol, fashion critic of *The Village Voice.* She calls her theory "fashion fascism" and she's alluded to it often in her column which has also branded certain designers as copyists and put-on artists.

The afternoon I visit her, Blair is packing to go off to Acapulco. She is a big rawboned woman with a Jewish Afro and an appealing lisp. Throughout our conversation she munches on poppy seeds.

"High fashion is dead," she tells me, "because the public got sick and tired of being dictated to."

"1970 was the year high fashion really fell on its ass. The big fashion fascists like Saint Laurent, John Fairchild of *Women's Wear* and certain big American manufacturers decided the mini must go. Don't forget the mini was the Sixties' f_____ you costume to the Establishment. The mini used just a tiny bit of material, no? And you couldn't wear a hat with a mini or gloves so those industries were dying. Even the shoe biz was in trouble. The rag trade definitely needed a shot in the arm.

"As soon as Paris created the midi in January, 1970," she goes on, "designers and manufacturers got on the bandwagon and not since Dior's New Look has a descending hemline raised such a furor. While Seventh Ave. was busily producing the midi and *Women's Wear* was pushing it every day on the front page the public was decrying the midi. Protest groups were forming, like G.A.M.S. (Girls/Guys Against More Skirts).

"Enormous fashion confusion ensued. The public refused to buy the ugly midcalf length and store owners all over the country were left with hundreds of midis unsold on the racks.

"And in spite of the enormous fake buildup by the fashion press . . . *Vogue, Bazaar,* and in particular *Women's Wear Daily* . . . the midi was just not purchased, except by women with fat legs.

"It was a ludicrous scene," Blair recalls. "I was writing for *Rags* at the time . . . the underground fashion magazine. We did an article about The Great Midi Conspiracy. The piece got a lot of reaction. We had reporters go into stores in Chicago and New York. They found out that salesgirls in places like Bonwit's had to go to educational meetings on the midi. They couldn't wear anything but midis on the job and they were forbidden to speak out against the midi if customers asked them.

"After that women stopped reading *Vogue* and *Bazaar* like they were bibles. They weren't into fantasy trips either. They were getting into their own heads. There's a direct connection between the midi debacle, the death of high fashion and the women's movement I think. I don't think John Fairchild or *Women's Wear* is totally to blame for the death of high fashion. Because the death of high fashion is really the death of unnecessary consumption. Of extravagant consumption."

John Fairchild

When I mention the midi crisis to Fairchild, the publisher of *Women's Wear,* he bleats, "Stop blaming me! Paris created the midi. We just reported on it. That's all we did. And if we happened to influence manufacturers and store owners it wasn't the newspaper's fault. All fashion operates in a circle. There are no new patterns or silhouettes. Women were ready to change from the mini to the midi. They'd gotten bored with the mini baby look. I refuse to be blamed for something that should be blamed on the 1970 recession. In the Fifties and Sixties women had orgasms when they tried on high-fashion dresses. Now the entire world is b-o-r-e-d with fashion. And the only fashion worth looking at is on the street.* Whatever *that* means.

"Kids are the purveyors of fashion today. Look at the popularity of jeans."

He begins to pout fiercely. "If I had to blame anybody for the manipulation of the fashion industry, which I suppose has something to do with the death of high fashion, I'd blame Eleanor Lambert. She has tried to get complete control of the fashion press in this country and she's succeeded . . . with the exception of *W.W.D.* and the New York *Times.* I feel sorry for Eleanor Lambert. She has a terrible lust for power."

---

*See "Fashion from the Streets," pp. 137–138.

Eleanor Lambert

Eleanor Lambert? She'd been a friend of my family's. I remember her as a tiny sixtyish blonde who always wore red shoes. She'd wanted to be a sculptress . . . had come to New York from Indiana in 1928 with only a pay-as-you-go cheap coat on her back. It fell apart within days of her arrival. She loved telling how "dirt poor" she was. At first she wrote fashion publicity copy before starting her own fashion p.r. firm and marrying Seymour Berkson, who was publisher of the *Journal-American*. Now the Lambert office bills $200,000–$250,000 a year and Eleanor has her jeweled fingers into everything in fashion, from the Coty Awards (the fashion industry's Oscars) and the Best Dressed List to her twice yearly fashion press week. During these weeks reporters from around the country gather in New York and view the collections of the "Fashion Mafia," a clutch of bigname designers Eleanor handles . . . Halston, Anne Klein, Mollie Parnis and Adele Simpson, among others.

"Eleanor's getting old now," says a former employee. "She keeps her power because she knows where all the bodies are buried in fashion."

The day I visit her office, Eleanor is late. Phones ring, secretaries and assistants wander about almost listlessly . . . past photographs of Chanel and President Eisenhower, past bound copies of *Vogue* and *Harper's Bazaar* . . . but the antique-laden office seems at a standstill. "I can't delegate authority," Eleanor tells me later. "I have to do everything myself."

One of the things she has to do is tabulate the Best Dressed List, which is why she's late. Her secretary informs me she's closeted in a room at The Plaza with Eugenia Sheppard, *Bazaar* editor Carrie Donovan and gossip columnist Suzy going over the 2000 ballots from supposed fashion authorities from around the country.

As soon as she arrives, Eleanor takes off her bright red shoes and announces that Mrs. Mick Jagger has just made the Best Dressed List. Two weeks before Bianca Jagger painted mustachios on both her cheeks. Are mustachios on women's cheeks going to be the newest fashion fad?

Eleanor doesn't answer. She demands to know what Fairchild has said about her. "Oh my Gawd, what's eating John?" she shrieks, as soon as I repeat his remarks about her lusting after power. "It's a free country but I don't control the press . . . never have and saying so doesn't make it true. I know why he's doing this to me. Because when we were speaking we used to lunch every week. John has a very French thing about lunch. That meal means everything to him. He lingers over it until the middle of the afternoon. Well, when we lunched together I was always late. But I couldn't help it. I have too much to do."

Had she ever heard the phrase "Fashion Mafia" and if so did she know she was considered its "Godmother?"

"Beg pardon?" Heavy-lidded eyes stare at me from a softly wrinkled heart-shaped face. "I've never heard that phrase. Never in my life. Does it have something to do with my 'lust for power'?" She giggles. "Powerful people, you know, are not supposed to have any souls."

Is it true you've deliberately confused the public by muddling the terms "haute couture" or "high fashion" with the work of the designers you handle? After all, they're not really practicing haute couture but are designing very expensive ready-to-wear.

She fixes on only one word in my question. "It was not deliberate," she says and swiftly changes the subject.

Charlotte Curtis

It is almost New Year's Eve when I drop by Charlotte Curtis' drab little office.

The most powerful woman on the New York *Times* seems subdued. She is dressed in grey cashmere and she chain-smokes. She has written about the 1970 recession, she has written about Radical Chic and how Henry Ford once pelted someone with Perrier water in the south of France. She tells me she began her career reporting on fashion.

"Clothes are a political statement," she says quietly. "They define who you are. They state your independence or dependence. Right now I'm ambivalent about fashion. The industry takes itself so seriously. I know they'd like The *Times* to be the bell ringer for fashion but we must keep things in perspective. I wish we could treat fashion more like Campbell's soup than a mystique. Status today isn't a wardrobe. It's an understated status . . . like a nutria sweater or a jean jacket with diamond cuff links."

Who killed high fashion?

"The kids," she answers at once. "They started questioning our values. Our system. The war. The bombing. Isn't that more important than the clothes we put on? I can't forget a story James Sterba filed from Afghanistan. He saw a naked child in the rubble; his only possession was a tin can. I should worry about getting a new mink? Fashion today is a question of priorities. Some women still take all morning putting on a dress. Clothes to me are something I put on my back to go to work in."

Suddenly she is singing to me across her desk, singing in a slightly hoarse Midwestern soprano. "Brighten up the corner where you live. . . ." She repeats the phrase. "It's an old Presbyterian hymn. That's what fashion should do for you . . . brighten up your corner . . . your lifestyle. Because fashion feeds off the individual before it ever becomes a mass phenomenon."

American designers, jet travel, urban warfare, women's lib, fashion fascism, the midi, John Fairchild, Eleanor Lambert, technology, the recession, amateurism, the kids or the mutating twentieth-century soul . . . all these have been mentioned as high fashion's killer, and for my part I can't decide which one of them to blame. Maybe all of them.

CLOTHING AND TEXTILES: SUPPLIES, PRICES, AND OUTLOOK FOR 1978

Annette Polyzou

Trends in Clothing Expenditures and Prices: 1960–77[1]

Two types of data can be used in examining clothing expenditures: (1) Aggregate data on personal consumption expenditures (PCE) are supplied annually by the Bureau of Economic Analysis of the U.S. Department of Commerce. These data, which are derived from business transactions, measure total expenditures in the United States and are part of the U.S. National Income and Product accounts. The PCE data are easiest to use when they are expressed on a per-capita basis (total U.S. expenditures divided by total U.S. population). (2) Household data on family expenditures are collected through nationwide surveys, such as the Consumer Expenditure Surveys (CES) of 1960–61 and 1972–73, conducted by the Bureau of Labor Statistics of the U.S. Department of Labor and the U.S. Department of Agriculture. CES data measure average family expenditures and are available for component population groups as well as for national totals. These data, however, have only been available at about 10-year intervals.

The two types of data are not interchangeable.[2] The PCE data are most useful in examining trends in clothing expenditures and the CES data are most useful in developing budgets or in helping families understand their expenditures. Nevertheless, examination of the data from both sources, between 1960 and 1977, shows similar patterns with respect to total expenditures for clothing and the percent of total expenditures spent on clothing.

Expenditures. Per-capita expenditures for clothing and shoes, as measured by PCE data, increased in both current and constant dollars during the period 1960–77 (table 1). In current dollars, per-capita expenditures for clothing and shoes were about 152 percent higher in 1977 than in 1960. Approximately two-thirds of this increase was caused by a rise in the level of prices and one-third by increased buying—a real increase of 51 percent in dollars of constant value. Such an increase in purchase of clothing and shoes during this period might be attributed to rising incomes as well as to a change in the composition of the population. Real disposable income was 89 percent higher in 1977 than in 1960, according to the U.S. Department of Commerce series on personal income and outlay.

The composition of the population during those years reveals an increasing proportion of individuals in the 14–34 age group (table 2). These individuals typically have high clothing expenditures that result from new clothing needs associated with sporting activities, dating, entering college, or beginning careers. Individuals in this age group also tend to be more fashion conscious than in other age groups and may thus accept fashion changes more quickly. The increase in 14–34-year-olds with gen-

erally high clothing expenditures was partially offset by a slight increase in the proportion of individuals age 55 and over. These people typically spend less on clothing than other individuals due to decreases in clothing needs and in income, which result from retirement from the labor force and from a reduced level of physical activity. Projections of the population for 1980 indicate that the composition will be virtually the same as that in 1976— the greatest proportion of the population will be individuals with the highest clothing expenditures. Thus, real increases in per-capita clothing expenditures, on an aggregate basis, are likely to continue at their present levels during the next few years and perhaps to increase as real disposable personal incomes rise. However, future increases are likely to be at a slower rate since projections indicate no further growth in the 14–34 age group.

As measured by the CES data, average family expenditures on clothing, materials, and services, including all laundry and drycleaning services, were 17 percent higher in current dollars in 1972–73 than in 1960–61 (table 3). In constant dollars, however, average family expenditures dropped by about 13 percent between 1960–61 and 1972–73. That drop might be attributed to a decline in family size. Data collected separately by CES and by the Bureau of the Census show a decline in average family size between 1960 and 1970. Smaller families generally buy fewer clothes. Data from the Bureau of the Census show that average family size continued to decline during the period 1972–73 through March 1977 from 3.51 persons to 3.37 persons. That decline suggests the possibility that family expenditures on clothing may have continued to decline in recent years.

Percent of total spending for clothing. In both current and constant dollars, the percent of total personal consumption expenditures (PCE) spent on clothing and shoes declined during the period 1960–77 (table 1). In current dollars, clothing comprised 8.2 percent of personal consumption expenditures in 1960 and 6.8 percent in 1977. In constant dollars, clothing comprised 8.1 percent of personal consumption expenditures in 1960 and 7.7 percent in 1977. Clothing, as a percent of total personal consumption expenditures, declined at a faster rate in current than in constant dollars because prices for the all-items category of personal consumption expenditures increased at a faster rate than prices for clothing.

Reprinted from *Family Economics Review*, Consumer and Food Economics Institute, Agricultural Research Service, U.S. Department of Agriculture, Winter-Spring 1978, pp. 34–41.

1. Preliminary figures for 1977—based on most recent data available during October 1977.
2. For a more detailed discussion of the differences in aggregate and household data, see *Family Economics Review* December 1970.

The CES data are consistent with PCE indications of a decline in clothing expenditures as a percent of total personal consumption expenditures. Clothing expenditures, as a percent of total consumption expenditures (table 3), were lower in 1972–73 than in 1960–61 in both current (7.8 versus 10.9 percent) and constant dollars (7.8 versus 10.2 percent).

The downward trend in clothing as a percent of total expenditures parallels a downward trend for nondurable goods in general. Expenditures have shifted away from nondurable goods toward durable goods, such as automobiles, furniture, and household equipment, and toward services. According to the PCE data, nondurable goods declined from 46 percent of personal consumption expenditures in 1960 in constant dollars to 39 percent in 1977, whereas durable goods rose from 12 to 16 percent and services rose from 42 to 45 percent during the same period. The CES data show a similar trend. The trend toward durable goods may be partially attributed to an increased rate of new household formation during the 1960–77 period, resulting from a greater proportion of individuals aged 14–34 years who either live away from home before marriage or get married and form new households. The formation of new households is typically associated with increased demand for durable goods and services, such as automobiles, housing, and household furnishings.

Attitudes towards clothing also have changed in recent years. Most individuals have adopted a casual lifestyle that has brought about a relaxed attitude towards clothing. Jeans have become a major influence on apparel, as have separates that provide variety through mixing and matching garments and allow inexpensive replacement of components. There has also been greater use of active sportswear, such as jogging suits, as streetwear. Consumers' interest has also shifted in recent years from faddish items to garments with basic utility and permanence. Trade sources expect consumers to purchase a few higher priced, better quality garments with more durability for long-lasting wear rather than many lower quality faddish items.

Clothing Expenditures and Prices During 1977

Consumer expenditures for clothing and shoes averaged $373 per person during the first three quarters of 1977, according to preliminary figures (table 1). Although that amount is $18 higher than the corresponding amount in 1976, nearly two-thirds of the increase resulted from a rise in the level of prices rather than from increased buying.

The price level for apparel and upkeep, as measured by the Consumer Price Index (CPI), averaged 4.6 percent higher during the first three quarters of 1977 than during the same period in 1976 (table 4). Increases among the three apparel subgroups averaged 4.6 percent for men's

and boys' clothing, 3.3 percent for women's and girls' clothing, 4.9 percent for footwear, and 5.2 percent for other apparel commodities. Such increases for apparel items were less than the 6.4–percent increase for all items of the CPI.

Retail sales of apparel were generally weak during the first quarter of 1977. Abnormally cold weather during January and early February caused an increase in home-heating fuel usage as well as a rise in fuel prices and in weather-affected food prices, thus reducing consumers' discretionary income for retail purchases. The severe cold did strengthen sales of sweaters, thermal underwear, hats, and gloves. As the effects of the severe weather abated and personal income increased substantially during the latter half of the first quarter, consumer spending rapidly increased. Strong sales of durable goods, mainly automobiles, major appliances, and furniture, indicated that consumers may have purchased such big-ticket items in anticipation of future price increases resulting from the rise in fuel prices. Consumers also invested in such home improvements as storm windows and home insulation, presumably to reduce energy usage.

This trend continued to be strong during the second quarter, affecting sales of automobiles, appliances, garden and nursery equipment, sporting goods, and related items. Various trade sources cited several possible reasons for the weak apparel sales during most of the second quarter:

- Consumers' resistance to higher prices of apparel.
- Consumers' strong interest in housing and automobiles.
- Consumers' concern about energy and long-term inflation.

Retailers responded to sluggish apparel sales by promoting aggressively and cutting prices in hope of creating some consumer interest. Retailers also kept inventories lean and depended on quick delivery of fast-moving items. Unseasonably warm weather during May created strong consumer demand for active sportswear and athletic footwear for all family members. Other factors that influenced the growth of active sportswear during this period included increased use of such sportswear as streetwear, increased attention on physical fitness, and continued emphasis on sports activities as social affairs.

The sales pattern of the third quarter again favored durables (especially automobiles) over soft goods, although apparel sales strengthened somewhat during this period. Consumers responded well to clearance prices on summer items and back-to-school merchandise early in the quarter. Retailers realized that consumers had been increasingly more price conscious throughout the year. Thus, they stressed price over fashion during the back-to-school season and offered basic merchandise such as corduroy and denim jeans, knit tops, flannel shirts, shetland pullovers, and down jackets and vests at competitive prices.

TABLE 1
Annual expenditures on clothing and shoes, 1960-77[1]

Year	Per-capita expenditures[2]		Percent of expenditures for personal consumption		Aggregate expenditures	
	Constant dollars (1972)	Current dollars	Constant dollars (1972)	Current dollars	Billions of constant dollars (1972)	Billions of current dollars
1960	203	148	8.1	8.2	36.6	26.7
1961	203	149	8.1	8.2	37.3	27.4
1962	209	154	8.1	8.1	38.9	28.7
1963	209	156	7.9	7.9	39.6	29.5
1964	222	166	8.1	8.0	42.6	31.9
1965	227	172	7.9	7.8	44.2	33.5
1966	239	186	8.0	7.9	46.9	36.6
1967	236	192	7.8	7.8	46.9	38.2
1968	242	208	7.7	7.8	48.6	41.8
1969	245	223	7.6	7.8	49.6	45.1
1970	240	227	7.4	7.5	49.2	46.6
1971	249	244	7.5	7.6	51.6	50.5
1972	264	264	7.5	7.5	55.1	55.1
1973	281	291	7.7	7.6	59.2	61.3
1974	279	308	7.8	7.3	59.1	65.3
1975	288	329	7.9	7.2	61.5	70.2
1976	301	355	7.9	7.0	64.7	76.3
1977[3]	306	373	7.7	6.8	66.2	80.9

[1]Data shown for 1960 through 1976 differ from data given in previous papers on the outlook for clothing and textiles. The revisions resulted from changes in definitions of personal consumption expenditures (other than clothing and shoes), statistical revisions of previous estimates, and revisions in population figures for 1975 and 1976. More detailed information can be obtained from the *Survey of Current Business* and *Current Population Reports* (see sources below).
[2]Calculated by dividing aggregate expenditures for each year by population figures for July 1 of each year.
[3]Preliminary figures—average of estimates for first 3 quarters of 1977 (i.e., seasonally adjusted quarterly totals at annual rates).

Sources: U.S. Department of Commerce, Bureau of the Census, 1977, Estimates of the population of the United States and components of change: 1940 to 1976, *Current Population Reports,* Series P-25, No. 706 (table c). U.S. Department of Commerce, Bureau of Economic Analysis, *Survey of Current Business* (tables 2.3 and 2.4), 1976, 56(1), parts I and II, and 1977, 57(7); and personal communication with the Bureau of Economic Analysis.

TABLE 2
Composition of population by age, specified years, 1960-80

Year	Total population (in thousands)	Percent of population by age group			
		Under 14	14–34	35–54	55–65+
1960	180,671	30	28	25	18
1970	204,878	26	32	23	19
1976	215,118	22	36	22	20
1980[1]	224,066	21	36	22	21

[1]Projections.

Source: U.S. Department of Commerce, Bureau of the Census, 1977, Porjections of the population of the United States: 1977 to 2050, *Current Population Reports,* Series P-25, No. 704, table h.

TABLE 3
Comparison of 1960-61 and 1972-73 Consumer Expediture Survey data[1]

Item	1960-61	1972-73
Current dollars:		
Average total consumption expenditure	5,054	8,282
Average expenditures on clothing, materials, and services	553	647
Clothing expenditures as a percent of total consumption expenditures	10.9	7.8
Average family size	3.2	2.9
Constant 1972 dollars:		
Average total consumption expenditures	7,328	8,282
Average expenditures on clothing, materials, and services	747	647
Clothing expenditures as a percent of total consumption expenditures	10.2	7.8

[1]1972-73 preliminary data.

Source: U.S. Department of Labor, Bureau of Labor Statistics, 1977, Changes in consumer spending patterns, *News* 77-428, pp. 1-5.

TABLE 4
Annual percentage increase in selected indexes of consumer prices, 1973-77

Consumer Price Index component	1973	1974	1975	1976	1977[1]
All Items	6.2	11.0	9.1	5.8	6.4
Apparel and upkeep[2]	3.7	7.4	4.5	3.7	4.6
Men's and boys' clothing	3.7	7.9	4.3	3.5	4.6
Women's and girls' clothing	3.5	6.0	2.4	2.8	3.3
Footwear	4.2	6.1	4.4	4.0	4.9
Other apparel commodities[3]	—	—	—	—	5.2

[1]Preliminary estimates—average for first 3 quarters of 1977 compared with the average for first 3 quarters of 1976.
[2]Also includes infants' wear, sewing materials, jewelry, and apparel upkeep services, for which indexes are not available.
[3]Developed in 1976 to include diapers, yard goods, earrings, wrist watches, and zippers.

Source: U.S. Department of Labor, Bureau of Labor Statistics, 1977, *News,* Consumer Price Index (monthly issues); and personal communication with the Bureau of Labor Statistics.

According to several trade sources, prices for most fall apparel items for men and women were 5 to 15 percent higher than a year ago. Higher prices of fall apparel mainly reflected increased costs of such natural fibers as cotton, wool, silk, and cashmere, as well as increased yardage for the fuller fashions for women—tiered and double skirts, full dresses, and big blousons. Consumers did not seem adverse to spending extra money for better quality apparel, which suggested that they may be viewing the purchase of apparel as an investment. Retailers cited some price resistance toward lower and moderately priced apparel during the fall season, and they responded with aggressive advertising and promotion and tight control of inventories.

The seasonally adjusted wholesale price index for apparel rose 0.7 percent during the period June through September. This indicates the probability of price increases for apparel at the retail level during the months ahead.

With higher prices of apparel, consumers may wish to take advantage of this year's fashion emphasis on separates and create ensembles from jackets, vests, sweaters, shirts, pants, and skirts coordinated by color, fabrication, or both. Consumers can also stretch their clothing dollar by using the separates concept to build on last year's wardrobe. Also, with the onset of cold weather, consumers can use apparel as an insulation against the cold and as an aid in saving fuel costs by layering garments and wearing sweaters.

Prices and Use of Fibers During 1977

U.S. per-capita mill use of natural fibers was lower in 1977 than in 1976, while mill use of synthetic fibers was higher. Estimated U.S. per-capita mill use of all fibers in 1977 (based on data for the first 9 months) is about 55.5 pounds, including 14.5 pounds of cotton, 0.5 pound of wool, and 40.5 pounds of synthetic fibers. This compares with 1976 per-capita use of 54.1 pounds, including 15.9 pounds of cotton, 0.6 pound of wool, and 37.6 pounds of synthetic fibers.

The natural look in clothing has continued to be important during the year, but high prices of cotton and wool, relative to prices of synthetic staple fibers, have influenced textile mills to achieve natural looks with blended fabrics containing a higher percent of synthetic fiber. This is apparent in the denim market, where mills are offering denims in 80/20 and 65/35 cotton/polyester blends. Blends now account for nearly 30 percent of the denim market. Even corduroy, which has traditionally been all-cotton, is being offered in blends of 84/16 cotton/ polyester and 50/50 cotton/polyester. Other natural-looking fabric blends available in the market for men's and women's clothing include polyester blended with wool, silk, linen, viscose rayon, and acrylic, as well as acrylic blended with wool.

Research in the area of textiles is focusing on the development of easy-care synthetic fabrics with a natural hand. Texfi Industries[3] recently introduced such a synthetic fabric—a lightweight all-polyester fabric coated with a finish to allow moisture absorption. Another recent development, air texturizing, fluffs up acrylic yarn to impart a mohairlike appearance to the fiber.

U.S. mill consumption of cotton for the first 9 months of 1977 was about 9 percent lower than during the same period in 1976. Mill use of synthetic staple fibers increased about 8 percent over 1976. The decline in mill consumption of cotton was attributed to the rather static textile activity and relatively high cotton prices in relation to synthetic staple fiber prices.

Mill-delivered cotton prices declined from a high of 83 cents per pound in March to 57 cents in September. This is about the same price that mills are presently paying for synthetic staple fiber. The decline in cotton prices during this period was mainly due to prospective abundant supplies of cotton in relation to weakening demand. The 1977 cotton crop was about one-fourth larger than the 1976 crop due to increased cotton acreage and favorable growing conditions during the summer. Diminished domestic demand for cotton is reflected in the decline in mill consumption of cotton, as previously mentioned. Foreign demand for cotton has also weakened. Exports of cotton during the 1977–78 marketing year are expected to total slightly below last season's 4.8 million bales. However, currently lower cotton prices are expected to stimulate U.S. mill consumption of cotton in 1978 and may reverse the trend toward cotton/polyester blends in the denim market.

Mill consumption of raw apparel wool during the first 8 months of 1977 was about 12 percent lower than during

the same period in 1976, reflecting a shift to higher synthetic fiber content in blends due to high wool prices. Average U.S. farm prices for wool declined, from a high of about 75 cents per pound in January to 71 cents in September, but were still above 1976 wool prices.

Shipments of synthetic fibers by U.S. producers during the first 8 months of 1977 were approximately 11 percent higher than in the same period in 1976, according to *Textile Organon* (September 1977). According to fiber producers, price increases during the year for selected acrylic, rayon, nylon, acetate, and polyester fibers mainly reflected increased costs of energy, raw materials, and labor. Currently, acrylic is benefiting from strong fall and holiday sweater sales; nylon is benefiting from strong sales of down nylon parkas, skiwear, and other sports outerwear; and polyester is benefiting from a revived interest in polyester/ rayon slacks as well as a shift in production from all-cotton to cotton/polyester denims.

---

3. Reference to a company name is used in this publication solely for the purpose of providing specific information. Mention of a company name does not constitute a guarantee or warranty of the company by the U.S. Department of Agriculture or an endorsement by the Department over other companies not mentioned.

REFERENCES

Erickson, A. 1968. Clothing the urban American family: How much for whom? *Monthly Labor Review* 91(1): 14–19.

U.S. Department of Agriculture, Economic Research Service. 1977. *Cotton and Wool Situation,* CWS–4 and CWS–12.

U.S. Department of Commerce. 1977. Recreation and business, the American connection. *Commerce America,* Sept. 12 issue, pp. 7–10.

U.S. Department of Commerce, Bureau of the Census. 1977. Households and families by type: September 1977. *Current Population Reports,* Series P–20, No. 282 (table 3); and personal communication with the Bureau of the Census.

——— Bureau of the Census. 1977. Estimates of the population of the United States and components of change: 1940 to 1976. *Current Population Reports,* Series P–25, No. 706 (table c).

——— Bureau of the Census. 1977. Projections of the population of the United States: 1977 to 2050. *Current Population Reports,* Series P–25, No. 704 (table h).

——— Bureau of Economic Analysis. *Survey of Current Business,* 1976, 56(1), Parts I and II (tables 2.3 and 2.4); 1977, 57(7) (tables 2.3 and 2.4); and personal communication with the Bureau of Economic Analysis.

U.S. Department of Labor, Bureau of Labor Statistics. 1966. Consumer expenditures and income total—United States, urban, and rural, 1960–61. BLS Report No. 237, Supplement 3, Part A, p. 2.

——— 1976. *Consumer Expenditure Survey Series: Diary Survey, July 1973–June 1974.* BLS Report 448–3, p. 11.

——— Bureau of Labor Statistics. 1977. Changes in consumer spending patterns. *News,* USDL: 77–428, pp. 1–5.

Whitehead, C.A. (ed.). 1977. *Textile Organon.* New York: Textile Economics Bureau, Inc. XLVIII(9), (table) p. 152.

Selected articles from the *Daily News Record, The New York Times, The Wall Street Journal,* and *The Washington Post.*

STRETCHING THE CLOTHING DOLLAR

Virginia Britton

To get the most for the clothing dollar, today's family has several alternatives—sewing at home, making home repairs and alterations, using handed-down clothing, purchasing used clothing, and careful shopping for new clothing. A family may use all of these alternatives at some time during a year. The method chosen for acquiring any specific item will depend on the type of item being acquired and its intended use, the urgency for saving money, the family's standards, the energy and skills of family members and their time and equipment, and the availability of local outlets.

Although most families acquire a major portion of their clothing as new ready-to-wear items, about one-fifth of the clothing acquired by families with low to moderate incomes comes from other sources. Specialists working with families can help them to take an objective look at alternative ways of obtaining clothing, develop flexibility and imagination in adjusting to changing conditions, and be ready to make speedy decisions to take advantage of unusual opportunities for acquiring needed garments.

Developing skills in shopping and in creating and caring for garments plays a key role in stretching the clothing dollar. The acquisition of skills and information increases a person's judgment of quality and appropriateness and can increase her or his willingness to shop widely for clothing and fabrics and to make use of other means of acquiring clothing for the family.

Paying for appropriate durability is important. How long and how hard will the garment be worn and for what types of occasions? Work clothes for construction workers, farmers, garage mechanics, and factory workers in heavy industry need to be highly durable to withstand severe daily wear and many heavy washings. Underwear, nightwear, and hosiery also need to withstand many wearings and washings. On the other hand, great durbility of the fabric, notions, and tailoring is not essential for garments that are likely to be rapidly outmoded, outgrown, torn, lost, or used infrequently. For example, infants' clothes may be outgrown long before they are worn out. Active children rip garments on nails and trees and lose gloves and boots, and even shoes and socks in warm weather. Some women quickly tear or snag their long hosiery. Garments for special occasions, such as parties, weddings, or graduation, may be worn seldom and may be outdated or outgrown before there are many opportunities for wearing them.

Sewing at Home

About 41 million persons in the United States probably do some home sewing in a year[1] and spend an estimated $4 billion a year for fabrics, patterns, machines, and notions.[2] Retail sales of yard goods for apparel rose from 636 million square yards in 1965 to 1,355 million square yards in 1974.[3] Sales of knit fabrics were 14 million square yards in 1967 and 623 million in 1974.

About 46 percent of U.S. households reported purchasing fabric in the 12 months ending June 1972, according to a nationwide survey of about 3,400 households interviewed by telephone for the USDA.[4] Twenty-one percent of these "buyer" households had two or more members that purchased fabric. Most of the fabric buyers intended to do their own sewing rather than having someone else do it for them. Fabric-buyer households averaged more members than nonbuyer households, and a higher proportion included children under 19 years of age. Buyer households averaged larger total income than nonbuyer households, but about equal income per capita. Nearly all of the fabric buyers were females, of a wide age span. During the year, the median purchase was five pieces of fabric for spring or summer clothing and two pieces for fall or winter clothing. Based on information on the last piece of fabric bought, the clothing was generally made for the same age group as the purchaser, which probably means for the buyer herself. However, a sizable proportion of the last fabric purchases by those 20 to 39 years was made into garments for children under 13 years.

Homemade clothing comprised about 2 percent of the quantity of clothing acquired in a year by families with low to moderate income, according to a survey taken in Des Moines, Iowa, in 1965–66.[5] However, broken down

Reprinted from *Family Economics Review,* Consumer and Food Economics Institute, Agricultural Research Service, U.S. Department of Agriculture, Fall, 1975, pp. 3–7.

1. Estimated from percentage of households with one or more purchasers of fabric (see footnote 4) and data from the U.S. Bureau of the Census on the number of households.
2. Hyde, N.S. A Pattern in the Home Sewing Industry? *The Washington Post,* February 16, 1975, p. L 1.
3. National Cotton Council of America, *Cotton Counts Its Customers,* Memphis, Tenn. Annual edition, June 1975, p. 89 ($25); and personal communication with G. Booker, Economic Research Department, National Cotton Council of America.
4. Kaitz, E.F., and Stack, T.M. *Consumers' Buying Practices, Uses, and Preferences for Fibers in Retail Piece Goods.* U.S. Dept. Agr., Market. Res. Rpt. No. 1013. Washington, D.C.: U.S. Government Printing Office, 1974. (Supply exhausted).
5. See article by Britton, V., *Family Economics Review,* pp. 3–5. September 1969.

by family member, homemade clothing amounted to 5 percent for wives, 4 percent for girls 2 to 17 years, 2 percent for female heads of families, 1 percent for infants, and less than 1 percent for boys 2 to 17 years and for male heads of families.[6] The survey included families who sewed and those who did not.

Reasons for sewing. Saving money is a major reason for home sewing. In the USDA survey mentioned above, 65 percent of the fabric buyers gave "cheaper, more economical" as one of the reasons for making garments rather than purchasing them ready made. "Better fit" was mentioned by 31 percent; "can make exactly what you want" by 29 percent; "creative satisfaction" by 28 percent; and "better quality, workmanship" by 16 percent. A few other reasons were mentioned occasionally, and some people gave more than one reason.

People who do not sew probably do not consider home construction of garments a choice activity. Some lack sufficient skills to meet their own standards for completed garments. Home sewing takes time which they need or prefer to use in other ways, and they can find acceptable ready-made garments in the stores. Futhermore, they feel more certain of its suitability when they are able to try on the completed garment before making any expenditure.

Money cost of home-constructed garments. The money cost of home-constructed garments varies greatly, depending on the cost of materials selected and the skill and aspirations of the home sewer. Persons with skill who sew at home for enjoyment or because the finished product is better suited to their needs may select more expensive fabric and trimmings than those who have limited skill or who sew to save money. Thirteen persons—mostly staff of the Consumer and Food Economics Institute (CFEI)—who had recently constructed garments at home were asked about the cost of these garments. This group had contructed 23 street dresses ranging in cost from $3 to $27; 15 pants outfits costing from $5 to $17; 13 party dresses for $6 to $22; and 8 pairs of slacks for $2 to $10. These costs, however, do not give any indication of savings because savings from home sewing depend to a considerable extent on the cost of the readymade garment that would be selected as an alternative to the home-sewn one.

Direct comparison of the cost of garments purchased at a retail outlet with an identical garment constructed at home is difficult, if not impossible. The fabrics and trimmings found on ready-to-wear garments are not generally available in fabric stores at the same time, and the styles are not always exactly duplicated in current patterns. Nevertheless, an estimate can be made of the cost of similar items by concentrating on simple styles such as those without special trim and mutiple fabrics.

In April 1975 shoppers from CFEI priced size 14 one-piece dresses and two-piece jacket-dress costumes of ma-chine-washable polyester knit at a local shopping center used primarily by moderate-income families. The shoppers also priced items of similar types available in large mail-order catalogs, and priced patterns, fabrics, and notions similar to those used on the ready-to-wear garments.[7] (No estimates were made of costs of power to operate equipment.)

The one-piece dresses were constructed of a one-color fabric, unlined, with set-in sleeves, and had self-trimming only (except for closures). The ranges in costs per garment for three types of one-piece dresses requiring different yardages of 60-inch fabric were estimated as follows:

Five dresses with short sleeves requiring about 1¾ yards of fabric—
Ready-to-wear . . . . $11 to $15
Homesewn . . . . $5 to $11

Five dresses with long sleeves requiring about 2½ yards of fabric—
Ready-to-wear . . . . $14 to $26
Homesewn . . . . $7 to $15

Five dresses with long sleeves requiring about 2¾ yards of fabric for coat styles or tucking and other features—
Ready-to-wear . . . . $20 to $40
Homesewn . . . . $8 to $16

The range in cost for the "duplicate' homesewn dresses was due primarily to choice of fabric which ranged from $1.74 to $3.99 a yard. Lesser differences were due to choice of pattern and some diversity in notions used on various garments.

The two-piece jacket-dress costumes consisted of a one-piece dress with set-in short sleeves and a jacket with set-in long sleeves. They were constructed of a single fabric with self-trim only and required about 3¼ yards of 60-inch fabric. The fabric costs ranged from $1.74 to $3.99 a yard for one-color fabrics and from $2.29 to $6.99 a yard for multicolor fabrics. The ranges in costs per costume were estimated as follows:

Two two-piece costumes (unlined) made of one-color fabric—
Ready-to-wear . . . . $28 to $38
Homesewn . . . . $9 to $19

One two-piece costume (lined jacket) made of one-color fabric—
Ready-to-wear $64
Homesewn . . . . $13 to $22

Four two-piece costumes (unlined) made of multi-color fabrics—
Ready-to-wear . . . . $15 to $56
Homesewn . . . . $11 to $29

6. These percentages are believed to be similar today.

7. Mary Lou Cooper, home economist, gave major assistance with the pricing.

Two two-piece costumes (lined jackets; one not marked "machine washable") made of multicolor fabrics—

Ready-to-wear .... $95 to $100
Homesewn .... $16 to $37

Other costs. The direct money cost of constructing clothing at home may help determine whether to sew at home or not. However, the other costs—time for doing the construction and the initial cost of acquiring the equipment necessary—should also be considered.

Estimates of time spent in the home construction of a garment are difficult to make because of interruptions and the use of scattered blocks of free time, and because shopping for fabrics and notions and preparing the fabric may be combined with other tasks. A previous USDA study of home-made clothing showed that the average time cost for constructing a size 14 cotton daytime dress was 2.9 hours. This garment, however, was made in a laboratory by a skilled seamstress who constructed the garments according to the pattern, with no alterations. Interruptions were carefully recorded and subtracted from the total. The CFEI sewers in 1975, of varied skills and interests, estimated that the street dresses they made last year took 3 to 12 hours, with a median of 7 hours. Median time was 6 hours for party dresses and 7 hours for pants outfits. The time spent varies according to the skill and standards of the sewer, the type of pattern, the necessity for altering the pattern for better fit or changing the design, the use of fabric that requires matching, and the equipment available.

The cost of equipment adds to the cost of home sewing. Home construction of garments may be done with relatively simple or elaborate equipment. The quality of the finished garment does not necessarily reflect the quality of equipment, nor does the amount of home sewing always parallel the price of the equipment.

New sewing machines priced by the CFEI shoppers ranged from under $100 for machines with no features other than straight and zigzag stitch to over $600 for machines with many added features. The buyer needs to consider how much she will be using the special features before investing the extra money. Acceptable garments are still being sewn in homes on quite old machines with only a straight, forward stitch. Of course, the special features may save time or improve the product.

In addition to the sewing machine, other equipment used in home sewing includes a steam iron, ironing board, sleeve board, shears, needles, pins, chalk, and hem marker. Many additional pieces of equipment are available to ease the job or improve the quality of the product.

Additional costs of home sewing are not usually considered. For example, the growing collection of fabrics stored in the attic or closet for some vague future use, the garments that have been started and never completed, the items that have been completed but not enjoyed or worn,

and the sewing machine and other equipment which are seldom used.

When does home sewing pay best? Home construction of garments probably pays best for persons with wants or needs that are not met by ready-to-wear garments in their price range; for persons who can construct garments for lower prices than the price of the comparable readymade garment; and for persons who sew frequently enough to spread the cost of equipment over many garments.

Persons whose needs are not met by ready-to-wear garments may prefer sewing even if the savings per hour are not high. For some, home sewing is a preferred leisure activity and the time spent for shopping and coordinating fashion fabrics, linings, interlinings, buttons, zippers, and other notions and the time and effort of perfecting skills may be considered time better spent than shopping for readymade garments.

Greater savings may be possible by constructing items such as street or party dresses, coats, and suits rather than "basic apparel" such as underwear or nightwear. The home sewer who can "build in quality" by replicating the more highly styled dress will save more than the sewer replicating a simple dress. However, a simple coat or raincoat with straight lines may be profitable to construct at home even with lining and interlining, as these garments are usually costly.

Leftover fabrics incorporated into new garments; fabrics and notions purchased at sales or as remnants; re-use of patterns, buttons and perhaps zippers; and omission of facings, linings, and interlinings when not required—all increase savings. Savings per hour may be increased by improving skills and by simplifying standards and techniques.

Making Home Repairs and Alterations

The skills of the home sewer can be applied toward repairing and altering clothing. Keeping clothing in a good state of repair increases its wearability and extends its useful life. The fit of garments can often be improved by simple alterations such as enlarging or releasing darts or changing hems on sleeves, pant legs, and skirts. This is true for those garments already owned as well as those newly acquired. Some home sewers have the skill and time to do extensive remodeling of garments for adults or children—a major recycling, "making something out of nothing," which can be a highly creative activity, as well as stretching the clothing dollar. On the other hand, time and money may be wasted in excessive remodeling of wornout garments or those that will not be used.

Using Handed-down Clothing

Handed-down clothing made up about 14 percent of the quantity of clothing acquired in a year by families with low to moderate income in the Des Moines survey, 1965–66. For infants, handed-down clothing totaled 33 percent of the amount received, including 21 percent from outside the family and 12 percent from inside. For girls 2 to 17 years and boys in the same age group, handed-down clothing amounted to about 20 percent—14 percent from outside the family and 6 percent from inside. Handed-down items, nearly all from outside the family, amounted to 14 percent of acquisitions for female heads of families, 9 percent for wives of male heads, and 6 percent for male heads.

Greater use of handed-down clothing can be an excellent way of stretching the clothing dollar for many families, particularly those with children. Exchange plans in schools or neighborhoods or among friends make important additions to the amounts available within families. Usefulness of the handed-down clothing is frequently enhanced by home repairs and alterations, plus laundering or cleaning.

Purchasing Used Clothing

Used clothing items that were purchased by the Des Moines families totaled only 2 percent of the amount of clothing acquired. Purchase of used clothing was relatively more important for adults than for children. Regardless of income, many families can profit by checking the shops that offer used clothing and those that rent clothing for an occasional formal use. (For local shops, see the YELLOW PAGES under "Clothing Bought and Sold" and "Formal Wear—Rental.")

Thrift shops and bazaars run by charitable and religious organizations offer used clothing for the family. Outgrown and excess clothing is generally contributed to the organization, and the proceeds after minimal costs are used for charitable purposes. The shops are simple and the personnel frequently volunteer their services. Children's clothing and adults' coats, suits, dresses, sweaters, and party clothes are available at fractions of their original prices, some of which may have been quite high. Thrift shops are especially useful for garments that are wanted for short-time wear such as maternity clothes, party clothes, and garments for graduation, vacation, or other special occasions; for rebuilding depleted wardrobes in an emergency situation; and for dressing rapidly growing children or teenagers who want a large variety of garments. Shirts, blouses, sweaters, skirts, slacks, and dresses may be found for $0.25 to $1, and 2- or 3-piece suits and

coats for $4. Some items are clean and ready for wear off the rack; others require some repairs or alterations or a good cleaning. A large unfashionable coat can provide beautiful fabric for remodeling. The lack of labels showing fibers and size (which some donors might pin on the garment) makes a greater demand on the buyer's shopping skills and judgment.

At a different level are resale shops for men or women offering elegant clothing that is slightly used at fractions of their original prices. Some of these items, such as designer fashions, elaborate party dresses, and furs, are placed on consignment at the shops by individuals who have worn the garment only a few times. Prices for items that are slightly used and fairly current in fashion may be about one-third of the price of a new item. Prices often range from $25 to $200, and special mark-downs are frequently offered.

Shopping for New Clothing

Most clothing is purchased new, readymade. Items purchased new by the Des Moines families amounted to about 70 percent of the total amounts of clothing acquired, but ranged from 33 percent for infants under 2 years to 81 percent for male heads of families. Other new clothing acquired by those families included gifts from outside the family (11 percent of total family clothing acquisitions—31 percent for infants), and items received as pay, bonus, stamp purchase, or prize (1 percent). Except for infants and little children, gifts are usually confined to the smaller items which need frequent replacement.

Clearance sales toward the end of the buying season or occasional midseason and early-season sales may offer sizable savings. A great variety of clothing has been available at special sales in recent months. Garments that are slightly soiled or in need of minor repairs are sometimes offered at reduced prices.

Other ways to save include comparative shopping among various retail outlets and using retail outlets that specialize in "basic" apparel and offer less than "full services," such as catalog chains and their stores, variety stores, and grocery supermarkets. Surplus stores operated by catalog chains offer sizable savings. Discount shops offer clothing from manufacturers' closeouts. Some factory outlets for overstocks of brand-name garments are located near the factories. However, these outlets do not offer full lines of clothing.

WOMEN'S SHOES: FOOT FETISH

Everybody in the shoe industry has a theory concerning why shoes are selling better than almost every other classification of apparel or accessories. All are trying to find a formula for continuing success. Success, however, is probably contingent on the combination of theories.

Excitement permeates the shoe industry. Not only do vendors and retailers expound on how great business has been and continues to be, but optimism about the future is limitless. Current optimism is easy to comprehend—1977 produced handsome retail increases for shoe merchants, with department stores averaging 15%, and for the first half of '78 department store merchants report increases of 20%. But above and beyond even current dollar increases, excitement about the future involves ingredients that in the industry's estimation puts them on the brink of an explosion that could quite possibly last for years.

The past fall/winter season's increases were not based solely upon the continuing sale of boots, and spring/summer increases were obtained without much help from espadrilles. For six months to a year numerous items and concepts have developed so rapidly that they are predicted to become full-fledged classifications, possibly even before spring '79. Shoes are said to be moving into the world of diversified fashion choices which will be the impetus for more women to build wardrobes of shoes rather than to buy shoes merely for replacement. According to a survey of working women a year-and-a-half ago, 70% of women even under the age of 30 bought shoes for replacement.

It may be an anomaly for the traditionally conservative shoe industry, that a few years back complained about a plethora of shoe choices, to be now lauding diversification. But retail success has a loud voice—customers are buying all manner of shoes. The question has become: are women more interested in shoes because the selection has widened or has the selection widened because women have become more interested in shoes? On this subject there is endless rhetoric.

One school of thought gives credit for the upward trend in sales of high-heeled, bare-open shoes to feet becoming the current sexual focal point. It is contended that one part or another of the female anatomy has historically been a sexual focal point, and the type of apparel accepted at the time has always been accepted because it enhanced that area of the body. Examples are cited: French empire partially bared and emphasized the bosom. Women during the 1860s and '70s pulled strings tight in their corsets to emphasize tiny waists. Gibson Girl blouses emphasized full bosoms and tiny waists. In the 1930s and '40s cheesecake photography pinpointed knees. The mini skirt focused upon legs and thighs and the focal point moved to

derrières when girls opted to wear fanny pants. And now it's feet. Of course there are those who snicker at the concept of feet becoming a sex symbol—"Feet aren't sexy; they're disgusting," says the sales manager of a shoe company. But a believer in the theory retorts, "It's all in the eyes of the beholder. Feet are far less disgusting than armpits, which were the focal point when sleeveless dresses and blouses were the rage."

Naturally there are those who expand the theory of feet by including legs. Some admit to being traditional 'leg men'. Overall, it is contended that interest in legs and feet has suddenly emerged because they were so long hidden by pants that grazed the floor. Although dresses and skirts have not overtaken pants as the most popular way to dress, increased acceptance has moved all eyes to legs and feet. And high heels are being more broadly accepted because they make legs look more shapely. However, the feet-first group (although they are not against any theory that might help sell shoes) points out that high-heeled, sexy shoes are also being accepted by women to be worn with narrower and shorter leg pants which do not reveal legs at all.

Nonetheless, the foot fetish contingent represents only one school of thought regarding women's renewed interest in shoes. A larger group which includes a higher portion of retailers is far more pragmatic. They point out that with all the noise about high heels, heels above 21/8ths are only 5% of retail shoe business and estimate that even 18/8ths to 21/8ths are somewhere between 15% to 20%. Boots, most of which are not high-heeled, are claimed to represent 35% to 40% of fall business, with 20% of those in weather-proofed boots for inclement weather. And when one gets to spring/summer, 60% to 75% of the business, they say, can be attributed to sport and casual shoes.

This summer the big winner was flat, or near so, fisherman sandals—a classification being greatly expanded for 1979 because of the inclusion of a greater variety of fashion. Merchants and vendors also cite other types of flat shoes as winners. One is the manly oxford look for which they credit "Annie Hall," and the other is active sportswear shoes (or sneakers, as we once referred to them). There are different ones for tennis, jogging, etc., and although one might expect the sports enthusiast to be building a wardrobe of them, it is claimed that women who are not even sports spectators are doing so as well. Merchants in the midwest claim they constantly see women in polyester pants wearing them at shopping malls. Although department store merchants currently attribute no more than 5% to this category in their regular shoe departments, "because they are sold everywhere at every price," they believe the category will become more important for them next year. Doctors both on and off TV have been warning about the bad effects of cheap, poorly-constructed sports shoes. Department store retailers believe women taking heed will be more prone to buy such shoes from them. But whatever type of flat or low-heeled shoe women are buying, they are said to be the best selling category and are not related, no matter how you slice it, to feet as sexual focal points.

With so many types of shoes and boots moving up at the same time, the pragmatists credit the movement simply to the fact that shoes have become an important accessory. Women always extract the currently most exciting accessory to update or embellish outfits they are wearing. It has been scarves or jewelry, handbags, belts—but none of these classifications according to shoe people look as exciting or as new as do shoes at this point in time.

Here is where students of the fashion school of thought step forward. They insist that shoe business is uptrending not because women suddenly decided to concentrate on their feet because they became a new sexual focal point, or because other types of accessories started to look dull. Since the largest share of fashion pundits are from the shoe market itself, they take full credit. "Women are buying shoes because we gave them a great selection of shoes to buy. We moved away from repetition and conservative shoe merchandising." Many shoe manufacturers (most of whom produce abroad) have hired ready-to-wear designers to design their collections. Although they like to push the name of the designer (even into a separate shop concept) in shoe departments in order to get the most volume for themselves, they admit that most customers don't buy shoes because of the designer's name but because of the styling. And although one might expect all designer shoes to be outrageously priced, by today's escalated standards many are moderately priced. The purpose of using designers was not necessarily to move lines into better, which is estimated to be at most 10% to 15% of total shoe volume. Designers brought, and are expected to continue to bring new ideas into the business in both styling and colorations. Since shoes, of necessity, must be designed before a ready-to-wear season, at least designers have some idea where fashion is going and shoes at long last are said to relate to apparel. Naturally the volume producers of shoes, like volume producers in any business, knock off the best sellers.

Although styling changes are said to be dramatic by shoe people, the most dramatic change involves the color palette. For the past couple of seasons, excellent retail sales were reported in three or four shades between bone and pale brown in moderate and better-priced shoes, and even neutralized shades of green, mauve and wine moved up in importance. The new color spectrum, to a lesser degree, also affected volume shoes, and next spring/summer this trend is expected to be dynamite. While new colors have been trending in, the traditional spring/summer standbys have been withering on the vine. Black patent died on the shelves this spring as did white this summer and very little of either is being planned for 1979.

It is said that vegetable dyes, widely accepted in ready-to-wear, have had the greatest impact on the changing color spectrum of shoes. Nonetheless, it may even be the consequence of a more open attitude by consumers about what must go with what. Since women are prone to wear whatever color handbag is already set to go when they wake up in the morning, no matter what outfit they decide to wear, many colors in shoes are being viewed as equally neutral by them. And if shoes are truly perceived as an important accessory, they can be the color accent that makes the outfit.

Drunk with the success of consumer acceptance of new styles and diversification, even more options will be offered to her in spring/summer '79. If a customer wants her feet to be sexy, besides high-heeled strip sandals and mules, she can choose city sandals that are more closed but have cutouts or perforations. If she can't walk on such high heels, she will find more mid heels and much of the selection, high or mid heel, is being made sexier by the use of ankle straps. If the customer loves flats, the ballerina has been added to the collection. If she loves boots, there are sexy, soft ankle-highs, and for the lover of western, there are mesh ones and open shanks that look like boots when worn with pants. The possibilities are endless. Now, if customers can find money to pay for all the choices for which they opt (shoes are not inexpensive), the shoe industry's optimism concerning its future should be limitless.

Podiatrists Rejoice

Try to make an appointment with an ophthalmologist; it takes six to eight weeks and then you wait until it's your turn. The same thing is true of other medical specialists, and very often dentists. It's even difficult to get an appointment for a haircut. But call a podiatrist and ask when you can come in, and the answer invariably is, "Can you get here immediately?" Not only has business slowed down appreciably for those currently in practice, but the future has looked so dismal that those worried about perpetuating the profession have formed groups to canvass colleges in order to entice students into the field.

This of course was not always the situation. Fifteen years ago, it was more difficult to get an appointment with a podiatrist than a dentist, and a number of them were earning as much money as medical doctors. The clients were primarily women who showed up at intervals of three to six weeks so they could walk comfortably for another three to six weeks. Skinny heels, at least 20/8ths high, were worn by all females other than those in the geriatric set and the grammar school contingent (when their mothers weren't looking). High heels weren't worn just because females wished to be taller, since they were also worn by women who were 5'8" or 5'9" or more, which to their chagrin made them much taller than 'he' was. It was just an accepted fact of life that if a woman wanted to be dressed like all other women, look right in her clothes, make her legs look more shapely, she wore high heels. The first thing a woman did when she walked into her home (even before taking off her tight girdle) was kick off her shoes. But even then she was in trouble, since wearing high heels all of the time shortened the calf muscles so that barefoot she walked on her toes. Yup, those were the good old days, the nostalgic days when podiatrists were in the chips. Every woman complained about some kind of foot ailment.

The youth revolution and mini skirts which introduced low-heeled shoes into the fashion spectrum brought high heels to a screeching halt. High heels were suddenly worn only on a rare occasion, generally with strict formal attire. Women whose feet had been killing them for years heaved a sigh of relief and began visiting their favorite podiatrist possibly twice a year. Most of the younger set today don't even know what a podiatrist does.

But all of this is about to change. The shoe industry, with input from the apparel prognosticators, has been pushing higher and higher, narrower and narrower heeled shoes for a couple of years now. This spring/summer more and more pairs have been sold, particularly to a young audience who consider them very chic and sexy. And the trend appears to be growing. Young women who did not know what a podiatrist was, may soon find out. One even grows suspicious that a podiatrist's lobby has gotten to shoe designers. However, watching young women clumsily wobbling along on high-heeled strip sandals and mules to which they are not accustomed, and occasionally falling off curbs, one must wonder whether it may turn into more of a boom for orthopedic specialists, who may very well get them first, than for podiatrists.

THE GENIE IN THE BOTTLE

Although the explosion of the fragrance business over the past five years has been much publicized, industry volume continues to be underestimated. In such a potentially large market, competition may well emerge from yet another source—the supermarkets.

Cleanliness has historically been considered second only to godliness in the United States. But, of late, there has emerged in this country a self-consciousness for personal hygiene bordering on the fanatical. If a product promises cleaner teeth, fresher breath or drier underarms, the American public is certain to give it a try. It is precisely this mania that has, in less than two decades, turned the domestic fragrance industry into a mass phenomenon.

Previously, for millenniums, fragrances were the property of the rich and the exalted. Cleopatra anointed her body with sweet smelling oils; Alexander the Great saturated his living quarters and his clothing with strong perfumes; Persians covered their carpets and couches with rose petals; and Nero showered his dinner guests with fragrances sprinkled from the ceiling of his banquet hall. Because of poor hygiene, rather than to enhance good hygiene, wealthy members of society covered their bodies' odors with varying degrees of essence. Queen Elizabeth I even perfumed her pets with imported scents.

Originally, Arabia supplied the world with flacons and fragrances. But by the early Renaissance, Venice had become prominent in the art of glassmaking; and from there,

this trade moved into other parts of Europe. By the late 1600s, French craftsmen had mastered not only the flacon business but also the production of refined fragrance. And, with the application of scientific methods to the art of perfumery, Grasse became the fragrance center of the western world, exporting products to half of Europe by the early decades of the 19th century.

France had taken its lead in the perfume industry and would hold this preeminence until the 1970s, at which time the American fragrance industry would introduce the first perfume to fit the changing lifestyle of the American woman. But until that time, America continued to look to France for the acceptable scents. At first, the rich alone partook of the French exports—for the masses still gave heed to their puritanical mores and looked upon fragrance as frivolity. It was not until post World War I, when American soldiers returned from Europe with French perfumes, that mass acceptance of fragrances even began to emerge in a noticeable way in this country.

Reprinted with permission from *RetailWeek* Incorporating *Clothes,* August 15, 1978, (c) 1978 PRADS INC.

Despite greater acceptance, from that point until this decade the fragrance business in America continued to rely, for the most part, on French imports. In spite of the fact that to be alluring opposed all Anglo-Saxon ethics, more and more American females began to be enticed by such designer fragrances as Chanel and by such provocative names as My Sin. So, what once was an acknowledged luxury for a select number of wealthy women, slowly became a part of the daily toilette of the not-so-privileged majority.

In the same way that fashion was to trickle down from the old couture system, first to be imitated by the crème of Seventh Avenue, then to be knocked off by the moderate-priced manufacturers, and finally to have the mass merchandisers follow suit, so also was fragrance to move from department and specialty store exclusivity to drug store availability; to move from the small numbers of women influenced by top fashion publications to the vast American public exposed to national television advertising.

This is not to say that the department and specialty stores' influence in setting a tone for the validity of fragrance is not paramount in the same way that it is in apparel. But it is to say that as the specialty and department stores have gained consumer acceptance for the higher-priced fragrances, this acceptance has filtered down to the masses, who are willing to purchase less expensive perfumes from the imitators. These, in turn, are trading off of the legitimacy established by the department stores and specialty stores.

Thirty years ago, the fragrance industry was an 'either/or' business. On the one hand, there were the expensive French perfumes with department/specialty store exclusivity. On the other hand, there were budget fragrances whose attraction lay only in price. But with the emergence of the moderate-priced lines, which offered an acceptable fragrance at an affordable price, the exclusive and the discount businesses have moved closer together.

By the 1960s, the American fragrance industry was beginning to gear itself up to compete with the French, using the only ammunition that was available—fitting fragrances directly into the American lifestyle. In that decade, with the introduction of Youth Dew, Estee Lauder gave American women a fragrant body oil that would last throughout the day and into the night. Previously accustomed to dabbing a short-lived fragrance on the neck, the wrists and behind the knees, women could at last hold a scent for hours without reapplication by using Lauder's revolutionary oil.

In that same decade, Revlon's Norell matched the French perfumes in terms of quality and packaging. Although it was a true imitation of French couture fragrance, Norell proved its point—America could also manufacture elegant perfume.

But as successful as Norell and Youth Dew were, the American fragrance producers were still off target. They had not yet fully realized to what extent America would carry its hygiene-conscious mania, and they were not yet aware of how the change in living patterns could be successfully exploited with a fragrance that fit a lifestyle.

Prior to World War II, the entire American cosmetic business revolved around lipstick, rouge and nail polish. But following the war, with the introduction of hair coloring, the industry began to expand its base. As never before, mass America was becoming overtly sexual, and cosmetic manufacturers would soon learn how to capitalize on this newly found freedom of expression.

It was not, however, until Charles Revson bought advertising time on the "$64,000 Question," and promoted his "kissing pink lipstick" on national TV that today's cosmetic business was born. Through this advertising promotion, Revson revolutionized the entire cosmetic industry. In one year, Revlon's dollar volume in cosmetics jumped from $32-million to almost $150-million. The world of mass marketing of cosmetics had been discovered.

Of course, there is no doubt that the Clairol advertising campaign—"only her hairdresser knows"—changed women's attitudes toward their personal appearance. It is even possible that Clairol may have had more to do with the emergence of the new woman than any other single manufacturer. Regardless, it is for certain that the increased acceptance of hair dye (which henceforth was to be called hair coloring) did more to make cosmetic business increase than anything else.

Meanwhile, the fragrance market remained in the hands of the French. And, if it was slow to follow the lead of the growing cosmetic business, this was merely because of the inadequacies inherent in the French system of marketing.

Throughout the latter part of the 1960s and into the 1970s, the role of the American woman was, once again, drastically altered. As more and more women entered the work force, the image being sought was no longer one of femininity and seductiveness. To the contrary, the American woman was wearing a pant suit to the office, going braless on weekends and joining the craze for health-oriented activities. Elegance did not fit into the newly discovered image. The new woman wanted not only to project cleanliness but also to smell naturally fit.

Once again Revlon geared itself up to meet the masses. By the early 1970s, Charles Revson gave birth to an idea that would change the entire American fragrance industry—an idea that would gain department store acceptance at the same time it gained mass popularity. In 1973, Charlie was born.

There is no doubt that Charlie became the sportswear of the fragrance business. It broke every rule that the

French couture fragrances had attempted to establish. Its very name mocked the seductive Parisian labels and their ornate flacons. Charlie did not intimidate middle America. No one talked about whether or not it projected a sophisticated image. No one really cared. Charlie smelled good; Charlie was priced right; and most of all, Charlie was with the times.

Department stores, drug chains and mass merchandisers alike gave Charlie the needed square footage. Revson advertised in fashion publications, in news print and on national TV. Within a brief period of time, Charlie climbed to the number one fragrance slot (where it still remains today) and Revson returned to the drawing board. By 1975, Revson gave Charlie a suitable mate: Jontue was introduced.

While Charlie was for the natural event, Jontue was for the more sophisticated occasion. Once again, as if to prove that the old days of the trickle-down theory were finished, Revson gave his new fragrance a French name that would connote romance, elegance and mystery—just as the expensive French fragrances had done from their beginning. But this time, like Charlie, Jontue was priced for mass America; and like Charlie, Jontue climbed the ladder to sit just below Charlie in the top spot.

This one-two punch by the top man in the cosmetic field was to revolutionize both the potential of fragrances and the nature of doing business within the industry. It was also to set in motion the imitators and speculators who were now aware of the notable dollars that could be made from perfume.

Today, the American fragrance industry—estimated to be worth in excess of $2-billion—is continuing to grow at an annual rate of about 10%. Since the beginning of 1975, 79 women's fragrances and 38 men's fragrances have been introduced by both professionals within the industry and amateurs from without. Many have been failures; some, like Just Call Me Maxi, disasters.

Yet, the frenzy for fragrances goes on, and with good reason. Generally speaking, only 30% of the dollars spent to produce a new fragrance goes into the actual making, bottling and packaging of that fragrance; the remaining 70% goes into promotion, overhead and profit. When compared with any other product in the cosmetic industry, fragrance—with this kind of cost factor—is by far the most profitable. And, to make matters better, there is little to be concerned about in terms of stock keeping units, since variations in size and color are of minimal concern.

Knowing this, the American fragrance manufacturer is no longer content to introduce a single fragrance every 10 years. With rapidly changing trends and total consumer acceptance of a fragrance that smells good, mass market manufacturers have found it profitable to bring out a new scent as often as every other year and design that scent to have a life expectancy of no more than five years. For the most part, at least in the mass market, classic fragrances are a thing of the past.

Nevertheless, no matter what the success story of a nationally distributed, mass fragrance might be, it will continue to be looked down upon by specialty and department store retailers. The reason is one of necessity. As the greatest percentage of fragrances turns to the mass market, in order to hold a healthy dollar share the conventional store is forced to demand stronger promotional backing as well as total exclusivity. With a fixed profit margin determined by the manufacturer, who for the most part runs the department and specialty store fragrance business, profitability in fragrances can only increase with an increasing sales volume. In perfumes, that volume can only come through the continual introduction of scents not yet offered in other retail outlets.

Luckily, by the 1970s, a new craze was brewing that would give the conventional store fragrance business the individuality that is its lifeblood. As French designers moved from ready-to-wear into men's wear, the American apparel designer emerged in the women's market. Within a short period of time the market became saturated with one prestigious name after the next. To further capitalize on their popularity, these American designers moved into every type of accessory.

Side by side with this, the cosmetic industry had also reached a saturation point in its line of merchandise. The solution was to exploit the successful American designers' names through the women's fragrance industry and the successful French designers' names throughout the men's fragrance industry.

The elegant women's fragrance business, which had been the province of the French, would now be opened to the American manufacturer who would continue to rely upon the French for quality and image in bottling and packaging. Men's fragrances, which for so many years primarily consisted of inexpensive after shaves, would now give the French designers a new market to exploit along with their success story in apparel. The department and specialty stores, which were quickly losing share of market to the mass merchandiser, were more than willing to invest their open-to-buy in these new designer items that would provide the needed exculsivity. This trend still holds true.

In turn, the fragrance manufacturers, both in men's and women's, still need the cachet of the conventional store in order to move their products on a mass basis into drug chains, discount stores, and other mass merchandising outlets. In the fragrance business, it has always been a question of one hand washing the other. The department and specialty stores control the exclusives; the mass merchandisers deliver the volume audience. It is this symbiotic relationship that has created the enormous profits for conventional stores in cosmetics and fragrances. Yet, at the same time, this relationship now appears to be losing ground as a direct result of national television advertising.

The success of Charlie was unique in that Revlon did not wait for a name to become established in conventional stores and then have the product finally distributed to mass merchandisers. Instead Revson attacked all fronts at one time. Top fashion publications gave Charlie the department and specialty store tone; TV introduced it to the masses. Thus the traditional rules of the fragrance business were sundered; however, it was clear that not everyone in the industry really understood the implications of this new thrust in marketing—albeit they all were certainly aware of the increases in profits and sales at Revlon.

The role of the drug store and mass merchandiser has also radically changed during the past 25 years. Years ago before there were shopping centers, the drug store carried the lesser-known brands of fragrances. It was generally a neighborhood operation, and volume potential was limited to the immediate area. There was no advertising other than in the store's window, and the product mix—give or take a soda fountain—primarily consisted of health and beauty aids, with a small number of fragrances stocked for Christmas and, to a lesser extent, for Valentine's Day and Mother's Day. Furthermore, the number of independent drug outlets made it difficult for them to be adequately serviced by manufacturers.

Meanwhile, the role of the mass distributors of inexpensive fragrances had already been captured by the five-and-ten-cent stores whose customer was the much less affluent female who could not afford to dab her neck with an expensive import.

Twenty-five years later, however, an entirely new retailing industry had appeared, and the mass discounters and large drug chains are a product of the evolution. Of greatest import was the emergence of computers, which facilitated shipping and purchasing, thereby greatly diminishing the problem of servicing drug accounts. Chain drug stores moved into almost every area of general merchandise, from blue jeans to liquor, from housewares to toys, and of course into the most profitable area of all—cosmetics, health and beauty aids, and fragrances. It was in the drug store that fragrances became ubiquitous. Because of this, and because drug stores often work on a shorter markup than the conventional, they have been able to capture a large share of the burgeoning fragrance field.

For the major fragrance manufacturer, drug stores are dream customers. They make no demands; and provided there is reaction from the national advertising, they will continue to allocate shelf space to a brand that checks out.

However, although drug store chains may account for a large share of the fragrance business, they still operate under the department and specialty stores' umbrella, where gift-with-purchase and purchase-with-purchase play a significant role in establishing a brand. In reality, most fragrance purchases are impulse gift buys. For this reason, conventional stores have designed the fragrance and cosmetic areas to be centrally located on the main floor in order to maximize the traffic potential and therefore stimulate sales.

By marking down fragrances and cosmetics, a department or specialty store would only be destroying the image it has worked to create. Hence, the fragrance and cosmetic manufacturers have come up with a type of sale better known as gift-with-purchase and purchase-with-purchase. Today, after years of popularity, this type of promotion is being cursed by the industry as a necessary evil, for it is like an albatross around each manufacturer's neck. Despite this, without gift-with-purchase and purchase-with-purchase, there would not be any means by which conventional stores could promote a brand, since they are unable to alter the suggested retail price because, in turn, that would destroy the brand by cheapening it.

Just how large the fragrance business is in this country is a subject which has been avoided by almost all concerned. Estimates range from $1-billion at retail including Avon to $1.4-billion at retail excluding Avon—an indication of just how fragmented the information is from the various outlets which provide fragrances to the public.

In reality, the fragrance business is in excess of $2-billion in women's alone. The bulk is divided among department stores, discounters, and drug chains—with department stores leading in total volume with approximately $550-million. But while department stores may do the largest share of the business, pressure is coming from discounters who contribute about $500-million and drug chains who do approximately $440-million in fragrances. Also in the running are Avon, with $240-million in domestic sales; the specialty stores, with about $120-million; the catalog/retailers, with approximately $130-million, and the general merchandisers, which contribute only about $50-million.

More disturbing to today's leading fragrance retailers is what the future holds for the supermarket giants. Already there have been attempts on the part of supermarket retailers to capture a slice of the cosmetic industry. There have even been some sluggish trial runs in the fragrance end of the business. If the time should come when supermarkets take a full-hearted leap toward capturing notable fragrance volume—and all signs seem to point in this direction—not only will the supermarkets compete with the conventional outlets on price, but more importantly the supermarkets will have the advantage of a consumer who visits their stores on an average of about 2.5 times a week.

If it is true that the future of the mass fragrance industry lies in convenience, what role will department and specialty stores play in the world of fragrances? More likely than not, conventional stores will continue to set the image to be imitated by the mass market. But, as the push to mass distribution continues, there is no doubt that department stores and specialty stores will be forced to become more selective, more promotionally-oriented and certainly more exclusive. The manufacturers in search of prestige will have to be willing to pay the price for this type of distribution.

Meanwhile, mass fragrance manufacturers will further capitalize on what really is America. As more women enter the work force, fewer females will have the leisure to wait for a line-girl's help to purchase a fragrance. It will be the function of the advertising campaign to explain a perfume's use and meaning. If the advertising and the scent please the potential customer, the fragrance will be picked up and paid for without any delay.

Department and specialty stores will still provide the cachet for the brand. But, in the battle for mass distribution, it may well be the supermarket that will take advantage of these new marketing concepts and will accomplish in fragrances what this retail sector has so ably accomplished in pantyhose—*i.e.,* domination of the market.

COLLEGE SURVEY: WOMEN'S MARKET

As the cost of a college education continues to rise and students get less and less financial help from home, categories other than school expenses must suffer. Apparel is one of these areas.

The signs of the times are inescapable. Even young adults whose eyes focus on the wonders of merchandise are thinking twice before they buy. The results of this year's survey of college women indicate that the priorities of life are being put into economic perspective. If students choose to go to college today, something in their budgets must yield. Love clothes or not, apparel has moved down within one year from 23% to 18% of students' annual expenditures, and students are planning to spend 17% less on clothes in '78 than they spent in '77 despite the fact that the same percent (57%) come from homes where family income is above $20,000.

The cost of a college education has indeed steadily risen, and fall '78 tuition hikes were recently announced. Students say they already spend 42% of their total incomes on school expenses, 5% more than last year and 12% more than in '76. As school takes a bigger bite of incomes, other categories must suffer. The only other category that increased as a percent of income dispersement was the car. Since it is most often a transportation necessity, there is no doubt its upkeep continues to escalate (3% of personal income in '76, it is now 8%). Except for clothes and entertainment/vacations all other categories such as cigarettes, toiletries, books, etc., remain constant from one year to the next, evidently because they are considered everyday necessities. Despite the fact that the tourist travel business is reputedly doing far better than the apparel industry, when it comes to college students the reverse is apparently true. While clothes maintained its share of college students' incomes in '77 and dropped 5% of its share this year, entertainment and vacations lost half of its share over the two years to become a 6% smaller share than clothes, particularly interesting in light of the fact that clothes showed 2% less of the income in '76 than

vacations/entertainment. Although not the highest priority on the list, at least clothes are considered a necessity.

And necessity may be the spur to make students, who have a personal and financial stake in their educations, part with their money. Help from home gets scarcer and scarcer each successive year. Today there are not too many families, even in the $20,000 and over bracket, that can any longer afford to take on total responsibility for the higher education of their children. Not unlike national statistics which claim that 51% of all women work, 55% of the mothers of college students work. Although the women's movement might like to include women of this calibre as 'career women,' only 12% have worked 20 years and 46% have worked less than five years. The shift back to the job market might also sound like mother-love but the majority of these women appear not to be working to help their children through college but for the primary purpose of maintaining an established standard of living for the family during an inflationary period.

By 1976, 46% of surveyed students were contributing to their tuitions; today 67% do. This year's students claim to pay 40% of their tuition and 21% of the students say they pay all of it. Seventy-two percent do not receive allowances from home, and even the 28% who do may receive a few dollars more per month but a smaller percent of them are allowed to vary the amount they receive according to need than could a year ago. Approximately the same percent of students work during summer vacations (87%) as did last year, but an additional 11% work part-time during the school year, bringing that figure up to 57%. Forty-seven percent work both during the summer vacations and part-time during the school year.

The most dramatic change in student's working commitments has taken place over a two-year span. In 1976, 40% less students worked during the summer and 48% less worked part-time during the school year. But even with so many students working to help maintain themselves, the '77/ '78 school year has not been the best year for young workers in the job market. Evidently many students found it difficult to find employment for all the hours they desired to work since average earnings are $425 less this year than one year ago.

Most students who attend an expo in Florida [the source of the statistics in this article] come from areas not that far out of reach, at least financially. As a result western areas of the country were not represented. From wherever they hailed, about 42% claimed to come from cities. Since a city can have under 50,000 residents or multi-millions, lifestyles can be very different. However since the greatest majority of our population live in either suburbs or smaller cities, this sample can be considered a good representation of majority residency. Nonetheless being college students, lifestyle, goals and specific pressures makes this sample unique.

But even within the sample, geographic locations show discrepancies. Except for annual income of students, an average of $1,145 in the northeast and $2,100 in the midwest, the northeast and midwest were not too far apart on any other results. The southeast, however, showed family incomes of $20,000 and over at 63%, 6% over the total sample. While only 28% of all the students receive allowances, 41% from this section of the country do. Only 51% of southeastern students contribute to their tuitions compared to 67% of total respondents. Whereas 55% of the mothers work, in the southeast 61% do, and 38% of them have worked more than 11 years compared to 30% for the total sample.

Why students select certain stores*

Merchandise attributes:
Like the merchandise	50%
Price	34%
Quality	32%
Sizes carried	3%
Brands	4%

Store attributes:
Reputation	4%
Service/saleshelp	3%
Unique appeal	3%
Charge cards	1%
Miscellaneous**	4%

*Totals exceed 100% due to multiple answers.
**Atmosphere, advertising, return policies.

College student income dispersement

School expenses:

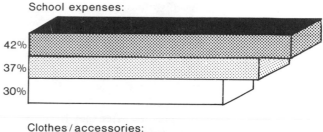

42%
37%
30%

Clothes/accessories:

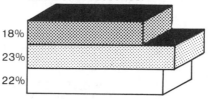

18%
23%
22%

Entertainment/vacations:

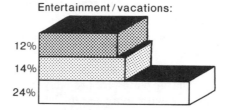

12%
14%
24%

Cosmetics/toiletries:

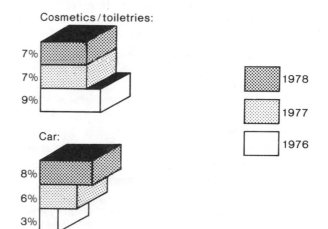

7%
7%
9%

▨	1978
▦	1977
☐	1976

Car:

8%
6%
3%

Hobbies/books/records/sports:

7%
6%
6%

Liquor/cigarettes/drugs:

6%
7%
6%

But even with a little more family help in the southeast, the overwhelming number of students are not having an easy time financing their educations. As a result academic and cultural acumen are far from current students' goals. Students who, from necessity, are learning the value of the dollar are planning to get as many dollars as possible back upon graduation. One-hundred percent of the students plan to work when they finish college and 86% plan to work after they get married. Even more interesting is that 70% plan to continue working after they have a family, quite a reversal from their mothers, 88% of whom did not work when they were born.

Since college students today must earn and pay their own way, they are no longer secondary customers as once they were when 'good ole dad' footed the bills. Family influence has little bearing on where and what they buy, except when they use family charge plates. One enigma this year is that 22% more students are permitted to use their parents' charge accounts than a year ago. Possibly parents who are unable to more actively contribute to expensive college educations salve their consciences by offering fringe benefits when the kids come home to visit. In any case most of these charge plates are probably from department stores. Yet, even with more parents' charge plates at their disposal, only 31% of their clothing is bought in department stores, a definite erosion from 47% in '76 and 38% last year. Over half of student apparel is purchased in specialty and specialty store chains, with specialty stores losing 5% as the specialty store chains gain the lost amount.

What makes students choose the stores in which they buy apparel? Fifty percent of them say it's because they like the merchandise. Almost equal in second place are price and quality of the merchandise. Students of course gave more than one reason for choosing a store, but even adding multiple answers all other answers combined were only 20%. Service, decor and reputation, although seemingly unimportant to college students may if fact be just

something they take for granted. Certainly specialty store chains which continue to get a stronger and stronger share of this business offer all the accoutrements. However, they also offer sharp merchandise at sharp prices, geared to junior customers. Department stores may be losing their share because they have been more concerned with simultaneously lifting the level of sophistication and price points of junior merchandise than concentrating on sharp merchandise at sharp price points. Those department stores that have recently been reporting better business in junior departments than in the rest of R-T-W admit that increases come from merchandise of this calibre. Obviously it's not only the college student who relates to such merchandise.

There is no doubt that college students are predominantly customers of junior departments and stores specializing in junior merchandise. Once again this year an overwhelming 81% of the survey respondents claimed to wear junior sizes, the exact percentage given last year. It is interesting, however, that 76% of this year's students cited pure junior sizes while of last year's sample, only 58% noted pure juniors with 23% claiming to wear split ticket junior and/or misses sizes. The most logical explanation for this shift is that the continuing emphasis on looser, less constructed silhouettes has enabled even fuller-figured or longer-waisted college students to don junior sizes, which most prefer because of more youthful styling and more reasonable prices. It is also possible, however, that more college students are now aware of the deceptively meaningless nature of double ticketing. Having learned that a size 9/10 is essentially no different from a plain old 9, more of this year's students may have simply ignored the second number in their responses. The same 19% of college students as last year still claim to wear pure misses sizes, a somewhat disheartening observation for those updated misses resources which for the past several years have attempted to capture the interest and ensuing patronage of a much younger customer.

Breakdown of items of clothing bought by students [women]

Item	Percent of total sample answering	Quantity bought 1977	plan 1978	Average price paid, 1977	No. Bought at regular price	reduced discount prices	Average no. of days per week worn: 1977	1976
Pants (other than jeans)	90%	5	5	$17.70	3	2	3	3
Skirts	89%	3	3	$17.21	2	1	1	1
Sweaters	91%	7	6	$17.65	5	2	0	0
Blouses/shirts	88%	7	7	$13.21	5	2	0	0
T-shirts	89%	6	5	$ 6.14	5	1	0	0
Dresses	91%	3	4	$27.14	2	1	1	1
Coats or jackets	90%	2	1	$63.27	1.5	0.5	0	0
Swimsuits	86%	2	1	$19.87	1.5	0.5	0	0
Special occasion or evening wear	77%	2	0	$46.06	1.7	0.3	0	0

But despite the high percentage of college students who wear junior sizes and the fact that about 80% of total respondents are of 'average' size (between 7/8 and 11/12), 29% of all college students still claim to have difficulties with fit. With more than half of these complaints based on the fact that students are equally split between too short and too tall, perhaps it might not be so unreasonable for more junior manufacturers to proportion their pants into short, regular, and tall.

Second to apparel proportions, most students' problems with fit related to their own unbalanced proportions. Among total college students in 1978, 15% wear a larger bottom size than top size, and 10% wear a larger top than bottom. (Since today's tops are increasingly voluminous, the latter percentage has dropped 18% from last year.) But while 25% of 1978 college students are not perfectly proportioned, only about 10% regard their situation as a problem. Those retailers, however, who have recently decided to carry only small- and medium-sized tops based on the preponderance of looser silhouettes in the market, might note that despite today's fashion emphasis on fullness, 21% of college students still wear large-sized tops, a percentage which is bound to get bigger as fashion gets slimmer.

While big and loose silhouettes continue to predominate both in showrooms and on selling floors, 55% of all college students in 1978 still prefer figure-revealing clothes. But since 22% actually favor big and loose, and another 18% are fond of both loose and fitted apparel (some according to their changing moods and others according to their changing weight patterns), perhaps the junior market should consistently offer both options simultaneously rather than their current practice of periodically discarding one for the other to render last year's styles obsolete. In light of the highly diversified nature of junior taste levels, those retailers emphasizing both loose and fitted apparel stand the best chance of hanging on to their share of the ever dwindling proportion of disposable income which college students allocate to apparel.

According to their reported unit purchases by college students in 1977, sportswear outsold dresses by more than 9:1, tops outsold bottoms (excluding jeans) by 2.5:1, and pants without jeans outsold skirts by almost 2:1, ratios which seem very much in line with those stocked by most junior departments last year. It is especially noteworthy however that in line with aforementioned demographic information, students from the southeastern section of the United States consistently purchased more items at higher retails than did the national average (*i.e.,* 6 pants vs. 5 nationally, 4 dresses vs. 3 nationally, 3 special occasion outfits vs. 2 nationally, etc.). Even for the total sample, however, it is probable that a number of students considered purchases made during the 1977-78 school year as part of both '77 and '78 figures, resulting in a disproportionately high number of items purchased annually.

Added to that, not all students answered for all classifications. No answers may well imply no purchases. Nevertheless, the relationship among specific categories remains constant as do the average prices paid.

Compared to last year's average retails, college students as a group seem far less willing to trade up than prices in the market would indicate. In fact, the only merchandise for which college students paid more in '77 than they did in '76 were skirts, dresses, and special occasion wear, categories which may have been relatively new in a good number of respondents' wardrobes. On the other hand, students spent significantly less in 1977 than in 1976 for pants, T-shirts, and outerwear, items which were obviously already part of most wardrobes and for which increased pricetags may have seemed greatly unjustified. (Although the decline in average outerwear retails, contrary to industry evaluation is more likely a reflection of a trend toward shorter length jackets and away from full length coats.) But while college students are planning to purchase fewer T-shirts and fewer outerwear garments in 1978 than they did in 1977, they still expect to buy the same number of pants.

The fact that college students have not lost interest in pants was reinforced several times throughout the survey. Among the 37% of students citing bottoms as 'hard to find' items, 48% indicated that great-looking and/or great-fitting pants are particularly difficult to locate, implying that they would purchase more if they could find more of them they liked. Only 9% said the same about skirts. Furthermore, in 1977 surveyed college students wore skirts once a week, dresses once a week, and pants three times a week. In addition, 70% of respondents claim to wear jeans from 4 to 7 days per week. Apparently, students are still changing into jeans after classes or social events (last year's survey indicated that 39% did so) and many of the skirts and dresses which students claimed to have purchased in 1977 apparently spent more time in closets than on campuses. While this may be of no immediate concern to the industry as long as sales continue, it is probable that with tight money, customers will stop buying those items which are least frequently worn.

Despite given retails which indicate that college students across the country remain extremely price-conscious, 60% to 85% of all items purchased in 1977 were allegedly bought at regular prices as opposed to reduced or discounted prices. While this seems high, it is possible that a store's special purchases are often considered regular priced by students who don't actually see numbers crossed out and rewritten. Nevertheless, if college students are in fact spending $17–$18 for regular priced skirts, pants, and sweaters, then most of the junior market offerings for fall '78 are obviously geared too high for these college customers.

In addition, many conventionals are oblivious to students' attitudes toward multiple purchasing. For while numerous junior departments across the country have virtually abdicated coordinates business, 80% of all college students still claim to buy tops and bottoms to go with each other, although they didn't indicate whether from coordinate groups or personally coordinated by them. But since 50% of total respondents still buy tops and bottoms as a single purchase, it seems that coordinates groups which are appropriately styled and priced may be as viable for junior selling as comparable separates.

Although it should hardly be a surprise to anyone in the industry, the greatest discrepancy between what customers want and what retailers provide continues to exist in the area of timing. While retail selling floors are traditionally replete with dark colored wools and sweaters beginning in July, a mere 3% of college respondents claimed to do their major purchasing at that time. Thirty-five percent of college students in 1978 indicated that they purchase most of their fall/winter wardrobes in September, a single month which received more votes than October, November and December combined. For while December remains the biggest volume sportswear month at retail, merchandise is apparently bought as gifts for these customers, not by these customers for themselves. They buy apparel for themselves primarily when they expect to wear it.

Spring/summer presents a slightly different picture featuring two distinct peak buying periods: March for spring purchases and then again in June. While this emphasis on June buying may be merely an indication of increased promotional purchasing, it is also possible that college students are buying in June for summer vacations. Sixty-six percent of responding students claim that they do buy clothes specifically for vacations, while another 10% hedged that they 'sometimes' do. Another explanation for the popularity of June purchasing may be for summer work wardrobes. Since 87% of college students work during summer vacations, and less than 30% receive allowances or have their own charge accounts, it's only logical that they must wait till they get home to use their parents charge plates, or else begin working to accumulate some cash.

Jeans: The Beat Goes On

Unlike most fashion trends which traditionally are supposed to last seven years, but today are frequently born, peak and die with far greater speed, college women's love affair with denim jeans appears to defy mortality. At a time when conventional retailers across the country bemoaned their weak jeans business which has only recently shown signs of life, and when one might expect students'

wardrobes to be glutted with jeans, respondents nonetheless claim to plan on purchasing still more in 1978. Though 48% of the respondents plan to limit their '78 jeans purchases to three pairs or less, 47% plan to buy four pairs or more. This is on top of the average of six pairs that students reportedly already owned last year, plus 1977's additional purchases.

Although many individual students indicated more than one brand preference for jeans, three brands were mentioned by 90% of the students, albeit not in equal proportions. No more than 6% of the students mentioned any other single resource, although 22 names were mentioned in total. Eight percent replied that they couldn't care less whose name was on their jeans.

When asked why they prefer the brands they mentioned, 58% of all respondents stated fit. Durability and style each appeared on 17% of the questionnaires, quality on 12%, comfort on 9%. Surprisingly, in a year of such limited disposable incomes for college students, price was the least important factor in choosing a brand appearing on only 5% of the questionnaires (total exceeds 100% due to multiple answers).

The consensus from the majority of students, most of whom had no serious apparent figure problems, was that they'd pay almost anything for a pair of jeans that fit well and were flattering. This claim is borne out by the fact that $19.09, the average price paid for jeans bought at regular price in '77 (the way most respondents maintain they buy jeans) is $2 higher than the price paid in '76. It's also higher than the average prices respondents are reportedly planning to pay for pants other than jeans ($17.70), skirts ($17.21), or sweaters ($17.65) in '78. In their quest for perfect jeans, the highest price respondents claim to have ever paid averaged out at $22.46 though individual responses to this question ranged from a low of $10 to a high of $36. It is interesting to note that not one student said she ever spent over $36, especially since French fashion jeans, highly touted for the young, sell at that price or higher. Only 11% of all respondents, in fact, were willing to spend $30 or over.

Despite what appeared to be a generally high level of awareness and enthusiasm regarding jeans, the majority of respondents either aren't all that knowledgeable or particular about fiber content. A scant 7% of respondents knew that the term 'blend level' pertained to the percent of cotton and the percent of polyester in their jeans, while another 6% related the term to the percentage of cotton alone. Meanwhile, 74% of the respondents stated that they didn't know what a blend level is, while the remaining 13% answered the question incorrectly.

The continuing importance of jeans

Jeans purchased in 1977:
- 46% of respondents bought 0-3 pairs in 1977
- 39% of respondents bought 4-7 pairs in 1977
- 14% of respondents bought 8 pairs and over in 1977
- 1% of respondents did not answer question

100%

What % were basic blue jeans:	54%
What % were fashion/fancy jeans:	46%
% of fashion/fancy jeans in denim:	56%
corduroy:	25%
other:	1%
did not specify:	18%

100%

Jeans bought at reduced or discount prices: 37%
- 86% of respondents bought 0-3 pairs at reduced or discount prices
- 9% of respondents bought 4-7 pairs at reduced or discount prices
- 2% of respondents bought 8 pairs and over at reduced or discount prices
- 3% of respondents did not answer question

100%

Average price paid for jeans in 1977:
- at reduced or discount price $12.87
- at regular price $19.09

Average highest price ever paid for jeans: $22.46

Expected jean purchases in 1978:
- 48% of respondents plan to buy 0-3 pairs in 1978
- 35% of respondents plan to buy 4-7 pairs in 1978
- 12% of respondents plan to buy 8 pairs and over in 1978
- 5% of respondents did not answer question

100%

Average number of days per week jeans worn in 1977 and 1978:
- 30% of respondents wore jeans 0-3 days in both years
- 70% of respondents wore jeans 4-7 days in both years

Nonetheless, it's primarily because of the magical, mystical attributes of denim that students favor jeans as they do, as evidenced by the fact that 54% of all jeans bought last year are claimed to have been basic blue denim, while of the remaining 46% pegged as fashion jeans, 56% of those were in denim.

Apparently what students mean by 'fashion' jeans isn't the same as the department store interpretation of this term since, despite the fact that a reported 46% of last year's jeans purchases involved fashion jeans, the most popular three brands, mentioned by 90% of the respondents, actually confine their offerings to relatively basic styles. Nonetheless, conventional department store retailers attribute a recent upswing in jeans business to increased sales of true fashion jeans from manufacturers who consistently failed to garner more than 6% of the votes when respondents were asked for their favorite brands.

Students' tendency to equate 'fashion' jeans with basic lines, coupled with the fact that only 17% of all respondents mentioned styling, the raison d'etre of true fashion jeans, as the reason they prefer a particular brand should serve as a signal to department stores. It appears that by concentrating so heavily on fashion jeans, and leaving offerings from the giants of the industry to specialty stores, department stores are abdicating college students' jeans dollars, which may well represent the most consistently loyal market for jeans. It's not only jean business department stores may be losing, since it's likely that students make other purchases at the stores where they buy their jeans. This may well account for the erosion of department store share of college apparel business from 47% to 31% in the past two years.

COLLEGE SURVEY: MEN'S MARKET

Current survey results answer several pertinent questions. First, jeans are and will remain the core of student wardrobes, only students will be buying fewer pairs. Next, apparel is less important to current collegians than past. And finally, a combination of these two facts signal future youth market shrinkage.

The dynamic evolutions within the youthful econo-styles, from the residually rebellious postures of the early seventies, to the more frivolously conventional attitudes of 1978, are partly measurable through the annual youth surveys. The first, initiated in 1974, captured a profile of kids in transition, pulled on the one side by the anti-establishment poses of their immediate forerunners and, on the other, by the repressed influences of the Nixon years.

Where, in 1969, a young man's choice of apparel—uniformly similar despite presumptions of individuality—represented political, cultural and even moral disenchantment, by 1974, young men described themselves as 'middle of the road' and defined apparel as reflections of personality, attainment, and prospects. While the wheel had not completed a full evolution, from the indifferent ivy apparel of the fifties, through the garment mortifications of the sixties, back to white shirt/chino respectability, the disc of public taste had completed a three-quarter turn by the middle of this decade.

The jean(s), the sixties' symbol of societal abasement, as well as equalization, remained nonetheless as the nexus in the youthful apparel transitions, only by 1974, this article of apparel was no longer a badge of revolution but rather a sign of functional particularization. By 1974, 65% of the survey respondents disagreed that jeans inferred a particular political alliance or disenfranchisement on the wearer's part. By 1974, the majority of young men were beginning to ally with the more frivolous cliches such as *clothes are a useful way to express ones' personality;* also *psychologically, a person feels better if he looks better,* and disagreeing with, for one example, *clothes are totally unimportant and a waste of time*—in fact, to this latter, 83% of the respondents disagreed.

Succeeding youth, those interviewed during 1975, 1976 and 1977 were the end-products of the transition, which middles were coincidentally at the center of this decade. For the typical youth, during these annums, clothing became increasingly important. In fact, apparel was their third most important expenditure, ranking closely with entertainment as a priority, although considerably below school-related costs.

But by 1978, there was another shift, both in attitude and in spending. Apparel slipped down to the number four slot in student expenditures. Ranking higher were school expenses, as usual, but then apparel spending was superseded by entertainment and automotive costs.

Does this change of attitude signal the beginning of another polarization? Or is it just a reflection of economic pressures? Or possibly of apparel boredom resulting from silhouette stabilizations and general repetitions? Or is it indicative of a level of garment saturation? Is this shift in percentage expenditures likely to be fixed in the future or is the repositioning of apparel in student budgets a warning to the apparel industry?

The equalization of household incomes, among this year's collegians; the lowering of student discretionary reserves; plus the proletarianization of apparel has weakened the effect of clothing as a primary symbol of status, of self-expression, or of econo-style positioning. Bored, disinterested or disillusioned, students are buying fewer garments than at any time since the institution of this survey. Ironically, they are paying about 30% more on typical apparel purchases than they were at the beginning of 1974, when the range of $8 to $10 was fairly representative of majority jeans purchases against the $11 to $13 and $14 to $16 levels of today. Ironic also is the fact that the valid silhouettes of 1974 are wearable today, so while the typical student is buying fewer units, his apparel ownership is paradoxically about 40% higher than his 1974 counterpart's, the result of accrual, in turn the result of high quality manufacturing (which often proves to be a retardation of, even an anathema to, replacement buying).

Generally retailers are going to have a harder time this year selling apparel to college-age students, according to findings of the 1978 college survey. First of all, both earnings and allowances are down from 1977, thus cutting amounts of discretionary income. Secondly, apparel purchases placed fourth on the priorities expenditures list tallied by college respondents this year. Already, the major apparel classifications have been affected by this lessening of buying power, and jeans, the pivot category, was first to be pinched.

Amounts of disposable student income decreased by over 20% in 1978, and the focus of priority expenditures has shifted. Still, the majority of these dollars are earmarked for school-related expenses, although this category is receiving about 4% less than in 1977, the result of student financial aid availability—these, including pa-

Priority of student expenditures
(How students spend their money)

	Northeast	Southeast	Midwest
School-related	34%	33%	33%
Automotive	16%	27%	15%
Entertainment	16%	17%	16%
Apparel	14%	7%	13%
Sports events / equipment	5%	10%	8%
Drugs / alcohol	8%	2%	9%
Records / stereo equipment	5%	3%	3%
Travel	2%	1%	3%
	100%	100%	100%

rental support plus loans and scholarships (see box). The big change in typical expense patterns has come from the realignment of a category which placed fourth in importance in 1976 and 1977: automotive expenditures. It jumped to a solid number two priority this year, pushing entertainment and apparel—both former second and third slot-holders—down another notch. In the past, automotive expenses claimed 9% to 12% of total spending, but now averages close to 20% nationally—the result of (1) higher fuel and maintenance costs; and (2) automotives becoming a youthful avocation, motorcycles included. Ironically, in relation to the rise in these costs, what kids spend on travel has lessened during the past two years. Where travel once ate up 5% to 7% of expenses, this category now claims only minimal percentages. This occurred, perhaps, because more students own and maintain their own vehicles, and use them instead of commercial transportation.

Getting less discretionary dollars are (a) entertainment, which moved from second place last year to third this annum; and (b) apparel, which fell another notch—and now occupies the fourth position. Even less important are (1) sports participations and equipment; (2) records and stereo components; and (3) drugs, alcohol, and cigarettes—all of which continue to fill even smaller niches than in past college surveys. Although expense percentages shift from year to year and region to region, this is the first annum in which apparel has not been in one of the top three positions.

Also changing is the student choice in point of sale preferences, now showing a marked allegiance for specialty outlets and a continuing loss in share of market for department stores. This, first apparent on the 1977 sampling, was concurrent with the slowing of conventional branch store developments as well as an increase in mail order chain and discounter penetration into key areas of the midwest and southeast. Since the regional demographics from these regions has remained relatively stable over the past four years, shifts in share of market can be attributed (1) to the fact that department stores continue to drag their feet in young men's; (2) to the assortments in most department stores; (3) to generally weak pre-

sentations and poor continuity at this level; (4) to increased consumer mobility, hence choice in point of sale; and (5) to the assumption of a stronger 'jeans' position by the mail order chains and discounters, especially among the outlet leaders within these designations. Because jeans are the most important, and frequent, wardrobe acquisition, the consumer determination in point of sale is often made on the basis of jeans brands (including the chain brands), jeans assortments, and jeans prices. It should, however, be noted that the low response recorded for discounters and chains is due to the facts that, first, students do not always admit patronage in these low-end outlets, and second, *because their purchase rate in these emporiums is not consistent.* Often, they shop the low-enders for an item, a basic or a commodity. But they *prefer and idealize* the conventional branded store. Above all, this age group is retail-insecure. Their purchase reinforcement comes from two directions— the legitimacy of brands (or the appearance of same) and peer approval, although few will admit to either.

In spite of the fact that catalog chains are third on the list of preferred shopping outlets, purchases from catalogs were higher this year than in the past. Here, respondents were asked to identify the type of catalog from which they made their most recent purchase, and, as expected, the majority (83%) of students cited Sears/Penneys/Wards as their top choices. In fact, only 7% named other catalogs, including those from department stores, and from some specialty operations, dealing in specific areas such as jewelry, sporting goods, etc. Most appeared satisfied with their purchases, which ranged from underwear, jeans, and vested suits to appliances, auto parts, and furniture. Only 9% of total respondents stated they would *not* purchase from these books again. Ironically, almost 100% of the negative responses were in regard to apparel purchases, where sizing problems were the most common complaints.

The largest response towards catalog usage came from the southeast—also the area with the highest primary shopping preference for major mail order chains. Lowest figures came from the northeast, which has traditionally been the weakest area for catalog buying, most likely because of the overwhelming density of all types of stores.

Total jeans purchased during past year

	Northeast	Southeast	Midwest
None	1%	5%	1%
1–3 pairs	60%	58%	62%
4–5 pairs	25%	24%	25%
6–7 pairs	8%	7%	7%
8–9 pairs	2%	2%	1%
10 and over	4%	4%	4%
	100%	100%	100%

Despite the industry reposturing in jeans, there has been no change in consumer attitude and only slight shift in the rate of purchase. Production curtailments and piece goods cancellations resulted from retail and wholesale accruals. (And industry pullbacks are now being viewed as treatments for saturated supply lines. While there has been a slight erosion in retail rates of sale, the loss in these unit transactions adds up to far less than proposed wholesale cutbacks. However, apparel analysts now say that as soon as the major retailers adjust their stock levels downward, and sell off aging issues, this market should show improvement. The anticipated retail dollar loss in now being quoted at 10%, or thereabouts.)

According to the student survey, jeans—especially denim—will continue as the core of purchases, wardrobes and wear time; are uniquely suited to the econo-style of the average student—more so than any other pants type. Whatever the sales attrition eventually totals, the loss will not be due to consumer dissatisfaction with the product. Nor will it be because the student is 'dressing up.' What has affected O-T-C activity, and what will continue to do so, however, is a combination of several factors. First, there was an artificial sales hump beginning last spring, due to price footballing on branded denims. During this period, student purchases went up, meaning that many of these kids are, like the retailers, temporarily *overinventoried*. While their wear time is identical to that of past surveys, their immediate needs and response have been curtailed by *high ownership*.

Next, the silhouette changes have caused a drop-off in flare leg sales, causing even higher totals on retail slow sell. Formerly an east coast predilection, the straight leg jean is now being cashiered nationally and according to this survey, almost 20% of recent purchases—within the last three months—were in this silhouette. But while a model change should have been the means of boosting jeans sales, the combination of short open-to-buy funds and mounting blocks of stock has limited retail investments to a core of basically styled straight leg numbers. Once retail assortments are expanded into fashion specializations, however, this nucleus of stocks should produce a much higher growth rate—*but* flares will show a concurrent decrease.

Finally, the O-T-C activation of certain slacks styles has caused a division of student spending. Although not yet a national factor, according to student answers, the tube slack has eaten somewhat into traditional jeans sales in the northeast, southwest and west coast—as have other types of casual slacks constructions—albeit not significantly. This is not interpreted as a sign that students are dressing up more than usual or that slacks will ever replace the jean. It is, however, an indication that collegians are willing to diversify their purchases and to buy items, even if applicable only to limited wear time. Obviously less susceptible to fashion change than the distaff customer, male students are nevertheless being exposed to broader retail selections, much of which they find acceptable to their particular econo-style.

On the general question of quantity of jeans purchased during the past school year, the majority of students—an average 60%—cited one to three pairs as their total purchases. About one-quarter of respondents bought between four and five pairs These purchases include a *majority of denim*—which showed even higher rates of purchase prior to the beginning of the school term—followed by corduroy, fatigue cloth, and twill. Denim appears to be holding position in this market. Between 36% and 45% of respondents claimed to have purchased their most recent pair of denims within the last month.

Although students consider themselves fashion-, rather than price-conscious shoppers, many agreed that they do look for bargains when shopping for jeans. This was obviously not the case last year when 45% of respondents claimed to have paid $16 or more for their last jeans purchase. In the past year, over 50% of college men bought from one to three pairs of jeans 'on sale.' The dominant price points were $16 and under—specifically, $11–$13 and $14–$16—covering more than 60% of all jeans purchased. Activity within $11 to $13 range has almost doubled.

When naming primary shopping outlets for jeans, not surprisingly, the great majority of youthful shoppers chose specialty operations, including jeans stores.

Not only have jeans-only operations claimed increasingly large numbers of youthful customers, but many of these outlets concentrate on bargain-priced incentives along with their fashion presentations. In fact, the jeans specialty operations are, dubiously, credited with originating the price footballing of the national branded jeans lines. When these jeans chains began promoting, competing stores had little choice but to follow, and within months, jeans which originally retailed for $13.50 were going for as little as $8.97 and $9.99 in many areas.

(For the balance of this year, it appears this price promotion trend will continue in certain regions, although with nowhere near the fervor or availability which characterized last year's price scaling. Jeans chains increased early fall 1977 volume to such a degree, by promoting these labels, that they say the price war could begin again this summer if only to cover some of last year's figures.)

Not only have fluctuating price points caused a stir in the jeans market, but fabrication was also a major issue for a time. However, as in other men's wear markets, the question of all-cotton versus polyester/cotton was more hotly debated by manufacturers, fiber companies, mills and retailers than by student consumers. In fact, most of these shoppers are hardly aware of what constitutes the fiber content of their jeans. College respondents were fairly evenly divided between those who *believed* their last jeans purchase was 100% cotton and those who simply didn't recall or didn't know or didn't care. And to the question of would they buy only 100% cotton denim, the majority of respondents—except in the southcast where cotton is an economic and emotional issue—said NO. This, compared to last year's reversal when the majority from the northeast and midwest elected to buy only all-cotton, and paradoxically the southeasterners chose blends. The only other difference between this year's poll and last year's, is that now after all the publicity, there are very few students who do *not* have an opinion on the cotton vs. blends issue.

As to fabric preference for jeans, denim, of course, surpassed all other categories. However, as in past years, corduroy remains a strong number two, in most cases followed by fatigue cloth and twill. Chino, gabardine, and knits placed last—but often it appears that college students consider only denim and perhaps corduroy suitable for jeans—all other weaves are automatically regarded as slacks fabrications.

Encouraging for retailers, the great majority of respondents said they would be willing to buy another pair of denim jeans *right away*—a definite plus for denims considering the fact that the majority of respondents also stated they had bought their most recent pair within the last month. Only minimal percentages of students admitted boredom with denims. (If not strictly bargain-hunters, students are definitely more price-conscious than those surveyed in past years: more than half the college men polled responded they would buy denims again only if they considered the selling price 'fair.' Lesser numbers were willing to spend a lot of money to get the 'right'style—and the least numbers cited price reductions as their only buying criteria.)

On style, especially in the northeast—most respondents say they buy chiefly basics (primarily because that's the straight leg emphasis)—compared to the same question two years ago, when students from this area agreed to owning at least one western style, but overwhelmingly vetoed the purchasing of another basic model. However, right now, the terms 'fashion' and 'basic'are more difficult to apply, except to the most detailed and trimmed garments or the plainest of westerns. Actually, most O-T-C jeans are basic in shape, with few deviations in silhouette except for leg modifications. The major difference between one and another is pocket or belt loop treatment, stitching and seam details. The highly detailed styles of a few years ago with leather insets, embroider, grommets, and multicolor stitching have passed out of vogue, replaced by basics.

With brand loyalty, there seems to be some shift in progress on the part of college students. Although from one-quarter to one-third of respondents claimed to buy jeans regardless of brand—compared to just 8% who were totally nonbrand-conscious in 1976—most students still search out specific labels. In fact, those students who buy 'certain brands only' represent 35% to 40%. This is a majority but far short of the 57% response last year. About one-third of the respondents were willing to buy *many* brands rather than limit themselves to one or two labels only. While brand loyalties have changed, and this is evident, labels are still an important aspect in determining eventual jeans purchases, as well as in choice of outlets. (While the major national brands gathered a predictable response in this survey, many of the secondary, fashion labels had a high purchase index as well.)

With more students working for their spending money, and with apparel slipping down to fourth place as expenditures, certain brands are, perhaps, becoming less important than price. So, even though students prefer to have a familiar label on their jeans, they are willing to buy differently than in past years.

Purchasing frequency of slacks has risen an average 42% in the zero to three-month time span during the last couple of years. In fact, over one-half of those units purchased within the last three months were actually bought within the last 30 days. A possible reason for this may be that purchasing was done in anticipation of weather changes as spring approached. Since the college student is spending less on apparel this year, his buying is done as the need arises. Or perhaps the reason is economics—*i.e.,* the loosening up of dollars in the past few weeks, after school expenses had been paid.

In an overall comparison of price points this year as opposed to last year—the activity in the $0 to $10.99 range is up 60%; $25-and-up is up 42%; but the $17 to $19.99 plateau is down by 48%. Taken regionally, the northeast has transacted the highest percentage at the lower price points ($0 to $10.99 and $11 to $13.99 combined)—29% as opposed to 17% in the southeast, and

Denim jeans: shopping attitudes

	Northeast	Southeast	Midwest
Would buy another pair right away	42%	62%	60%
Has enough	31%	27%	28%
Is tired of denim jeans	5%	1%	1%
Will buy replacements only	22%	10%	11%
	100%	100%	100%

Purpose of denim jeans

	Northeast	Southeast	Midwest
Knock-around pants	55%	49%	62%
Fashion and look	45%	51%	38%
	100%	100%	100%

Prices of denim jeans

	Northeast	Southeast	Midwest
Will spend a lot	41%	40%	31%
Will buy only if price is 'fair'	55%	50%	66%
Will buy only 'on sale'	4%	10%	3%
	100%	100%	100%

Styling of denim jeans

	Northeast	Southeast	Midwest
Buys a variety of styles	27%	37%	38%
Buys mainly basics	63%	53%	54%
Buys what friends buy	10%	10%	8%
	100%	100%	100%

Importance of brands

	Northeast	Southeast	Midwest
Buys certain brands only	32%	40%	41%
Shops around and buys many brands	35%	33%	34%
Buys regardless of brand	33%	27%	25%
	100%	100%	100%

Fiber content: most recent denim jeans purchase*

	Northeast	Southeast	Midwest
100% cotton	45%	53%	49%
Cotton blend	8%	7%	6%
Don't remember	47%	40%	45%
	100%	100%	100%

*Respondents were told to answer this question only if they 'thought' they remembered the fiber level. Otherwise they were told to check off the answer 'don't remember.'

Would you buy only 100% cotton denim?

	Yes	No	Doesn't Matter
Northeast	35%	62%	3%
Southeast	51%	46%	3%
Midwest	40%	59%	1%

19% in the midwest. This may be because competition, hence, promoting, is more competitive in this densely populated region of the country. The $14 to $16.99 price points remain strong in all areas and about the same percentage as last year, 25% of business, was transacted here. The strongest price range in the southeast and midwest is that of $20 to $24.99, with an average of 30% of sales as opposed to the northeast where this price range accounts for only 15% of the business. Also, the northeast customer shops more often in specialty stores, especially pants chains, than his midwest and southeast counterpart—20% more.

If this student is calling anything other than denim jeans a slack, as he has in the past, then the jean look in other fabrications—which specialty stores are most likely promoting alongside with their denims at price points under $13.99—would also account for the strength of the lower price points in the northeast. However, students in the northeast have the *least brand loyalty.*

(Concerning the increase of slacks purchases in the $25-and-up price range, perhaps one reason for the increased activity is natural fibers, the use of which raises the price of a pair of slacks. In fact, when the students were questioned as to whether they would buy slacks which have to be drycleaned, it was an almost even yes/no split, with the southeastern students providing the most resistance to drycleaning, and the northeasterners indicating the least. It is the preference for easy-care slacks, however, which accounts for the large increase of knit pant ownership in the southeast. Other factors influencing knit slacks ownership are weather and (since a large part of the knit slacks are manufactured in the southeast) there is a large retail market. Overall ownership in knit slacks has increased from 15% to 46% since last year, with the northeast index dropping by 5%. Of those who own knit slacks, however, most are satisfied, and from 4% to 18% *more* students, than last year, say they will buy another pair.)

While figures of ownership of knit pants may look impressive, this fabrication is a small part of what today's college student owns in the category that he calls 'dress' pants. The majority of students questioned consider *anything* other than blue denim, a dress pant. In terms of fabric preferences, corduroy came in second to denim, in all constructions, as the most popular.

As to whether students will buy another pair of slacks before they purchase jeans, the majority say NO; their next purchase will be jeans.

Concerning the importance of brands in slacks, in 1976 only 12% looked for particular brands in this construction (or in what they term slacks construction). In 1977, this figure rose to 18%. In 1978, while the students did not state that they look for a particular brand, 15% to 24% said that their last purchase was from a branded slack line; 22% to 32% purchased from major branded *jeans* lines which also produce casual slacks. From 22% to 33% did not remember the brand of their most recent slacks purchase, even though in the majority of cases, this had been made within the last three months, with over one half of that amount purchased within the last 30 days. Obviously, slacks brands make less of an impression on students than jeans labels—probably because over three-quarters of their bottoms purchases are jeans Also, in most young men's stores and departments, there has been poor continuity of branded slacks stocks. In addition, many students cross over into men's areas for this purchase.

Outlet preferences for slacks varied significantly from sources cited as *primary* shopping outlets. Specialty stores picked up several percentage points in 1978 and apparently, these, from department stores. The largest came in the northeast.

Initial survey results signal a change of attitude at the student level. Without having compromised their integrity, collegians are now shopping with a new set of purchase criteria. Where once price was only marginally important as a transaction stimulus, it is now *very.* Where fashion changes motivated this consumer to increase his purchase index, now the effect is diluted and the student is buying less. In fact, his whole focus has changed and now this male is spending money on different gratifications. Already, the pillar jeans and slacks business has softened.

Have these repositioned spending priorities affected other categories of apparel as much as bottoms? Preliminaries show both a yes and no.

WHAT CONSUMERS OF FASHION WANT TO KNOW

A Study of Informational Requirements and Buying Behavior

Claude R. Martin, Jr.

This article reports the results of an experiment with consumers of fashion goods to determine their information requirements in making a purchase decision. It lends support to the new wave of consumerism and the resulting demand for increased product information, especially for information about price and the physical characteristics of the product.

The practice of marketing under a cloak of ambiguity appears to be diminishing with the rise of consumerism and marketers' continuing exploration of the consumer's decision-making process. No longer is the sole purpose of marketing to tailor the product to meet the marketer's preconceived idea of the consumer. Marketers are now faced with the obligation to recognize the consumer's need for information about the product and assist him in satisfying this need. The principal causes for this added obligation are two: the blossoming recognition on the part of marketers of the role information seeking plays in consumers' decision processes and the role goverment has played in directing that consumers' informational needs be fulfilled.

The marketing literature is rich with material about the content of information supplied to the consumer. There is also much research relative to the uses of information resources. However, identification of the kinds of information which the consumer requires—or, at least, wants—to make his purchase decisions is significantly sparse. A review of the literature and personal interviews with retailers indicate that this sparseness is particularly evident in the area of fashion goods, especially in women's and men's ready-to-wear clothing.

Research Design

The department store members of what is called Research Group "B" of the Bureau of Business Research at the University of Michigan have committed support both financially and otherwise to explore the customer's need for information as well as other aspects of the decision process. One of the projects in this continuing program was recently completed at Myers Brothers' department store in Springfield, Illinois. Women from throughout the Springfield area were invited to participate in an experimental program concerning the purchase of fashion goods.

First, each woman was shown a line drawing of a shirt dress that had a very basic style. The criterion of a basic style evolved from a pretest conducted in January 1970, in Ann Arbor, Michigan. The test was designed to prevent any substantial patterns of nonresponse which a garment styled for a particular age group might create. Each

woman was told she could assume that the dress fit her correctly but that she could *not* assume any other information about the dress. Then she was asked whether, on the basis of the drawing only, she would purchase the dress. After responding to this question, she was informed that she would be permitted to learn some facts about the garment, and she was given the following list of nine factors of information that would be available to her:

  Price
  Color
  Content of material
  Store (where the garment could be purchased)
  Brand name
  Department of store (where garment could be purchased)
  Instructions for care of garment
  Salesgirl's evaluation of style
  Salesgirl's evaluation of quality

The participants did not have to select any information, they could stop at anytime they wished in the selection process, and they were permitted to choose a maximum of five factors. The content of the information selected could be different for different women. For example, two women could choose "Brand name" as a factor that would influence their purchase but receive two different brand names as information.

Finally, the women were asked again whether they would buy the dress and for what reason. The experiment was then repeated with another dress and a coat. These garments were also presented as having a basic style.

Research Findings

The participants in this study represented a broad range of ages and socioeconomic status, and none of the segments in these spectrums were "loaded."

The responses of the participants were assigned to a matrix showing pre- and postinformation buying decisions

From "What Consumers of Fashion Want to Know." *Journal of Retailing,* Vol. 47, No. 4, Winter 1971–1972, pp. 65–71, 94. Reprinted by permission of the publisher.

(Figure 1). The object of this matrix was to examine the potential differences, based on informational needs, among the nine types of decisions within the matrix. The sample examined was 243 purchases, and this potential constraint on the size of individual matrix cells caused the blending or mixing of the nine decisions into larger units. Thus we examined the differences between participants whose behavior did not change after the experiment (the diagonal line in the matrix) and those whose behavior did change (the other six positions in the matrix). Then we examined the differences between those whose behavior changed positively (boxes 1, 2, and 3 in the matrix) and those whose behavior changed negatively (boxes 4, 5, and 6 in the matrix).

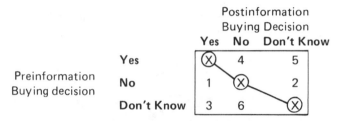

Figure 1. Preinformation and Postinformation Buying Decision Matrix.

Overall Results

The participants, in answering why they made their buying decision, heavily emphasized the information supplied in the experiment. Only 25 percent indicated that style was the prime reason for the decision, while 67 percent reported that information they had requested about the garment was the prime factor in their decision. In all, 55 percent of the participants said price was the prime element in their decision.

Table I shows the aggregate percentage of participants by their choice of information factor. The results indicate the relative importance of price and physical characteristics, such as color and material, as opposed to the psychological factors of the decision, such as brand, store, salesgirl's evaluation of quality and style, and location within store. Table II emphasizes this relative importance by showing the percentage distribution by the order in which the informational factors were selected. The fact that 62 percent of the participants wanted to know the price as the first "bit" of information they received and the subsequent distribution by order of choice show the added importance of the factor of price over the two physical characteristics of color and material.

Changers vs. Nonchangers

The findings point to price as the major factor that distinguishes persons making a change in their decision from those persons who remained committed to their original purchase decision. Of those who examined the price

TABLE I
Percentage of Participants Requesting Information Factors

Information Factor	Overall Percentage of Participants Requesting the Factor
Price	86
Color	74
Material content	64
Brand name	44
Store identification	35
Garment care	35
Department of store where sold	16
Salesgirl's evaluation of quality	9
Salesgirl's evaluation of style	9

TABLE II
Percentage of Participants in Order of Choice of Information Factor Selected

Factor	Choice				
	1	2	3	4	5
Color	12	34	28	14	8
Material content	13	24	19	16	8
Brand name	6	9	12	17	20
Price	62	22	13	4	··
Store identification	2	3	10	20	18
Department where sold	1	2	3	4	15
Garment care	2	5	12	17	15
Salesgirl—quality	1	··	2	4	8
Salesgirl—style	1	··	1	4	8

factor, price was the primary influence on 78.1 percent of the women who changed their decision and on 37.1 percent of those who did not change their decision. Price was the first "bit" of information requested by 67.7 percent of those who changed and 53.7 percent of those who didn't. The difference between both sets of percentages is significant at the .05 level.

Positive vs. Negative Changers

The pretesting resulted in the hypothesis that those who make a positive change make greater demands for information—that is, they require more "bits" of information—than those who make a negative change in their decision.

We assigned a series of weights to informational choices of all participants in the rank-order in which the information was selected. For the informational factor selected first we assigned a weight of 5, and then, in descending order, the weights of 4, 3, 2, and 1 for the second through fifth choices. Thus, if 20 persons selected price as a choice they would receive a weighted score of 100 (20 × 5).

The participants making a positive change in their decision used 88.3 percent of the potential weighted score, while those making a negative decision used 75.1 percent of their potential score. This difference is significant at the .05 level.

When the weighted score measure is used for all informational factors, there are no significant differences between the two groups who changed their decision except in the area of material content and color. Those who changed positively use these physical factors more heavily than do those who change negatively. The results of using the weighted score measure are shown in Table III, and reinforcement for the difference between the decision changers is seen in Table IV, which details the percentage of participants who continue to seek information through the first of three choices. This again indicates that positive changers use more informational factors in their decision process than do negative changers.

Table V gives the informational factors that each of the three types of participants—positive changers, negative changers, and nonchangers—chose in the rank-order in which they were selected. There are no apparent differences in the order of importance of the types of information for the three classes of participants.

Analysis of Results

The participants in this experimental study indicated that they used information supplied by the seller when buying fashion goods. A significantly large number of people described the information received as a prime factor in their buying decision. A ranking of the informational factors by importance of use shows that price and the physical properties of the garment contribute to the buying decision more than do psychological factors.

The element of price is significant in distinguishing those who change behavior as a result of the information received from those who do not alter their decision process. Among the consumers who did make a change, those who changed their behavior in a positive direction used more "bits" of information than those who changed negatively. Further, the positive changers used information about the physical characteristics of the material and color of the garment more heavily than did the negative changers.

Conclusions

The object of this study was not to examine fully the criteria for choice in buying decision for fashion goods, but rather to identify the different informational requirements that different buyers of ready-to-wear clothing demand in the process of making their buying decision.

The relative unimportance of psychological factors, especially brand names, is in sharp contrast to the emphasis

TABLE III
Weighted-Score Percentages

Informational Factor	Positive Changers	Negative Changers
Brand name	20.0	24.0
Price	85.0	88.9
Material content*	65.0	49.8
Color*	66.0	53.3

*Significantly different at the 5 percent level.

SOURCE: Samuel Richmond, *Statistical Analysis* (2d ed.; New York: Ronald Press, 1964), pp. 205-6.

TABLE IV
Percentage of Participants Seeking
Information Through Three Choices

Choices	Positive Changers	Negative Changers
1	100.0	97.8
2	100.0	82.2
3	85.0	60.0

TABLE V
Rank-Order of Weighted Scores of Five Most
Favored Information Factors

Rank-Order	Positive Changer Factor	Score	Negative Changer Factor	Score	Nonchanger Factor	Score
1	Price	85	Price	200	Price	588
2	Color	66	Color	120	Color	400
3	Material	65	Material	112	Material	299
4	Brand	20	Brand	54	Brand	197
5	Store identification	29	Store identification	21	Store identification	104

which much fashion advertising puts on the importance of brand names.

The results of this study add some support to the rising trend called consumerism: The results show that information about price (first) and about the physical properties of fashion clothes (second) is in large part the basis for a consumer's buying decision: therefore, his demands for such information are consistent with his behavior. What's more, the study shows that those who move toward a positive buying decision apparently need more information than those who move toward rejecting a garment. This latter finding is significant for marketers. It reemphasizes their new obligation to make available to a susceptible market target the information necessary to make buying decisions.

READING THE LABELS ON APPAREL AND HOUSEHOLD TEXTILES

William L. Mauldin and Marianne S. Beeson

Labels and hang tags on textile products include a wide variety of descriptive terms and instructions to the consumer. This information can be very helpful in selection, in purchase, and during use and care of textile items.

Textile labels can also be confusing and may be ignored by some consumers. So much information is given it may seem overwhelming. The meaning of some technical terms may not be understood. Or the ability to relate textile information to individual needs and wants may be lacking. In some cases labels are actually unclear, containing conflicting instructions or incomplete information.

In general, however, it is not difficult to understand the terms used to describe textiles and their care. Federal legislation and rulings regarding textiles and voluntary efforts by the industry have made it possible to know, for the most part, what to expect on textile labeling. But in rapidly changing markets which are heavily influenced by fashion and by technological changes, the updating of your consumer knowledge is necessary from time to time as new types of textile products become available.

Careful attention to labeling can increase satisfaction with apparel and household textile products. Most textiles can be damaged or ruined by improper use and care. This can be a sad experience when a daughter's favorite sweater is no longer wearable. Since some textile items represent a large investment, reduction of wear life can mean a serious financial loss as well. We usually expect such items as carpets, rugs, draperies, curtains, slip covers, upholstery fabrics, bedspreads, and blankets to perform satisfactorily over a period of several years before they have to be replaced.

The information provided on textile labels and hang tags offers factual knowledge about the products, which can make purchasing decisions easier and help you to obtain maximum use and enjoyment.

For those responsible for laundering and cleaning clothes, one of the most common problems used to be knowing exactly what care procedures were required. This information was usually given on hang tags, but they were of course removed by consumers prior to wear. Highly organized individuals were able to file the tags with a description of the garment, but most of us had problems locating the instructions whenever the garment needed cleaning.

A new Federal Trade Commission (FTC) ruling, which went into effect in July 1972, now requires that care instructions be permanently affixed to the garment on a label sewn in, adhered, or stamped onto the garment. Thus, directions for care are located where they can be used most effectively.

The ruling applies to all articles of wearing apparel which require care and to fabrics sold by the yard. Some items are exempt from the ruling: articles priced at $3 or less which are completely washable, footwear, and items to cover the head and hands.

The FTC has granted several additional exemptions upon petition from manufacturers under conditions where "utility or appearance would be substantially impaired by a permanently attached label."

Some of the labels may be fold-over or loop labels on which instructions continue around the loop of the label. Consumers should be sure to read the entire label.

If a garment is packaged and the label not easily visible, the care instructions should be repeated on the package itself or on another prominent tag. Intent of the ruling is to have care instructions available at the time of purchase, as well as the time of actual care, thus making it possible to compare products in terms of care required. The cost and convenience of care should be considered in reaching purchasing decisions.

For piece goods, labels are ordinarily offered to the consumer with the purchase of fabrics. The consumer should check the label to see that it contains the same care instructions as those printed on the fabric bolt or attached hang tag.

One system of label distribution uses a number code. You can check the number code on the end of the fabric bolt to be sure it corresponds to the number on the care label.

Since the care labels for piece goods are usually separate from the fabrics and distributed by the sales person, mistakes can be made. Consumers should ask for a care label if it is not provided. It is the consumer's important responsibility to attach the care label to the garment after it is made.

It is also the home sewer's responsibility to keep track of the label which is intended for a particular fabric. When several different fabrics are purchased at one time or when fabrics are stored before being made into garments, you may find it necessary to tape or pin the appropriate label to the edge of the fabric piece.

Care of the home constructed garment will not be successful unless all the fabrics, findings, and trimmings are similar in regard to care. Linings, interfacings, and trims must be selected with care requirements that are compatible with the care needed for the garment fabric. A

Reprinted from *The 1973 Yearbook of Agriculture: Handbook for the Home.* U.S. Department of Agriculture, Washington, D.C.: U.S. Government Printing Office, 1973, pp. 311–316.

CONSUMER CARE GUIDE FOR APPAREL
American Apparel Manufacturers Association

	When Label Reads:	It Means:
MACHINE WASHABLE	Machine Wash	Wash, bleach, dry and press by any customary method including commercial laundering and dry cleaning
	Home launder only	Same as above but do not use commercial laundering
	No Chlorine Bleach	Do not use chlorine bleach. Oxygen bleach may be used
	No bleach	Do not use any type of bleach
	Cold wash Cold rinse	Use cold water from tap or cold washing machine setting
	Warm wash Warm rinse	Use warm water or warm washing machine setting
	Hot wash	Use hot water or hot washing machine setting
	No spin	Remove wash load before final machine spin cycle
	Delicate cycle Gentle cycle	Use appropriate machine setting; otherwise wash by hand
	Durable press cycle Permanent press cycle	Use appropriate machine setting; otherwise use warm wash, cold rinse and short spin cycle
	Wash separately	Wash alone or with like colors

	When Label Reads:	It Means:
NON-MACHINE WASHING	Hand wash	Launder only by hand in lukewarm (hand comfortable) water. May be bleached. May be dry cleaned
	Hand wash only	Same as above but do not dry clean
	Hand wash separately	Hand wash alone or with like colors
	No bleach	Do not use bleach
	Damp wipe	Surface clean with damp cloth or sponge
HOME DRYING	Tumble dry	Dry in tumble dryer at specified setting—high, medium, low or no heat
	Tumble dry Remove promptly	Same as above but in absence of cool down cycle remove at once when tumbling stops
	Drip dry	Hang wet and allow to dry with hand shaping only
	Line dry	Hang damp and allow to dry
	No wring No twist	Hang dry, drip dry or dry flat only. Handle to prevent wrinkles and distortion
	Dry flat	Lay garment on flat surface
	Block to dry	Maintain original size and shape while drying
IRONING OR PRESSING	Cool iron	Set iron at lowest setting
	Warm iron	Set iron at medium setting
	Hot iron	Set iron at hot setting
	Do not iron	Do not iron or press with heat
	Steam iron	Iron or press with steam
	Iron damp	Dampen garment before ironing
MISCELLANEOUS	Dry clean only	Garment should be dry cleaned only, including self-service
	Professionally dry clean only	Do not use self-service dry cleaning
	No dryclean	Use recommended care instructions. No dry cleaning materials to be used

lining labeled "Do not dryclean" used with a garment fabric labeled "Dryclean only" would cause an obvious problem.

Because care labels on garments are necessarily brief, additional information may be needed in order to know more about garment care. The chart with this chapter may be used as a reference.

The Flammable Fabrics Act (1967) has broadened the scope of textiles legislation to include the development of Department of Commerce (DOC) Flammability Standards for certain textile products.

At the present time children's sleepwear (sizes 0–6✕), fabrics intended for children's sleepwear, carpets and rugs, mattresses and mattress pads are covered under standards.

It is expected that additional standards will be developed to apply to other textile products, such as children's sleepwear in sizes 7–14, girls' dresses, blankets, draperies, and upholstered furnishings.

The standards specify laboratory test methods that subject textile products to sources of fire somewhat related to household situations which can cause textiles to burn.

For example, burning cigarettes are the source of ignition in the test for mattresses and mattress pads, since smoking in bed is a frequent cause of fires. Textiles which meet the various standards may char, or burn very slowly, or not burn at all under the test conditions.

For products that meet the flammability standards, the consumer may be protected from undue hazard from textiles flammability. However, prevention of burn injuries and deaths will also continue to depend upon safety precautions. Do not become careless about sources of fire just because some textiles on the market are now flame-retardant or resistant to fire.

Flammability is referred to on labeling of textile items covered under the present DOC standards. When a standard becomes effective there is often a "period of grace" during which products may be marketed which do not meet the standard so long as cautionary labeling appears.

In the case of children's sleepwear, prior to July 1973, garments which did not meet the standard were labeled "Flammable (does not meet U.S. DOC Standard FF-3–71). Should not be worn near sources of fire."

Rugs and carpets larger than 24 square feet must meet the flammability standard and will bear a label "Approved. Meets or exceeds Federal Flammability Standard DOC-FF-1–70." Rugs less than 24 square feet and bath mats must carry warning labels if they do not pass the flammability test.

Care instructions on flame resistant textiles should be strictly followed. Characteristics of these products can be changed drastically by improper care, often to the point of making the fabric highly flammable. In particular, the effect of flame-retardant finishes on fabrics can be counteracted by soap and hard water mineral deposits on the fabric.

You may see labels cautioning, "Do not use soap. Launder with phosphate detergent." This procedure is needed in order to allow the flame-retardant finish to remain effective. There is a concern about households in areas which have banned the sale of phosphate detergents in order to lessen water pollution problems. At present the dilemma is not resolved.

To protect consumers from false advertising and misbranding of fiber content of textile products, Congress enacted the Textile Fiber Products Identification Act in 1958. The Act covers wearing apparel and household textiles. An important provision is the requirement that textiles be labeled or otherwise identified by percent of each fiber present, by weight, in amounts of 5 percent or more.

Fibers must be listed in their order of predominance, each fiber designated by its generic name. Cotton, wool, silk, and flax are the names used for the major natural fibers. The Act provided for establishing generic names for the manmade fibers, classifying them according to chemical composition as

acetate	metallic	rayon
acrylic	modacrylic	rubber
anidex	nylon	saran
azlon	nytril	spandex
glass	olefin	triacetate
lastrile	polyester	vinal
		vinyon*

Consumers should learn to recognize fiber generic names and realize that there are likely to be several trade names for the same type of fiber.

This knowledge can make comparison shopping easier since the performance and care required for fibers with the same generic name can be expected to be very similar when used in the same type of product. However, keep in mind that fiber content is only one of many factors which determine characteristics of the final product.

Other Federal legislation has been enacted to prevent deception in labeling of furs and wool. The Wool Products Labeling Act of 1939 requires fiber content labeling by wool type as defined below:

• Wool—fiber from the fleece of the sheep or lamb or hair of the Angora or Cashmere goat (or hair of the camel, llama, alpaca, and vicuna) which has never been reclaimed from any woven or felted wool product
• Reprocessed wool—fiber which has previously been manufactured into a wool product but has not been used in any way by the ultimate consumer
• Reused wool—fiber reclaimed from wool products which have been used by the ultimate consumer.

The term "virgin wool" was not defined in the original Act, but it is used on labels to refer to new wool fiber which has never previously processed. None of the terms which describe wool type indicate anything to the consumer about quality or grade of the wool fiber.

The Fur Products Labeling Act of 1951 prevents deception by requiring labeling of the true English name of the fur-bearing animal and other provisions.

Designation of fabric weight may appear on labels and be useful in comparing textile products or in determining suitability of fabric to season of the year. Fabrics for men's suits and work clothes, draperies, tents, and camping equipment are sometimes described by weight in ounces per square yard or ounces per linear yard.

Thread count of fabrics is usually given on labels as a single number (for example, 180) representing the total number of warp and filling threads or yarns per square inch, although two numbers may also be used. A thread count of 95 × 85 means 95 warp yarns and 85 filling yarns per square inch.

---

*Since the publication of this article, the FTC has approved two additional generic fiber classifications: aramid and novoloid.

Thread count is often labeled on sheets, pillow-cases, and draperies, and can be used as an indicator of durability in comparing items of the same fiber content and fabric construction.

Often trade names are among the most visibly prominent words on textile labels. The manufacturer of the item may be identified in characteristic printing style and trademark symbols. It is possible for a single item to carry trade name labeling for almost every step in the manufacturing process: fiber trade names, yarn processes or finishes, fabric mill, fabric finishes, and end product. In addition, the retailer's name may be included.

The names, and particularly the mailing addresses, of manufacturers give consumers several sources, in addition to the retailer, from which to seek adjustment in case of product failure. Unsatisfactory performance believed to be the fault of the manufacturer and not due to misuse or improper care by the consumer should be reported.

The best recourse for complaints is usually the store from which the item was purchased. But if this proves unsatisfactory, the manufacturer should be contacted and given a precise and honest account of how the product failed to perform.

Industry representatives repeatedly say that one of their continuing problems is the lack of adequate consumer "feedback." Producers need consumer reaction in order to know how to improve their products.

Product guarantees are relatively new in the textile field. Some textile products carry labels describing terms or conditions of a guarantee. Read carefully! Most of the guarantee programs require you to keep the sales slip and the guarantee tag and return them with the garment in order to claim replacement or money refund if the product fails to perform as stated in the guarantee.

In summary, textile labeling offers a wealth of information to the consumer, whose responsibilities are to read and understand labeling, follow directions given and communicate with retailers and manufacturers regarding performance of their products.

FOR FURTHER READING

Blanford, Josephine M. and Gurel, Lois M., *Fibers and Fabrics,* NBS Consumer Information Series 1, issued in November, 1970. Available for 65 cents from Superintendent of Documents, U.S. Government Printing Office, Washington, D.C. 20402.

A *Dictionary of Textile Terms by Dan River Mills, Inc.,* eleventh edition, 1971. Single copies available free from: Public Relations Manager, Dan River Mills, Inc., P.O. Box 6126, Station B, Greenville, S.C. 29606.

The following publications may be obtained from Consumer Information, Public Documents Distribution Center, Pueblo, Colo. 81009:
Clothing and Fabric Care Labeling. 1972. 7 pp. 036A. Free.
Look for That Label. 1971, 8 pp. 039A. Free.

SPOTTED CATS IN TROUBLE!

Norman Myers

Spotted cats of the world are in trouble. Potentially serious trouble. Just how serious is a matter of debate among concerned, knowledgeable people. Some say there will be a crisis within five years. Others say there will be none for a decade or more. Still others declare that the crisis has already arrived. But trouble is undeniably brewing. And American women are partly responsible.

The worldwide trade in skins has been estimated at one-half million per year, of which 70 percent eventually arrive in the United States. Most are sent abroad again as coats or accessories, but many end up on the backs of American women. A huge proportion is made up of ocelots, of which around 130,000 are finding their way to the United States.

Between one-third and one-half of the world's 20,000 leopard skins have also been coming into the United States. The International Union for the Conservation of Nature (IUCN) believes that 10,000 leopards are taken out of Africa every year *on license,* which is reckoned to be the maximum that they can bear while still maintaining their numbers. The IUCN suggested a few years ago that there were 60,000 being taken out without license;

experts on the spot estimate that in some regions the legitimate exports may constitute only one percent of all leopard-skin exports.

Until very recently, fur traders and fur wearers ran into opposition they could ignore. Now it looks as if those who object are becoming less silent; possibly they are also becoming more of a majority. They don't agree that the rights of furcoat wearers are minority rights which others shouldn't interfere with. And they are saying so. Perhaps 1971 will be the year things get done.

Already you are forbidden from using spotted cat skins if you live in California. If you are a member of the 11,000-strong Furriers Joint Council and its affiliated members across the United States, you don't use them either. The same holds true for members of the London-based International Trade Federation. And the United States' Endangered Species program now forbids the importation of skins which are declared endangered in the country of origin.

But these bright spots are few. Cat-fur coats are still in great demand, and the more expensive and exclusive they become, the more potent they are for propping up failing egos.

The problem, moreover, is no longer simply a question of ego or taste. There is now enough available evidence to draw tentative conclusions about the current welfare of spotted cats. The picture is considerably less than heartening.

Fewer adult cats. There are fewer full-sized leopard and jaguar skins available—possibly the adults are being removed faster than they can be replaced. Jaguars exist at only one pair per 100 square miles, and one pair will not produce more in a lifetime than will make one top-quality coat. Ocelots are evidently in the same trouble—local hunters now have to travel about 500 miles to find the remaining ocelots and jaguars.

In Somalia, the leopard is almost extinct. Somalia contributed 443 of the 17,490 leopard skins the United States imported in 1968. In 1969, Ethiopia contributed 2,768. Kenya exported 3,422 to the United States, though it has been estimated that less than one in ten were obtained at the source legitimately.

In 1968, India exported several times as many leopard skins to the United States as the rest of Asia put together, 3,660. (When the total dropped to 895 in 1969, following a commercial ban by India, the numbers in nearby Nepal rose from 95 to 1,773.)

Also in trouble in Africa, leopards vary in number from habitat to habitat. In the Nairobi National Park, it is thought there are six in the forest area, and eight in the stretch of savannah eight times as big. In the 7,000-square-mile Kruger Park in South Africa, there are believed to be around 650. In the 5,600-square-mile Serengeti, there may be only half as many. A report in Kenya has found that game wardens outside the parks consider the prospects for leopards to be extremely bad and steadily getting worse.

Cheetah figures are rather more exact, since the animal is not as elusive. There are only 250 of them in Kruger Park, and they are declining—not from poaching but from shifts in the total ecological scene. The estimate for the Serengeti is 150. The 3,168 cheetah skins imported into the United States alone in 1968 and 1969 would account for as many of them as would be found (at Kruger/Serengeti rates) over almost 100,000 square miles of Africa.

In Peru, one region alone accounted for 138,000 ocelots, worth about $25 each, during a 20-year period. The total turnover for other creatures—monkeys, caimans, parrots, peccaries, capybaras and others—amounted to two-thirds

of a million dollars in 1966 for Iquitos, Peru, a town of 50,000 people. (All of these animals were apparently being overhunted and could scarcely sustain such killing for long.) In addition, Peru's total export of jaguar skins probably clears out the best part of 80,000 square miles *each year.*

Officials in every country I have visited in Africa and South America stress they would find it much easier to enforce prohibitive legislation if the demand could be reduced overseas. As long as demand increases, they find it very difficult to implement the best-intentioned legislation within their own countries. Each nation is taking the steps it thinks appropriate, though the measures vary from area to area.

In fact the countries which supply spotted cat skins to the world face problems far more complex than those of the consumer nations. While Americans and Europeans are being asked to decide whether fur coats are important to them, whether the economics of the fashion industry and the importers and the tastes of buyers will bear changing, far poorer or less stable nations are wondering: What do you tell a hunter whose only livelihood is the price of a jaguar or leopard skin? What do you tell him when the pressures of exploitation have made even this cash crop impractical to locate and bring in? And even if your laws say that the cats must be protected, how do you police thousands of miles of Amazon jungle or African bush?

A world with fewer spotted cats would not be the same world. It would be a world enriched for those who want something to cover their transparency. It would be an added luxury to those who already have a great deal of material comfort.

And the world would be sadly different for those who love spotted cats. A leopard is more than its outward appearance. If it were plain gray, or as chameleon-colored as those who follow the latest fashions, or as naked as those who seem to need a leopard skin more than the leopard does, it would still be a remarkable animal. It is so much at one with itself you cannot have *part* of a leopard.

Not that you have to see a leopard in the wild to know what it is all about. Most people won't go to Africa, and most who go to Africa won't see a leopard, since it is too stealthy, too leopardlike. But most people can still sense what makes a leopard a leopard.

Many people, however, are now being asked to give up something to ensure the survival of a creature which must remain a mere idea for them. They are asked to give up what seems to be something dear, beyond sparing, considering the record so far.

IT'S FUN AND FASHIONABLE TO BE FAKE

Phyllis Feldkamp

Conservationists can justifiably feel encouraged. The circle of people in fashion that sets the pace in international style does not think it is chic any more to use or to wear the skins of threatened animals, and is making its views well known. Increasingly, this group is turning to simulated or "fake" furs for the wild look.

At least this is the case in the United States and in Great Britain, where most of the people who evaluate the trends, design the furs, and actually determine the course of fashion are listening and responding to the conservationists.

Since 1965 when Jacqueline Kennedy Onassis, then Mrs. John F. Kennedy, was given a Somali leopard coat which set her admirers off on a rush to buy coats of all varieties of spotted cat, such furs have plummeted from top status. Today they are often "negative status symbols."

Women like Joan Simon, wife of the playwright Neil Simon, have stopped wearing their endangered specie furs, even though Mrs. Simon's husband gave her a baby leopard coat four years ago. Other well-known women are active in various militant organizations. And several name designers and furriers—notably New York's Oscar de la Renta, Chester Weinberg, Jacques Kaplan of Georges Kaplan, Mr. Fred of Fur & Sport, Ben Kahn and Philadelphia's André Ferber of Jacques Ferber—will not handle any of the pelts, feathers, or skins of vanishing birds, reptiles or mammals.

Media responding. Now the wildlife conservation campaign that began to mount in force some two and a half years ago is succeeding. The September 1, 1970, issue of *Vogue* magazine contained a full-page editorial taking a stand against furs from imperiled wildlife. Written in part by Diana Vreeland, *Vogue's* editor-in-chief and perhaps America's most influential fashion authority, it advised readers about the availability of clothes made from ranch-raised or population-controlled animals.

Said *Vogue:* "We are deeply concerned about preserving animals threatened with extinction. . . . You won't see in the pages of *Vogue* any fur you can't buy, wear and enjoy with a clear conscience." In October *McCall's* followed suit with a feature on "Furs for the Woman with a Conscience."

Editors refuse pictures. Many fashion editors—and I am one of them—on daily newspapers in America and England will not print pictures of coats made of leopard or cheetah or any skin known to be listed in the Red Data Book of the International Union for the Conservation of Nature and Natural Resources. And we welcome new information from scientists on the current state of endangered wildlife.

Consciousness has yet to be raised on any comparable scale in Europe. It is reported that the West German Furriers Association has put its own voluntary ban on the skins known in the trade as "spots," but the Germans are in the minority. Although the husbands of the queens of England and the Netherlands, Prince Philip and Prince Bernhard, are outspoken in their conservationist views, the public on the Continent is largely indifferent. When designers or furriers and the women they dress are made aware of the conservation crisis, their reaction is often a defensive, negative one, like that of Gina Lollobrigida: questioned about the tigers used for one of her coats, she quickly rationalized, "I didn't kill anything."

When spotted furs are modeled—and they frequently are in Rome and Paris buyer-press couture presentations—some of us in the audience object audibly. At the Mila Schoen opening in Rome—she is one of the greatest Italian designers and her clothes are among the world's most expensive—were an even dozen rare, superior quality spotted furs.

"They can't be real," we decided, after we had interrupted the applause. "They must be superb fakes."

When I asked her which they were after the show, Signora Schoen was offended. To her the idea that anybody would think she would touch an imitation was unspeakable.

Other designers are not quite of the same mind. Valentino, who is internationally famous as Rome's number one couturier and who counts Mrs. Onassis among his best customers, also showed a few of the diminishing specie skins. However, on his visit to America last fall, he was interested to hear the U.S. fashion community's position, and seemed sympathetic to our stand.

Marc Bohan, haute couture designer and artistic director of the house of Christian Dior, the Paris name that carries the greatest weight on a worldwide basis, showed several magnificent spotted furs in his collection. One was a white mink full-length cape completely lined with Somali leopard. The house was very pleased with it and the public relations director offered me a color transparency of the cape to run in my newspaper. She was surprised when I declined the offer and explained why. In January of this year when the spring-summer collections were shown in Paris, I was offered still another photograph of a spotted fur at Dior. This time the coat was a combination of black astrakhan and fine leopard skin. Not that Dior should be singled out for showing a couture coat of endangered animal skins. The shop windows of Paris modistes and furriers are filled with clothes made of jaguar, tiger, ocelot, Somali leopard, alligator and crocodile skins.

Both these European designers may in time stop using these furs. They have already noted the examples of their American counterparts, whom they respect and with whom they are friends.

"I make furs and I definitely do not use any of the endangered skins and I will not use any on coats or fur trimming," says Oscar de la Renta. Socially, De la Renta is a friend of Valentino's and a member of the rich international jet set that can afford costly luxury furs.

Most people in fashion reject the idea that fake furs can substitute for real, because aesthetically it is distasteful to put the real and the fake on the same level. There is no sense trying to talk oneself into believing that a furry fabric made of some coal tar derivative is ever going to take the place of the soft, natural, deep-piled original, anymore than plastic daffodils, however well made, can supplant the real flowers. Like anything pretending to be something it is not, factory-made fur succeeds best for fashion purposes when it does not ape the genuine article too cleverly; when, to borrow an expression from the costume jewelry ads, it is "frankly fake."

Synthetic furs can be warm, amusing, chic, even elegant, so long as they are honest. Some of the most attractive fakes are the obvious ones—long or curly-haired fabrics that suggest fur without straining to imitate it literally. American designers Donald Brooks and Calvin Klein, and Paris couturiers Pierre Cardin, André Courrèges, and Emmanuel Ungaro, have all employed furry material.

The most lifelike imitations in fashion this year have been animal skin patterns printed on chiffon, silk, cotton poplin, and velvet. In no way can they replace the function of fur as a garment to keep one warm but they do serve to please the eye.

Introduced on the market this past season was another type of fur that might be described as a "real fake." Jacques Kaplan made a series of white ranch mink coats stencilled, by a special process, with the markings of leopards, jaguars, zebras and tigers. Keplan once ridiculed the pleas of conservationists. But one night at dinner he heard the whole preservation story from Alfred Barr, director of the Museum of Modern Art in New York. Kaplan was converted and let the world know by running a large ad in *The New York Times*.

Meanwhile, laws have been passed—in particular the Federal Endangered Species Act prohibiting the importation of endangered specie skins—and state laws are in the making.

Looking at the overall situation, it would seem that the conservation movement has made great strides where fashion is concerned. However, in the course of writing this article, I realized there is still a considerable way to go. Turning on our television set to "The Lucy Show," I found the other side of the picture: actress Jayne Meadows coming on screen in a leopard skin coat.

A DEMOCRACY OF CLOTHING

Claudia B. Kidwell and Margaret C. Christman

By the twenties the ready-to-wear clothing industry had reached full maturity. Domestic and imported fabrics in a panorama of colors, patterns, and textures were available by the millions of yards. A labor force of divergent skills provided adequate manpower. Machines that could cut hundreds of layers of fabric at one time, machines capable of sewing thousands of stitches a minute, machines that could press any part of a garment with crispness and dispatch were at the disposal of the manufacturer. The manufacturing process itself was structured with a flexibility that allowed for organizational patterns which ranged from imdividual handwork to assembly-line technique. All the elements for successful mass production were in place.

No man or women in America was so remote as to lack the opportunity to buy the products of this gargantuan industry. In every city and town across the land, department and specialty stores paraded the fruits of prolific manufacture. Mail-order catalogs did the same for those who might lack access to a commercial center. Thanks to the genius of American production and distribution there were few Americans who did not have the means of dressing reasonably well, and at moderate cost, immediately at hand.

Such was the perfection of mass manufacture that from across the room a man's $50 suit looked much like a $250 suit, and only an eagle eye could tell if the fashionable "little nothing dress" was custom or ready-made.

One midwestern businessman remarked in the twenties, "I used to be able to tell something about the background of a girl applying for a job as a stenographer by her clothes, but today I often have to wait till she speaks,

Reprinted from *Suiting Everyone: The Democratization of Clothing in America* by Claudia B. Kidwell and Margaret C. Christman. Washington, D.C.: United States Government Printing Office, 1974, pp. 165–203.

shows a gold tooth, or otherwise gives me a second clew." At about the same time a clothing dealer complained that working-class men were "no longer content with plain, substantial low-priced goods, but demanded 'nifty' suits that look like those every one else buys and like they see in the movies."

The democracy of clothing was at hand. The developments over the next fifty years would serve only to widen the clothing choice.

Men's clothing continued to be manufactured in the large factories of Rochester and Chicago and in smaller establishments in Philadelphia, Boston, Baltimore, St. Louis, Dallas, Kansas City, and other places.

In the twenties the women's clothing industry moved west from New York's Lower East Side to Seventh Avenue. This area of midtown Manhattan, comprising some twenty city blocks, became and was to remain the focus of the female fashion world. Even though, as the years went on, a large share of the billions of female garments produced annually were sent outside to be sewn, Seventh Avenue remained the nerve center of the women's garment industry, the mecca to which buyers from all over the country came on semiannual pilgrimage.

At about this time The Charles William Stores said in their catalog:

"As all roads lead to Rome, so all fashion inspiration reaches New York eventually. Paris sends wonderful creations in frocks and blouses and lingerie, a thousand and one ideas that bear the stamp of that artistic race and exhale the perfume of rare beauty. London contributes fashions in that garment that American women seem to love the best of all—the tailored suit—and also sends smart hats to match, and from Berlin come wonderful coat styles. The Philippines offer embroideries, veritable cobwebs of fine underwear; and Japan, that wonderful country of little people and great accomplishments sends rich fabrics, sumptuous embroideries, kimonos that ravish the eye for color and design, and a hundred silken treasures of the East. Occident and Orient without stint pour their riches into New York, the heart of the fashion world. . . . Does New York merely receive—not give? New York gives generously. With marvelous talent she takes the best of other countries and makes of them something better for her own. She selects, adapts, combines, transforms all she has received, evolves from them wonderful new things, and gives them to America.

Beginning in the thirties a fashion influence from a new source, namely California, was manifest in both men's and women's clothing. Out of the less formal lifestyle of the West, perhaps out of the lingering frontier attitudes of individuality and independence, out of the louder tones of a newer civilization, out of the vivid colors of a sun-drenched landscape came a casual clothing which Americans made peculiarly their own. It is symbolic that California's first clothing manufacturer was Levi Strauss, who in 1850 began the production of jeans, the most American of all garments, which in his day spoke to the

pragmatic need for durable clothing and which in ours has come to speak to the point of social equality. Following Strauss came White Stag, Catalina, Jantzen, Cole of California, Pendleton Woolen Mills, and others—makers of bathing suits and sports clothing, garments which even the French acknowledged were done better by Americans than by anybody else. The French designer Schiaparelli said in a New York interview in 1940, "It is amazing what America does with reasonably-priced clothes, especially sports clothes. So much taste." And Christian Dior, *Time* reported in 1955, said that "the la mode sport in America is beyond doubt excellent."

Whatever the location, the business of clothing Americans was, in the most fundamental terms, the business of figuring out exactly what it was the consumer wanted. Only those who guessed right could long survive.

The Best-Dressed People

Michael Harrington said in *The Other America* (1962), "It is much easier in the United States to be decently dressed than it is to be decently housed, fed or doctored." Harrington, bemoaning the fact that clothes make the poor invisible added, "Even people with terribly depressed incomes can look prosperous. There are tens of thousands of Americans who are wearing perhaps even a stylishly cut suit or dress, and yet are hungry." Harrington wrote that "for a variety of reasons, the benefits of mass production have been spread much more evenly in this area than in many others."

It was this benefit of mass production that gave Americans the reputation of being the best-dressed people in the world. It may be that as individuals, Americans fell short of the highest sartorial perfection, but taken as a whole, Americans in this century have been a most extraordinarily well-dressed citizenry.

Even during the depression of the thirties people were able to keep up appearances. A woman expending only $2.95 for a skirt and $1.95 for a blouse and another $2.95 for a sweater could achieve a neat and stylish "no price" look.

As for the men, the ready-to-wear clothing industry had long been accustomed to providing for them what one writer called "the proud uniform of a democratic society." Soviet leader Nikita Khrushchev took note of this equality of male dress as he described his meeting with Governor Nelson Rockefeller in 1959. He said in his taped reminiscences that Rockefeller "certainly wasn't dressed in cheap clothes, but I wouldn't say that he was dressed elegantly either. He was dressed more or less like other Americans." Khrushchev was astonished that "not just a plain capitalist, but the biggest capitalist in the world" was dressed just like everybody else. The other side of the coin, of course, was that everybody else was dressed like Rockefeller.

Over the years the garment industry continued to turn out low- and medium-priced garments,which by and large offered value for the money and which displayed a higher level of taste than did most mass-production items. *Vogue* was not far off the mark when it said in 1974 ". . . in America, to be well dressed is a matter of taste and choice rather than price and place."

It was sometimes noted that Americans were the best-dressed people because they were the most appropriately dressed people. American designers and manufacturers made it their business to concentrate on what might be called the commonplace needs, making a great selection of functional clothing to meet the needs of an active people.

As early as 1923 E.L. Patterson, writing in the *Ladies' Home Journal,* assessed the situation:

> . . . see the average American woman at any time anywhere. Look at her in the country, or in the suburbs, in her smart straight skirts and sweaters, see her about her household tasks in her neat and efficient apron dresses or ginghams; look at her in the city in her cloth frock, her tailor-made suits, her smart topcoat; or see her at tea in her simple, dark crepe, pretty hat and well fitting shoes; or watch her at dinner, or at the play—never overdressed, but training her silks or velvets with an air well poised, but not self-conscious.

On the other hand the author, while conceding that the English woman when dressed for a formal function was "perfectly turned out," pointed out that the same lady at tea or any kind of semisocial occasion would appear as a "dowd-or-dowager." Of the Frenchwoman she wrote, "in her afternoon or evening toilette . . . you rest your gaze on one of the most alluring of creatures, finished with such elegance of detail a woman of less bien soignée feels crude." But then, "if you want to see a sight that would cause to stand on end every hair in Dame Fashion's 'transformation' have one look at a Frenchwoman in her sports clothes: If she is playing golf the chances are that she will be wearing a garden hat wound with the seven veils of Salome, a draped Something that might be a house gown; and sandals with Louis-the-Umteenth heels."

The article concluded, "In the last analysis the well-dressed woman is she who is suitably dressed, according to her purse and activities."

Not only could all Americans be dressed in approximately the same manner, but thanks to the incredible developments in "easy-care," "easy-wear" fabrics, all Americans could look equally well-groomed. Starting with nylon in the forties the parade of synthetic-fiber fabrics exploded in the fifties and sixties, making possible a wardrobe of garments that made few demands on the wearer. Drip-dry, machine-washable, durable-press, wrinkle-free fabrics were truly "miracles of comfort and accommodation," particularly to those who had lived in the dark ages when a whole day might needs be set aside for ironing. In the sixties knitted fabrics that stretched with body movement gave a new dimension of comfort and the look of a custom fit as well. No longer was a crisp, clean appearance the mark of the leisure class. The gentleman in a wash-and-wear suit could look as well turned out as the man who enjoyed the services of a personal valet; the woman with dresses in synthetics and knits could appear to be—depending upon her age—debutante or grande dame.

The Fashion Machine

In the twenties, with the growth of mass communications, a whole new concept was instilled into the minds of Americans, the idea of clothing obsolescence. Even though previous generations had been concerned with being in fashion, style changes moved at a comparatively slow rate and the durability of clothing remained a major consideration. By the twenties, however, the clothing industry, having an unlimited capacity for production, found that to make maximum utilization of its resources, it must stimulate buying by introducing change as frequently as possible. What can now aptly be termed the "fashion industry" embarked, therefore, on an all-out campaign to impress upon everyone the need to dress in the very *latest* styles. To be out of style was to be ridiculous.

Most people responded to the drumbeat of fashion—in part because of the overpowering nature of the Fashion Machine, and also in part because, as a nation, Americans were receptive to change and to novelty. As *Vogue* put it in 1938, "We are a clothes-crazy people—restless and acquisitive about fashion as everything else."

To mass production and mass distribution had been added mass fashion information. No one in this wide land need ever suffer for want of knowledge of "what they are wearing." As *Vogue* said, "the sticks are wiped out." "New fashions are hustled into every cranny of the country."

The image of the fashionable male was kept in constant view as men's brand name clothing was advertised nationally. However, because the status of a woman, far more than the status of a man, was determined by clothes, the story of fashion promotion is overwhelmingly the story of the female side of things. Fashion, someone once said, is the great equalizer of women.

The reporting of Paris fashions became a gigantic operation in the twenties. Elizabeth Hawes, who later became one of the first American designers to get her name before the public, noted that there must have been over a hundred American reporters covering the Paris couture openings in 1926.

Virginia Pope, writing for the *New York Times,* began also in the twenties to scout the New York garment district for news of styles and trends. With Mrs. Pope as fashion editor, the *New York Times* became the first newspaper to allocate funds for fashion photography and artwork.

It was not long before newspapers all over the country carried, in addition to fashion advertising, columns of fashion commentary as well. Trade publications, such as *Men's Wear* and *Women's Wear Magazine,* alerted American manufacturers and retailers to the latest fashion trends.

America has more fashion magazines than any other country in the world. Other magazines of a more general nature regularly carry fashion features. All of them carry pages and pages of fashion advertising.

Between all of the periodicals it is hard to think of any consumer group that has been overlooked. *Vogue* helped the woman of "more than average wealth and refinement with their clothes and social life." *Harper's Bazaar,* said *Time* in 1967, "aims at stylish women in Des Moines and Omaha as well as New York and San Francisco." *Vanity Fair,* which came out as *Dress and Vanity Fair* in 1913, had, as one of its aims, "a worthy forecast as well as an accurate reflection of the best [apparel] that is favored by men and women of taste." The *Ladies Home Journal* and the *Woman's Home Companion* catered to middle-class American women who might never have occasion to see an original French design. The *New Yorker* and the *New York Times Magazine* provided well-written, sometimes provocative fashion news for a more sophisticated audience. *Life* and *Ebony* illustrated the "newsy" fashion happenings, allowing those without the time or inclination to keep up with the nuances of fashion to be aware of the salient developments. *Time, Newsweek, Business Week,* in reporting regularly on events and people in the world of fashion, did the same for their readers. *Cosmopolitan, McCalls, Redbook, Collier's, Good Housekeeping,* and *Women's Day* all faithfully devoted many pages to helping the average American housewife dress well and in the latest styles. Even the literary *Harper's* and the *Atlantic Monthly* offered occasional observations on the passing scene. *Fortune, Holiday,* and *Sports Illustrated* reported fashion notes of specific interest to their readership.

In the thirties began a number of magazines aimed directly at that segment of society which was becoming the prime purchaser of clothing, girls and young women. *Mademoiselle,* established in 1935, was intended for the college audience and stylish young career women on a limited budget. *Glamour,* published first in 1939 as *Glamour of Hollywood,* was subtitled "For the Girl with a Job." *Seventeen* began as the movie magazine *Stardom* in 1942. Jessica Davies, in *Ready-Made Miracle* (1962), in her description of *Seventeen,* remarks, "In this generation, girls begin to be seventeen when they are thirteen or fourteen, it appears."

To enlighten the male, *Esquire* was founded in 1933 with the announced aim of "the establishment of elegance." To which Arnold Gingrich, a founding editor, has added in the recently published *Esquire's Encyclopedia of 20th Century Men's Fashions,* "a bizarre aim it must have seemed in an era when Presidents were photographed fishing in derby hats." The allied publication, *Gentlemen's Quarterly,* was begun in 1957 for distribution through men's wear stores, but later came to be sold on the newsstands. *Playboy,* which dates from 1953, brought high-style fashions to the attention of a diverse audience.

The fashion show was a popular diversion by the twenties and served well the function of fashion propaganda. One such event is described by Robert and Helen Lynd in their sociological study of Middletown (Muncie, Indiana) They noted, "On two successive nights at one of these local shows a thousand people—ten-cent store clerks, tired-looking mothers with children, husbands, and wives—watched rouged clerks promenade langourously along the tops of the show cases, displaying the latest hats, furs, dresses, shoes, parasols, bags and other accessories, while a jazz orchestra kept everybody 'feeling good.' "

Far and away the greatest vehicle for fashion indoctrination has been the movies. "More and more," it was said in 1932, "do we absorb our fashion information by pictures rather than by text. And what pictures are so graphic, so easily understood and followed as those that move, talk, and generate fan mail?" In the thirties almost everybody went to the movies, many people, taking advantage of cheap entertainment in depression days, every week. For the first time in history the common folk everywhere could see in action a whole gamut of clothing worn by people of varying physical types. Each person could find his own resemblance in one or more of the bright and shining stars and thus use this figure of glamour as his personal fashion guide. Added to the film themselves was constant publicity in newspapers and magazines plus a whole great world of movie magazinedom, which supplied the avid readers with details about the stars' private wardrobes.

The designer Adrian, who dressed the stars and other women, too, since he manufactured high-priced ready-to-wear clothing, said in a 1933 interview in the *Ladies' Home Journal* that motion pictures were becoming the Paris of America and "when women see the stars in pictures they can use them as their fashion guides." He went on to say that "Garbo's reaction to clothes, her individuality in spite of prevailing trends, appeals to and fires the imagination of American women. Her influence on style has been more far-reaching than any other actress." "Norma Shearer," he added, "looks her truest self in simple tailored things, to which she gives great style." He described Joan Crawford as "the essence of sophisticated young America. She expresses a great deal of freedom in her dress." Myrna Loy, Adrian said, "always looks best in simple sports clothes." Ethel Barrymore he referred to as a sweeping personality with complete lack of limitation. "No train is too long or too heavy for her to manage. No earrings are too long, nor hat too ponderous."

Silver Screen told its readers in October of 1932, shortly after Joan Crawford appeared as "Letty Lynton" clad in an Adrain-designed dress with wide pleated flanges at the shoulders, that "Some old fossils may still look to Paris for their fashions, fads and furbelows, but you and I know that Paris isn't even a stand-in to Hollywood. . . . Paris may decree this and Paris may decree that, but when that Crawford girl pops up in puffed sleeves, then it's puffed sleeves for us before tea-time." The columnist Wes Colman added that those sleeves you saw in *Letty Lynton* really "aren't so bad once you get used to them. Rather graceful, too, if you go in for shrugs and embraces, both of which are 'comme il faut' this season when you are feeling nonchalant and naughty."

Continuing the fashion report from Hollywood we learn that "At the opening of her picture 'Strange Interlude,' Norma Shearer appeared in an organdy-velvet ensemble with sleeves that were puffed by Adrian, and we might say, completely puffed. Now don't let me catch you going to that country club dance next Saturday night without your puffed sleeves." Further, it was observed, "Robert Montgomery and his scarf practically put the tie and collar man out of business, and I must say the Clark Gable turtle neck sweater hasn't helped the tie industry either. All the boys go for the Gable sweater in a big way and no place is too good for one. Turtle necks can be found at the Ambassador and Roosevelt patios and the Brown Derby any old day. . . . No one seems to know who started the blue flannel slacks fad but try to walk one block in Hollywood without seeing them. Early in the season Garbo was seen lunching at the Roosevelt in blue flannel slacks, and about the same time Joan Crawford was seen wearing them on the Metro lot. And everybody is wearing them now—especially dames with big hips— which is just too bad."

The Fashion Machine sent Americans in pursuit of the stars and other beautiful people. Thanks to the efficiency of the whole fashion industry, however, whatever was perceived to be the ultimate in beauty and desirability was at the command of the common man. In the twenties French fashions were coveted, and although every American woman could not have a Paris gown every woman could have a copy or an adaptation, at fairly reasonable cost, of the creations of the great French couturiers. It had been the genius of Coco Chanel to make simple, functional clothing the prevailing fashion, thus enabling American mass manufacture to bring an unprecedented equality to the dress of American women. Almost any woman in America could buy a "Chanel" at prices ranging from $3.75 to $375.

In 1930 the *New York Times* reported that the French designer Jean Patou had deliberately made his new designs "uncopiably intricate" in order to keep them out of the hands of the American mass producers. The *Times* went on to say that nothing could keep the latest fashions out of the hands of the "smart little working girls" of America. The newpaper concluded, "When practical clothes are the style, they will wear them. But they recognize no distinction of society, nationality, or money when it comes to fashion. If frills are the thing in Paris, they will be worn in every office in America."

Dorothy Shaver, then vice president of Lord & Taylor, urging in the early thirties a recognition of American design and designers and deploring the single-minded interest in French fashion, looked back on the recent past and said, "Every woman could not have an original. But they could have copies of Paris gowns; and have them they would. They poured into the stores demanding a Chanel, or a Patou, or a Lanvin. The great names of the Parisian haute couture, over night it seemed, were on the lips of women from the tip of Cape Cod to the Golden Gate." But, said Miss Shaver in July 1933, "To us on the firing line, it became increasingly evident that the never-ending flow of "ready-to-wear" with which this country is so abundantly supplied, could not possibly all have derived from Paris. Every little side street shop has chic, wearable models. Every small town in this country has crisp, fresh, smart-looking clothes that have somehow been translated into the American vernacular. . . . Behind this vast productive activity, creative talent was turning out fashions worn by the bulk of American women. Unwept, unhonored and unsung, were hundreds of artists and designers doing pioneer work."

In the thirties, however, few Americans were interested in American designers, anonymous or named, and were less impressed by the famous French designers than they were by their new idols, the motion picture stars. In their image, clothing was made for all. "The snappiest outfit in Ginger Rogers' wardrobe," complete with autographed label, could be ordered from Sears at $6.94. "Hollywood," Sears told customers in 1934, "has gone Taffeta 'crazy' " and for $3.98 customers could buy a "fine, crisp, swishy All Rayon Taffeta frock just like Loretta Young's." Copies of the gown designed by Jacques Fath and worn by Rita Hayworth when she married the Aga Kahn in 1949 could be bought at Macy's for $18.74. Sixteen other stores also carried the dress in brown, black, and bride's blue.

Men could look like Clark Gable in turtle neck sweaters and shirred back jackets; or like Douglas Fairbanks Jr. in double-breasted green plaid suits.

For those swept up in the romance of royalty, copies of the dress Mainbocher designed for Wallis Simpson's 1937 wedding to the Duke of Windsor could be had in a full range of sizes and at all prices. Copies of this particular dress by Mainbocher were sold at $10.75, and Elizabeth Hawes notes in *Fashion is Spinach* (1938). "You could tell by the looks on the faces of the American girls who wore them that they really felt beguiling."

Following World War II came Dior's "New Look" and fashion attention was concentrated on high-style French fashion once again. Three months after Dior presented his celebrated line in the spring of 1947, American dress manufacturers, using rayon instead of silk, were mass-producing copies. Time/Life reports that a million dresses were made up within weeks.

In the sixties the Jacqueline Kennedy look was the popular aspiration, and with sleeveless, collarless dresses in fashion, anyone could be a beautiful person at rock-bottom prices. Phyllis Levin wrote in *The Wheels of Fashion* (1965), "If there is such a thing as a classless dress it is the one without sleeves. It reached the summit of its popularity in 1961 and rode radiantly in and around the White House while it also bundled into the subways without regard to price, fabric, color, or size."

Fundamentally, during most of the sixties, London's Chelsea borough was where it was at, and American manufacturers saw to it that American males could have all the panache of the Beatles, and American females could have Mary Quant's London "working girl" look that shook up the fashion world of the decade.

Freedom of Choice—To Each His Own Thing

"The World," said columnist Dorothy Dix in the twenties, "judges us largely by appearance. If we wish to be successful we have got to look successful." In 1967, in an interview in *Time* magazine, the West Coast designer Rudi Gernreich, proclaiming that dress should never again dominate the woman, went on to say, "Clothes are just not that important. . . . They're not status symbols any longer. They're for fun."

Beginning in the mid-sixties, clothing mores underwent a most remarkable transformation in the direction of a new freedom. "A person should wear what they want to wear—it's no one else's business," cried the voice of modern youth, and more and more the world agreed "to each his own thing."

The old unwritten rules of proper dress for every occasion have been revised or dropped altogether. Dress codes have been abolished in colleges and high schools almost everywhere. Social pressures for prescribed "correct clothing" have diminished. Although there are those who continue to deplore the wearing for business "clothes one would wear to work in the yard or for recreational activitiies," most business and governmental officials have come to conclude in the words of one such that "There are differing circumstances which affect one's dress choices, which is the reason that prescribing standards is of no avail. It is obviously a matter of personal taste and judgment." No doubt about it, an increased tolerance towards differing styles of dress can be sensed almost everywhere. People had come to be accepted for what they are rather than for what they wear. Within the bounds of decency, freedom of choice carried the day.

Fashion itself has been becoming freer and less inhibited. "We have passed that thing in fashion where we all have to dress alike," said Halston in May 1970. And Bill Blass in that same year noted, "We live in a fascinating era, because you can go to a party and see everything from shorts, to pajamas, to evening skirts to anything. There is no longer a dictatorship in fashion."

For 150 or so years men had been dressing inconspicuously, and the most that could be said for a well-tailored man was something to the effect of "quiet good taste." As *Time* put it in 1964, "For the average American male over 30 fashion is something for other people—females, fops, and perhaps the Duke of Windsor." But even as this was written, the Beatles, who, incidentally, had appeared earlier in suits designed by Pierre Cardin, were exposing American males not only to new styles, but more importantly, to new attitudes towards dress. George Frazier, writing in *Esquire* in October 1968, noted that "It is impossible to exaggerate what the Beatles have wrought in men's fashions." Their influence, he said, "liberalized the male animal and inspired him to investigate the new." For the first time since Beau Brummel, men could take a frank interest in clothes without fearing a threat to their masculinity, and could, if so inclined, dress adventurously. The peacock look—color, sumptuous fabrics, fancy shirts, lace and eyelet embroidery—was in its most flamboyant aspects the domain of the young. However, since the young were the ones spending money for clothes, the manufacturers' response to this dominant consumer community also resulted in the modification of the styles offered to their elders. The result, in terms of the past, was an extraordinary choice of colors and fabrics and styles. It was up to each individual male to decide how much or how little of the new culture he was willing to absorb. Russell Lynes, writing in *Harper's* in 1967, concluded that "It does still take a great deal of summoning up of the ego for most men to wear flashing colors." The chairman of Hathaway Ellerton M. Jette, however, expressed the "peacock revolution" in the framework in which it was made acceptable to most men. He advised men never to wear a white shirt before sundown. They "look like murder by midafternoon" he said. "And furthermore, they are a pitiful abdication of individuality."

Nina Hyde, fashion editor of the *Washington Post*, reflected on results of the "men's clothing revolution." She wrote on March 4, 1973: "On the one hand the 'alternate culture' freed men from wearing what was expected of them and made it acceptable to dress in work clothes or wear velvet to the office if they cared to. It also freed their heads to discover the pleasure of wearing elegant clothes, well cut and in fine fabrics."

Women in the past ten years, be they "sex kittens" or "liberated," have made extraordinary advances in freedom of dress. Dr. Martin Marty of the University of Chicago was quoted in *Time* in December 1967 as proclaiming shorter skirts "a mark of the new freedom." He went on to say, "Girls in the New Left wear them. Young Republican women wear them. Matrons wear them." Still more liberating was the wearing of pants. Just as skirts went up gradually, so too was the acceptance of pants an evolutionary process. Overcoming the ancient abhorrence of pants as "a stride along the path to masculinity" was not easy. Even as pants and pant suits began to be made in elegant materials, it continued to be stipulated that they were suitable only for informal occasions. Norman Norell, for example, said that he made them for country and travel but not for city wear. Into the late sixties women in formal pant suits continued to be barred from some of New York's status restaurants. By the seventies the bifurcated garment had, however, won general acceptance for all occasions, thus giving women an increased freedom of movement and an additional degree of comfort.

The rejection, in 1968, of the midi was hailed on all sides as an indication that today's woman, with consciousness raised, will never again be a sheep to fashion. Interestingly enough, this landmark declaration of independence from fashion, if indeed that is what history will prove it to have been, was not so much in rebellion against the imposition of a new fashion as it was in support of retention of one of the most obviously sexist fashions of all time. In any case, women were assured by all the voices of fashion authority that this was the age of the INDIVIDUAL, and that they were free to define their own lifestyle and to pick and choose among a smorgasbord of fashions. There was a common agreement that clothes should be functional, practical, easy to wear and care for, and that they should express one's personality.

Fashion for both sexes was, in the words of Gernreich again, "a kind of flaunting of one's personality." And although the sight was frequently unaesthetic, the principle of freedom of choice was well served. Many were repelled by the sight of the untidy young dressed monotonously alike in shirts and jeans, but this unisex look marked a new equality in the relationship of the sexes. The vulgarity of "too fleshy bodies" not well covered was a disturbing sight to others but perhaps a source of comfort to the perpetrators. Thick-legged matrons in miniskirts were seen by some as the ultimate obscenity, but if women felt the younger for it, what difference did it make? Certainly many, both men and women, were spectacles indeed in stretch pants and see-through shirts—and these, perhaps, in garish disordant colors. Who can deny that the freedom to suit oneself has, as someone put it, "opened the floodgates to the Sartorial Philistines." But the whole blatant scene, representative as it surely is of the great variety of choice freely open to Americans of differing tastes and lifestyles, is an eloquent statement of the full and complete democratization of clothing.

We make no pretense to knowing what's ahead. Maybe the old formalities will reassert themselves. Perhaps those who scorn the amenities of dress will find that clothes are, after all, important to morale. Others who are now "into clothes" may come to hold dress subordinate to other interests. Feminists who now call for "inoffensive plainness in women's dress," may find that once the seduction principle has been conclusively laid to rest that finery need not be thought of as sexual lure. Perhaps, as the equality of male and female roles becomes better understood, both sexes can comfortably use clothing to enhance their respective sexuality. Fashion may become as important to men as it has been to women. Or perhaps men will forget about it altogether. People may come to look upon clothing as investments to keep and to wear all their lives. On the other hand, they may come to desire clothing cheap enough to be soon discarded. As a nation, we may take more interest in clothes or we may take less. It seems probable, however, that there will never be an abdication of individual choice. Few are likely to write to a department store or mail-order house saying, "Here is the money and my measurements. Send me clothes."

TEXTILE FIBERS TO TEXTILE PRODUCTS

Marianne S. Beeson with Bennie E. Beeson, Jr.

It seems appropriate to close these discussions of many factors determining what people wear with a survey of how the actual garments you and I are wearing came into being. Allow to fade into the background all of those dozens of cultural and psychological influences which resulted in each of us selecting what we are wearing at this moment and which motivated our purchases of these clothes in the first place. We are left with a fascinating story in itself—the transformation of fibers into clothes.

The route of textile raw materials through numerous steps in processing can be described in economic terms. Each manufacturing operation can be a separate business operaion. These businesses require capital investment in plants and machinery, labor to operate the machinery, management to make decisions about how much and what to produce, inventories of raw materials and stocks of their particular products to fill orders, plus the ability to distribute the products to their customers.

As businesses, manufacturers and producers must be responsive to the demand of their direct customers, those who buy the products and perform other steps in the manufacturing process. For example, a yarn spinner's customers are, primarily, the weaving and knitting mills which produce fabric from yarns. Yarn producers attempt to provide yarns that meet the requirements of weaving and knitting mill customers *or* attempt to convince their customers that the yarns they produce are what the mills want. Thus, each business along the marketing chain must appeal to its direct customers.

In the broader analysis, demand for any intermediate product is derived from the demand for the final product. Therefore, in promoting a yarn or a fabric, the manufacturer of one of these intermediate products may decide to attempt to increase demand by directing attention to a user at a stage in processing beyond its immediate customers and closer to the final product. The spinner of a high fashion, loopy mohair yarn, for instance, might promote the product to a coat manufacturer, even though the coat manufacturer will not buy yarn from the spinner. The spinner is hoping that the apparel producer will demand from its supplier, the fabric finishing mill, fabrics made of this particular yarn. If the spinner's promotion is successful, the fabric finishing mill will order from the weaving mill, fabrics woven with the mohair yarn, and the weaving mill will place an order with the rewarded spinner.

It has become increasingly common for manufacturers of intermediate products to appeal to the ultimate consumer in an effort to increase demand for their products. You and I do not buy fibers from DuPont or Eastman or Celanese. Yet among the advertisements we see in newspapers and magazines and on television are ads paid for by fiber producers. They do not show us their products in the form in which they sell it—fiber in filament or staple form; they show us an end-product—a shirt or a blouse or a sheet. The fiber companies do not make the end products, but they hope that we will be persuaded by advertisements to buy products containing their particular brands of fiber. Thus, derived demand may be increased for all of the intermediate products containing that fiber, as well as for the fiber itself.

The flowchart (page 209) best tells the story of the business of textiles and apparel and how textile raw materials are converted into the garments we buy.

Fibers

Natural Fibers

The flowchart shows producers of man-made and natural fibers and leather. Natural fibers are those found in nature in a fibrous state. Natural fibers have in common some method of cleaning, that is processes to separate the fibers from other naturally formed substances, dirt, and trash.

Cotton and flax are vegetable (cellulosic) fibers. Cotton in a major agricultural crop in the United States and is grown primarily on irrigated lands in the Southwest and in the Mississippi Delta area of the South. Harvesting and cleaning of cotton require removal of the cotton boll from the plant and any plant materials adhering to it and then *ginning,* the separating of cotton fibers from the seeds. Cotton is packaged in large bales at the cotton gin, and after grading procedures it may be bought by a yarn manufacturer, who will perform several operations including *carding* and possibly *combing* prior to spinning the fiber into yarn.

Carding involves drawing a lap of fibers over a large cylinder covered with protruding wires. The process aligns the fibers parallel to each other so that they will more readily accept spinning. Combing continues the alignment of fibers to the point that the short fibers are separated out, thus forming a finer, smoother yarn when spun.

Flax, a cellulosic natural fiber, is formed in the tough, woody stem of the flax plant. Considerable hand labor is required for the several processes used to separate fiber from the rest of the plant. Once separated, flax fibers are prepared for spinning similarly to cotton. There is virtually no commercial production of flax for fiber in the United States. In the Pacific Northwest and the Great Plains States, flax is grown for seed, linseed oil being important in a number of markets. Almost all of the relatively small quantity of flax used in the United States for apparel and home furnishings fabrics is imported from such countries as Belgium, Ireland, and Canada. Fabric made from flax is called *linen.*

Silk and wool are animal (protein) fibers. Wool refers to the fleece of sheep and lambs as well as that of the Angora goat (mohair fiber), the Cashmere goat (cashmere fiber), and Angora rabbit (angora fiber), and other animals such as alpaca and camel.* However, the fleeces from animals other than sheep and lambs are often referred to as specialty hair fibers or specialty wools.

In addition to cleaning processes to remove trash and dirt, the preparation of wool includes washing to remove natural animal oils. The wool grease or lanolin obtained from the cleaning process is used in cosmetics and pharmaceuticals. Wool fiber is carded in a manner similar to the cotton carding process.

After initial carding of wool, fibers are handled differently depending upon whether they will be made into *woolen* yarns or *worsted* yarns. To obtain the characteristically fuzzy appearance and soft hand of woolen yarns and fabrics,

. . . one thin film or sliver of wool is placed diagonally and overlapping another sliver to give a crisscross effect to the fibers. This permits the fibers to be disentangled and some-

---

*See page 197 in "Reading the Labels on Apparel and Household Textiles."

what parallel and at the same time provides a fuzzy surface to the yarn. After this carding process, the woolen slivers go directly to the spinning operation (1, pp. 242–43).

Wool which is destined for worsted yarns and fabrics is put through a combing operation to remove short fibers and further align the longer fibers parallel. The fibers are spun on a worsted system, which draws out and twists the fibers more tightly than the woolen spinning system. Worsted yarns, and fabrics made of worsted yarns, are finer, smoother, and have a hard hand as compared to woolen fabrics, which are bulkier and softer.

FLOW OF TEXTILES FROM PRODUCERS TO CONSUMERS

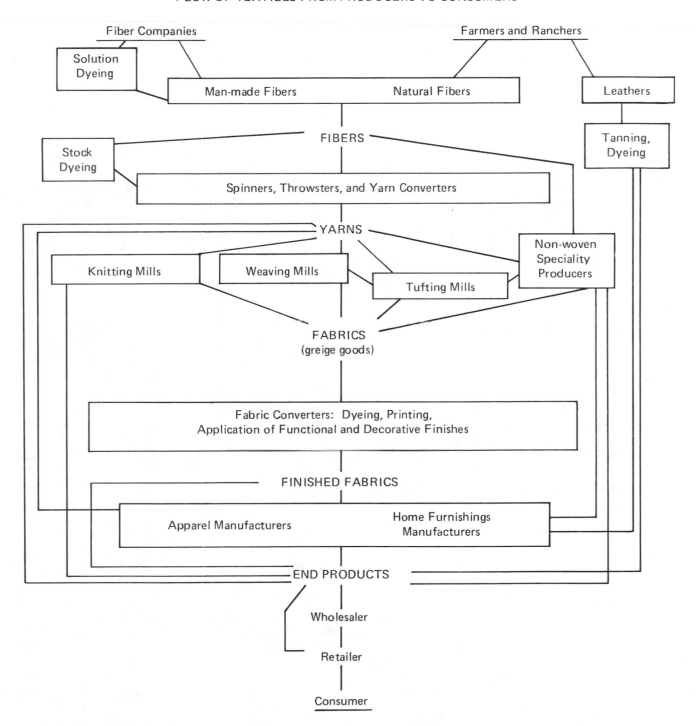

Source: Freely adapted from "Flow of Man-Made Fibers from Producer to Consumer," *Man-Made Fiber Fact Book*. New York: Man-Made Fiber Producers Association, Inc., 1969, pp. 8-9.

In spite of being a relatively expensive fiber, most consumers own and continue to buy a few wool garments, particularly coats and suits. The fashion picture determines whether the crisp, tailored look of worsted fabrics or the soft, fuzzy look of woolen fabrics will predominate in wool garments on the market. Thus, manufacturers of wool yarns must make accurate and **early** fashion predictions in order to meet the demand of their customers. Otherwise, a yarn manufacturer can be "stuck" with too much yarn that customers are not ordering and too little yarn of the type in greater demand. Early in the manufacturing process, markets for products must be secured.

Silk is produced in nature in a form different from that of the three other natural fibers discussed. The silkworm forms silk *filament,* along with gum substances, to make its cocoon. Wool, flax, and cotton are *staple* fibers, that is fibers of relatively short length that can be measured in inches or centimeters. Filament refers to fiber in a long, continuous strand—long enough to be measured in yards or meters. Silk is the only natural filament of the major natural fibers. It was the silkworm which the early man-made fiber pioneers studied so carefully in their efforts to develop machinery that would duplicate the silkworm's extrusion of filament.

The steps necessary for obtaining silk fiber from the cocoon are first to soften the *sericin,* the gum that holds the cocoon together, usually with warm water, and then to unwind the cocoons. Because each silk filament is so extremely fine, several are grouped together as the cocoons are unwound.

There is no commercial silk production (sericulture) in the United States. The history of colonial America records many attempts to raise silkworms along with mulberry trees for their food and to establish silk industries. None was of lasting success, and all of the very small quantity of silk used in this country is imported. China, Japan, Korea, Thailand, Italy, and France are leading producers of silk.

Leather is made from the hides of a number of animals, with beef cattle supplying the major portion of United States hides. While leather is not a textile fiber, it is used for apparel and apparel trims in addition to the more traditional uses in gloves, belts, handbags, wallets, and, of course, shoes. As the flowchart indicates, after tanning and dyeing, leather goes directly to apparel and home furnishings manufacturers to be converted into consumer products. A small quantity of leather may be sold through retailers for home sewing.

Natural fibers, then, are the products of nature, obtained from plants which are cultivated and from animals which are raised and herded by the natural fiber producers—farmers and ranchers. Research and development and promotional functions of fiber production cannot be undertaken effectively by these producers acting as individuals. In additon to their trade associations, natural fiber producers depend on government sponsored research and services to assist in such areas as improving animal breeding stock and testing of new plant varieties, pesticides, and herbicides. Development of new cotton and wool products and new markets for cotton and wool are also considered in some research projects of the U.S. Department of Agriculture. For instance, the slack mercerization process for producing stretch cotton fabrics was developed at the USDA Southern Utilization Research and Development laboratories in New Orleans during the early 1960s. Stretch diapers made by this process have proved to be a successful product in the marketplace (as successful as any cloth diaper can be against current competition of nonwoven disposable diapers).

Trade associations financed by the natural fiber producers are active in research and promotion. Cotton, Inc., with headquarters in Raleigh, North Carolina, is the fiber research facility for cotton producers, offering technical assistance to the industry and promotional efforts for cotton. The Wool Bureau, Inc., performs the same services for wool producers. The International Silk Association (USA), Inc., and the Belgian Linen Association are examples of trade associations representing overseas producers as they promote the use of these fibers to intermediate producers, to fabric and apparel designers, and to retailers and consumers.

Man-made Fibers

The producers of the major man-made fibers are giant chemical companies, which also provide other chemical products. Tires, explosives, photographic film, and gasoline are a few of the other products from chemical firms which make textile fibers as well. As suppliers of chemicals for dyeing, finishing, and other textile operations, many fiber companies are active in several phases of the textiles and apparel industries.

Man-made fiber producers, rivals with each other and with the natural fiber producers, have been responsible for the very intense and pervasive types of promotional activities which have now been imitated by other segments of the industry. Since several companies produce generically the same fibers, it is advertising and promotion within the industry and to the consumer which attempt to establish product differentiation and to carve out a market for a particular brand name of fiber. The man-made fiber companies make a strong commitment to research and development. Their technical assistance programs provide engineering and scientific data (and engineers and scientists when necessary) on every aspect of handling their own brand of fibers, from yarn production to cutting and sewing, and even to dry cleaning and laundering procedures. Thus, testing laboratories are another part of the structure of a typical fiber company.

As long as it does not require any sharing of trade secrets, the fiber companies work together in an association, the Man-Made Fiber Producers Association, Inc. The preparation of educational materials is one of the functions of the Association.

Among the raw materials needed by the fiber companies are natural gas and petroleum-derived chemicals for the synthesizing of long chain polymers such as nylon, polyester, acrylic, olefin, and synthetic rubber. For the cellulosic man-made fibers—rayon, acetate, and triacetate—a source of cellulose is needed, usually wood pulp from spruce, pine, or other soft woods.

Glass is a mineral fiber, produced for the most part by companies which make plate glass and other glass products. Metallic fibers are also mineral in nature. Most metallic yarns on the market are thin strips of aluminum foil sandwiched between layers of plastic film.

The actual formation of most man-made fibers is accomplished by forcing a thick, syrupy solution of the fiber-forming substances through tiny holes in a *spinneret,* a metal device, often made of platinum, which bears some resemblance to a shower head, only smaller. As the filaments emerge from the spinneret, they are hardened or solidified by a chemical bath, warm air, or cool air. The size and shape of holes in the spinneret determine size and cross-section shape of the man-made filaments.

Due to the nature of the production process, man-made fibers begin their existence as filaments. However, fiber producers proceed to prepare man-made fibers in a form suitable to the needs of their customers. Single filaments (*monofilaments*) are used in products calling for sheerness, such as hosiery. Two or more filaments may be twisted together to form *filament yarns.* Large groups of filaments may be put together without twist and then cut or broken into short lengths, or *staple.* Staple fibers may be used in conventional spinning operations or in loose or bat form for pillows, or as the insulative inner layer in jackets, comforters, and the like.

Unique to the man-made fibers is the fact that they can be dyed before the filaments are formed. Pigments may be added to the fiber-forming solution before it is extruded through the spinneret. *Solution dyed* fibers and the products made from them can be extremely resistant to fading, because the color is actually a part of the fiber. However, solution dyeing reduces the color flexibility of manufacturers farther along the marketing chain, since the color of an end product must be determined before the fiber is produced. Solution dyed fibers have fewer uses in fast-changing apparel markets than in home furnishings, where the interval between fashion "seasons" is longer and colorfastness is also a highly desirable property.

Before being spun into yarn, fibers of different generic type may be blended. A large variety of fiber blends is possible, and there are many reasons for blending two or more fibers in a product. One reason is to improve performance characteristics of the product by allowing the desirable properties of one fiber to compensate for certain weaknesses in another. A very common blend on the market is polyester/cotton. Polyester contributes ease of care and durability properties to the product, and cotton offers absorbency and comfort. To accomplish a polyester/cotton blend prior to yarn spinning, polyester staple fiber is mixed with cotton fiber according to a predetermined weight ratio; for example, 65 percent polyester/35 percent cotton or 50 percent polyester/50 percent cotton. After blending, the two fibers are treated as one when they go on to yarn spinning operations.

Fibers may be dyed in the fiber stage, as the flowchart shows. *Stock* or *fiber dyeing* is one technique used to obtain heather yarns and fabrics, that is a mottled effect due to the use of different colored fibers in the yarn, often several shades of the same color. Stock dyeing is not very common because it is more costly and for the reasons discussed in connection with solution dyeing.

Yarns

Although some fibers go directly into fabric forming operations to produce such items as nonwoven interfacings and textiles that are sometimes called webs, most fibers go into yarn production. As the flowchart shows, spinners, throwsters, and yarn converters are the textile producers responsible for yarns.

Spinners produce spun yarns from short fibers. Throwsters, by the application of twisting machines can alter filament yarns to make them suitable for such fabric constructions as crepe, or can add to filament yarns such special characteristics as bulk or stretch. Yarn converters, who may also be throwsters, dye or otherwise prepare yarns for fabrication, as do integrated weaving mills (2, p. 8).

Processes to form carded and combed cotton yarns and woolen and worsted wool yarns have been briefly discussed in relation to those fibers. The essential operations for conventional spinning of any staple fibers are *drawing* out the fibers into a fine strand and *twisting* to help the fibers adhere to each other.

Man-made filament yarns may be the product of fiber companies and sold directly to fabric mills. However, for apparel uses, most man-made filaments are further processed (the job of the throwster) to impart texture to the otherwise smooth, silk-like filaments. *Texturizing* may be designed to add bulk or stretch or to alter the hand and appearance of filament yarns and resulting fabrics.

All of the major man-made fibers except rayon have some degree of heat sensitivity. This *thermoplastic* nature makes them receptive to texturizing processes using heat to shape the filaments. When curls, kinks, or loops are heat set in a thermoplastic filament, bulk or stretch is also "set" into the product.

Yarn converters may perform plying operations, that is twisting together two or more single yarns to produce a *ply* yarn. Ply yarns may be required by fabric makers seeking to design a fabric with greater strength and durability than would be possible with comparable single yarns. Yarns may also be combined or plied for novelty effects. Slub and bouclé yarns are examples of novelty yarns that contribute surface texture and design interest to a fabric.

Yarns are sometimes dyed before they are made into fabric. Plaid, striped, and checked fabrics can be produced by combining yarns of different colors in fabric construction. However, *cross-dyeing* is a relatively new development which makes it possible to fabricate plaids and similar patterns by using yarns of different fiber types instead of different colored yarns. Yarns of different fibers or different fiber types may be woven or knitted according to a plaid pattern for example; then in the dyeing process, the various fibers or fiber types become different colors due to unlike chemical reactions between dye and fibers. Thus, the same fabric can be dyed into several different color combinations by the use of a number of separate dye baths. Cross-dyeing technology permits color flexibility in the finished fabric, whereas with yarn dyed plaids and stripes, the only way to obtain another color combination is to start the fabric construction process over with a new assemblage of colored yarns. (With a yarn of different fibers or fiber types, cross-dyeing can produce heather effects ordinarily achieved by stock dyeing.)

From the yarn producers, fabric mills have a wide choice of yarns—thick, thin, fuzzy, smooth, stretchy, bulky, loopy, soft, hard, and so on. A small quantity of yarns is sold through retailers to consumers who produce their own fabrics by knitting, crocheting, and handweaving. Sewing thread is also a type of yarn that can be bought for home sewing. Packaged in much larger quantities, the same sewing thread can go into commercial garment manufacture.

Fabrics

While there have been exciting new developments in fabric formation technology, weaving and knitting still account for the majority of fabrics produced. Both woven and knitted fabrics are an arrangement of yarns.

Weaving is the right angle interlacing of two or more sets of yarns accomplished on a *loom*. The loom allows for one set of yarns (*warp* yarns) to be held under tension and parallel to each other. Certain warp yarns are raised and/or lowered on the loom permitting *filling* yarns to be inserted at right angles to the warp. When other warp yarns are then raised and/or lowered and the filling returned between the warp, interlacings are formed.

There are many variations and types of weaves depending on the number and spacings of interlacings between warp and filling yarns. A *plain weave* is formed when the maximum number of interlacings occur. If some warp or filling yarns are regularly allowed to skip or *float* over corresponding filling or warp yarns without interlacing, a *satin weave* results. If placement of the floats is such that a stairstep or herringbone pattern is formed by the weave, it is called a *twill weave*. Using the three basic weaves—plain, satin, and twill—numerous variations and combinations are possible.

The fabric mill controls closeness between yarns (expressed as thread count or yarns per square inch) and chooses the weave type according to design and end-use of the fabric. For example, the floats of yarn that appear on the surface of a satin weave permit greater light reflection from the yarn. A plain weave breaks up the surface of the yarn with frequent interlacings, which reduce reflectance. Thus, if a lustrous or shiny fabric is desired, a satin weave is a better choice than a plain weave.

Knitting is a method of fabric construction in which one or more yarns are formed into a series of interlocking loops. The loops of knit fabrics, as compared to the right angle interlacings of wovens, make knits more flexible, stretchy, and conforming to the body. Within the loops of a knit, yarns have room to shift, and the loops can elongate or become distended in response to stress—hence the comfortable "give" of knit garments.

Knit fabrics have somewhat different characteristics depending on the type of knitting machine used to produce them. *Warp knitting* involves one or more sets of yarns arranged parallel to each other, something like the way warp yarns are arranged on a loom for weaving. Each warp yarn on the knitting machine is interlooped with adjacent warp yarns. (There are no filling yarns as in the weaving process.)

Filling knits are produced by looping one or more yarns across the previous row, in either a circular manner (tubular knits) or from side ot side. Hand knitting is an example of filling knitting. Double knits are usually produced as circular filling knits. Later the tubes are slit open to make a flat fabric.

Filling knits are as a rule more stretchy than warp knits. Double knits, even though they are also filling knits, are made relatively stable and less stretchy by the double knitting process.

Unlike weaving, some knitting machines allow the fabric to be shaped or fashioned into garment sections at the same time the fabric is being formed. You may have observed someone hand knitting a sweater and "decreasing" the width of the fabric when the armhole is reached. The knitting machine is also able to increase or decrease fabric width. Since there is no cutting of fabric and very little sewing needed, some knitting mills also produce finished knitted garments like sweaters. Underwear and hosiery are commonly finished at the same mill where the fabric is knitted. Other knit fabrics proceed to fabric finishing mills for operations similar to woven goods.

Tufting is a fabric forming method of limited importance in apparel, but it accounts for most of the carpeting produced in this country. For tufted pile fabrics and carpeting, a ground fabric, either woven or nonwoven, is fed into a machine that resembles a giant sewing machine with hundreds of needles. Each needle is threaded with yarn, and the needles punch the yarn through the ground fabric, leaving loops on the surface. The loops may be cut or left uncut or finished in some combination of cut and uncut pile. Tufting is many times faster than conventional woven pile constructions for carpeting, a factor which is reflected in the price of carpeting. For some home builders, it is less costly to lay wall-to-wall carpeting over subflooring than it is to construct a finished floor over the subflooring.

Fabrics as they leave the loom or knitting or tufting machines are called *greige* (gray) *goods*. Although they may have been dyed in the yarn or fiber stages, most fabrics require some type of finishing to prepare them for manufacture into apparel or home furnishings products.

Fabric Finishes

Fabric converters accept geige goods from the fabric mills, dye or print them, and apply a wide variety of functional and decorative finishes.

Piece dyeing is the term used to describe dyeing in the fabric stage. It is the most frequently used method of dyeing. Solution dyeing, stock dyeing, yarn dyeing, and cross-dyeing have been discussed previously.

Of the many ways used to print design on fabric, *roller printing* is the most common. For roller printing, a copper cylinder is engraved with the part of a design that is to be printed in one color. For each color used in the design, a separate cylinder is prepared. The fabric to be printed is fed onto a large cylinder with the printing cylinders arranged around it so that the fabric passes between the large cylinder of the printing machine and the smaller printing cylinders. As the fabric goes through the machine, the printing cylinders pick up color paste and press it onto the fabric at the engraved areas of the printing cylinder. The same rollers may be used to print thousands of yards of fabric. Of course, color combinations in the print design may be varied by changing the color paste supplied to the printing cylinder. Engraved rollers are sometimes sold to other printing firms and used to print another line of fabrics.

Embossing is an example of a decorative finish. An engraved copper roller, much like those used for roller printing, is used to press a design into fabric, creating a raised or sculptured effect. For fabrics made of thermoplastic fibers, the roller is heated to soften the fibers and "set" embossed patterns.

Of the many finishing processes that serve to improve the functional properties of fabrics, those that result in durable press or permanent press products have attained prominence in the market. Consumers have come to expect shirts, blouses, dresses, sheets, and other apparel and household textiles to be laundered, tumble dried, and ready to wear or use **without** ironing.

Durable press finishes involve the application of synthetic resins to the fabric, which is most often a blend of polyester/cotton. Curing of the resin may be done after the garment is completed so that creases and pleats are set by the curing process. The garment manufacturer performs the last step of fabric finishing in this method of curing. Completed garments are placed on hangers or racks which move through curing ovens. (I remember shopping at a garment factory outlet and finding in a rack of raincoats one that had apparently fallen off the hanger during its trip through the curing oven. The resin finish was set by the heat of the oven while the raincoat lay crumpled on the floor; it was a mass, or a mess, of permanently pressed wrinkles!).

Finished fabrics are ready to go on to manufacture into apparel products or household textile items. Some products, especially household items such as sheets and pillowcases, tablecloths, and the like, require a minimal amount of cutting and sewing. Such products are likely to be completed in an integrated operation—beginning with greige goods, for example, and ending with packaging and shipping to retailers.

A few fabric and finishing mills design fabrics specifically for the home sewing market. These fabrics go to the consumer through a retailer. However, most home sewing fabrics are the "leftovers" from the previous season—those that were not bought by apparel producers.

End Products: Apparel

Apparel manufacture is a study in assembly line methods. The industry is labor intensive, making use of specialized machines which generally require continuous operation by workers. Although there have been a few efforts to develop automated equipment for some garment assembly processes, automation could hardly be described as a trend at this point.

Cutting of fabric into garment pieces is one of the specialized jobs in apparel production. Several dozen layers of fabric are mechanically spread on a cutting table. The cutter uses a power blade to cut around pattern pieces and through the many layers of fabric. Cut garment sections are assembled in bundles to be transferred to *sewing* operations. The bundles are sometimes shipped great distances, even to other countries, for sewing. Since the cost of labor is a considerable portion of manufacturing costs, in some cases apparel producers find a cost advantage in contracting with an apparel jobber in a low-wage country, such as Taiwan, Hong Kong, Korea, or Puerto Rico. Even with the addition of air freight transportation, production costs may be reduced in some situations.

Commercial sewing of apparel is not unlike home sewing exept that, in moderate or low priced lines especially, assembly is simplified as much as possible, hand sewing is eliminated, and sewing machines are geared to operate several times faster than the ordinary home sewing machine. Sewing machine operators receive the garment bundles from the cutters and perform one type of operation before passing a set of bundles on to the next station. For example, a worker may sew side seams on jeans all day, day after day. She (only rarely "he") is paid on a production rate, or piece rate, that is according to how many dozens of side seams she completes per day.

Pressing and inspection are additional apparel operations, other than cutting and sewing. From the garment factory, apparel may be shipped to wholesalers, who may handle the distribution of several lines, or directly to retailers.

You and I can purchase apparel through a number of different types of retailers—department stores, specialty stores, mail order catalogs, discount houses, variety stores, factory outlets, drug stores, supermarkets, and even vending machines. A significant volume of retail sales of a particular item means that the right decisions were made made by the store buyers, the apparel producers, the fabric finishers, the fabric mills, yarn producers, and fiber producers.

From fibers to consumers the route of textiles and apparel products is a complex one. There may be changes in the years ahead—new fibers, new production methods, and new ways for consumers to make purchases. Here are some predictions from the editors of *American Fabrics* (3, p. 86).

- The development of a *new generic fiber* which will have the ultimate properties . . . the comfort of cotton, the loft and warmth of wool, the dye brilliance of silk, the performance and ease-of-care of polyester. It will be antistatic, lightweight, soil and flame retardant.
- *Direct fabric formation* (nonwovens) will achieve parity with knit/woven fabrications and create a new level of production *economics* and style *aesthetics*.
- *Automated custom clothes* will be ordered at retail counters. Your size will be electronically recorded and stored, and the product will be computer-produced for prompt delivery. Electronic knitting or rapid direct fabric formation will produce full fashioned/contour molded custom fit products *on the spot*.
- *Shopping revolution*. The store comes to your home. Retailers will bring products to you via electronic presentation—video, film, holographs . . .
- *Computer line connections will tie-in to manufacturers warehouse terminals, instantly updating inventory simultaneous with sale. The consumer's purchase action will trigger a computer controlled network which will transmit a chain reaction encompassing sales transaction information, in-store item replenishment, shipping orders to field warehouse and reorder command to manufacturer. The era of the order-taking salesclerk will have passed.*

Whatever changes are made in the production of textiles and apparel and in whatever direction technology takes us, we are fairly safe in also predicting that the creation of apparel will continue to be an *art,* a *science,* and a *business.* What we wear will (1) be obtained through a business transaction, (2) represent achievement in science and technology, and (3) provide a source of aesthetic satisfaction.

REFERENCES CITED

1. Potter, M. David and Corbman, Bernard P., *Textiles: Fiber to Fabric,* fourth edition. New York: Gregg Division/McGraw-Hill Book Company, 1967.
2. *Man-Made Fiber Fact Book.* New York: Man-Made Fiber Producers Association, Inc., 1969.
3. "The Next 100 Issues—Things to Come 1974–2001," *American Fabrics,* spring, 1974, No. 100, p. 86.

INDEX